Sheetfed Offset Press Operating

by
Lloyd P. DeJidas
and
Thomas M. Destree

Graphic Arts Technical Foundation
4615 Forbes Avenue
Pittsburgh, Pennsylvania 15213
United States of America
Telephone: 412/621-6941   FAX: 412/621-3049
Telex: 9103509221   Cable: GATFWORLD

© 1988
Graphic Arts Technical Foundation
All Rights Reserved

Library of Congress Catalog Card Number: 88-81903
International Standard Book Number: 0-88362-116-9

Printed in the United States of America

Order No. 1525

A catalog of GATF text and reference books, Learning Modules, and audiovisuals may be obtained on request from the Graphic Arts Technical Foundation at the address given at the bottom of the title page.

Contents

1. Introduction to Offset Lithographic Presses   1
2. The Printing Unit   15
3. The Inking System   43
4. Dampening   69
5. Sheet Control   101
6. Packing and Printing Pressures   141
7. Blankets   161
8. Plates   183
9. Paper   199
10. Ink   219
11. Premakeready   251
12. Makeready   261
13. The Pressrun   279

Glossary   303

Index   323

Foreword

Designed to supplement press operating manuals and formal apprenticeship programs, GATF's *Sheetfed Offset Press Operating* provides both novice and experienced press operators with valuable information to improve productivity and print quality. Theoretical and practical how-to information have been combined in a single volume. In addition, pertinent material from other GATF sources, such as the one-week Sheetfed Offset Press Operating workshop, Learning Modules, Research Project Reports, and Technical Services Reports, has been included.

The concepts presented in this book are applicable to most sheetfed presses. However, the actual press adjustments must be made following the press manufacturer's recommendations.

Although this book is the most comprehensive discussion of sheetfed press operating ever compiled by GATF, several other GATF publications cover certain subjects in more detail. Among these are the following textbooks:

- *Safety for the Graphic Arts*
- *Solving Sheetfed Offset Press Problems*
- *Solving Offset Ink Problems*
- *Lithographic Press Operator's Handbook*
- *What the Printer Should Know about Ink*
- *What the Printer Should Know about Paper*

Lloyd P. DeJidas, GATF Production Department director and facility manager, and I have worked closely to develop a comprehensive book on press operating. Robert J. Schneider, Jr., an assistant editor in the Publications Division, wrote the chapters on paper and ink. The entire manuscript or portions of it were reviewed for technical accuracy by the following GATF personnel: Nelson R. Eldred, John E. Peters, John H. Pohlgeers, Raymond J. Prince, and Murray I. Suthons. Assistant editors Ann L. Mertz and Deborah L. Stevenson helped with the editing of the book. Illustrations for the book were drawn by Matthew E. Spangler and Mary Alice O'Toole, who also prepared the mechanicals. Numerous equipment manufacturers contributed photographs.

Thomas M. Destree
Publications Editor

1 Introduction to Offset Lithographic Presses

Offset lithography, a planographic printing process, requires an image carrier in the form of a plate on which photochemically produced image and nonimage areas are receptive to ink and water, respectively. In addition, the image on the plate must be right-reading; i.e., it is oriented the same way that the printed image will be.

Following are the basic steps involved in printing by offset lithography:

1. Plate with photochemically produced image and nonimage areas is mounted on a cylinder.

2. Plate is dampened with a mixture of chemical concentrates in a water-based solution, which adheres to the nonimage areas of the plate.

3. Plate surface is contacted by inked rollers, which apply ink only to the image area of a properly dampened printing plate.

4. Right-reading inked image on the printing plate is transferred under pressure to a rubber-like blanket, on which it becomes reversed (wrong-reading).

5. Inked image on the blanket is transferred under pressure to a sheet of paper or other printing substrate, producing an impression of the inked image on the paper.

An **offset lithographic press** is a mechanical device that dampens and inks the printing plate and transfers the inked image to the blanket and then to the printing substrate. A **sheetfed offset lithographic press** is a printing press that feeds and prints on individual sheets of paper (or other substrate) using the offset lithographic printing method; the operation of such a press is the focal point of this book. A **web,** or **webfed, offset lithographic press** is a press that prints on a continuous web, or ribbon, of paper fed from a roll and threaded through the press.

A modern sheetfed press reaches speeds of 10,000–12,000 impressions per hour (i.p.h.), whereas a web press reaches speeds three or four times greater. Both types of presses are increasingly being controlled from remote consoles, from which the operator can adjust inking, dampening, and circumferential and lateral register; control ink density; and monitor dot gain.

Sheetfed Press

A sheetfed press consists of a feeder, one or more printing units, transfer devices to move the paper through the press, a delivery, and various auxiliary devices (such as a control console).

The printing unit of a sheetfed offset lithographic press generally consists of three primary cylinders and systems for dampening and inking the plate:

- **Plate cylinder,** a cylinder that carries the **printing plate,** a flexible image carrier with ink-receptive image areas and, when moistened with a water-based solution, ink-repellent nonimage areas
- **Blanket cylinder,** a cylinder that carries the **offset blanket,** a fabric coated with synthetic rubber that transfers the image from the printing plate to the substrate
- **Impression cylinder,** a cylinder running in contact with the blanket cylinder that transports the paper or other substrate
- **Dampening system,** a series of rollers that dampen the printing plate with a water-based dampening solution that contains additives such as acid, gum arabic, and isopropyl alcohol or other wetting agents
- **Inking system,** a series of rollers that apply a metered film of ink to a printing plate

In addition to one or more printing units, a press also includes the following:

- **Feeder,** which lifts and forwards the sheets of paper or other substrate from a pile to the first printing unit
- **Transfer devices** (often auxiliary cylinders with sheet grippers), which facilitate sheet transport through the press
- **Delivery,** which receives and stacks the printed sheet

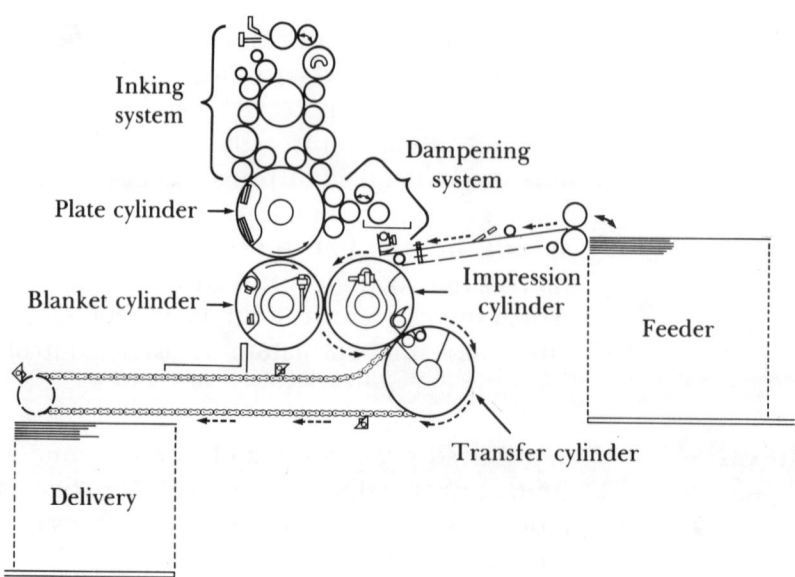

A single-color sheetfed press

Introduction to Offset Lithographic Presses

Press Configurations

A variety of sheetfed printing presses are available. These presses can best be classified according to their offset press cylinder configurations (arrangements), although the placement of the feeder and delivery are also important considerations in the design of a press. For sheetfed printing, the printing unit cylinders are arranged in three basic ways:

- The single-color sheetfed press, in which there is one set of printing cylinders arranged to print only one color on one side of each sheet as it passes through the press
- The multicolor sheetfed press, in which more than one color is printed on one side of a sheet during a single pass through the press because there is more than one printing unit
- The perfecting sheetfed press, in which sheets are printed on both sides during one pass through the press

Single-Color Press

A press consisting of a single printing unit, with its integral inking and dampening systems, a feeder, a sheet transfer system, and a delivery is called a **single-color press.** Normally, it can print only a single color in any one pass through the press. On some presses, the inking system can be modified—split—with ink fountain and ink roller dividers so that two or more colors can be printed at one time. On these presses, the same printing plate is used, and the colors are widely separated.

A single-color press can also be used for true **multicolor printing,** the printing of two or more colors, often one over another. Multicolor printing on a single-color press requires that the sheet be fed through the press as many times as there are colors to be printed. After each printing, the just-used plate is removed and the inking system is thoroughly cleaned. A new plate is mounted on the plate cylinder, and the inking system is filled with the next color. The sheet of paper is run through the press again and printed with this new color. (Multicolor printing on a single-color press is dependent upon **dry trapping**—the ability of a dry, printed ink film to accept a wet ink film over it. The wet ink dries by oxidation polymerization.)

The printing unit of the single-color sheetfed press is sometimes described as an "open unit." The plate cylinder, blanket cylinder, and impression cylinder are usually arranged in a near right-angle relationship. This arrangement is common for three reasons:

The most common arrangement of the plate, blanket, and impression cylinders for single-color printing

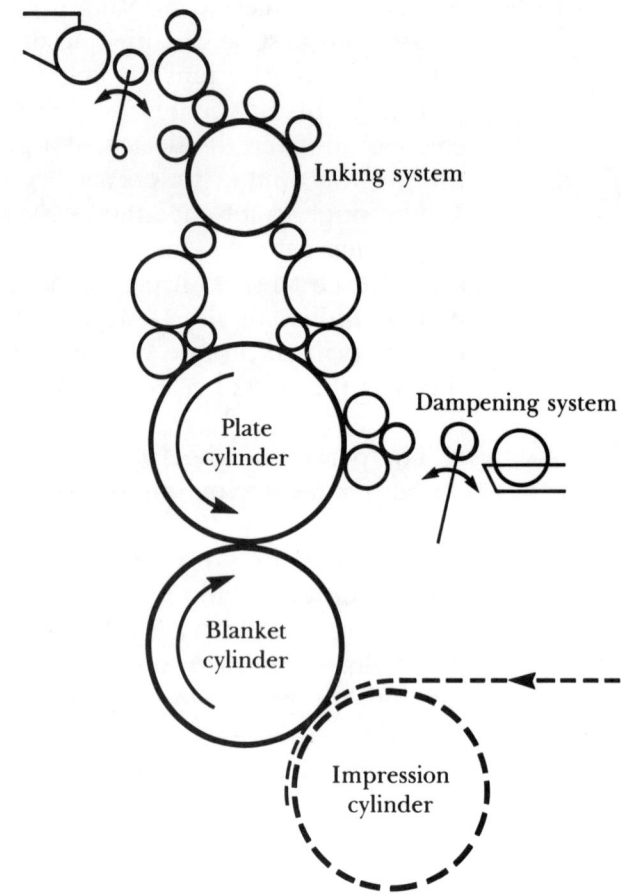

- To reduce the overall height of the press
- To make it easier to feed the paper into the impression cylinder grippers
- To make it possible, by movement of only the blanket cylinder, to throw all three cylinders out of contact with each other.

There are exceptions to this nearly right-angle (L-shaped) arrangement of cylinders. With one type of metal decorating press, the cylinders are stacked directly above each other so that the rigid metal sheets can pass through the printing nip (the line of contact between the blanket and impression cylinders) without being bent around the impression cylinder. Another exception is a press that has a single, oversized cylinder that is used as both the plate and impression cylinder. Yet another exception is a press that has a single oversized cylinder functioning as the impression cylinder for two printing units.

Multicolor Press   A press consisting of several printing units (each with its own inking and dampening system), a feeder, a sheet transfer system, and a delivery is called a **multicolor,** or **multiunit, press.** A multicolor press can have two, three, four, five, six, or more printing units. Multicolor presses are capable of **wet trapping,** the ability of a wet, printed ink film to accept another wet ink film printed over it.

In the larger press sizes, the printing units are almost identical and are arranged in tandem. With some of the other two- and four-color presses, one printing unit may be higher than the other to obtain better accessibility.

When placed in tandem, the open-unit type of single-color sheetfed press becomes a multicolor press, capable of printing a different color on each unit. One or more transfer cylinders are placed between units to transport the sheet from one printing unit to the next. Some presses have three transfer cylinders between units, while other presses have a single, double-size transfer cylinder. An odd number of transfer cylinders is needed between units so that the side of the sheet to be printed faces away from the impression cylinder.

Oliver 258 two-color sheetfed press
Courtesy Graphic Systems Div., Rockwell International

In another multicolor sheetfed press design, sometimes called the "semiopen design," a single (common) impression cylinder serves two pairs of plate and blanket cylinders. The

(Text continues on page 10.)

6 Sheetfed Offset Press Operating

Courtesy Heidelberg Eastern, Inc.

Heidelberg Speedmaster five-color sheetfed press

Introduction to Offset Lithographic Presses 7

Courtesy Komori America Corp.

Lithrone 26 four-color sheetfed press

8 Sheetfed Offset Press Operating

Courtesy Miller Printing Equipment

Miller TP104 six-color sheetfed press

Introduction to Offset Lithographic Presses 9

Miehle-Roland four-color sheetfed press of the semiopen design

Courtesy Graphic Systems Div., Rockwell International

printed sheet is held by the common impression cylinder and successively brought into contact with each blanket. A press consisting of two semiopen units, then, would be capable of printing four colors on one side of the press sheet in a single pass.

Perfecting Press

Most sheetfed presses can print on only one side of the sheet in a single pass. For the other side to be printed, the entire paper pile must be turned over and the paper run through the press a second time. There is, however, a type of sheetfed press that can print on both sides of the sheet in a single pass. The printing of at least one color on both sides of a sheet in a single pass through a press is called **perfecting;** any press that can do so is called a **perfecting press,** or **perfector.**

The most common sheetfed perfecting press is called a **convertible perfector.** Special transfer cylinders tumble the paper end for end between printing units so that the other side of the sheet is printed by the second unit. This type of press usually has the capability, through transfer cylinder adjustment,to print either two colors on one side of the sheet or one color on each side in a single pass through the press. (Other color combinations are also possible.)

With another type of sheetfed perfecting press, the blankets from two printing units are in contact, with the paper passing between the two blankets. This type of press is called a **blanket-to-blanket press,** because the two blankets are in contact. No impression cylinder is needed; each blanket acts as the impression cylinder for the other. (Most web offset presses print blanket-to-blanket.)

A two-color convertible perfector
Courtesy Graphic Systems Div., Rockwell International

Notice the extra-large transfer cylinder. See pages 26 and 27 of chapter 2 for information on how a convertible perfector operates.

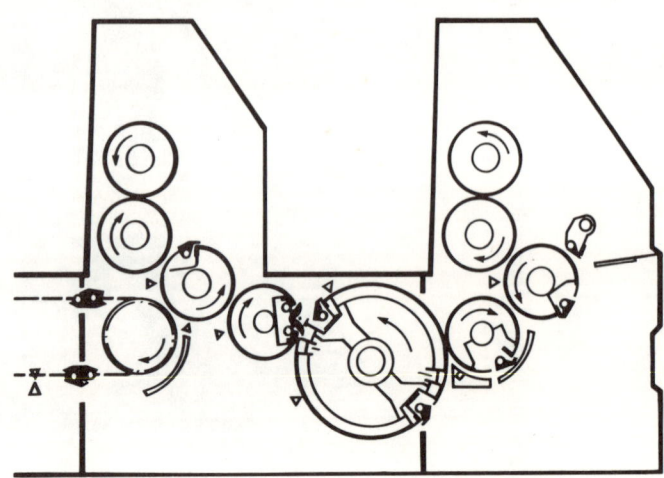

Introduction to Offset Lithographic Presses   11

Komori Sprint 26 two-color convertible perfector
Courtesy Komori America Corp.

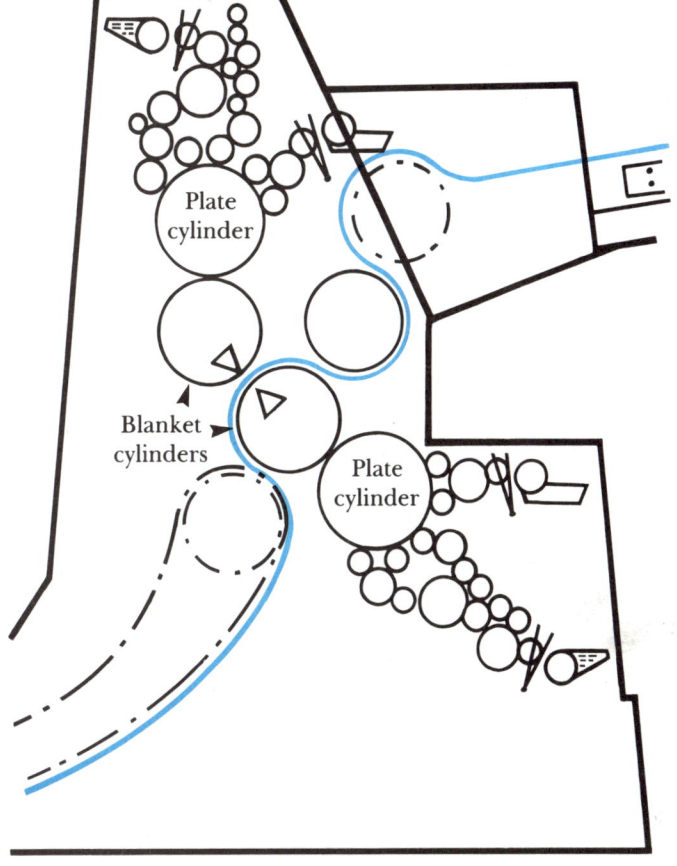

A blanket-to-blanket sheetfed perfector
Courtesy Graphic Systems Div., Rockwell International

Proofing

A **proof press** is a printing machine used for making a **proof,** a trial print from a plate, film negative, or film positive to verify correctness and quality. It usually has most of the elements of a production machine, but not the automatic features for sustained production.

The most commonly used proofing presses have a flat bed for holding the plate and paper and a rollable blanket cylinder. The blanket cylinder rolls over both, picking up the image from the inked plate and laying it down on the paper.

In the older types, the plate was dampened and rolled up (inked) by hand. The blanket cylinder rolled on bearers and gear racks. The cylinder was necessarily heavy in order to apply sufficient pressure, and on larger presses, it took two people to roll one. Later, this cylinder was put in a carriage that enabled additional pressure to be put on it, and a gear reduction crank made it easier to roll. Next, the carriage became power-driven. Still later, automatic dampening and inking systems were installed.

Proof presses are used less and less. Some proofing is done using a press similar to the one used for production, or even the same one. Most proofing is done photomechanically using light-sensitive papers (principally to proof single-color printing), colored films, or photopolymers. This procedure is called **off-press proofing.** Two basic types of proofs are used for multicolor or process-color proofing:

- **Single-sheet proof,** where the printing colors are built up on a base through lamination and toning or other processing
- **Overlay,** or **multiple-sheet, proof,** where pigmented or dyed sheets of plastic are registered to each other and taped or pin-registered to a base

Small Offset Press

Generally, any press smaller than 11×17 in. (279×432 mm) without bearers (hardened metal rings attached to the ends of the cylinder or to the cylinder's journal) is called a **small offset press,** or, more often, a **duplicator.** Duplicators started out as office machines using the offset principle. They are extremely simple, but they have developed into efficient offset presses that fill many printing needs. Many are being used for multicolor work.

The gap between "duplicators" and the more heavily built offset presses is being filled by some new presses. These have the simplicity of the duplicator plus many of the quality features of the larger presses.

Introduction to Offset Lithographic Presses 13

Multi 1860 GPC two-color small offset press
Courtesy AM Multigraphics

ATF Super Chief 2217 two-color small offset press
Courtesy ATF-Davidson Co.

14 Sheetfed Offset Press Operating

Total Copy Center

Total copy centers have become very popular in the past few years. Such systems are capable of printing both sides of a sheet of paper in a single pass through the press. The copy is automatically fed into the system, a photo-direct plate is exposed, and the programmed number of impressions is made. After the count is reached, the plate is ejected, the blanket is washed, and the next plate is automatically mounted and wetted with fountain solution while the previously printed copies are being collated.

In addition to total copy centers that print using the offset lithographic principle, total copy centers that use a variety of nonimpact printing technologies (such as electrophotography and ink jet printing) to produce the image have started to offer competition. However, the speed, image resolution, and color capabilities of these systems are generally inferior to those of conventional printing processes, although remarkable advances in image quality have been made in the past decade.

A.B. Dick Model 1700 computerized duplicating system
Courtesy A.B. Dick Co.

2 The Printing Unit

The printing unit is the section of the offset lithographic press where the print is generated and applied to a substrate, usually paper. On a single-color offset press, the printing is accomplished by means of a three-cylinder unit. The three cylinders are the plate cylinder, blanket cylinder, and impression cylinder. It does not matter how these cylinders are arranged as long as the proper cylinders touch. The cylinders must be brought together under pressure in order to transfer the ink, and they must be released to stop printing. The line of contact between cylinders is called the **nip.** The contact pressure is roughly 200 lb./sq.in. (1,380 kilopascals).

Panel opened on the operator's side of a printing unit on a Miller TP104 press

On a multicolor press, the printing is accomplished by a number of three-cylinder units with auxiliary sheet-transport cylinders between units.

Plate Cylinder

The **plate cylinder,** which is usually the uppermost cylinder of the three, carries the printing plate. Since the plate is frequently changed, this cylinder has to be easily accessible.

The plate cylinder has four primary functions:
- To hold the lithographic printing plate tightly and in register
- To carry the plate into contact with the dampening rollers that wet the nonimage area
- To bring the plate into contact with the inking rollers that ink the image area
- To transfer the inked image to the blanket carried by the blanket cylinder

The plate cylinder consists of a metal body ground to close tolerances in diameter. On sheetfed presses, it is not a complete cylinder but has a depressed gap (about 20% of the circumference) running across the cylinder to accommodate the plate clamping bars. The gap also permits the inking system to recover before the next press sheet is printed. In addition, the gap compensates for the feeding of sheets individually instead of as an unbroken stream: each sheet is stopped on the feedboard and moved laterally, but the cylinders continue to rotate, reducing the amount of cylinder surface that can be used for printing.

At each end of the plate cylinder is a **bearer,** a hardened metal ring attached to the cylinder body or journal. On many presses, the bearers of the plate cylinder run in contact with the bearers of the blanket cylinder during printing. The diameter of the bearer is the **effective diameter** of the cylinder and is the same as the **pitch diameter,** i.e., the working diameter, of the gear attached to the journal.

The plate cylinder is driven by this gear, which is, in turn, driven by a similar gear on the blanket cylinder. The cylinder gears may be spur (on older presses) or helical. A **spur gear** has teeth cut straight across the gear, and a **helical gear** has teeth cut at an angle. A spur gear used as a plate cylinder gear nearly always has a **backlash gear,** a thin second gear bolted to it to reduce **play**—free or unimpeded movement— between gears. Presses that print with the plate and blanket cylinder bearers out of contact always have helical gears to reduce gear play and provide a smooth drive.

The Printing Unit 17

Spur gears *(left)* and helical gears

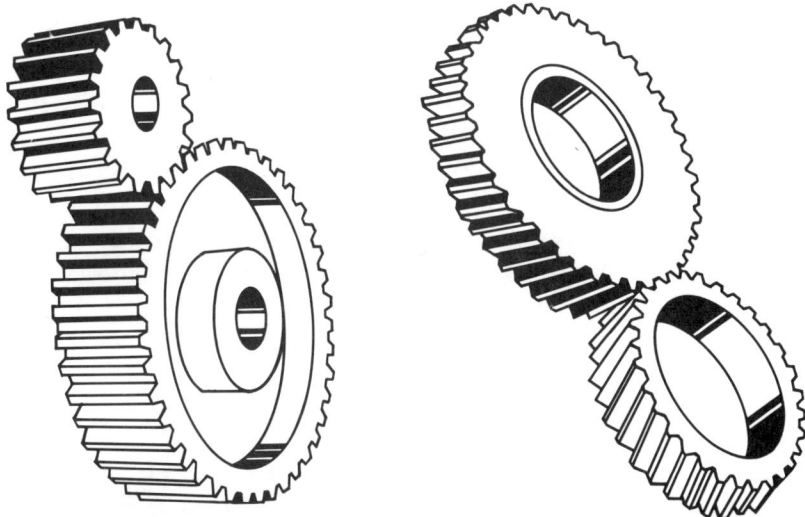

Gear end of a plate cylinder from an older sheetfed press

Notice the spur gear and how it is attached to the plate cylinder

The plate cylinder gear has several slotted holes. It is bolted directly to the cylinder body just beside the bearer or, more commonly, to a flange on the cylinder journal outside the press frame. (By being located outside the press frame, the gear remains cleaner and better lubricated.) Loosening of the bolts allows the cylinder to be moved forward or backward in relation to the lead or gripper edge. This movement is desirable in order to adjust the front margin of the sheet or change the position of the plate. (Most multicolor presses have a register mechanism that makes lateral or circumferential register moves while the press is running.)

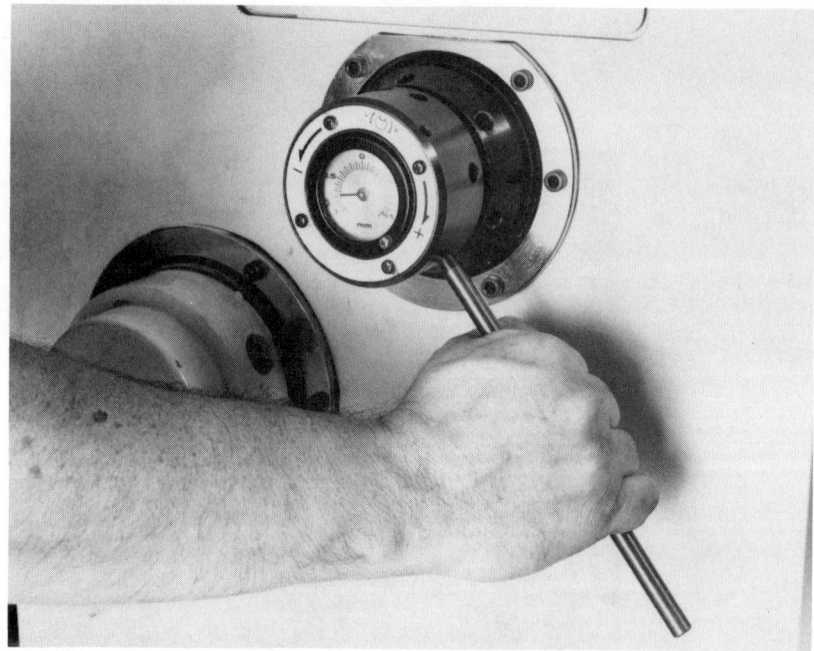

A press operator making a minor circumferential register move (±0.04 in. or ±1 mm) on a Komori sheetfed press

The body of the plate cylinder is smaller in diameter than the bearers. The difference between the radius of the body surface and that of the bearers is called the **undercut.** The undercut provides space for the plate and its **packing**—paper or other material that is placed between the plate and cylinder to raise the plate's surface to printing height or to adjust cylinder diameter to obtain image fit in multicolor printing. The amount of undercut is usually stamped in the cylinder gutter or the cylinder gap of both plate and blanket cylinders. These stamped values can be used to establish basic packing amounts for the cylinders in the absence of a press operator's manual.

Cylinder undercut

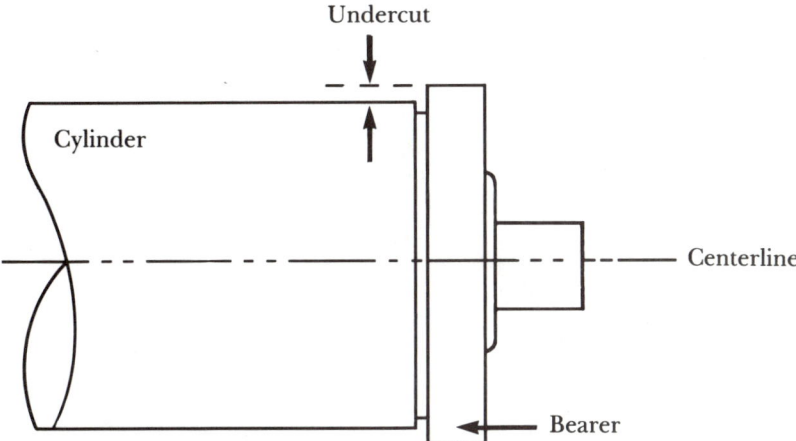

On some plate cylinders, a **start-of-print line,** a horizontal line that indicates the limit of the printing area, is engraved in the gutters about an inch behind the cylinder's leading edge. From that line toward the leading edge of the cylinder, the radius of the cylinder is progressively reduced to form a slight ramp. This ramp allows the inking and dampening rollers to mount the plate smoothly when the press is running at higher speeds. When the plate is in position on the cylinder, all image areas should be behind the start-of-print line.

A **plate clamp** is a device designed to first grip the edge of the plate and then pull it tight against the cylinder body. Plate clamps have widely varied designs, but they all do the same thing. Some clamps are quick-release; a simple twist of a cam actuates the grip. Others are segmented and operate independently. All clamps have provisions for moving the plate circumferentially and laterally in order to position the print on the paper.

Increasingly, plate cylinders are equipped with register pins. The pins on the plate cylinder correspond with holes punched in the printing plate. Such a plate-positioning system reduces the amount of cylinder adjustments necessary to properly position the printing image.

Blanket Cylinder

The **blanket cylinder** carries the printing blanket and has two primary functions:
- To carry the offset rubber blanket into contact with the inked image on the plate cylinder
- To transfer, or offset, the ink film image to the paper (or other substrate) carried by the impression cylinder

Press operator adjusting a quick-release plate clamp

It is very similar to the plate cylinder because it has a gap, gutters, bearers, a gear, and bearings. However, it does not have clamps like a plate cylinder does. Instead, it has one or two reels for holding and stretching the blanket tight. With some presses, the blanket ends are attached to bars, which, in turn, are mounted to reels.

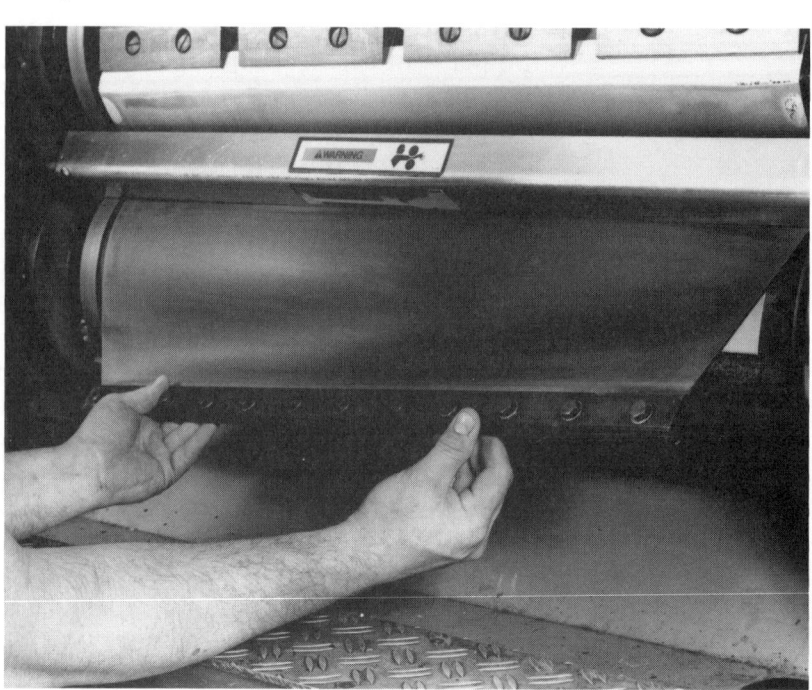

A blanket, attached to blanket bars, being mounted on a press

The reels rotate to tighten the blanket against the cylinder. The rotating mechanism is either a worm gear or a ratchet-and-pawl device. Premounted bars are an option on all presses.

Press operator tightening the blanket reel

The position of the blanket cylinder in relation to the other cylinders must be adjustable for two reasons: to bring it in and out of contact with them, and to compensate for variations in substrate and packing thicknesses. When contact between the cylinders is broken, the blanket cylinder is backed away from the other two cylinders, but the distance is not great because the gears on the cylinders must remain in mesh. However, the distance is sufficient to permit plates to be mounted and washed without getting the blanket dirty, and to allow the blanket to be washed or changed without any solvent getting on the plate. It also allows the press to idle without transferring the image on the plate to the blanket. Eccentric bushings permit this movement of cylinders.

The distance between the blanket cylinder and the impression cylinder must also be adjustable to accommodate different thicknesses of substrate and blanket packing. This distance is adjusted by another pair of eccentric bushings. Adjusting the position of the blanket cylinder relative to the impression cylinder does not affect the relationship between plate and blanket cylinders.

On single-color presses, the blanket cylinder gear is generally the driving gear for both of the other cylinders. It is driven by a pinion in the drive train from the main motor. The blanket cylinder gear is attached to the cylinder in much the same way as the plate cylinder gear. It is adjustable, but only for press timing purposes. The press operator never adjusts the position of this gear.

The body of the cylinder is undercut to accommodate the blanket and packing. The blanket cylinder does not have a ramp like the plate cylinder does; its radius is constant from leading to trailing edges. With some presses, particularly those that print with the plate and blanket cylinder bearers out of contact, the undercut is deeper to accommodate two blankets plus packing.

Impression Cylinder

The **impression cylinder** carries the paper into the printing unit, and contact pressure from the blanket cylinder transfers the print to the paper. It too has a gear and gap. The gap accommodates the gripper shaft on which are mounted the gripper fingers that hold the sheet during printing. The grippers hold the unprinted paper in register as the cylinder turns and presses it against the inked image on the blanket cylinder.

The blanket cylinder (with blanket mounted) *(top)* and impression cylinder viewed from the delivery end of a single-color press

Notice the gap between the impression cylinder body and its bearer.

The body of the impression cylinder is not undercut but is approximately the diameter of the bearers of the other two cylinders. The impression cylinder bearers are, in fact, undercut and are used only as paralleling devices when setting up the press.

There are two basic mechanical designs for varying the clearance between the blanket and impression cylinders to accommodate different thicknesses of stock. In the first design, the impression cylinder is mounted on a set of eccentrics. A shift of the eccentrics by an impression lever moves the impression cylinder toward or away from the blanket cylinder. The second method uses two sets of eccentrics, but these are on the blanket cylinder. The inner set adjusts the blanket-to-plate bearer pressure and actuates automatic on-and-off printing contact. The outer set moves the blanket cylinder only in relation to the impression cylinder.

Transfer Cylinder

After printing, the impression cylinder transfers the paper to another cylinder that moves the paper between printing units or carries it to the delivery. The paper-transport cylinders between printing units are called **transfer cylinders.** An odd number of transfer cylinders are placed between printing units.

A transfer cylinder may be covered with a variety of materials to avoid marking the wet ink. One of these is a frictionless, ink-repellent coating applied to a base material that is then adhered to the existing transfer cylinder. The cylinder is then covered with a loose-fitting, ink-repellent cloth net that moves freely between printed sheet and transfer cylinder. This rub-free movement reduces marking, and the ink-repellent surfaces reduce the chance of ink redepositing onto the press sheet.

As a stopgap measure, some press operators apply adhesive-backed ⅛- or ¼-in. (3- or 6-mm) foam insulation to the portions of the transfer cylinder that correspond to nonimage areas of the press sheet. The foam supports the image areas above the cylinder surface, preventing marking. The foam insulation must be replaced for each new job.

Some presses come equipped with an **air-transport,** or **air-cushion, drum,** instead of the typical transfer cylinder. An air-cushion drum is a device that supports the sheet on a cushion of air to lessen the chance that ink will smear on the press sheet. One air-cushion drum, for example, has a ribbed

24 Sheetfed Offset Press Operating

"Mark-less" Super Blue system for preventing marking of wet ink

Transfer and delivery cylinders that contact the wet side of a sheet are coated with a frictionless, ink-repellent substance and covered with a loose-fitting, ink-repellent cloth net.

P = Plate cylinder
B = Blanket cylinder
I = Impression cylinder
T = Transfer cylinder
D = Delivery cylinder

Courtesy Printing Research, Inc.

An air-transport, or air-cushion, drum
Courtesy Graphic Systems Div., Rockwell International

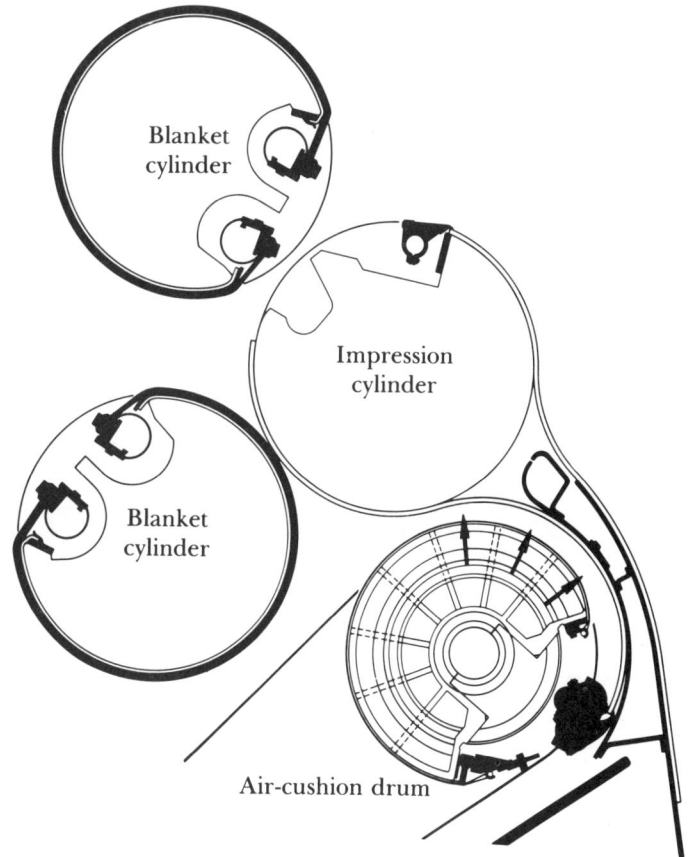

aluminum core covered with an air-permeable jacket. Air flows through this jacket, cushioning the printed sheet above the drum's surface.

In one type of perfecting press, three transfer cylinders are used between printing units: a conventional transfer drum immediately after the previous printing unit's impression cylinder, a large-diameter storage drum that can hold two press sheets, and a turning drum with two sets of grippers. On the storage drum, the tail, or trailing edge, of a press sheet is taken by the grippers of the turning drum. At the same time, the grippers of the storage drum open. During this transfer from one drum to the other, the tail edge of the sheet becomes the leading edge, and the just-printed side of the sheet is placed against the impression cylinder of the next printing unit. In single-sided printing, the three cylinders act as conventional transfer cylinders—that is, the lead edge of the sheet is transferred to the next cylinder.

(Text continues on page 28.)

26 Sheetfed Offset Press Operating

Sheet turning in three phases on a M.A.N.-Roland convertible perfector
Courtesy Graphic Systems Div., Rockwell International

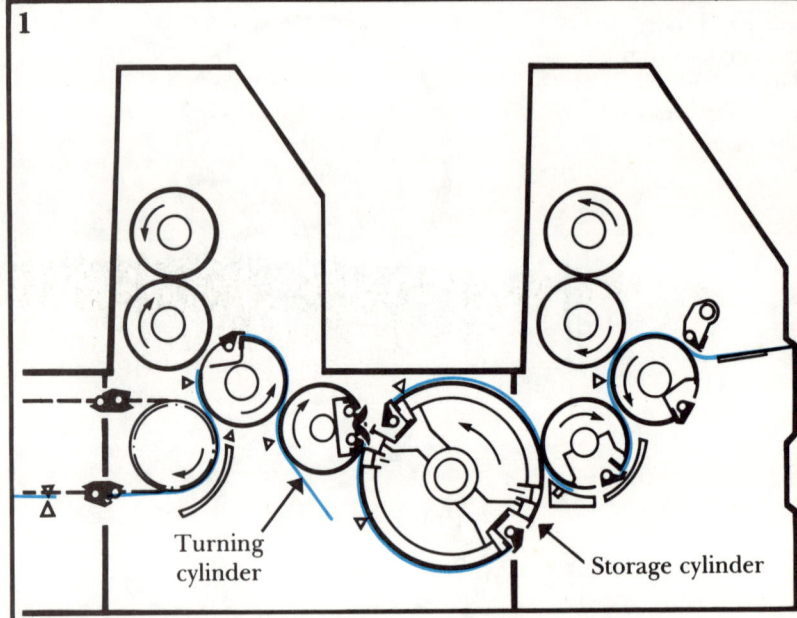

Two straight-forward sheets are on the large-diameter (storage) cylinder. The tail edge of the lower sheet is taken by the grippers of the turning cylinder; at the same time, the grippers of the storage cylinder open.

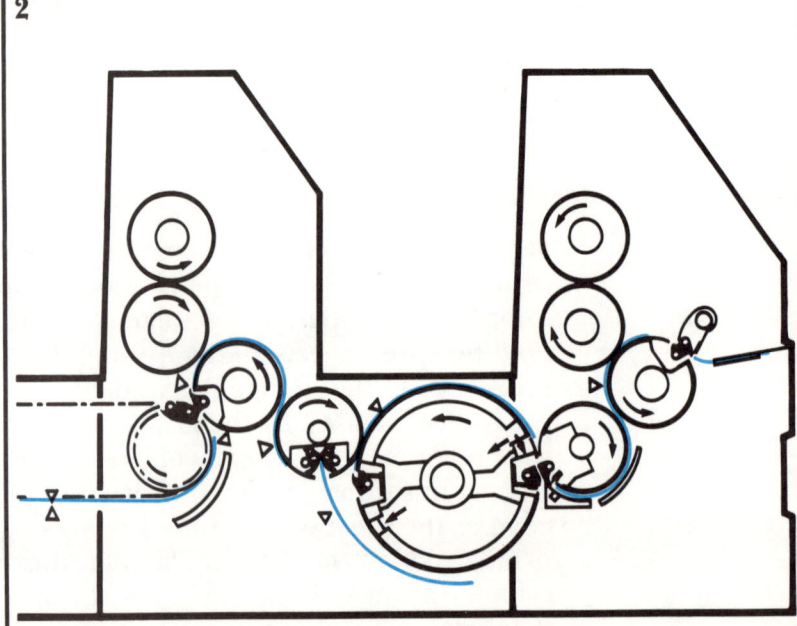

The sheet is held by the grippers of the turning cylinder. The tail edge of the sheet becomes the leading edge.

The Printing Unit 27

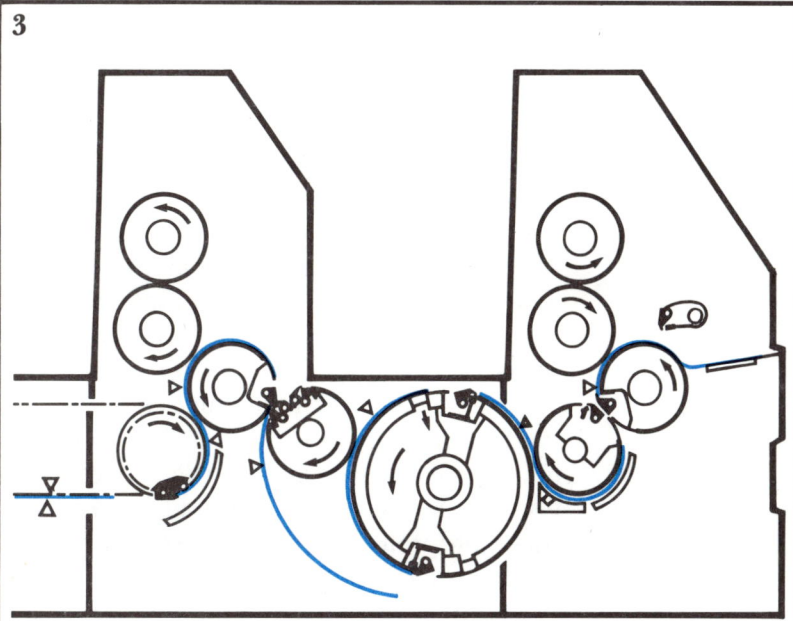

The sheet is transferred to the impression cylinder grippers in the second unit for perfecting.

Sheet travel on a M.A.N.-Roland convertible perfector set for single-side printing
Courtesy Graphic Systems Div., Rockwell International

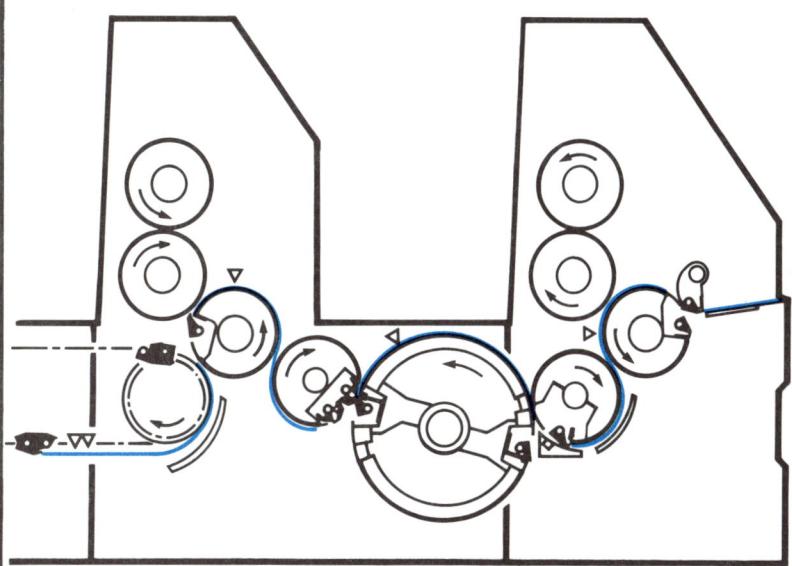

In single-side printing, the leading edge of the sheet travels directly from the storage cylinder to the turning cylinder, which now acts as an intermediate transfer cylinder.

Delivery Cylinder

The cylinder after the last printing unit, although technically a transfer cylinder, is called the **delivery cylinder.** This cylinder powers the chain delivery and coordinates the transfer of the printed sheet from the last impression cylinder to the delivery gripper bars attached to the two delivery chains.

The most common delivery cylinder consists of a shaft on which a series of disks, or **skeleton wheels,** are mounted. The wheels can be moved laterally to support the wet sheet in nonprinted areas. If they are not positioned properly, the press sheet can become marked with ink.

An alternative system replaces the skeleton wheels with a solid delivery cylinder that is first coated with a frictionless, ink-repellent material and then covered with a loose-fitting, ink-repellent cloth netting that moves freely between printed sheet and delivery cylinder, reducing or eliminating the tendency to mark.

Another alternative is the Track Eraser from Dahlgren International, Inc. In this system, a rotating air scoop (on the same shaft as the original skeleton wheels) generates a cushion of air that guides and supports the sheet. The air scoop alone is sufficient for most situations. However, either two side guides or two plastic or aluminum wheels can be used to assist the air scoop. Two side guide assemblies, each consisting of a spring-loaded plastic wheel, are attached to the tie-bar near the impression cylinder. The side guides are adjustable so that they can be positioned at the edges of the sheet. The plastic or aluminum wheels, on the same shaft as the scoop, are normally positioned at the extreme edges of the sheet. There is a 1/8 in. (3 mm) gap between the wheels and the impression cylinder.

Cylinder Setting

Setting the cylinders is a part of preventive maintenance, not a part of makeready. The procedures for setting the cylinders on a bearer-contact and non-bearer-contact press are discussed.

Cylinder Setting on a Bearer-Contact Press

Bearer pressure is an important part of cylinder setting on a **bearer-contact press,** a press that runs with the bearers of the plate and blanket cylinders in contact. The bearers perform several functions:
- They act as an alignment device. When bearers touch at both ends, the blanket cylinder and plate cylinder are in perfect alignment.

- They protect against excessive gear wear. When the bearers are touching, the gears mesh perfectly. The pitch lines of the two cylinder gears are running together just as they were designed to do, and it is impossible to jam the gears together beyond the pitch line and cause excessive wear. When the pressure is off and the press is idling, the bearers are apart and the teeth are not fully meshed. But at this time the press is not under load, and there is little strain on the gears.
- They act as a gauge for measuring the actual height of the plate or blanket when packed. They represent the effective diameter of the cylinder, and if necessary, the cylinder undercut can be determined from them.
- They help to smoothly transfer power from one cylinder to another. Since all running gears have clearance between the teeth and are subject to wear, a smooth flow of power between gears is impossible. Properly set bearers roll together smoothly and overcome backlash between spur gears or run-out between helical gears. If the bearers are not in firm contact, gear streaks sometimes appear.

To make bearers really effective it is necessary that they be forced together under pressure by the bearings. Just the weight of the upper cylinder forcing the bearers together is not enough. The pressure between bearers must be greater than the pressure between plate and blanket to prevent gear streaks.

In many printing plants, the setting of bearer pressure is considered a factory service technician's work. However, if necessary, the bearers can be set by the following method prefaced by these cautions:

- Obtain the press manufacturer's instructions and follow them.
- Be particularly careful with presses that have solid sleeve bearings in which the cylinders rotate, rather than ball or taper roller bearings. Such presses can be severely damaged if excessive bearer pressure is applied. The setting of these presses, usually of European manufacture, requires a light touch.
- Lubricate the cylinder bearers sufficiently after setting.
- Stop the press every hour for the first few shifts to check for excessive warmth in the bearing area.

1. Locate the adjustment that moves the blanket cylinder toward the plate cylinder. There is one on each side of the press. This adjustment is usually a turnbuckle; it changes the

length of the rod that moves the eccentric bushings of the blanket cylinder.

2. Make sure the plate and conventional blanket are packed to their correct working height.

3. Lift the blanket and increase the packing slightly with a thin sheet—about 0.003 in. (0.07 mm). Refit and tension the blanket.

4. With both blanket and plate cylinder bearers absolutely clean and dry, apply *thin* thumbprints of ink at several spots around both blanket cylinder bearers. The ink used must not be fast-drying. If necessary, the ink can be thinned (reduced) slightly with machine oil.

5. Isolate the sheet detectors, start the press, and turn on the impression. After two or three press revolutions, release the pressures and stop the press.

6. Look for the transfer of the thumbprints to the plate cylinder bearers. If there is no transfer, the cylinders must be adjusted. If there is a light impression only in the gap, the cylinders must be adjusted slightly. If there is a good, even impression in the gap and around the bearers on the gear and operator's sides of the press, no adjustment is necessary. It is a good idea to release the pressures during adjustments and reapply pressures to check the transfer.

7. Once bearer pressure is satisfactory, remove the extra sheet from the blanket and engage the sheet detectors.

Thumbprints that have transferred from the blanket cylinder bearer *(bottom)* to the plate cylinder bearer *(top)*

Cylinder Setting on a Non–Bearer-Contact Press

Setting the cylinders of presses that run without bearer contact is relatively straightforward. The setting mechanisms to adjust cylinder positions are similar to those on other presses.

The procedure for setting the cylinders of non–bearer-contact presses is as follows:

1. Slightly overpack the blanket, particularly on older presses.

2. Pack the plate correctly and adjust the blanket-cylinder-to-impression-cylinder pressure to apply approximately 0.004-in. (0.1-mm) squeeze to the impression cylinder *without* paper.

3. Refer to the operator's manual to determine how much gap is necessary between the bearers for normal packing heights.

4. Select feeler gauges of the same thickness, single pieces if possible. A **feeler gauge** is a thin strip of steel ground to precise thickness and marked accordingly.

5. With the bearers absolutely clean and dry, isolate the sheet detectors and roll the press into pressure.

6. Stop the press with the blanket in contact with both the plate and impression cylinders.

7. Shut off the power to the press.

8. Insert the feeler gauges between the bearers of plate and blanket cylinders. If the cylinders are set correctly, the feelers will be snug between the bearers. They should be just movable with a strong pull and should retain a new position after being moved from side to side. Gradual adjustment to achieve this setting should be done with the cylinders off pressure, and tested with the pressures reapplied.

9. When satisfactory settings are found, remove the extra packing, engage the sheet detectors, and reset the blanket and impression pressure to normal.

On one or two types of popular European presses, the distance between the plate and blanket cylinders can be altered by moving the plate cylinder, which is mounted in eccentric bushings. After adjusting this type of press it may be necessary to reset the inking rollers to the plate.

Paralleling Blanket Cylinder to Impression Cylinder

The procedure described for setting the plate/blanket cylinder relationship of a non–bearer-contact press can be applied to the blanket/impression cylinder relationship by adjusting the appropriate controls.

In all cases, the press manufacturer's instructions must be followed to ensure long press life. Procedures given by manufacturers for adjusting cylinders and bearer pressures must be clearly understood and executed, even if they differ from those presented here.

Maintenance

The upkeep of the printing unit requires strict attention, particularly regarding lubrication. On many presses, a considerable amount of lubrication is done automatically. Oil reservoir levels in these automatic oiling systems must be maintained. Other presses are manually oiled or greased and require regular servicing. The lubrication of the printing unit is usually simple and therefore often overlooked. The bearings of the blanket-tightening reel, as well as the pawls or worm gears, need lubrication. The gripper shaft bearings and the cam follower should be lubricated. The moving parts of the plate clamp must be kept clean and lubricated with a good grade of clinging-type lubricant. Manufacturer's specifications should provide the necessary information concerning lubricants.

The cylinder gears that do not run in oil baths must also be lubricated with a grade of grease recommended by the manufacturer. Before new grease is added, the gear teeth should be cleaned down to the bottom of each tooth to remove any particles of ink, paper, lint, or gum that have accumulated.

The linkages and levers that throw pressure on and off must be clean and well oiled. Oil holes and threads of adjustment screws must be kept clean. Eccentric bushings should be lubricated thoroughly. At every oil hole or grease fitting, excess oil or grease should be removed with a rag. Any damaged grease fitting should be replaced to ensure proper lubrication.

Bearers should always be clean and dry. Materials such as gum and ink get on the bearers. If left there, they gradually start to damage the bearers when they are in contact.

Many presses have cylinders that are chromium-plated or skinned with stainless steel to avoid rusting. When cylinders do rust, the rusted areas can develop into high spots causing extra pressure. The cylinders should be kept clean. Any rust should be removed with nonabrasive scouring pads, and the area coated with a thin film of oil. Never use files, razor blades, or coarse abrasives to clean the cylinders.

Presses equipped with infrared (IR) or ultraviolet (UV) dryers require special lubricants because of the heat buildup caused by the dryers. Normal lubricants would break down in such applications.

The labeling of grease fittings to ensure that the proper lubricant is used

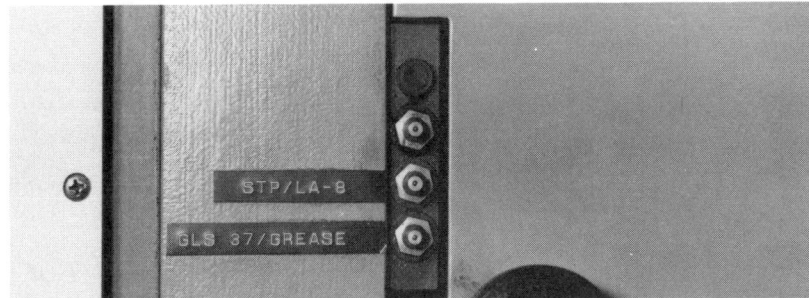

Caution: Lubricating and cleaning must be done only when the press is stopped. Excess oil should be wiped from the press to prevent it from running onto the floor, where it will be hazardous. Absorbent socks, designed to control hazardous materials, can be placed in the oil drip pans to absorb waste oil. Socks should be replaced once a month, or as necessary.

An absorbent sock, manufactured by New Pig Corp., placed in an oil drip pan to absorb waste oil

Preventive maintenance. The primary objective of a preventive maintenance program is to keep equipment in top operating condition and to prevent breakdowns. GATF's Technical Services Report 7230 discusses the subject of preventive maintenance and includes a series of maintenance checklists, which are reproduced on pages 34–38. In developing the report, GATF reviewed maintenance programs in hundreds of plants and studied service manuals provided by many press manufacturers. Five time-related preventive maintenance checklists and a malfunction report were then developed.

(Text continues on page 39.)

Daily maintenance checklist

DAILY

Daily Maintenance Checklist
Press No. _____

☐ Review malfunction report for the last 24 hours.
☐ Oil daily lubrication points.
☐ Grease dampener roller bearings.
☐ Check oil level in **all** gear boxes, machine drives, central lubricators.
☐ Clean and desensitize all chrome rollers in dampening systems.
☐ Clean plate and blanket bearers.
☐ Clean electronic detector eyes.
☐ Check cleanliness of dampener covers.
☐ Check condition of blankets.
☐ Check condition of plates.
☐ Check level of dampening solution in reservoirs.
☐ Measure pH and conductivity of dampening solution.
☐ Measure alcohol percentage, if alcohol is used.
☐ Measure plate-to-blanket squeeze.
☐ Measure ink film thickness.
☐ Clean sponges and pails. Refill pails.
☐ Pick up wastepaper.
☐ Dispose of empty containers.
☐ Clean up oil and ink spills.
☐ Return all tools to proper locations.

End of Shift

☐ Empty and clean ink fountains.
☐ Clean ink roller train.
☐ Clean impression cylinder.
☐ Check malfunction report.
☐ Stripe ink form roller.

WEEKLY

Weekly Maintenance Checklist for Month of _____, 19__
Press No. _____

Person performing maintenance must initial each operation on date performed.

Operation	Date	Date	Date	Date
1. Drain and flush all dampening systems and recirculators.				
2. Inspect all covered dampener rollers.				
3. Inspect all ink and dampening form rollers and check form roller settings.				
4. Wash all plate cylinders and impression cylinders with solvent and wipe down with lightly oiled rag.				
5. Blow off entire press (dry) and wipe down with clean rags.				
6. Clean all filters in feeder, delivery, decurler, and vacuum cleaner systems.				
7. Wipe down feedboard and wax, check feeder valves, replace suckers if worn, inspect feeder tapes for wear. Replace worn tapes; clean glazed tapes.				
8. Blow off delivery bars and wipe off spray powder. Clean and check all suction wheels.				
9. Brush spray powder off unit and check tube gap.				
10. Wash all open feeder and delivery gears.				
11. Oil and grease all weekly lubrication points.				
12. Lightly oil all feeder tape conveyor rollers that are not automatically lubricated. Oil blanket lockup reels.				
13. Grease infeeds and all grippers in impression cylinders, transfer cylinders, and delivery gripper bars.				
14. Lubricate delivery chains.				
15. Lubricate ink fountain rollers.				
16. Lubricate inking and dampening systems.				
17. Grease and oil feeder heads and all side guide and front guide mechanisms.				
18. **General cleanup.** Pick up all trash around press and on platforms. Sweep floors and platforms, wipe up all oil, and clean up ink spills. Clean drip pan dry. Empty rag cans and trash cans.				
19. Clean shelves; return chemicals, tools, and ink to proper location for use. Clean washup trays, buckets, and sponges and return to proper location for use.				
20. Fill washup bottles and solvent containers. Refill grease guns and oil cans.				
21. Check supply of spare blankets and covered dampening rollers.				
22. Update information on Malfunction Report.				

500-HOUR

Part 1

500-Hour Maintenance Checklist, Performed _____, 19__
Press No. _____

Operation	Performed by	Remarks and Additional Repairs Required
1. Check durometer and condition of all ink and water rollers. Replace all damaged rollers and remove glaze from hardened rollers. Clean roller ends and check journals for wear before installing.		
2. Clean press side frames and roller sockets while rollers are out of press and apply light film of oil.		
3. Reset all ink and dampening system rollers.		
4. Check oil level in all self-oscillating ink and dampening oscillators.		
5. Remove all ink fountain blades, inspect for wear and damage, and replace with new or reconditioned blades where necessary. Clean all keys, lubricate key screws, and parallel blade.		
6. Clean and inspect all washup blades.		
7. Clean all cylinder bearers and check for proper bearer pressures. Reparallel cylinders and reset bearer pressures.		
8. Clean ink, rust, gum, etc., from the body of all plate, blanket, and impression cylinders and apply a light film of oil.		
9. Clean cylinder gaps and cylinder ends. Clean plate clamps and reset.		
10. Spray-clean all pickup, impression, transfer, and delivery grippers. Clean gripper pads and check settings. Reset as necessary. Replace badly worn gripper pads. Check for broken compression springs and replace as necessary.		
11. Clean all oil pump filters. Clean regulating valves on all suction and air blast pumps.		
12. Vacuum dust from all electric motors and wipe clean. Clean dust filters on electrical controllers and press control consoles.		
13. Remove powder from antisetoff spray unit; blow out powder and air lines; clean nozzles. Clean etched roller, set tube gaps, and check tubes for brightness. Clean or replace tubes as necessary.		
14. Clean feeder pickup, forwarder, and side guide mechanisms; lubricate side guide positioning shaft.		

(Checklist continues on page 37.)

500-HOUR

Part 2

500-Hour Maintenance Checklist, Performed _____, 19__

Press No. _____

Operation	Performed by	Remarks and Additional Repairs Required
15. Check sensitivity of sheet detector; clean and lubricate.		
16. Clean and lubricate jogger mechanisms.		
17. Clean and inspect hoist mechanisms.		
18. Grease and oil all 500-hr. (red) lubrication points.		
19. Clean and lightly grease all exposed springs and spring rods.		
20. Clean and lubricate all exposed gears on cylinder ends and elsewhere.		
21. Spray-clean and lubricate delivery chains. Check chain tension.		
22. Complete all repairs on malfunction list since last major maintenance period.		

SEMIANNUAL

Semiannual Maintenance, Performed _____, 19__

Press No. _____

Every third 500-hour maintenance and in addition to that maintenance.

Operation	Performed by	Remarks and Additional Repairs Required
1. Drain oil in feeder and delivery pumps and refill. Inspect for wear and repair as necessary.		
2. Remove feeder separator pistons and air valves. Clean, lubricate, and reinstall.		
3. Clean and lubricate feeder clutch; clean and repack feeder universal joints.		
4. Check oil levels in **all** gear boxes. Add or replace as needed.		
5. Inspect brakes and brushes on all press drive motors. Clean interior of all electrical controllers, drive cabinets, and press control consoles.		

ANNUAL

Annual Maintenance, Performed _____, 19__
Press No. _____

Every sixth 500-hour maintenance and in addition to that maintenance.

Operation	Performed by	Remarks and Additional Repairs Required
1. Inspect press by a qualified service technician (might be the manufacturer's technician) for overall wear.		
2. Drain all press oil reservoirs, clean filters and pumps, and refill.		
3. Drain and refill all gear boxes in main drive.		

MALFUNCTION REPORT

Press No. _____

Keep this form at press at all times.
Write down all repairs and special maintenance required.

Date	Operator	Problem, or Work Required

Cylinder Low Spots

Cylinder low spots are more common than may be imagined. Even newer presses can have this fault as the result of flawed metal in the cylinders. A wad of paper, a rag, a screw, or even the bent up corner of a sheet of cardboard passing through the cylinders can cause a depressed area. The damaged area can be larger than supposed; e.g., a small setscrew makes a visible dent in both impression and blanket cylinders, but it also makes a depression larger than the dent that cannot be visually detected.

The following procedure can be used to find low spots in the cylinders:

1. Pack the plate and blanket cylinders normally. Put an old plate on the plate cylinder.

2. Ink up the dry plate completely.

3. Print a solid to 20 press sheets.

4. Decrease the impression pressure by 0.002 in. (0.05 mm) and print another 20 sheets. Repeat this step until no ink is transferred to the paper.

If a low spot appears anywhere on the press sheet, wash and reverse the blanket end for end. If the low spot comes in a different place, the blanket is at fault. If the spot is in the same place on the press sheets, one of the printing cylinders has a low spot or is misaligned. Therefore, a factory service technician should be contacted.

Safety

Safety must be stressed not only near the press but also in the pressroom as a whole. Following is a list of precautions that will make the pressroom a safer place to work:

- Never operate a press with cylinder guards removed.
- Do not override the interlocks that stop the press when the guards are raised.
- Inch the press carefully when working on a plate or blanket.
- Always lock the press on "safe" when working on a dangerous part of the press.
- Do not wear loose-fitting clothing, ties or necklaces, open-toe shoes, or shoes that will not offer adequate protection from dropped objects or chemical spills.
- Avoid the use of large, unfolded rags. Instead, use smaller rags or fold the larger rags into smaller sections.
- Remove finger rings to lessen the chance of having fingers crushed. Do not wear watches or bracelets.

40 Sheetfed Offset Press Operating

Press operator lifting press guard to gain access to the blanket for cleaning

Notice that the press operator is wearing protective gloves.

Nip guards between plate and blanket cylinders to prevent the operator's fingers from entering the in-running nip

- Pull long hair back when working on a plate or blanket to avoid getting it caught in the ink rollers.
- Keep steps and platforms clean and free of oil and obstructions.

The Printing Unit 41

- Wear safety goggles and gloves when handling hazardous chemicals.
- Understand and interpret the Material Safety Data Sheet that should accompany each chemical purchased.
- Understand the symbols/labels used with the Hazard Materials Identification System (HMIS).
- Become familiar with emergency first-aid procedures for the chemicals used.

Press operator pouring solvent onto a properly wadded cleaning rag

Notice the HMIS label on the safety can.

3 The Inking System

An inking system, or inker, consists of the following parts:
- **Ink fountain**—a pan that contains the ink supply
- **Ductor** or **ductor roller**—a transfer roller that alternately contacts the ink fountain roller and the first roller of the ink train, often an oscillating drum
- **Oscillating drums, oscillators,** or **vibrators**—driven rollers that not only rotate but oscillate from side to side, distributing and smoothing out the ink film and erasing image patterns from the form roller
- **Intermediate rollers**—friction- or gravity-driven rollers between the ductor and form roller that transfer and condition the ink; often called **distributors** if they contact two rollers and **riders** if they contact a single oscillating drum
- **Form rollers**—a series of three to five rollers that contact the printing plate and transfer ink to it

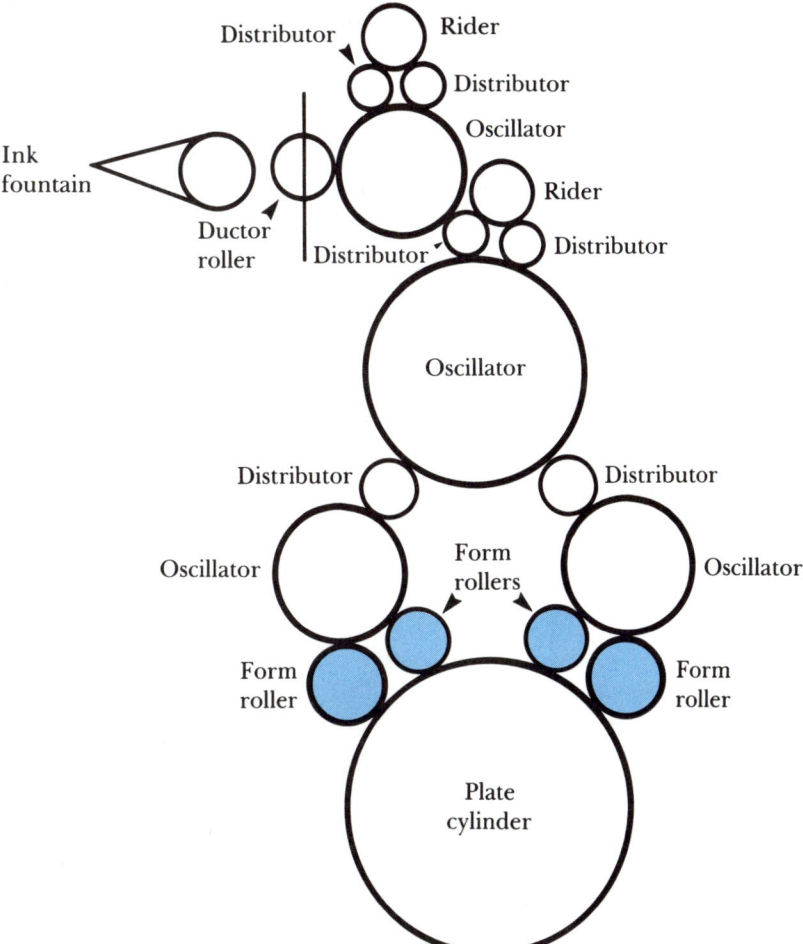

Typical inking system

Ductor, intermediate, and form rollers are very often made of a synthetic rubber such as vinyl (polyvinyl chloride), Buna-N (a copolymer of butadiene and acrylonitrile), or polyurethane. These substances are applied to a steel rod or tube that forms the roller shaft.

The ink fountain, the trough that holds the ink supply, is formed by the **fountain roller,** which is a metal roller that turns either intermittently or continuously, a **fountain blade,** which can be a spring steel plate, steel segments, or plastic approaching the fountain roller at an angle, and two **fountain cheeks,** which are vertical metal pieces that contact the fountain roller edges and the fountain blade edges to form an ink-tight trough. One press manufacturer has replaced the fountain blade with a disposable sheet of polyester that is held in contact with the fountain roller by a series of small cylinders lying parallel to it. Each cylinder has bearers at the ends. The space between bearers, about 1¼ in. (32 mm), is undercut and eccentric. As the cylinder rotates, more or less ink can pass to the fountain roller because the undercut of the eccentric roller increases or decreases. This produces controllable bands of ink on the fountain roller, which are blended by the oscillators. Each cylinder is adjusted by an individual motor controlled from the press console, which has an illuminated display showing the fountain profile.

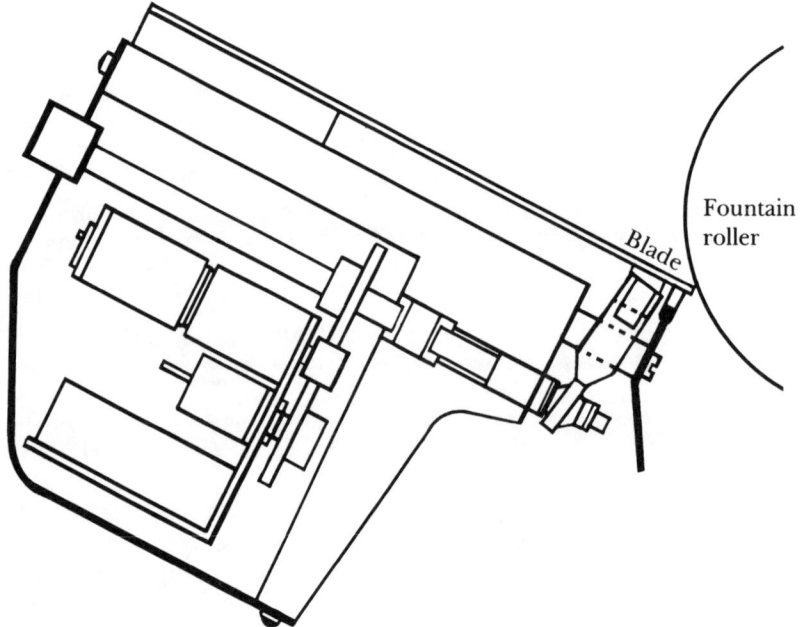

Single ink key for a remotely controlled ink fountain with a continuous blade
Courtesy Miller Printing Equipment

As the fountain roller turns, the majority of the ink in the fountain is held back by the fountain blade, which is set very close to the fountain roller. The distance between the blade and the roller is adjusted by means of **fountain keys,** a series of thumb screws (ink fountain keys) or motor-driven screws or cams behind the blade. This adjustment varies the ink feed across the press according to the demands of the plate.

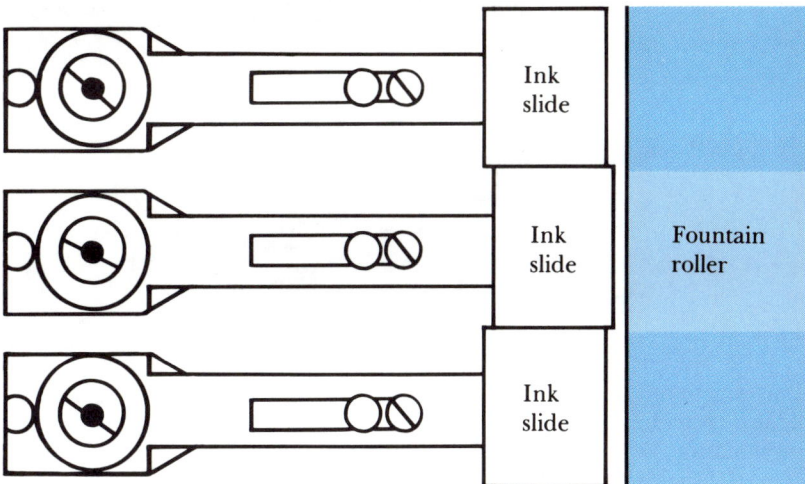

Ink slide for a Miehle-Roland sheetfed press
Courtesy Graphic Systems Div., Rockwell International

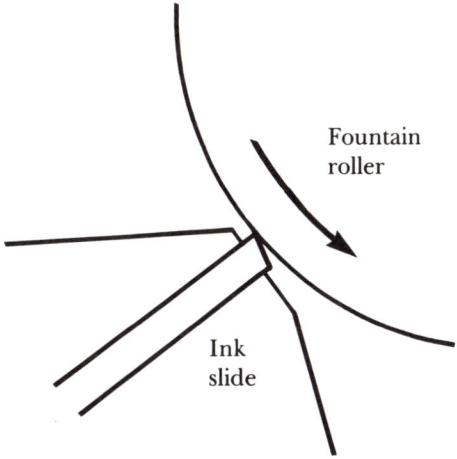

The overall adjustment of ink feed is controlled in one of two ways. If the fountain roller is the type that turns intermittently, the degree of rotation can be determined with a ratchet mechanism that varies the number of teeth exposed to the pawl. If the fountain roller turns continuously,

46 Sheetfed Offset Press Operating

Inking fountain on a Heidelberg Speedmaster press

Press operator adjusting ratchet mechanism

dwell—the length of time that the ductor roller contacts the fountain roller—can be varied with a dwell cam mechanism.

The ductor roller feeds a metered amount of ink from the fountain to the full roller system by alternately contacting the ink fountain roller and the first oscillating roller. Depending on the design of the system, the ductor roller contacts the fountain roller once or, more usually, every other or every fourth revolution of the plate cylinder. Ductor timing is related to the reversal of the oscillator, which is operator-adjustable on some presses. A properly timed ductor roller contacts the oscillating roller when the form rollers are in the plate gap or the trailing edge of the plate. **Ductor shock,** the vibration sent through the inking system when the ductor first contacts the oscillating roller, does not interfere with print quality as long as the form rollers are over the plate cylinder gap when the initial contact is made.

The heavy ink film is fed onto the oscillating roller and is then worked down into a smooth film by the rest of the inking system.

The oscillating drums are usually made of steel tubing covered with copper, ebonite, nylon, or other oil-receptive material that is resistant to roller stripping caused by dampening solution chemicals. The oscillators change lateral direction at least once for every revolution of the plate cylinder, which helps inking control by smoothing out the ink film and reducing banding. Oscillating rollers are driven by gears or chains, which indirectly power all other rollers by surface contact. The surface speed of the drums is the same as that of the plate when the plate is packed to manufacturer's specifications.

When the press trips off due to a missed sheet or when it is tripped off by the press operator, the form rollers lift from the plate automatically. At the same time, ink feed from the ink fountain ceases because the ductor roller does not contact the fountain roller. When printing is to resume, the rollers are brought back into contact with the plate either automatically or manually, and ink feed is resumed.

One weakness of the inking system is that the form rollers become slightly overloaded with ink during the interval when the cylinder gap passes them. During this interval they make one complete revolution. Ink continues to be fed to them but there is no plate to receive it. This slight overload is discharged on their first revolution over the plate and is sometimes noticeable as a rise in ink density on the first several inches (centimeters) of the sheet that suddenly ends in a visible streak. To partially compensate for this roll-out, the ink form rollers are varied slightly in diameter, which tapers the streak to an acceptable level.

Another weakness is the loss of controlled ink displacement when the press idles. As long as the press is running and printing, the fountain settings deliver a controlled amount of ink to each area of the plate. When a press idles for a few minutes, the oscillators tend to even out the supply of ink across the rollers. When the press starts up again, the areas of heavy demand on the plate are slightly starved and the light-demand areas get too much. This problem continues for only a few sheets, but it does cause variations. In high-quality work, these sheets are often removed from the delivery and discarded.

Some presses have an **oscillating form roller,** which is a roller substituted for the first and, sometimes, fourth (last) form rollers to reduce ghosting. This form roller oscillates (moves laterally, or side to side) at a rate different than the adjacent oscillator to smooth the ink film. The oscillation of the form roller can be turned on or off by the press operator.

Ink Film Thickness

The thickness of the ink film on the rollers is a very important consideration in printing. The thickness should always be measured using the oscillator above the last form roller. **Caution:** The press must be stopped and put on safe whenever ink film thickness is being measured.

A **wet ink film thickness gauge** is a device that permits the measurement of the thickness of the ink film on a roller. The most common gauge is essentially a roller with the center portion ground away to varying depths around the circumference. It is rolled over the ink surface until a point is reached where the ink just fails to penetrate to the bottom

Interchemical (Inmont) wet film thickness gauge with holder
Courtesy Gardner Laboratory, Pacific Scientific Co.

An inking system equipped with an oscillating ink form roller, which reduces ghosting when substituted for the first form roller
Courtesy Graphic Systems Div., Rockwell International

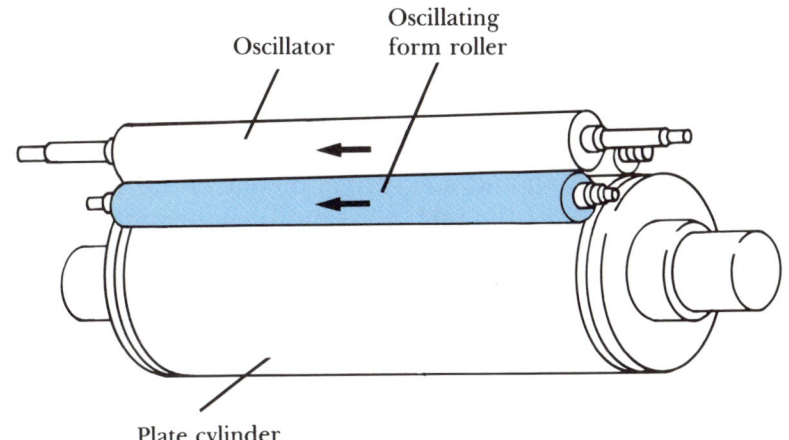

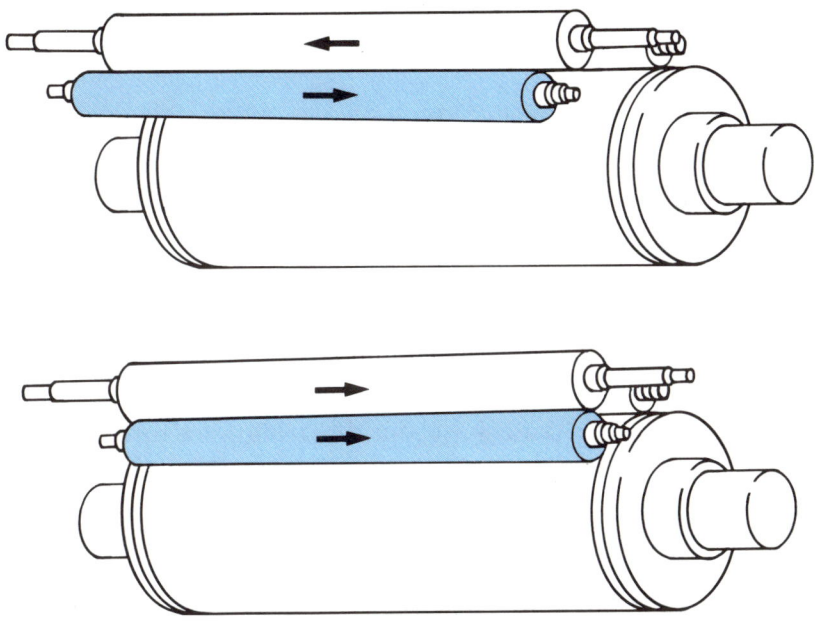

An oscillating ink form roller, the Ghost ContRoller™, from AirSystems, Inc., shown in the press

recess. At this point the corresponding number of the scale around the side of the gauge gives the thickness value.

Typical ink film thickness on a lithographic press is 0.2–0.4 mils (0.0002–0.0004 in., or 0.005–0.010 mm), depending on the ink color and printing sequence. The press operator should measure and control the amount of ink being carried by the inking system for more precise control of ink density and color, and to avoid problems related to excessively thick or thin ink films.

Common problems resulting from an excessively thin film of ink are low color strength and color saturation, low gloss, incomplete coverage of paper, picking, and hickeys. Also, ink/water balance is difficult to achieve.

Common problems resulting from an excessively thick film of ink are increased ink consumption, ink setoff, drying problems, slight degradation of light colors, graininess of print due to irregular dot gain, excessive emulsification of ink, and low contrast in the shadows due to dot gain.

Setting Rollers

In the inking system, few things are more important than setting the form rollers correctly. Roller streaks and many other problems can often be traced to poorly set rollers, so carefully follow the manufacturer's instructions for setting them.

Setting Form Roller to Oscillator

A form roller is usually mounted in brackets that pivot around the shaft of the oscillating roller that it contacts. The pivoting bracket permits the form roller to be set to the plate—without disturbing the form-roller-to-oscillator setting. The bracket also permits the raising and lowering of the form roller without affecting any roller setting.

It is not advisable to use single strips of paper to test for contact, because friction from the surface of the rollers will affect the "feel." The use of three strips of paper is a better method. The smoother paper helps eliminate the effect of friction on the "feel" of the pulled strip, allowing for a more accurate pressure reading. The outer strips should be about twice the width of the center strip, which is the one that is pulled to set the roller.

Following is a typical procedure to set a form roller to the adjacent oscillating roller:

1. Locate the adjustments and determine which way to turn them for inward and outward movement. The operator's manual usually contains this information and

The Inking System 51

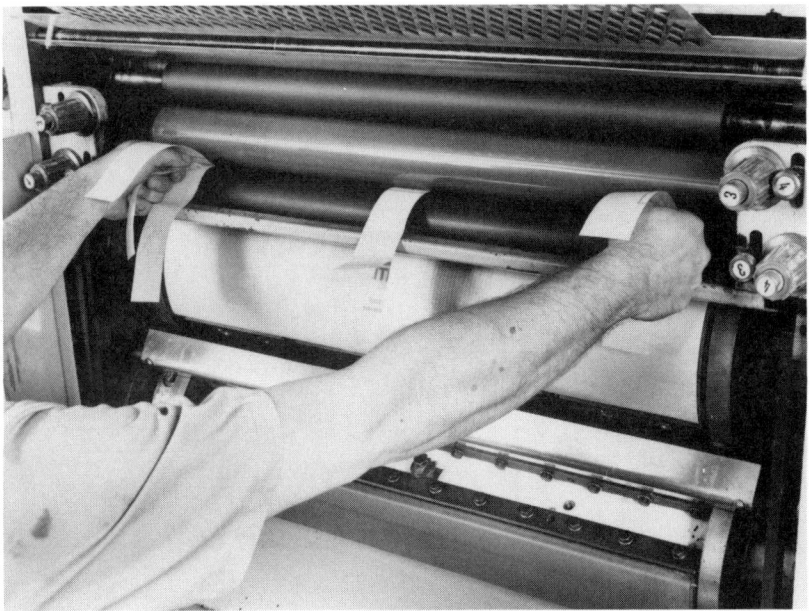

Press operator using strips of paper to set the form roller to the oscillator

sometimes illustrates the settings. The adjacent machine guard may also have this information.

2. Assemble the tools needed to make adjustments.

3. Cut nine strips of 0.002-in. (0.05-mm) packing paper, three about 12 × 1 in. (300 × 25 mm) and the other six about 12 × 2 in. (300 × 50 mm).

4. Assemble the strips into three sandwiches: each 12 × 1-in. strip is placed between two 12 × 2-in. strips. Insert a sandwich near each end of the form roller and in the middle of the roller.

5. Jog the strips into the oscillator and form roller nip. If the strips become trapped between the intermediate rollers in the ink train, excessive drag (resistance) results.

6. Adjust the distance between the form roller and the oscillator until the strips are gripped firmly. Remember that adjusting one side of the press will affect the setting on the other side.

When checking for pull on the strips, use only one hand and pull the center strip straight from the point of contact. There is no description of the right drag; one must develop the feel through experience. However, a **roller-setting gauge,** a device that shows the amount of pressure exerted by pulling the strip, can be used. A widely used procedure is to initially set the rollers using the three strips of paper and then to fine-tune the setting using two strips of paper and a roller-setting gauge.

52 Sheetfed Offset Press Operating

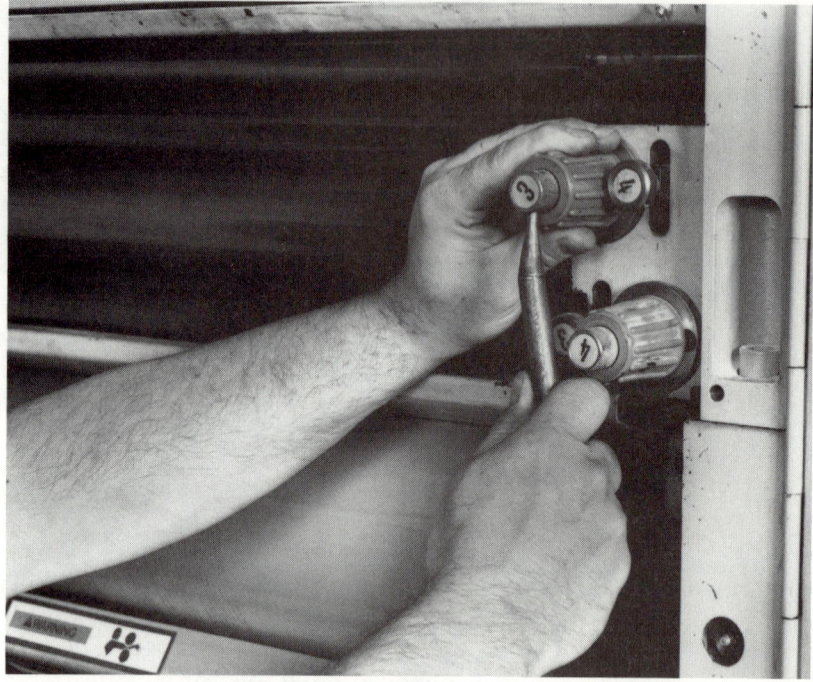

Press operator adjusting the pressure between a form roller and an oscillator

Setting Form Roller to Plate

To set the form roller to the plate, follow the same procedure described above, but position the form roller over the plate. Form rollers should be set slightly heavier to the oscillator than to the plate so that they are driven by the oscillators rather than by the plate.

Final checking of settings can be done using the **picture method,** which is an inked impression of the roller setting:

1. Ink up the rollers.

2. Pack the plate to printing height, gum it, dry it, and move it under the form roller to be tested.

3. Carefully lower the rollers to the plate, making an ink transfer.

4. Lift the rollers and turn the cylinder until the printed stripes are visible.

The required width of the stripe should be stated in the operator's manual. If not, a rough rule of thumb is to allow 1/16 in. (1.6 mm) of stripe for every 1 in. (25.4 mm) of diameter. For example, a 4-in. (101.6-mm) diameter roller should produce a stripe on the plate about 1/4 in. (6.3 mm) wide.

The stripe should be as even as possible in width throughout its length. Depending upon the age and condition of the form rollers, width may vary. A stripe that is fat at the ends may mean that the roller ends are swollen. A

The Inking System 53

Stripes on the plate from the form roller

Notice the unevenness of the stripes, indicating that both form rollers must be adjusted.

Press operator checking the width of a stripe on the plate using a roller stripe gauge

stripe that is fat in the middle may indicate shrunken roller ends or, more likely, too tight form-roller-to-oscillator settings. In circumstances where the inking system has deteriorated, a compromise setting will have to be made.

Settings between form roller and oscillator can be rechecked at this time:

1. Run the press for several seconds with the form rollers off the plate.

2. Stop and allow the press to stand for about 15–20 sec. Then inch the press, just moving the cylinders 2–3 in. (50–75 mm).

An impression of the form roller at rest against the oscillator will be seen on the oscillator roller. This impression should be inspected with the same criteria as a stripe to the plate, i.e., even and about the same width. The stripe on the oscillator should be slightly wider than that on the plate, to ensure that the form roller is set slightly harder to the oscillator.

Press operator using a stripe gauge to check the width of a stripe on the form roller

The picture test for roller settings can be repeated for all form rollers by removing the distributor rollers for clear viewing of the inner ink form rollers.

Many press operators gauge the form-roller-to-plate setting by the degree of bounce they can see or feel at the roller ends when the rollers cross the plate cylinder gap while the press is printing. It is risky to rely solely on this method even with a great deal of experience and a thorough knowledge of the machine's behavior. Some of the things that can affect the bounce are roller durometer; shock transmitted from the other side of the roller; play and wear in roller brackets, bearings, and linkages; and the presence or absence of a plate cylinder lead-on ramp. In short, it is better to set the form rollers as directed and use bounce as a gauge for testing accuracy or mechanical deterioration in the system.

In addition to bounce, **endplay,** the undesirable lateral movement due to poor fit between roller shaft and roller bracket, should be monitored. Endplay occurs as the oscillators change direction, usually as the plate cylinder gap passes beneath the rollers. As they change direction, the oscillators will move the form rollers sideways if there is play between the roller shaft and bearing or bracket. A very slight amount of endplay is acceptable. However, if the movement is more than about 1/64 in. (roughly 0.4 mm), it should be reduced; otherwise it will increase as the assembly wears, and in severe cases can cause slurring, excessive plate wear, and roller streaking. Some presses have a mechanical adjustment to reduce the amount of endplay. If no adjustment is available, shims can be used, but follow the directions in the press operator's manual for the proper procedure. The endplay must never be reduced so much as to strain the assembly or cause rapid wear, roller drag, or roller hangup that prevents the roller from being lowered properly.

Setting the Ductor Roller

On most presses, the ink ductor roller must also be set. Usually, this roller is only adjusted in one direction—either to the ink fountain roller or the receiving oscillator. Its movement is controlled by springs or cams. Use the following procedure to set the ductor roller:

1. Make sure that the ink system is clean.

2. Manually engage the ink feed mechanism.

3. Inch the press until the ductor roller has fully completed its stroke to the roller against which it is to be set.

4. Insert paper strips and proceed as for form roller setting. Make sure that the spring-controlled setting in the reverse direction still results in proper ducting.

Operation

The mechanical operation of the inking system is relatively straightforward. Most of the skill required lies in the setting of the rollers and the fountain.

On most presses, the automatic raising or lowering of the form rollers and the engaging or disengaging of ink feed can be manually overridden. This allows the plate to be rolled up without applying pressure.

The amount of roller oscillation can be adjusted on some presses, though in normal commercial printing this adjustment would be related to a specific problem.

The setting of the ink fountain is dictated by the demands of the plate. However, there are some basic fountain setting considerations. Care should be taken when changing the blade from a relaxed position (e.g., after removing, cleaning, and replacing the blade or fountain keys for maintenance following instructions in the press operator's manual or after a job with particularly heavy ink coverage) to a running position. The blade should be reset gradually, starting at the center of the fountain and moving to the outside edges. This method allows the blade to rise gradually on all the keys and avoids the distortion that would occur if setting started at one end and moved to the other.

As previously mentioned, the amount of ink running through the press is controlled in two ways. Across the press (laterally), it is controlled by the fountain keys; this setting reflects plate demands. The overall ink feed may be increased or decreased by varying the distance that the fountain roller rotates (sweeps) before being contacted by the ductor or by varying the length of time that the ductor roller contacts (dwells) against the fountain roller. During press makeready, it is necessary to establish a basic fountain setting from which the running setting can be fine-tuned. The accuracy of this basic setting depends heavily on the press operator's experience. The important point is the overall ink feed. In general terms, it is desirable to have a long sweep of ink feed to the ductor roller with a corresponding thin film of ink on the fountain roller. This relationship allows sensitive response to slight adjustments of both fountain key and ink feed. For example, if there were twenty points of adjustment on the ink feed and the form to be printed was of moderate coverage, it would be advisable to set the ink feed at ten to twelve points and adjust the fountain keys to correspond with this sweep.

During that portion of the makeready devoted to establishing color on the run, the sweep should be kept as constant as possible, with the fountain keys used to establish color. When a job is being printed, subtle increases or decreases of color can be achieved by raising or lowering the ink feed by one point. If the fountain is sweeping at four points instead of ten, a decrease of one point theoretically reduces the ink feed by 25%, which means that fine control of color on the press has been lost. In short, avoid extremes in one setting by increasing or decreasing the other.

Inking System Problems

Originally, inking systems were driven by the cylinder drive gears. When the gears became worn and noisy, they contributed to gear streaks. Any jarring, bumping, or interruption of the smooth inking of the plate is apt to cause a streak. To reduce this possibility, ink drives are now made independent of cylinder driving gears.

Roller Streaks

Most roller streaks are caused by glazed rollers or by rollers that are set too close to the plate or too far from the oscillators. A roller that bumps noticeably at the gap is set too hard. In some cases, the form rollers sag so much in the center or are so misshapen that they will not touch the plate without a bump.

There is a difference between a bump that is easily visible and a bump that is mainly felt through the roller end or bracket. As mentioned earlier, this latter procedure is used by some press operators as a gauge of roller setting. When a roller bumps too hard as the leading edge of the plate contacts it, its ink film ruptures. As a result, a streak appears on the roller and will be transferred to the plate at the end of the first roller revolution.

Glazed Rollers

Several serious problems can originate from glazed rollers. **Glaze** is a combination of oxidized roller surface, embedded ink pigment, dried ink vehicle, and gum from the fountain solution. It is generally a result of improper cleaning. In addition, rollers harden as they age; a combination of hardening and glazing seriously reduces the efficiency of the inking system. Hard, glazed rollers cannot adequately feed themselves with ink from the oscillator or intermediate rollers. This inability to feed properly increases starvation problems such as ghosting, roll-out (where there is a distinct drop in ink density as the rollers complete their first revolution over the plate), and drop-off (where there is a gradual loss of density from gripper to back edge of the sheet). If the press has any tendency to streak, streaking will definitely show up with hard, glazed rollers because they lack traction against both the printing plate and oscillator. Skidding also occurs; it not only slurs the print but wears the plate as well.

When rollers are only slightly glazed, their condition can be improved by scrubbing them with roller-compatible solvent, hot water, and a commercial rubber rejuvenator and using a blanket and roller abrasive pad. Deglazing should reduce the hardness of the roller by about 10 durometer units. If the hardness does not decrease, the roller should be reground or replaced. Regrinding should be done by a roller manufacturer according to press specifications.

Improper cleaning of the rollers results from poor roller settings, a worn washup blade, or inadequate solvents. If the rollers are not contacting each other properly, dissolved inks will not transfer properly up the roller system to the washup blade. A worn washup blade should not be used. The moderate cost of replacing these blades can be lost many times over in long washup times, increased glaze and roller deterioration, and the eventual scoring of or damage to the adjacent oscillator due to the use of excessive blade pressure.

A frequent cause of glazing is an improperly formulated solvent. As a cost-saving measure, a general purpose industrial solvent may be used and may appear to do the job initially. However, the removal of ink from the system is not enough. There are several other substances that must be removed from the rollers, e.g., ink additive compounds and emulsified fountain solution components, especially gum. These are often left behind by common solvents, and contribute to glaze. Washup solutions specially formulated for lithographic rollers are recommended. Several of these are two-step solutions; the first solution should be a water-miscible solvent. The extra cost of these solutions is quickly recovered in faster washup times, the use of less solvent, and easier color changes. If low-grade solvents are used, a good detergent-type glaze-removing solvent should be applied to the rollers once or twice a week.

In addition to the proper solvents, the washup technique is also significant:

1. Gum and dry the plate to protect it against stray drips.

2. Turn the press on and run it at medium speed, usually about 5,000–6,000 i.p.h. on newer presses.

3. Apply a little solvent across the rollers away from the washup blade to soften the ink.

4. Gently engage the washup blade to the oscillator roller, increasing pressure until contact is achieved.

5. Add solvent to one side of the ink system at a time, being careful not to allow the other side to become too dry. In this way, roller skidding, drips, and excessive buildup of ink at roller ends are avoided.

6. Apply solvent with a squirt bottle to various points of the roller system away from the washup blade. To avoid waste and drips, do not apply more solvent than can be held at the nips of the rollers.

7. Continue applying solvent periodically until the fluid running into the drip tray appears clear, and the rollers are clean. Do not be tempted to run a finger or a rag across the edge of the washup blade while it is working.

8. When the rollers are satisfactorily clean, release the washup blade while the press is still operating. Occasionally, if the washup blade is released on the run, a buildup of ink behind the blade will run back into the rollers, meaning that they have to be washed again.

Fountain Blade Problems

The ink fountain blade can also cause problems. The blade must be removed and cleaned occasionally. Dried ink accumulates on the underside of the blade, preventing the ink fountain keys from touching the blade.

When the blade gets wavy or worn, color control becomes very difficult and the fountain responds inaccurately. Blades become wavy when fountain keys are screwed in too tightly. The edge of the blade wears unevenly and becomes scalloped, which is particularly evident at the extreme corners of the fountain blade. Sometimes, the fountain roller becomes scored.

It is not necessary to jam the keys up hard to stop the flow of ink at a given point. They need only be tightened until a thin film of ink is on the fountain roller. Do not squeeze the ends of the duct, where there is no printing, until the duct roller is clean. Such a practice causes the blade to wear or the fountain to leak at the corners.

Sometimes the keys are too tight to start with, or they become tight through lack of maintenance.

Roller Problems

The ductor roller is often overlooked as a source of trouble. In some ways this is the most important roller in the train because it is the first roller to carry ink.

If the ductor roller has a low spot in it, or if it is out of round or out of adjustment, uniform inking is impossible. This roller must be free turning (to a certain point), carefully adjusted, and true in every respect.

When uneven printing occurs and nothing else seems to correct it, the rollers in the inking system should be checked using the "picture" method.

On older presses with steel-covered oscillator rollers, **roller stripping** is a common problem. It occurs when the rollers lose their affinity for ink and fail to carry it. Roller stripping is caused by the desensitizing agents in the dampening solution—the gum-acid combination primarily—that help nonimage areas to refuse to take ink. If stripping occurs, the

60 Sheetfed Offset Press Operating

A roller that is stripping

gum and acid content of the dampening solution should be reduced.

Washing up the rollers and applying copperizing solution helps temporarily. If practical, it would be advisable to have the roller electroplated with copper.

Maintenance

Mechanically, the inking system gives very little trouble if properly maintained. It must be lubricated properly to prevent excessive wear in bearings and linkages. The oscillation mechanisms work particularly hard and, therefore, should be lubricated and examined for wear frequently. All inker drive components that are not pressure-lubricated should be cleaned and lubricated regularly.

Roller Removal and Replacement

When rollers are removed from the press, their ends should never be "thumped" on the floor. Such a practice could bend the roller shaft or cause the ends of the roller shaft to flare out, preventing the easy removal of bearings or damaging the bearings. Rollers should be placed on a vertical rack when removed from the press and stored for a long period.

Even if the best washup solutions are being used, the rollers should be removed once in a while to remove ink

The Printing Unit 61

An ink cuff at the end of a roller

The ends of a roller being cleaned to prevent the buildup of dried ink

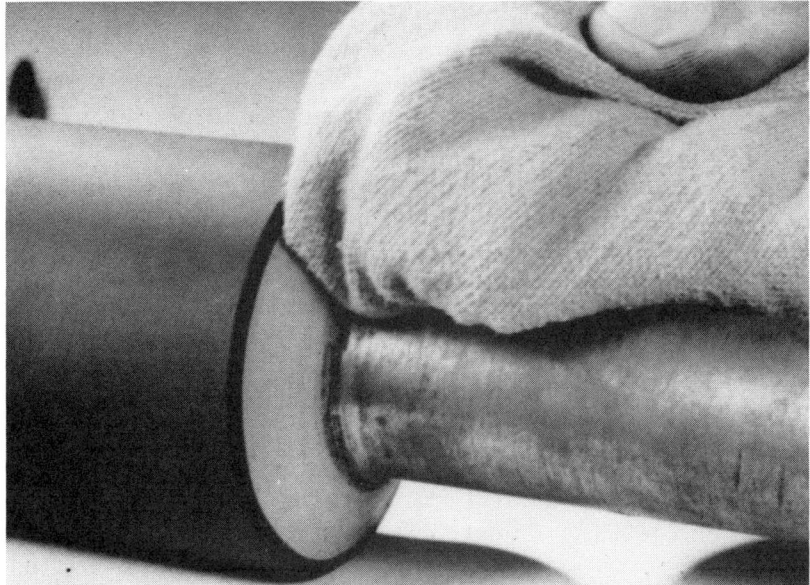

cuffs (a buildup of ink at roller ends), to inspect for replacement, to lubricate or replace bearings, etc.

Too often a set of rollers is put into a press and left there until all the rollers in the set are worthless. Eventual replacement is costly—both in money and time—because an entire set of rollers must be purchased and the time needed to replace all the rollers is extensive. Therefore at least a few spare rollers should be kept for each press. The spare rollers can be used to implement a simple system of roller rotation, which maintains the inking system at a high level of efficiency. Other advantages of roller rotation are that little time is needed to change only one roller and the cost of roller refurbishment is steady and controllable. The condition of the rollers should be examined weekly, and the worst one or two removed. A machine log book should be maintained, indicating which rollers are involved.

The removed rollers are replaced with the corresponding spare rollers. When replaced at this frequency, the rollers are unlikely to become densely glazed or pitted. So instead of re-covering the rollers, a light skim grinding will probably bring them back to a like-new condition. A roller may accept several skim grindings and polishing before re-covering is necessary; this considerably extends its useful life. Reground rollers then become spares for the next change. Where form rollers are concerned, larger ones that have been ground down can replace smaller form rollers on some presses, assuming that enough composition remains. Rollers should always be ground by someone specializing in this work, otherwise considerable damage to the roller can result.

New rollers should be inspected upon receipt. Items to check are the roller's trueness, its durometer, its diameter (because roller diameter must be very precise), its length, and the quality of its surface. A cast roller sometimes has an imperfect surface due to the casting process. A roller having any defect should be returned to the manufacturer.

Roller Storage

Spare rollers should be stored properly. The surface of a roller is sensitive to light and hardens due to the oxidation caused by the light. Ideally, rollers should be stored in a cool, dark area, standing on end in racks, and away from sources of heat and from electric motors.

There is a danger in storing rollers on racks horizontally for long periods. Longer rollers, particularly, become eccentric, or out-of-round, because the roller's composition covering flows downward. No adjustments can permit an eccentric roller to perform efficiently on press. If the rollers must be stored horizontally, each one should be given a quarter turn periodically, at least once a month.

If a roller is stored vertically, the composition of the roller will flow toward the lower end. The roller settings can be adjusted to compensate for the slightly enlarged roller end.

In addition, a vertically stored roller should be turned end for end periodically to minimize the effects of the composition's flow on the roller diameter.

Roller Hardness

Roller hardening is caused by several factors. Age is the most common cause, but such things as fluorescent light, sunlight, heat, and solvents that draw plasticizers from the roller compound also cause roller hardening.

The instrument that measures the hardness of roller compounds is a **type-A durometer.** The durometer measures the compound's resistance to a spring-loaded probe in units indicated on a dial or scale. On a scale of 0–100°, 100° indicates an inflexible surface such as cast iron. The durometer of a newly manufactured roller varies considerably—depending on where the roller will be used and on how the roller was made. For example, a form roller has a slightly lower durometer reading than an ink distributing roller. Typically, a roller's durometer will increase 10–15° during its useful lifetime. Beyond these hardnesses, the roller becomes less and less efficient, and contributes increasingly to ghosting and roll-out problems—particularly if glaze is present. The roller's durometer can often be reduced by using a commercial deglazing solution. If deglazing does not solve the printing problems, the roller manufacturer should be consulted.

Shore durometer
Courtesy Gardner Laboratory, Pacific Scientific Co.

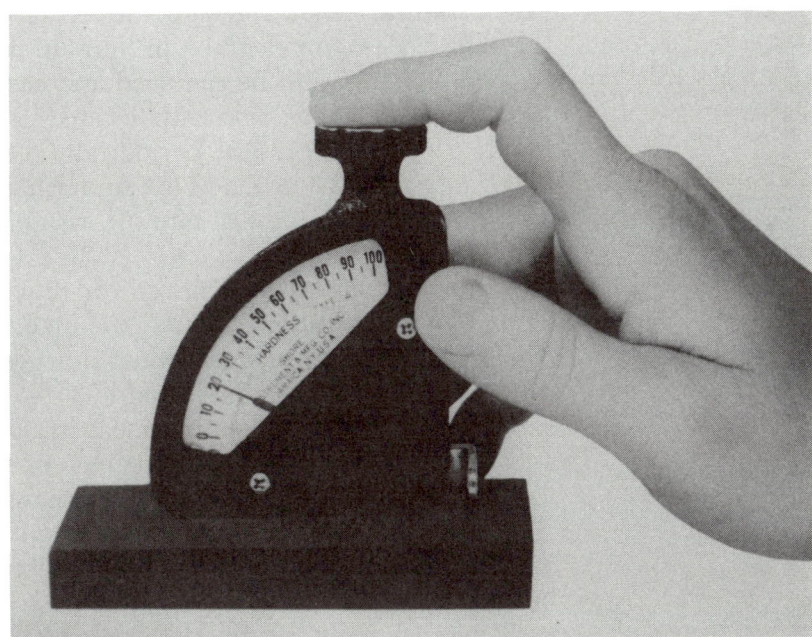

Two type-A durometers
Courtesy Rex Gauge Co., Inc.

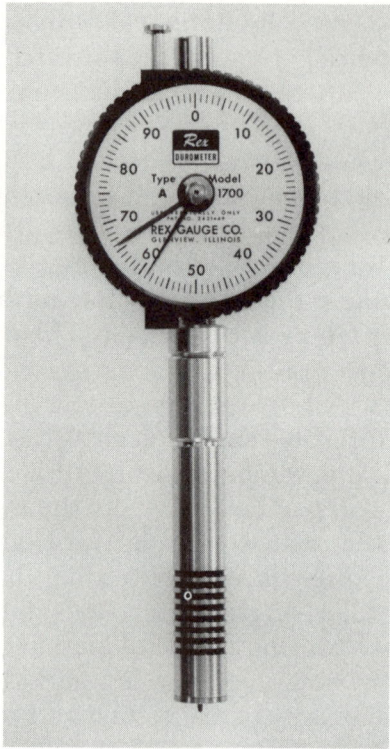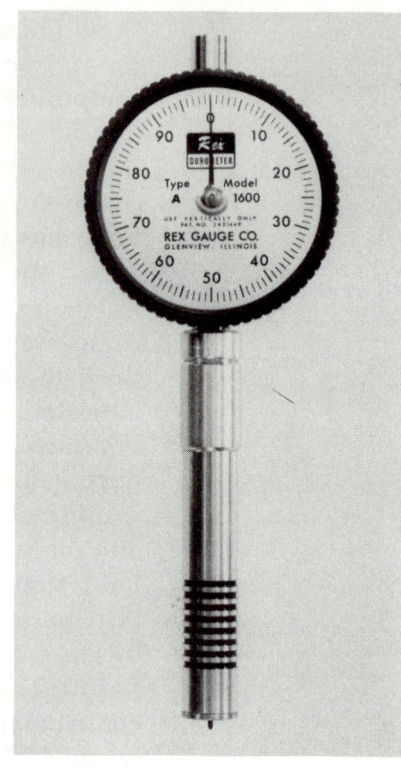

System Cleanliness

General cleanliness of the inking system is important. Ink cuffs should not be allowed to build up on the roller ends to the point where they break off on the run, causing hickeys. **Pipe** or **knife rollers,** small-diameter hard rollers, help to keep the ink system clean by picking up ink skin particles, lint, etc. They should be removed and cleaned periodically.

Many presses have drip trays located underneath the ink fountain. These should be periodically removed and cleaned. Any "stalactites"—hardened ink underneath the fountain that can break off and fall into the system—should also be removed.

Whenever rollers are removed for replacement or deglazing, the rods that connect the inker sideframes should be cleaned. Roller bearings should be checked for wear or dryness. At this time, it is a good idea to clean the roller-supporting sockets and setting mechanisms with a paintbrush and solvent, and to check for freeness of operation.

Many ink fountains have a blade assembly that can be removed easily for cleaning and replaced to the same setting as before. An adjustment for the forward positioning of the blade is also provided. If it is necessary to adjust the blade to the fountain roller, all the keys must be fully backed away from the blade. The blade should be adjusted according to manufacturer's instructions.

Fountain keys should turn smoothly and easily. If they do not, they may be damaged, insufficiently lubricated, or clogged with dry ink. Simple one-piece keys can be placed in a can of solvent and soaked while the threads in the fountain frame are cleaned according to the press manufacturer's directions.

Some inking systems have modular fountain keys. These modular keys are complex assemblies and are best left to a mechanic for servicing. These modular keys must be replaced in the press in precisely the same position from which they were withdrawn.

Ink Agitators

A common auxiliary device attached to many inking systems is the ink agitator. Inks of certain body characteristics tend to back away from the fountain roller, which means that the press operator has to stir the ink every few minutes. An **ink agitator** is a revolving cone-shaped device that moves from one end of the fountain to the other keeping the ink soft and flowing. It also reduces the formation of a skin on ink in the fountain, helping to reduce hickeys. Additionally, it helps control color variation by keeping the ink conditioned.

Fountain Splitters

For split fountain work where one color has to come quite close in location to another and oscillation cannot be reduced to zero, fountain splitters can be used. These small devices act like miniature washup machines. They are about 1 in. (25 mm) wide, and they clean off any color that works its way into the 1-in. (25-mm) splits.

Hickey-Picking Rollers

A **hickey** is a print defect that often appears as a void of ink or as a small, sharply defined solid area surrounded by a white halo. Hickeys are caused by solid particles that stick to the plate or blanket, e.g., ink skin, a chip of roller composition, a particle of antisetoff spray powder, cutter dust, paper fibers, or paper coating. The specific cause can sometimes be determined by removing the contaminant from the inking roller, plate, or blanket with a piece of clear adhesive tape. The tape is placed on a flat surface and cut in half, permitting particle identification.

The best solution to a hickey problem is to remove the cause of the problem. However, even in the cleanest pressroom, hickeys will still appear. Mechanical devices can be used to lessen the hickey problem. For example, a special "hickey-picking" roller can be added to the inking system to help remove hickeys from the plate during printing. There are several models available, all working on a similar principle. The surface of the roller appears to be fuzzy, due to the embedding of synthetic fibers, which may be plastics, elastomers, etc. This roller picks off the hickey as it appears or hides the white ring by filling it in with ink. Its efficiency depends on periodic maintenance. Depending on the type, maintenance may include removal from the press and cleaning following the manufacturer's instructions.

Checking the durometer of a Ryno® hickey-picking roller
Courtesy Jomac Roller Co.

Due to the fibrous nature of the roller's surface, it is best to install the roller as the first roller over the plate. If that space is occupied by a combination dampening/inking form roller, the hickey-picking roller should be placed in the second or third contacting position. If it is installed in the fourth or last position over the plate, mottling could appear in solids and dense tones. Wherever the roller is installed, its settings to both the oscillator and plate should be somewhat lighter than if it were a conventional roller. In addition, the nap of the fibers depends on the position of the roller in the ink train. If the hickey-picking roller is in the first ink form roller position (the one closest to the dampening system) the roller should have coarse-nap fibers. The farther back the hickey-picking roller is, the finer napped the roller should be, so that roller patterns do not show.

The Inking System 67

Fountain Height Monitors

Available as an auxiliary device on some presses, a **fountain height monitor,** or **ink leveler,** is an ultrasonic sensing device that checks the height of ink moving over the agitator. It signals a pneumatic ink pump to pump ink into the fountain when a certain level is reached.

It eliminates manual ink replenishment and reduces waste caused by color variations and print density inconsistencies. Some ink levelers are constructed so that they can be easily moved to another printing unit if the color sequence is changed.

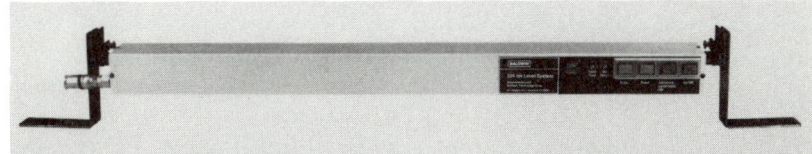

Ink leveler
Courtesy Baldwin Technology Corp.

Ink Consumption Counters

An **ink consumption counter,** a common accessory on web presses and some folding carton presses, is a device placed in-line with an ink pump to measure ink flow and, hence, consumption. It provides an accurate measurement of the amount of ink consumed on any one printing job.

Air Curtin

A recent innovation in press inking systems is the use of an Air Curtin™ to remove excess moisture from the inking system. An air bar directs streams of low-pressure air against a strategically located roller to evaporate the excess water.

Air Curtin™, available from AirSystems, Inc.

Notice that the Air Curtin has been installed to remove excessive moisture on the down side of the inking system.

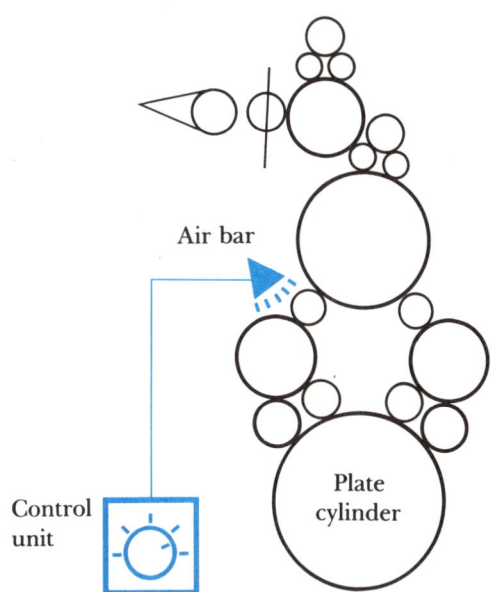

4 Dampening

The dampening system on a lithographic sheetfed press applies a water-based **dampening,** or **fountain, solution** to the printing plate before it is inked. Its major objective is to provide fast and complete separation of the image and nonimage areas of the plate; i.e., to prevent ink from becoming deposited in nonimage areas. Offset press operators have to control both ink and water and balance one against the other for good results. Ink, plate, press speed, paper, temperature, and relative humidity are the principal factors that influence the need for various dampening solutions.

Dampening solution is applied to the printing plate in a number of ways, most of which are discussed later in this chapter.

Dampening Solution

Dampening solution is a water-based mixture specially formulated to dampen lithographic printing plates before they are contacted by the inking rollers.

Composition of a Dampening Solution

Dampening solution composition varies for a number of reasons. A metallic or fluorescent ink, for example, may require an alkaline dampening solution. Most dampening solutions, however, are acidic with a pH between 4 and 6 being typical. The dampening system itself also influences the composition of the dampening solution. For example, some dampening systems require the use of a percentage of alcohol (or alcohol substitute) due to the method of applying the solution to the printing plate. Sometimes, in a conventional dampening system, the use of such an *additive* improves print quality although its presence in the dampening solution may not be essential.

In general, a dampening solution will consist of the following ingredients:

- **Water,** with minimal impurities.
- **Acid** or **base,** depending to a large extent on the ink being used. Acids used include phosphoric acid, acid phosphate compounds, citric acid, or lactic acid.
- **Gum,** either natural (gum arabic) or synthetic, to **desensitize** nonimage areas, i.e., to make them prefer water instead of ink.
- **Corrosion inhibitors,** to prevent the dampening solution from reacting with the plate. Magnesium nitrate is sometimes used; it also acts as a scratch desensitizer and **buffer**—a substance capable of neutralizing acids and bases in solutions

and thereby maintaining the acidity or alkalinity level of the solution.
- **Wetting agents,** such as isopropanol or an alcohol substitute, which decrease the surface tension of water and water-based solutions.
- **Drying stimulator,** a substance—e.g., cobalt chloride—that complements the drier in the ink. Drying stimulator is an additive that is used only if ink is not drying fast enough. Typical concentrations are 1–2 oz. of stimulator per gallon (8–16 mL per liter) of dampening solution.
- **Fungicide,** to prevent the formation of mildew and the growth of fungus and bacteria in the dampening system.
- **Antifoaming agent,** to prevent the buildup of foam. Foam can interfere with the even distribution of dampening solution on the dampening rollers.

Suppliers of dampening solutions provide a premixed (usually proprietary) one-step concentrate that contains all of the additives, except for the water and the alcohol or alcohol substitute, although some also include the alcohol substitute. Printers dilute the one-step concentrate with water, adjust its pH and conductivity to acceptable levels, and then add the

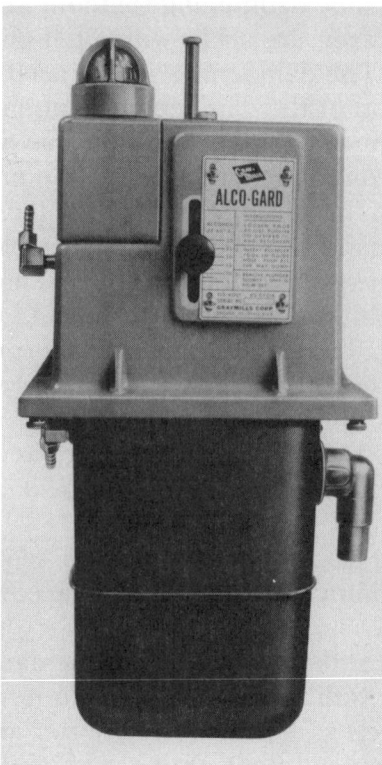

Alco-Gard *(left)*
Courtesy Graymills Corporation

Refrigerated circulator *(right)*
Courtesy Baldwin Technology Corp.

alcohol if needed. The manufacturer of the dampening system will indicate whether alcohol is necessary for the successful operation of the dampening system.

One-step dampening solution concentrates already contain a natural or synthetic gum. Two-step concentrates require the addition of gum. This extra step is an inconvenience, but it permits the press operator to control the gum/acid ratio. The concentrate's supplier usually indicates the amount of gum to be added. The addition of 0.5–1.0 oz. of gum per gallon of dampening solution (4–8 mL per liter) is common.

Local water conditions affect the dampening solution. Hard water requires a stronger acid than does soft water. Some concentrates are formulated especially for a certain type of water. In some cases, water conditioning may be necessary. Ion-exchange systems can be used to soften or demineralize the water.

Alcohol

When discussing dampening systems, the word "alcohol" means 98% pure isopropyl alcohol (isopropanol, or IPA). However, many of the alcohol substitutes are technically alcohols (although they can also be surfactants). Therefore, to avoid confusion, whenever the term "alcohol" is used, it will refer to isopropyl alcohol.

The use of alcohol in dampening systems is common, but the U.S. Environmental Protection Agency (EPA) has increased the pressure to use alcohol substitutes. In recent years, numerous alcohol substitutes have been introduced, with varying degrees of success.

Including alcohol in the dampening solution became popular for several reasons:

- **Easier control of the press.** Alcohol allows the press operator more time to devote to other aspects of quality control. Ink/water balance can be attained more rapidly, and quality signatures can be produced more quickly at startup.
- **Reduction of the surface tension of water.** Alcohol is a wetting agent. By reducing the surface tension of the water, the alcohol helps the water to wet the dampener form roller evenly, requiring less dampening solution. A thinner film of solution will keep the nonimage areas of the plate clean. Alcohol also helps to properly spread water over the ink on rubber or bareback form rollers that apply both ink and dampening solution to the plate.
- **Rapid evaporation.** Less dampening solution is carried to the blanket due to the rapid evaporation of alcohol.

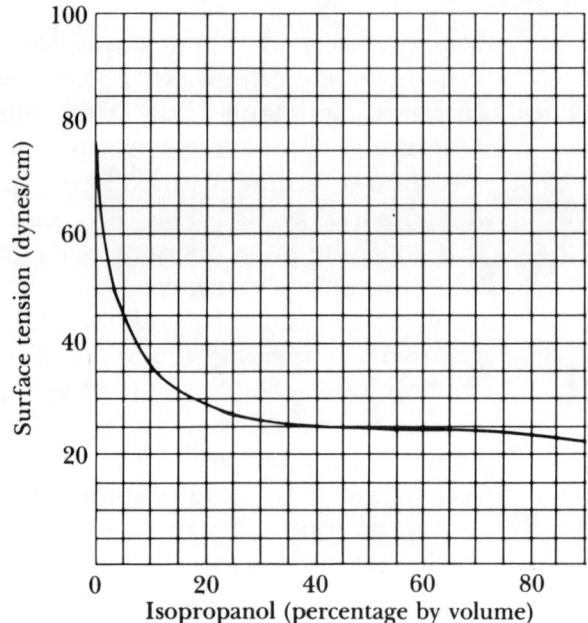

The effect of isopropanol on the surface tension of water

Consequently, less moisture is transferred to the printing paper, and ink drying is faster.

• **Reduction in contamination of system components.** The use of alcohol reduces the tendency of ink to emulsify. It also minimizes **snowflaking,** the tiny, white, unprinted specks that appear in type and solids. Snowflaking occurs when water becomes **emulsified** (dispersed) in the ink.

• **Reduction of time and materials.** With alcohol in the dampening system, quality printing is achieved sooner after startup. This saves paper, ink, and time. In addition, since less dampening solution is needed on the printing plate, less ink is required, resulting in decreased consumption of dampening solution and ink.

Hydrometer readings at various alcohol percentages and solution temperatures, using a hydrometer calibrated for 60°F

	Solution Temperature				
Percent Alcohol in Solution	**50°F** 10.0°C	**60°F** 15.6°C	**68°F** 20.0°C	**75°F** 23.9°C	**80°F** 26.7°C
0	0.9997	0.9991	0.9982	0.9973	0.9966
15	0.9809	0.9808	0.9802	0.9795	0.9793
20	0.9765	0.9769	0.9757	0.9745	0.9737
25	0.9723	0.9710	0.9703	0.9688	0.9671
35	0.9598	0.9570	0.9552	0.9532	0.9518

Despite alcohol's numerous advantages, several disadvantages may lead to constrained usage:
- **Expense.** Alcohol is more expensive than alcohol substitutes and conventional dampening solutions.
- **Toxicity.** Alcohol is highly toxic if ingested orally.
- **Flammability.** Alcohol is flammable and must be stored in approved, fireproof containers.
- **Irritability.** Alcohol fumes can be an irritant, especially in pressrooms without adequate ventilation.
- **Volatile organic compound (VOC) emissions.** Alcohol is a VOC that contributes to the formation of ozone in the atmosphere.

Storage and Handling of Isopropyl Alcohol and Other Flammable Liquids

Many chemicals and materials used in the printing industry can cause fires or explosions. Other chemicals are toxic and can harm the user through skin contact or inhalation. Isopropanol is both flammable and toxic.

Fire prevention practices are essential when handling flammable materials like isopropanol. Isopropanol must be kept in fireproof cabinets or rooms and stored in clearly labeled, approved safety containers; all sources of ignition should be removed from this area. The flame-arresting screen in the spout of these containers should be left in place. Bulk storage of flammable liquids is regulated by specific U.S. Occupational Safety and Health Administration (OSHA) standards. If possible these liquids should be stored in buildings other than the printing plant. Only immediately required quantities (limits are set by OSHA standards) should be brought into work areas. A practical rule of thumb is to keep no more than a day's needs in the work area.

The storage area must be away from any exits or escape routes; it must be well-ventilated, cool, clean, and orderly; and it must allow for grounding of the bulk containers. Smoking is prohibited in the areas where flammable liquids are stored, handled, or used.

All bulk containers should be bonded and grounded to prevent static electricity sparks. **Bonding** is the elimination of a difference in electrical potential between objects, while **grounding** is the elimination of a difference in electrical potential between an object and the ground.

Hazardous chemicals must be stored in properly labeled containers using the Hazard Material Identification System (HMIS). In addition, all users of chemicals in the plant must be familiar with the Material Safety Data Sheet and first-aid procedures for each chemical. Protective gloves, goggles, and aprons must be used when handling hazardous chemicals.

Alcohol Substitutes

Alcohol substitutes generally do not have any of the disadvantages of isopropyl alcohol, but using an alcohol substitute is more complicated.

Following are the principal advantages of alcohol substitutes:
- Less volatile than alcohol
- Used in lower concentrations (5% or less)
- Meets the Control Techniques Guideline (CTG) recommended by the Environmental Protection Agency (EPA)
- Odorless

The disadvantages of some alcohol substitutes are numerous, but continuing research and development may solve some of these:
- Increased paper debris on the blanket
- Buildup of dampening solution on the blanket
- Incapable of being mixed directly with concentrated gum and etch
- Increased drying time in some cases
- Occasional roller stripping
- Difficulty in running with nonabsorptive substrates, such as plastic papers

Dampening Solution pH

For a dampening solution to perform effectively, its acidity or alkalinity must be controlled not only during the initial mixing of the solution but also during the pressrun. If the proper level of acidity or alkalinity is maintained, quality printing should be easier to produce.

Acidic solutions. A dampening solution having an incorrect acid level or a solution in which the acid level changes excessively during a pressrun can cause several serious printing problems. Among these are slow drying or nondrying of ink, plate scumming, plate blinding, and roller stripping.

The gum arabic film protecting the nonimage areas of the plate is slightly acidic; however, it requires additional acid to adhere properly. The acidic compounds added to the dampening solution enable the gum arabic to cling to the nonimage areas of the plate.

Insufficient acid in the dampening solution lessens the gum's ability to adhere to the plate. Eventually, ink starts to replace the gum in nonimage areas, causing **plate scumming,** the pickup of ink in nonimage areas of the plate. Scumming can be caused by excessive acid if it attacks the plate metal and the protective coating. This type of scumming appears darker and more uneven than scumming due to insufficient acid.

Excessive acid also causes **plate blinding,** the loss of ink receptivity in the image area. The extra acid attacks the plate in the image areas, causing the image to deteriorate.

Another problem associated with excessive acid in the dampening solution is **roller stripping,** the failure of ink to adhere to the inking rollers. Stripping that occurs at the beginning of a pressrun is usually caused by glazed roller surfaces, and stripping that occurs during a pressrun is probably caused by an excessively acidic dampening solution.

Poor drying or nondrying of ink can be caused by excessive acidity. Drying problems can arise independently of scumming, blinding, and stripping problems and become obvious only after the completion of the pressrun. Excess acid reacts with the cobalt drier in the ink, rendering it practically useless as a drying stimulator.

Alkaline, or base, solutions. Most dampening solutions are slightly acidic. Some dampening solutions, however, are alkaline, particularly those for offset newspaper presses. These alkaline solutions do not contain a desensitizing gum and are made more basic by adding sodium carbonate or sodium silicate. An alkaline dampening solution sometimes contains a **sequestering agent,** a substance that prevents the calcium and magnesium compounds in the solution from precipitating, and a **wetting agent,** which lowers the surface tension of the water in the dampening solution.

Alkaline dampening solutions work best on newspaper offset presses or on converted letterpresses using the direct-lithography system:

- Roller stripping seldom occurs on inker rollers.
- Blankets do not become glazed because there is no gum in the solution.
- Fungus does not grow in the fountain pan.
- Aluminum plates run clean and do not need to be gummed up, even for overnight.
- Ink dot scum, a problem that occasionally occurs on

aluminum plates run with an acid dampening solution, does not occur.

In spite of these advantages of alkaline solutions for newspaper presses, almost all commercial offset lithography is done using acidic dampening solutions. The use of an alkaline solution in commercial offset lithography often results in the production of foam in the dampening solution, excess water emulsified in the ink, and bleeding of some pigments into the dampening solution, causing tinting.

pH measurement. pH—the potential of hydrogen—is a relative measure of a solution's acidity or alkalinity. **pH** is the negative logarithm of the concentration (in moles/liter) of the hydrogen ions in a solution.

If the pH of a solution is 7, it is neutral; it is neither acidic nor alkaline. A solution with a pH of 5 is slightly acid; a pH of 3 is considerably more acidic. The lower the pH reading, the more acidic a solution is. The opposite is true as the pH rises above 7. Thus, a solution with a pH of 8 is slightly alkaline, while one with a pH of 10 is considerably more alkaline, or basic.

Since the pH scale is logarithmic, a solution with a pH of 3 is 10 times more acidic than one with a pH of 4. Similarly, a solution with a pH of 3 is 100 times more acidic than one with a pH of 5.

As a general rule, an acidic dampening solution should have a maximum pH of 4.0 and a minimum pH between 4.5 and 5.5.

Three general methods are used to measure the pH of a solution. One colorimetric method of pH measurement depends on the color change of indicator dyes added to the solution. Each indicator changes color over a range of about two pH units. To determine the approximate pH of the solution, three dyes are used: one to determine the maximum pH, one to determine the minimum pH, and the last one to determine the approximate midpoint between the maximum and minimum pH levels.

Another colorimetric method of pH measurement depends on the color change of dye-impregnated papers. The widely used litmus paper strips permit quick reading but not pinpoint accuracy. Short-range pH testing papers have an effective range over a shorter portion of the pH scale and, consequently, are accurate to within 0.3–0.5 pH of the actual pH value.

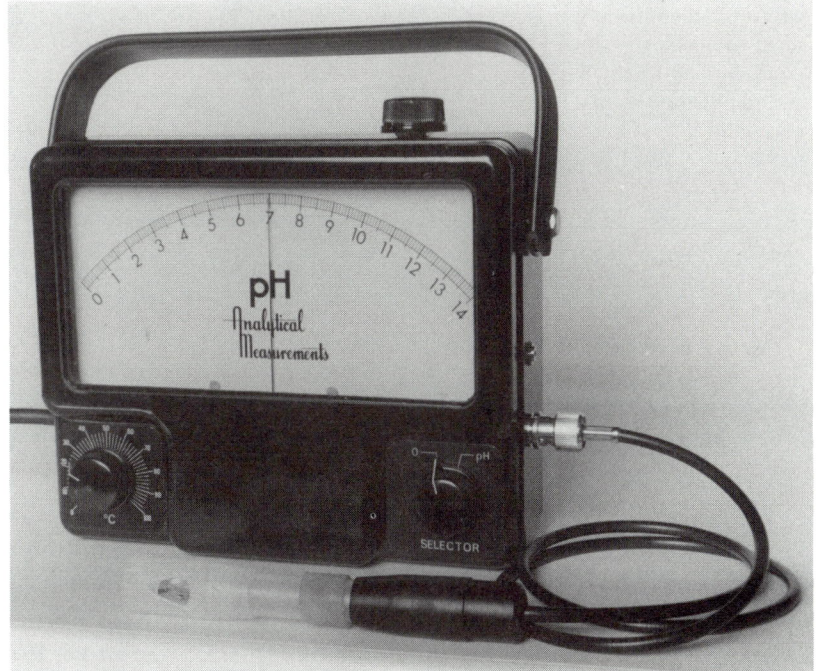

Model 707 pH meter
Courtesy Analytical Measurements, Inc.

The most accurate method of measuring pH uses electronically operated meters. Although more expensive than indicator dyes and pH papers, some pH meters are accurate to within 0.01–0.05 pH.

Additional information on the use of indicator dyes, pH papers, and pH meters can be obtained from the manufacturers or suppliers.

Conductivity of a Dampening Solution

Conductivity is a measure of the capacity of a material to conduct electricity. Extremely pure water is a very poor conductor of electricity. As materials dissolve or go into a solution, they form ions and the water becomes conductive. The conductivity of water increases directly with increases in the amount of dissolved matter (ions). Low (partially) ionizable materials such as alcohol and gum arabic are poor electrical conductors and usually lower conductivity of dampening solutions.

Pure water approaches a conductivity of 0 micromhos. Typical tap water might have a conductivity of 200 micromhos or more. As the amount of dissolved matter increases, the conductivity increases directly in a straight line. Thus, conductivity is commonly used as a measure of water purity. Soft water has a conductivity of 0–225 micromhos, and hard water has a conductivity greater than 450

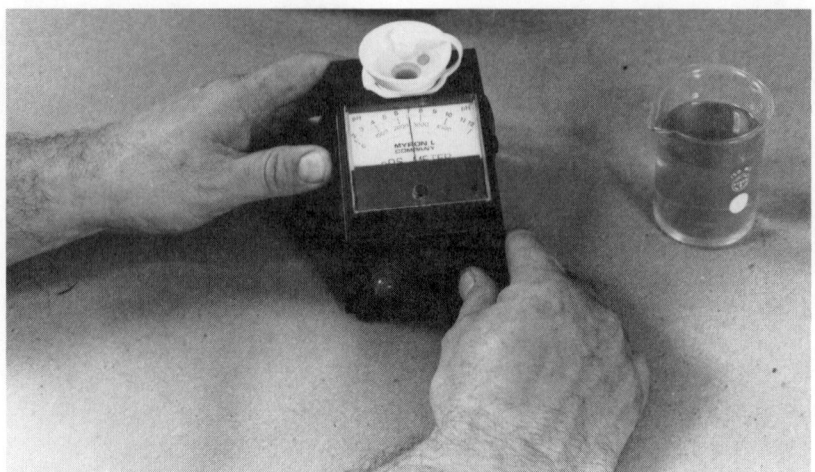

Myron L meter being used to measure the conductivity of a sample of dampening solution

micromhos. The relationship between water hardness and conductivity varies somewhat, depending upon the specific minerals and compounds in the water.

If the conductivity of different amounts of dampening solution concentrates in water is know, it is easy to measure the strength of a solution by measuring its conductivity. The following procedure can be used to develop a graph that plots conductivity and pH against concentration:

1. Measure the conductivity and pH of the water normally used to make the dampening solution. Place water in a clean 1-gal. (3.8-L) bottle.

2. Add 1 oz. (29.6 mL) of fountain solution concentrate. Remeasure both conductivity and pH. Record these values.

3. Add another ounce (2 oz. total) of fountain solution concentrate and remeasure both conductivity and pH. Repeat this process until the amount of fountain solution concentrate added exceeds the manufacturer's recommendations.

4. Plot these values on a graph that has concentration (oz./gal. or mL/L) on the horizontal axis and conductivity and pH on the vertical axis.

A similar graph can be developed if alcohol is also used in the dampening solution. New graphs must be made whenever the water or fountain solution concentrate changes.

If the conductivity of the dampening solution is known, the amount of either dampening solution concentrate or alcohol can be read directly from the graph.

The most important factor in preparing dampening solution is to make sure that it is the proper concentration. Most acidic dampening solutions are buffered so that, as the amount of concentration increases, the pH drops initially but then levels off, while the solution's conductivity increases in a straight line. Thus, conductivity is better than pH for determining the amount of concentrate in the dampening solution. However, the pH must still be measured, because the pH must be between 4.0–5.5 for good printing.

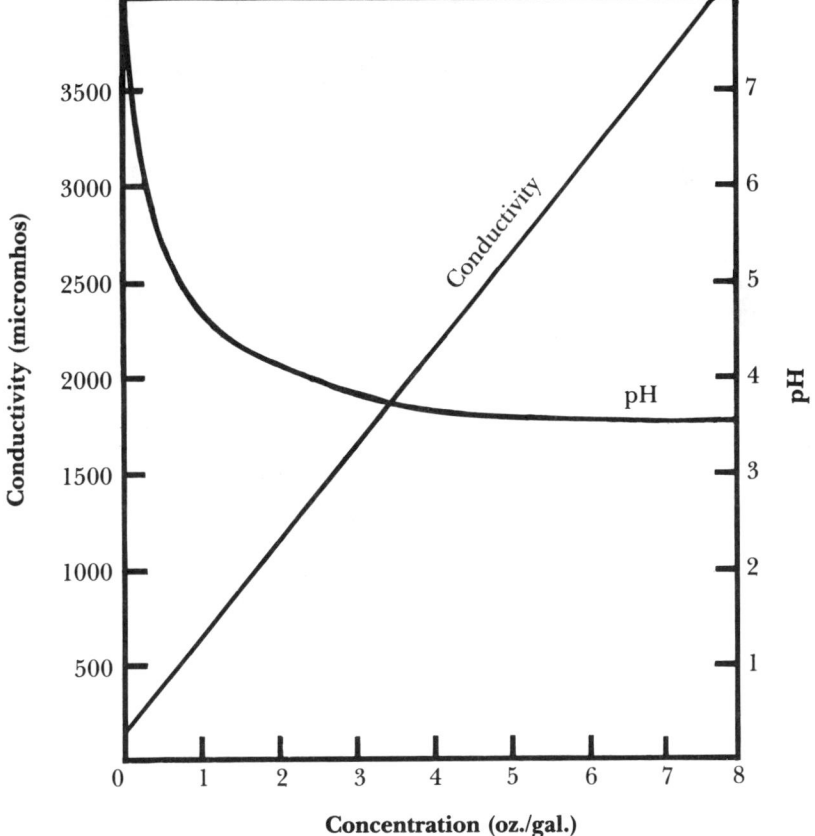

Graph of concentration vs. pH and conductivity for a hypothetical combination of dampening solution concentrate and water

With neutral dampening solutions and neutral (pH 7) water, the pH of the solution is constant, regardless of concentration. Therefore, conductivity must be used to measure the concentration of neutral or slightly alkaline dampening solutions.

Any unusual conductivity readings justify rechecking the conductivity of the water and the dampening solution concentrate. It is normal for the conductivity to increase during the pressrun because materials from the ink and paper contaminate the dampening solution. Therefore, conductivity measurements should be made before the dampening solution is used on the press.

Conventional Dampening Systems

Dampening systems used for sheetfed offset lithography are classified into two broad categories: the intermittent-flow (ductor, or conventional) and continuous-flow.

The intermittent-flow dampening system, usually referred to as a **conventional dampening system,** consists of the following:

- **Water pan,** or **fountain,** which holds the dampening solution to be fed to the plate
- **Fountain pan roller,** which rotates in the fountain and carries dampening solution on its metal surface
- **Ductor roller,** which intermittently contacts the fountain roller and an oscillator roller, transferring the dampening solution

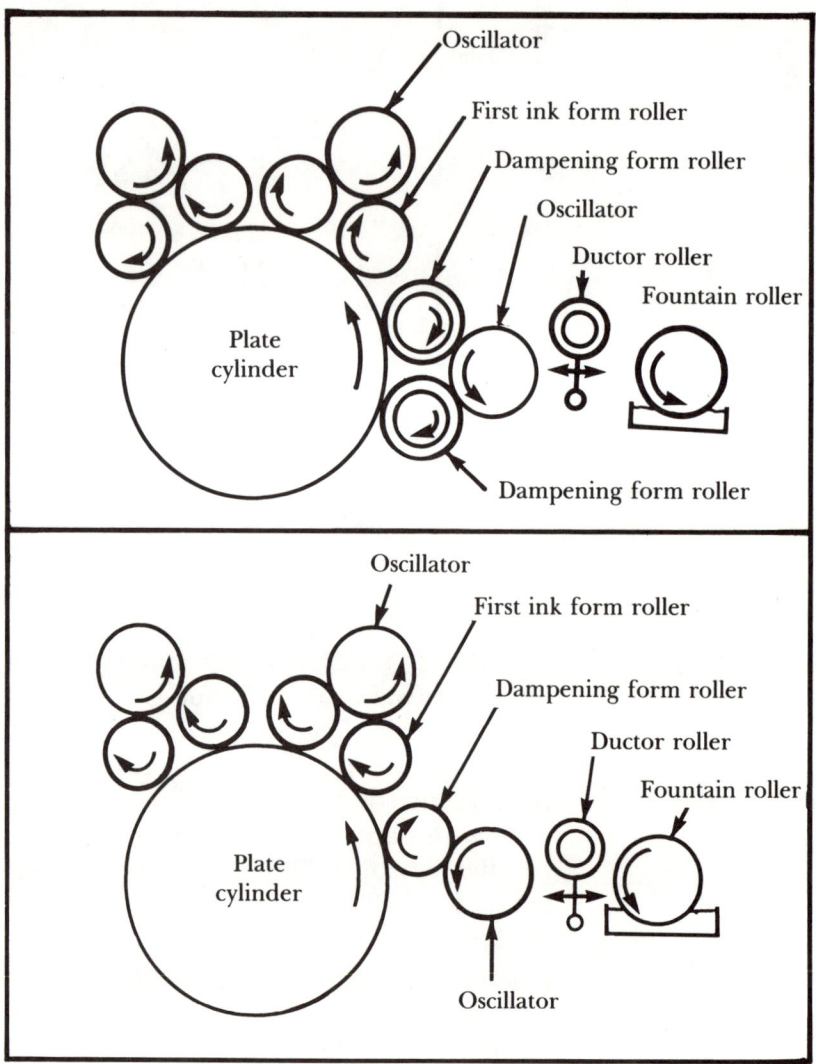

Conventional, or ductor-type, dampening systems using covered form and ductor rollers *(top)* and using a bareback form roller *(bottom)*

- **Oscillator roller,** which oscillates from side to side to even out dampening across the press
- **Form roller,** which transfers dampening solution from the oscillator roller to the printing plate

The design of a conventional dampening system resembles that of an inking system. A supply of dampening solution is held in a fountain. A chrome-plated or treated aluminum fountain roller rotates in the fountain. As the roller turns, it draws a film of dampening solution onto its surface. On some presses, this roller is covered with cloth to increase its solution-holding capacity. It is usually driven by its own motor, separate from the main press drive, or by a variable-speed drive off the press. The fountain roller is operated through gear reduction, because if it is operated at press speed it would sling solution all over the press area. All other rollers in the conventional dampening system are operated at press speed.

A ductor roller is a roller that alternately contacts the fountain pan roller and the oscillator roller. It transfers dampening solution from the fountain pan roller to the surface of the oscillator. The ductor roller is made of a plasticized-rubber compound and is always covered, often with a molleton fabric, to increase its solution-holding capacity.

The oscillator roller, chrome-plated or treated aluminum and power-driven, has a dual purpose: it drives the dampening form rollers by direct surface contact and its lateral oscillation equalizes water feed across the press. The rotational surface speed of the oscillator is the same as that of the plate when the plate is packed to manufacturer's specifications. There is no setting adjustment on this roller; it is permanently fixed in the dampener unit frame.

The form rollers apply dampening solution directly to the plate. Most presses have two form rollers. Form rollers are contact-driven rubber rollers, covered with a cloth or paper sleeve or run bareback. They contact both the oscillator and the plate.

The conventional dampening system is an intermittent-feed system. Dampening solution does not move continuously from the fountain pan to the plate. The amount of solution in the dampening system is lowest just before the ductor contacts the oscillator. Dampening solution surges through the system when the ductor makes contact. These surges make it difficult to control the conventional dampening system, and the problem is more serious here than in the inking system because the dampening system has very few rollers. Because the problem is inherent in the design, the press operator must learn how to control it.

Roller Covers

Absorbent cloth and paper dampener covers help to provide more continuous dampening by increasing the solution-carrying and solution-storing capacity of the rollers. The covered rollers act like sponges, absorbing excess water (becoming reservoirs) and giving it up when the supply becomes low. The dampening flow to the plate varies less, and less total solution is delivered. The advantages of increased volume capacity are better control and minimum dampening solution delivered to the plate.

In order to further enhance the carrying capacity, the operator sometimes puts a double cover on the roller, with the undercover made of cotton or flannel.

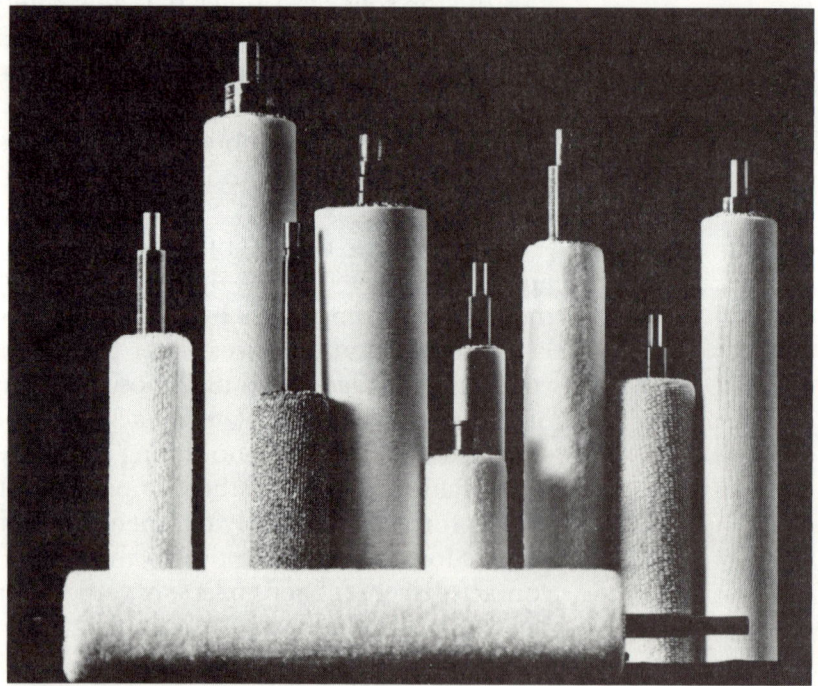

An assortment of dampener covers
Courtesy Jomac, Incorporated

The problem with large-capacity dampening systems is that they respond slowly to changes. If the press operator wants to increase the amount of dampening, the speed of the fountain roller is increased. On the other hand, if the operator wants to cut back on the level of dampening, it is necessary to turn the dampening supply off and let the press

A variety of dampening sleeve products
Courtesy REL Graphic Systems and Marketing Corp.

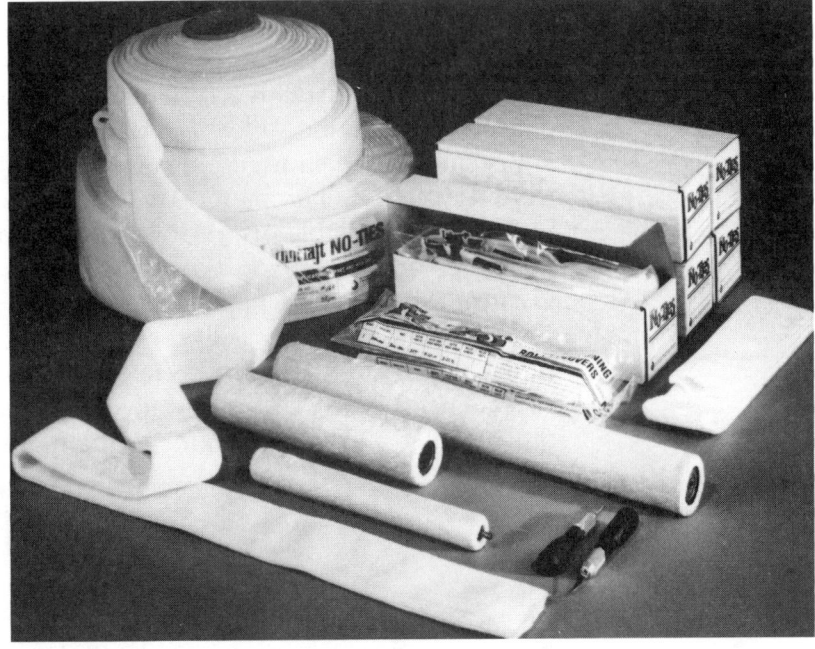

reduce the amount of dampening solution in the system. In both cases, skill is required on the part of the operator to make the change without producing waste.

Cloth (usually a fabric called molleton) is a widely used material for covering dampening form rollers. It is woven as a sleeve, slipped over the roller, and tied at the roller ends. Molleton has a relatively long nap and is good for storing water. However, it releases lint when new and easily becomes greasy. In addition, depending on how dirty or greasy the

Shrink-type dampener cover
Courtesy Jomac, Incorporated

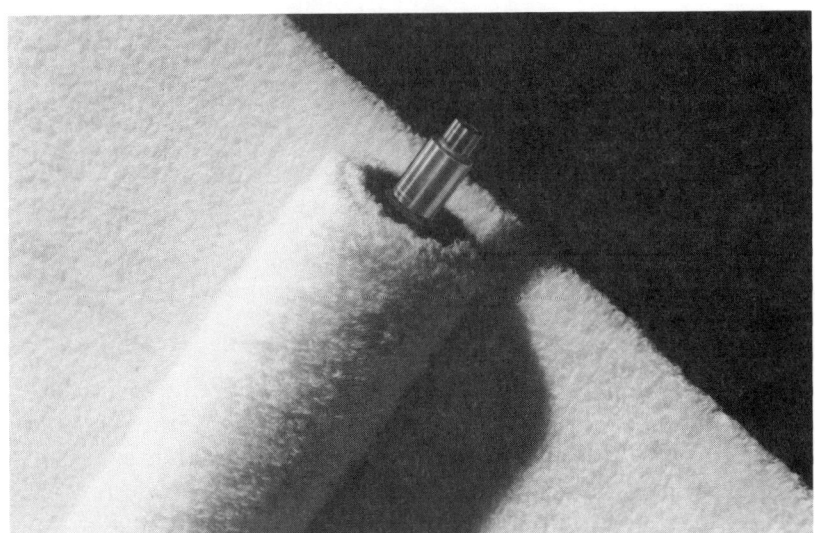

cover gets, its thickness can vary; this changes the effective radius of the roller. In effect, this changes the roller setting, which makes it difficult to maintain a uniform film of dampening solution unless the dampener rollers are reset.

Because of the shortcomings of cloth covers, paper covers were developed. The paper used is a special vegetable parchment, available originally as strips for winding around the roller or presently as tubular sleeves. Probably the greatest advantage of paper covers is that when they get dirty (as all covers inevitably will) they are easier to clean or replace than cloth. Paper covers are also less grease-absorbent. Because of their limited water-storage capacity, they require a skilled operator to maintain balance.

3M ductor sleeve
Courtesy 3M

Another dampener covering material that has proven successful consists of a randomly laid blend of 50% rayon fiber and 50% fusible fiber that serves as a binder to hold the rayon fibers in place. Loosely held rayon fibers permit the construction of a seamless sleeve. Rayon is hydrophilic and easily accepts water, but it does not hold excessive amounts that might cause flooding. When immersed in water, the sleeve shrinks tightly onto the roller. With a smoother surface than molleton, rayon sleeve material responds more quickly to press adjustments.

Adjustments to a Conventional Dampening System

Setting the pressure between the various dampening rollers is critical. The form roller's contact with both oscillator and plate is adjustable. Contact between form rollers and oscillator must be just enough to transfer dampening solution and driving action, and no more. If the contact is too weak, dampening solution will not transfer properly and the power-driven oscillator may fail to drive the form rollers at full speed. On the other hand, too much contact pressure will also fail to transfer dampening solution. Instead, the solution will be wrung out of the covers just as though they were passed between the rollers of a wash wringer. Plastic feelers or mechanical gauges should be used to determine the proper adjustment.

In most cases, the pressure between the dampening form roller and the plate should be less than that between the form roller and the oscillator. A tight setting can "squeegee" dampening solution off the plate and increase plate wear. The ideal setting exerts just enough pressure to smoothly transfer an adequate amount of dampening solution to the plate.

As in the inking system, the oscillator is the reference point used in setting the rollers. It must be parallel to the fountain roller and to the plate cylinder. Alignment should be checked periodically as part of long-term maintenance. If the oscillator is not parallel, the press operator should not attempt to reset it. Such settings are extremely critical and should be made by a manufacturer's service technician.

The pressure between the form roller and oscillator is set with smooth strips of 0.002-in. (0.05-mm) plastic. Sandwiches of three strips are placed between the form roller and the oscillator. A sandwich is put about 3 in. (76 mm) from each end, and another one or two are placed near the middle. The middle strip, about 1 in. (25 mm) wide, is pulled to gauge or judge the roller pressure. The outer two strips, each about 2 in. (50 mm) wide, help to remove the effect of friction on the tension. If roller covers are clean and soft and the oscillator clean, the middle strip should pull out with a resistance of about 0.5 lb. (0.2 kg).

Sandwiches of strips are also used to set the dampener form roller to the plate. A properly set, concentric roller with a soft cover should not "bump" at the plate cylinder gap. Running the press fully engaged with the dampening system on helps to show the action of the roller at the gap.

Modern dampening systems have a disengaging device to back the form roller away from the plate during gumming and other operations. If the system is in good mechanical order, the form rollers may be backed away from the plate and brought back into contact repeatedly with no change in setting. On some systems, the form rollers may even be removed and replaced without the settings being changed. Many systems are designed so that dampening feed can be stopped while the form rollers stay in contact with the plate. Stopping the ductor or fountain roller stops dampening feed; this ability can be helpful to the press operator in some situations.

Poor dampening at the roller ends causes many problems. The plate may catch up (start taking on ink in nonimage areas) at the sides or the ends of the cylinder. The ends of form rollers are often smaller than the rest of the roller if the ends of the molleton sleeve are drawn down too tightly. Poor contact with the plate often results.

The ductor can be set using the following procedure:

1. Inch the press until the ductor is at maximum pressure against the oscillator.

2. Insert a single plastic strip at three points between the two rollers.

3. Test for drag.

4. Inch the press until the ductor touches the fountain pan roller.

5. Again, insert a plastic strip at three positions between the two rollers. Equal drag indicates correct setting and alignment. Readjust the ductor, if necessary, according to instructions in the press operator's manual.

Metering Dampening on a Conventional System

All dampening systems meter, or control, the dampening solution fed to the plate. With a conventional system, metering is done in two, sometimes three, ways.

One way is to control the rotation of the fountain pan roller. The fountain pan roller can be adjusted for faster or slower rotation. On some presses, fountain roller rotation is controlled through a ratchet or clutch arrangement similar to that found on the inking system fountain roller.

A second method of metering dampening solution is to adjust the length of time the ductor dwells against the fountain roller. When the fountain roller rotates at high speed and the ductor dwells against it for a comparatively long time, dampening solution is put on the entire surface of the ductor. On the other hand, when the fountain roller turns slowly and the ductor dwells for a short time only, a narrow band of water is deposited on the ductor. These are, of course, extreme settings. The important thing is that the flow of water to the plate be as continuous and uniform as possible.

A third means of metering dampening feed involves the use of special tabs, squeegees, or rollers. The devices, called **water stops,** are set against the surface of the fountain roller. The pressure exerted by the water stops controls the flow of dampening solution across the rollers and is equivalent to adjusting the blade in the ink fountain. Water stops are commonly used to reduce the amount of solution reaching heavily inked areas of the printing plate.

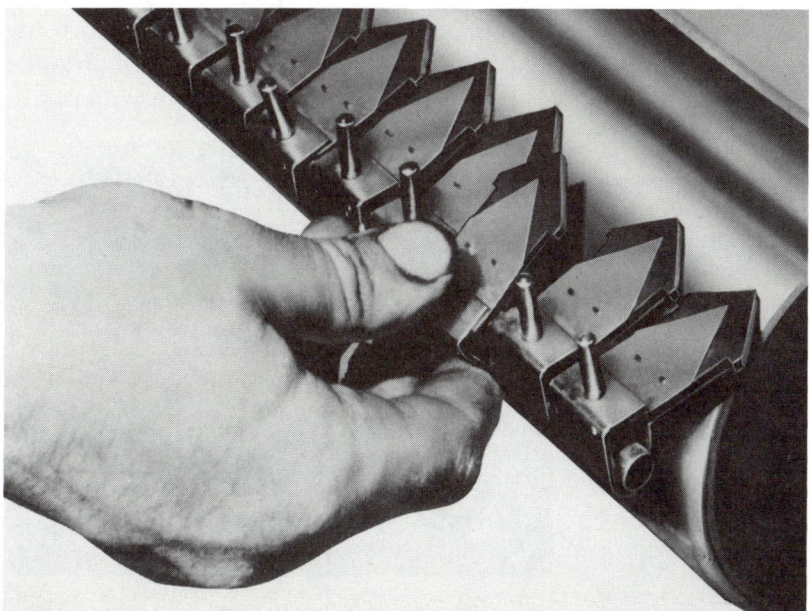

Press operator adjusting a water stop
Courtesy Baldwin Technology Corp.

Bareback Dampeners

Some press operators change the conventional dampening system by running the dampeners **bareback,** i.e., without cloth or paper covers. A system with bareback rollers is more sensitive (responds more rapidly) to changes in the rate of rotation of the fountain roller or to changes in the length of time that the ductor dwells against the fountain roller.

Alcohol (5–10%) or a substitute is usually added to the fountain solution to help bareback dampeners run efficiently. Alcohol reduces the surface tension of water, in effect making it "wetter." The reduced surface tension helps the uncovered rubber roller in picking up solution and wetting the plate.

Continuous-Flow Dampening Systems

The other major category of dampening systems for sheetfed offset lithographic presses is the continuous-flow dampening system. It is divided into two basic categories: plate-feed and inker-feed. In inker-feed systems, the dampening solution is fed indirectly through the inking system, while in plate-feed systems it is fed directly to the plate. Some continuous-flow dampening systems incorporate features of both plate-feed and inker-feed systems. The trend in the industry is toward plate-feed systems.

Continuous-flow systems eliminate some of the dampening control problems associated with conventional systems because the dampening solution is no longer supplied intermittently. A very important advantage of these systems is their rapid response to changes in fountain settings. This fast response is largely due to the absence of storage capacity in the system because the form rollers are not covered.

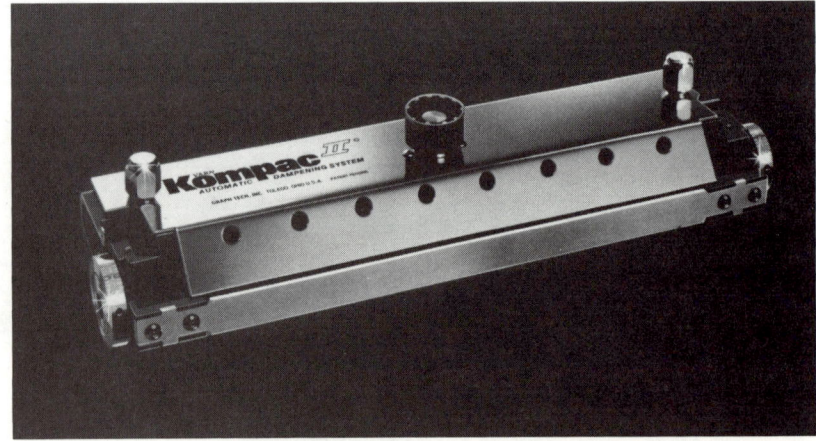

Varn Kompac II automatic dampening system for small offset presses
Courtesy Varn Products Co.

Inker-Feed Systems

An inker-feed, or integrated, system is quite different from conventional and plate-feed systems. One of its principal features is using the first inking form roller as a combination inking/dampening form roller. Another feature is the absence of a ductor roller.

An inker-feed dampening system often consists of two rollers that deliver dampening solution to an ink form roller.

One is a chrome-plated steel roller, and the other is a soft roller that meters (controls) the thickness of the dampening solution film on the hard roller. The line of contact between the two rollers is called the **metering nip.** Depending on the particular press requirements, either roller could be the fountain roller. They are driven independently of the press,

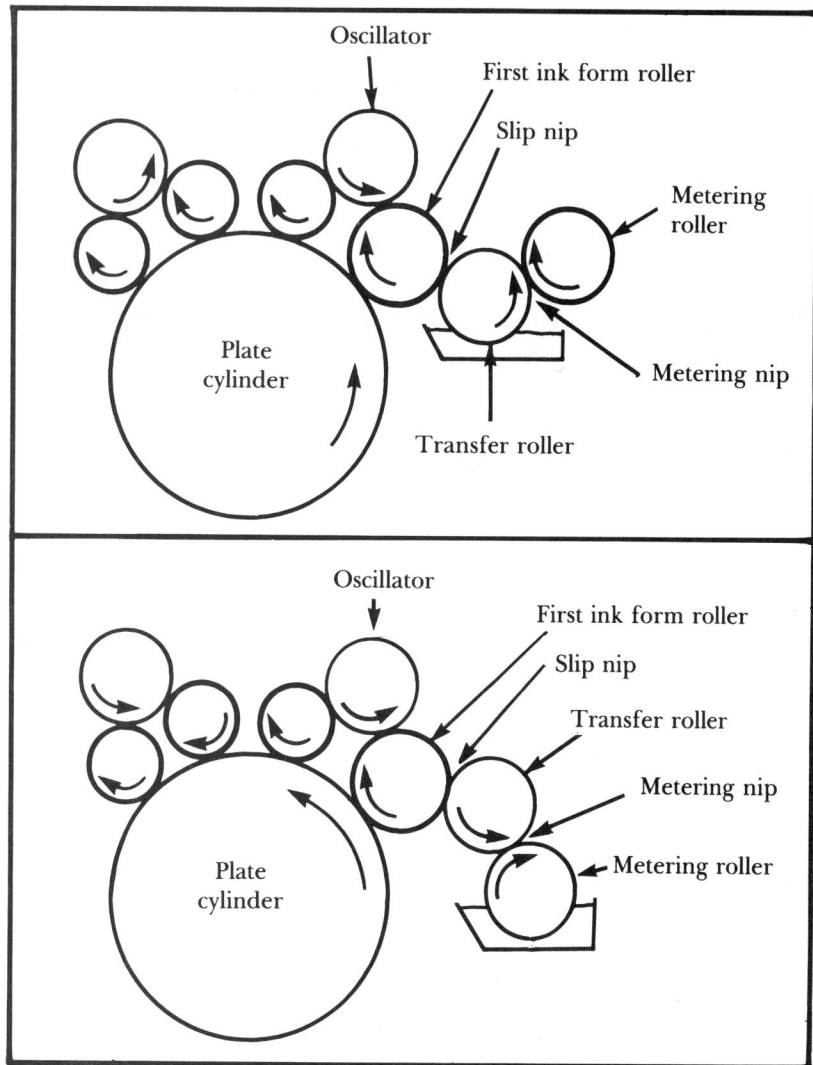

Two configurations of the Dahlgren inker-feed dampening system

and their surface speed is not the same as that of the plate. The hard roller rubs against the first ink form roller, which transfers the dampening solution directly to the plate. Dampening solution supply is controlled indirectly through speed control of the two rollers and the adjustable squeeze between them.

An important consideration of an inker-feed dampening system is that the dampening solution film must lay smoothly on top of the already inked form roller. The wetting properties of either alcohol (5–20% by volume) or a satisfactory substitute assist in the formation of an even film of dampening solution.

Setting the rollers on an inker-feed system is different from setting the rollers on a conventional system. The inking form roller is set heavier to the plate because it is considerably softer and larger in diameter than those in a conventional system. Follow the manufacturer's specifications for the stripe width that the inking form roller should leave on the plate when the picture method of roller setting is used.

Plate-Feed Systems

In addition to inker-feed dampening systems, there are several plate-feed continuous-flow systems. Unlike an inker-feed system, which uses the first ink form roller for dampening, these systems all have separate dampening form rollers. As with the inker-feed system, each has a metering nip formed between a soft metering roller and a hard chrome roller. Because these two rollers are driven independently of the press, there is also a slip nip. Usually, the roller farthest from the plate can be skewed to modulate

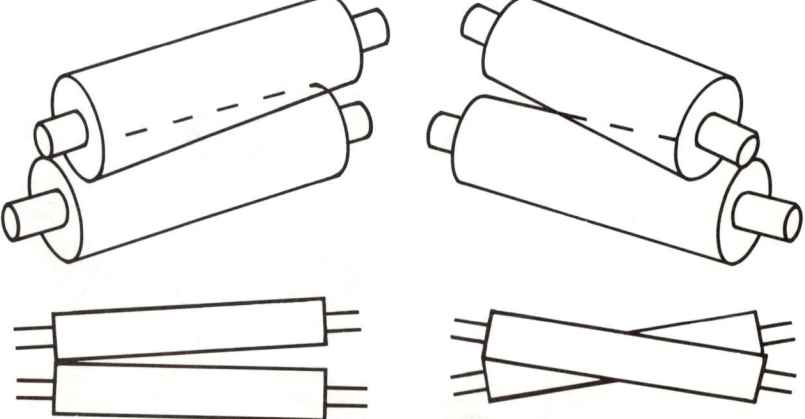

Adjustments at the metering nip on a Roland-Matic dampening system: rollers skewed to get more dampening at the end *(left)* and rollers angled to either reduce dampening at the center or increase dampening at both ends *(right)*.

the water feed across the press. These systems have either a metering roller or a water pan roller.

Most plate-feed continuous-flow systems also require the use of alcohol in the dampening solution.

Epic Litho/Dampener plate-feed continuous-flow dampening system

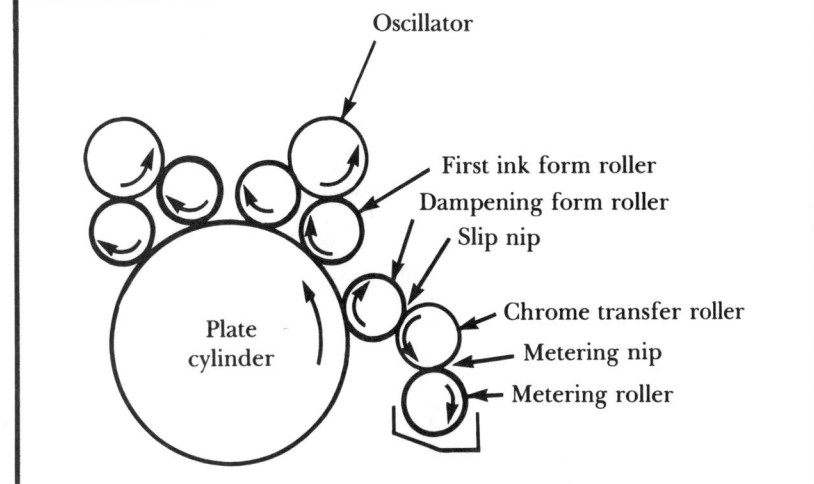

Roland-Matic plate-feed continuous-flow dampening system

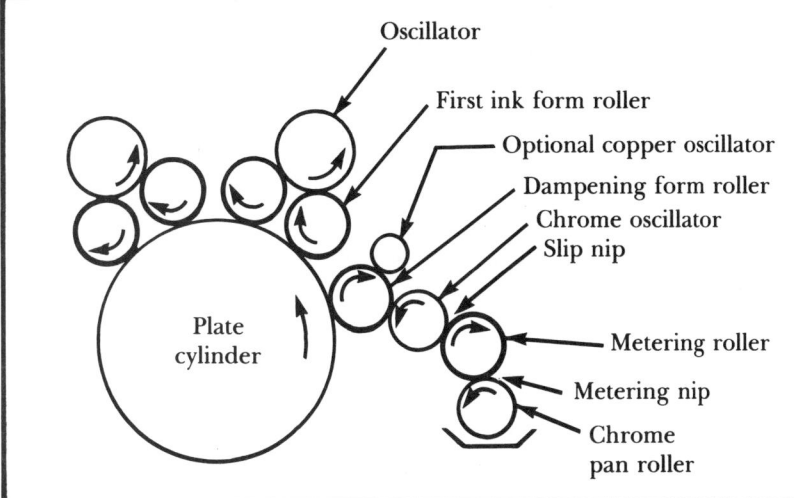

Miller-Meter plate-feed continuous-flow dampening system

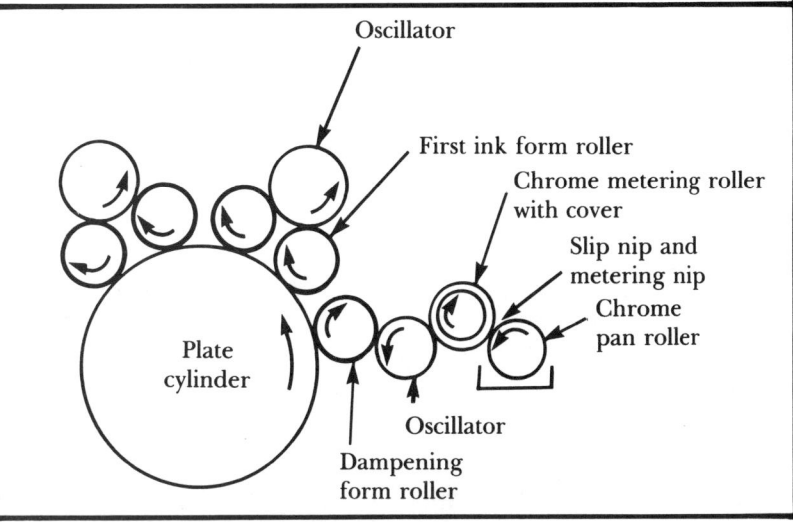

92 Sheetfed Offset Press Operating

Combination Continuous-Flow Systems

A combination continuous-flow dampening system incorporates features of both inker-feed and plate-feed systems. In a combination system, an oscillating or vibrating bridge roller contacts both the dampener form roller and the first ink form roller.

Heidelberg Alcolor continuous-flow combination dampening system

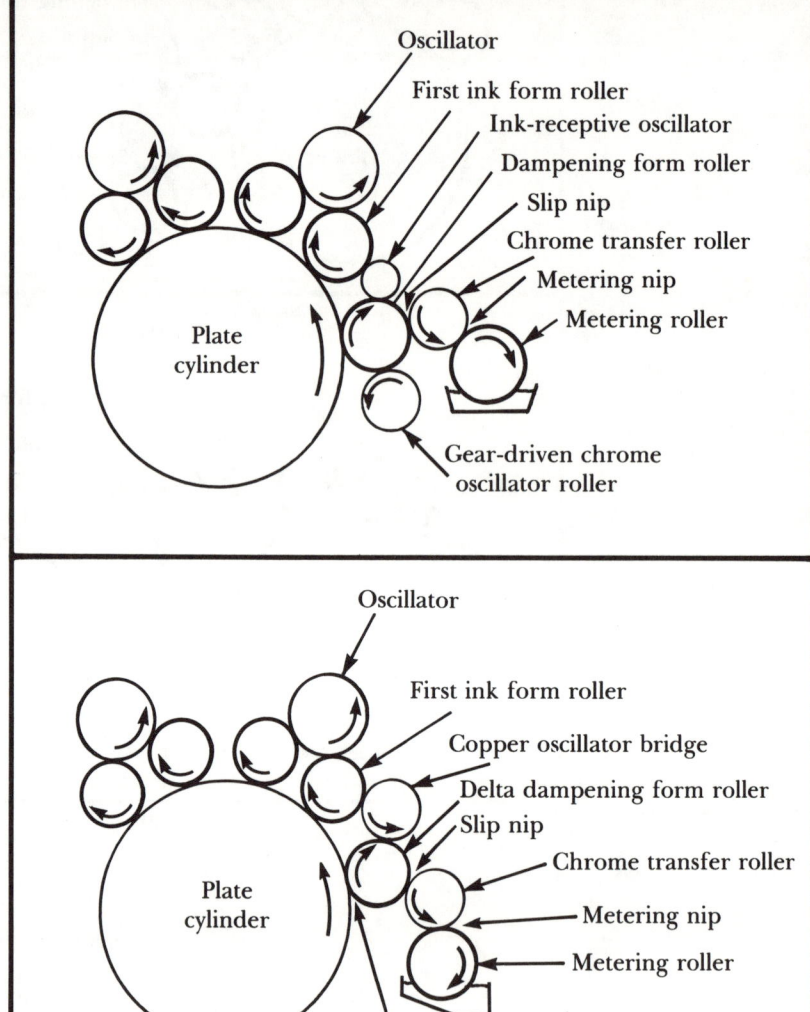

Epic Delta continuous-flow combination dampening system, which has a dampening form roller driven at a slower speed than the plate

The Epic Delta system consists of an oscillating bridge roller and a form roller that is driven at a slower surface speed than the plate. The differential speed results in a scrubbing action on the plate, giving the system a hickey-elimination feature. The bridge roller can be used either as a rider or as a connection between the dampening form roller and the inking system.

Another combination system has rollers that cannot be skewed to control dampening distribution. With this system, an air flow pattern (with water stops and an air bar) is used to achieve—as well as possible—an even distribution across and around the plate cylinder. At startup, the dampening form roller is contacting the plate ("on impression"), the ink form rollers are "off impression," and the bridge roller is in place, feeding dampening solution to the inking system. As a result of the bridge roller carrying dampening solution to the inking system, ink/water balance is quickly achieved.

Critical Metering Nip

All continuous-flow dampening systems have a metering nip (formed by a chrome transfer or pan roller and a resilient roller) that distributes the dampening solution into a thin, even film. The two rollers are geared to each other and run at almost the same surface speed. The thickness of the metered dampening film at the nip *exit* is dependent on the hardness of the resilient roller, the pressure exerted between rollers (determined by roller settings), and the viscosity of the dampening solution. An increase in the viscosity of the dampening solution results in a thicker metered film, and vice versa.

Reverse Slip Nip

With most continuous-flow systems, one of the rollers at the metering nip rotates clockwise and the other rotates counterclockwise. As a result, the surfaces of the two rollers are traveling in the same direction at the point of contact.

However, there are several dampening systems in which both rollers rotate in the same direction (both clockwise or counterclockwise). Consequently, at the point of contact, the two rollers are rotating in opposite directions, producing a **reverse slip nip.** The objective of this system is to reduce the interaction between dampening solution being fed to the plate and the solution returning from it.

A reverse slip nip produces a wiping action that is intended to prevent the flow of dampening solution through the nip. Theoretically, all of the metered dampening solution is carried to the printing plate, and all of the return solution is carried to the fountain pan.

Systems incorporating a reverse slip nip can operate with a relatively low alcohol concentration—5–10%. In addition, response to changes in dampening feed rate is quickened

Sheetfed Offset Press Operating

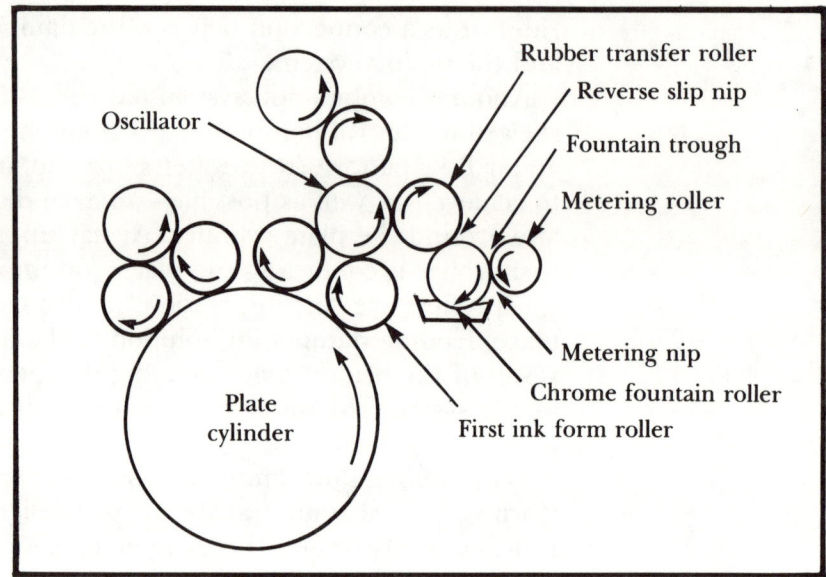

TG Color inker-feed continuous-feed dampening system with a reverse slip nip

due to the elimination of interaction between the metered film and the return solution. The elimination of interaction also results in a linear relationship between the speed of the metering rollers and the feed rate.

Refrigeration

Refrigerating the dampening solution has three principal advantages: a reduction in hot-weather scumming, the maintenance of a constant operating temperature, and reduction of alcohol evaporation.

Hot-Weather Scumming

Although metal plates and improved inks eliminated many printing problems associated with hot weather, hot-weather scumming was not one of them. **Hot-weather scumming** is the tendency of ink to print in nonimage areas when the dampening feed rate is too low. Hot-weather scumming is more properly referred to as **tinting,** the bleeding of ink pigment particles into the dampening solution, which increases as the temperature increases. This problem can be eliminated by controlling the temperature of the solution.

Constant Operating Temperature

Refrigeration of the dampening solution helps maintain a constant feed rate of dampening solution to the plate, independent of the temperature of other parts of the press or the surrounding air. A constant feed rate helps to maintain consistent print quality and reduce waste.

Temperature affects viscosity of the dampening solution. This relationship is particularly noticeable at the metering nip. Variations in temperature results in variations in the metered film thickness, which affects the level and consistency of print quality.

Reduction in Evaporation of Alcohol

Refrigeration permits the cooling of the dampening solution to temperatures below, say, 50–55°F (10–13°C) instead of the typical operating temperature of 68°F (20°C). Reduced operating temperatures are particularly important with dampening systems that use alcohol. The lower temperature reduces the amount of alcohol that evaporates from the dampening solution. As a result, alcohol consumption can be reduced as much as 50%, and less alcohol will be in the pressroom atmosphere.

Although cooling an alcohol-based dampening solution is thought to improve print quality, several problems could be introduced:
- The formation of dew in the fountain pan, which could drip onto the paper causing paper deformation. The fountain pans on new presses are insulated.
- An increase in the tack of printing inks, resulting in **picking**—the delamination, splitting, or tearing of the paper surface due to an ink film's resistance to being split between blanket and paper.

Maintenance

Like all mechanical devices, the dampening system should be properly lubricated and cleaned. Worn bearings or adjustments must be repaired or replaced, and corroded or uneven roller stocks must be turned down. Worn or bent spindles must be repaired. No press operator can obtain good dampening with rollers that are not cylindrical.

The dominant maintenance problem on conventional dampening systems is caused by the roller covers. They become greasy and ink-permeated during running, consequently failing to carry water adequately. When covers become dirty, hard, or threadbare, they must be replaced. Paper sleeves are easier to change than cloth covers.

When removing a covered roller from the press for any reason other than to replace the cover, the press operator must make sure that the ends of the roller are not reversed when the roller is reinserted. A roller reversed end for end will rotate in the opposite direction in relation to its cover, and the cover will be twisted. A cloth cover will become baggy and begin to lint, and a paper-strip cover may actually begin to creep. To prevent these problems, some press operators mark one end (e.g., the operator's side) of all covered rollers.

A mixture of one part 85% phosphoric acid to thirty-two parts 14° Bé gum arabic solution, called **1:32 gum etch,** can be used to desensitize a chrome-plated roller to make it water-receptive. After the gum etch is applied, the roller's surface should be polished with a dry cloth.

The smooth metal surface of the oscillator can become greasy. The press operator can sometimes see it because the film of dampening solution on the oscillator's surface will be broken. Such a roller should be thoroughly rinsed with a grease-cutting solvent. The solvent should then be washed away with water, and the roller gum-etched. The gum etch should be rubbed down to a smooth film and allowed to dry. The roller should then be dampened to see if the dampening solution beads. If it beads, the cleaning operation should be repeated. If the solution does not bead, the roller is ready for operation. Several proprietary solutions are available to clean the oscillator.

A recent innovation in dampener rollers is the ceramic-coated roller that is offered as an alternative to chrome-plated rollers. The ceramic-coated roller helps to reduce or eliminate the common problems associated with chrome-plated rollers, such as streaking, etching, and gumming. The proprietary ceramic coating is tougher and more damage-resistant than chrome and will not become grooved or

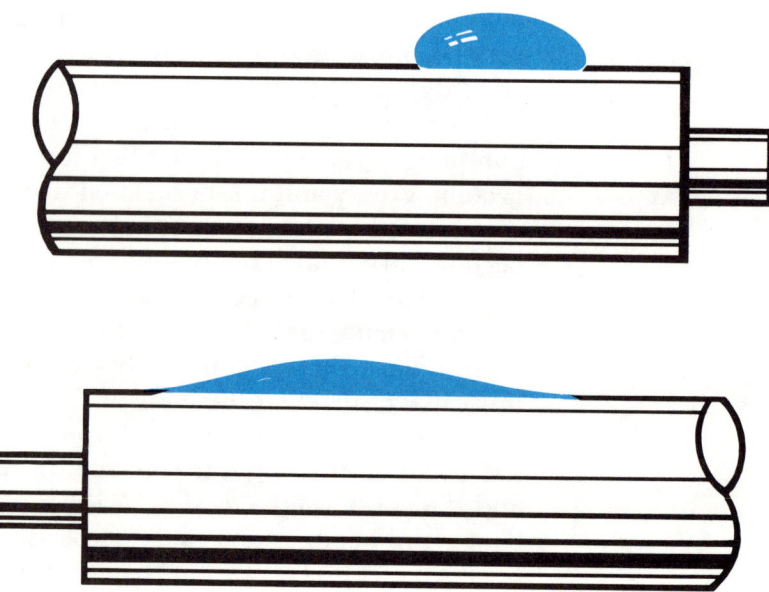

Water beading on a chrome-plated roller *(top)* and water spreading on the surface of a ceramic-coated roller *(bottom)*
Courtesy American Roller Co.

scored. The ceramic surface is naturally hydrophilic (water-loving) and, therefore, does not require gum etching treatments. Other advantages are minimized streaking, improved solution transfer, and greater durability.

Operating Problems

The greatest problems that face the press operator in the operation of the dampening system are uneven dampening across the plate and inconsistent dampening during a run. Uneven dampening across the plate has a number of causes. The two most common causes are dirty dampening rollers and improper roller settings.

Molleton dampener covers develop a twist after the press has run a few thousand impressions. This twist is not harmful. In fact, it tends to tighten the cover and compensate for any stretch that occurs in the molleton. If the roller is removed from the press and accidentally replaced in a reversed position, the twist reverses and the cover becomes baggy, resulting in uneven dampening.

Improperly adjusted dampening form rollers and ductors cause many problems. It is absolutely necessary to see that all contact points are adjusted properly. Each form roller and the ductor must be checked at least at four points. Each end of each form roller must properly contact both the plate and the oscillator. Each end of the ductor must properly contact the oscillator and the fountain roller.

If the spindle bearings are good, the spindles and the stocks are straight, round, and true, and the covers are clean and unworn, proper adjustment is not difficult. If the system is in good order, properly adjusted, and properly operated, even dampening across the plate is ensured.

Uneven dampening throughout the run is generally caused by poor operation of the dampening system. It can stem from frequent stopping of the press or sudden changes in atmospheric conditions. A sudden change in relative humidity may cause a setting that was good at 9:00 A.M. to be extremely poor at 11:00 A.M. It is seldom that an early-morning setting will do for a whole-day's run in a plant that is not air-conditioned. A draft from an occasionally opened door may also affect dampening characteristics.

It is not unusual for a plate's demand for dampening solution to change during a day's run. After 15,000–20,000 impressions, the desensitizing film on the plate may change to such an extent that extra dampening solution is needed to keep it clean.

Uneven dampening can cause serious problems. A large part of a job can be ruined before uneven dampening is discovered. If the plate becomes too dry locally or all over, **catchup**—ink in nonimage areas of the plate because of a lack of dampening solution—is likely to occur on the plate, and those sheets must be discarded. Even when there is no actual catchup, there may be a strengthening of color or a slight thickening of halftones that prevents those sheets from matching the others or the proof.

The beginner must make a thorough study of all aspects of dampening. Dampening becomes less difficult as knowledge and experience are gained.

Generally, most dampening problems result from too much solution on the plate. Too much solution causes an excessive amount of dampening solution to become emulsified in the ink. To compensate for these problems, the press operator often increases the ink flow, a second mistake. The result is a poor job and often a ruined plate. The job may not only be poor in appearance but may also be ruined entirely.

Too much dampening solution on the plate affects the entire inking system. Dampening solution can be found on the rollers of the ink train. The gum and acid in the dampening solution desensitizes these rollers so that they refuse to take ink. The ink itself can emulsify so much dampening solution that it prints light. This emulsion of ink and dampening solution has too little affinity for paper to print a good, full impression. Halftones are grainy, and solids are weak. Running more ink will not cure the condition.

Running too much dampening solution and too much ink plays havoc with the drying characteristics of the job. The ink on such a job will smear for days after printing. The moisture picked up by the paper will further retard drying, because the moisture is trapped between the sheets and raises the humidity of the air that is trapped with it.

Too much moisture transferred to the paper from an over-dampened plate also causes register problems. Paper stretches across the grain between colors. Excessive stretch of this type requires a shift in packing, which may ruin register and also cause slurring. If the moisture pickup of the paper is uneven or if the moist paper dries out around the edges of the piles between printings, achieving close register will be almost impossible.

The basic requirements of good dampening are as follows:
- A well-desensitized plate
- A clean dampening system that is perfectly adjusted
- The proper dampening solution
- A sound knowledge of the system and how it works

The press operator has very little to do with the kind of plate to be used, except to recognize a poor plate and report it. The press operator should know when the plate is at fault and be able to distinguish between a poor plate and poor handling of the dampening system.

The dampening system should always be kept clean and properly adjusted. Covers should be soft and water-receptive. Metal rollers should be clean and desensitized so that they will carry an unbroken film of dampening solution. Only enough solution to keep the plate clean should be run. Dampening feed should be carefully adjusted and controlled throughout the run. Only the necessary amounts of alcohol, gum, and acid should be used. The pH of the solution should be tested frequently. Manufacturer's instructions for the proper setting of dampening rollers should be explicitly followed.

5 Sheet Control

One often overlooked requirement of successful offset press operation is the smooth and consistent flow of paper through the press. Two conditions must be met for satisfactory flow of paper:
- The paper must be reasonably flat and free from any pronounced tendency to curl, and it must be properly piled and lined up in the feeder.
- Proper adjustment and timing of all sheet-handling elements must be maintained.

Poor sheet control can necessitate frequent press stops, resulting in color variation and ink/water imbalance. Plate problems can stem from press downtime, and getting the press back into balance can result in paper waste.

Sheet control on sheetfed presses involves four basic subsystems:
- **Feeder section,** where paper is removed from the top of a pile table, forwarded on a feedboard to front stops, laterally positioned on the feedboard, and fed into the first printing unit
- **Infeed section,** where the sheet is transferred from the registering devices of the feedboard to the first impression cylinder of the printing press
- **Sheet transfer section,** where the sheet is moved between impression cylinders of a multicolor press
- **Delivery section,** where printed sheets are jogged and stacked one on top of another

The first portion of the sheet control system that the press operator is concerned with is the feeder section. Two basic types predominate:
- **Stream feeder,** where a number of sheets of paper traveling slower than press speed overlap on the feedboard
- **Single-sheet,** or **successive-sheet, feeder,** where only one sheet of paper (traveling at press speed) is on the feedboard at any instant

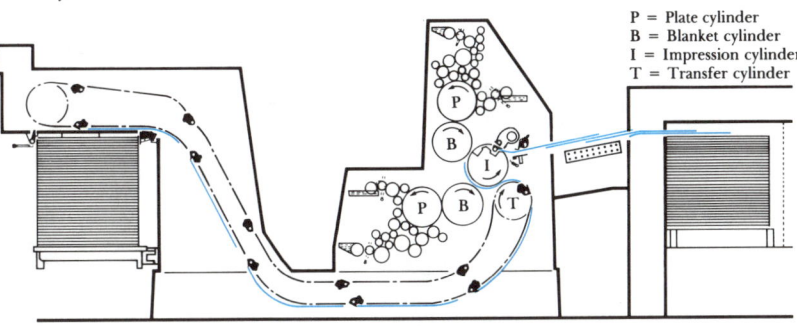

Sheet flow through a two-color press that has a common impression cylinder
Courtesy Graphic Systems Div., Rockwell International

P = Plate cylinder
B = Blanket cylinder
I = Impression cylinder
T = Transfer cylinder

Sheet flow through a
two-color convertible
perfecting press
*Courtesy Graphic
Systems Div., Rockwell
International*

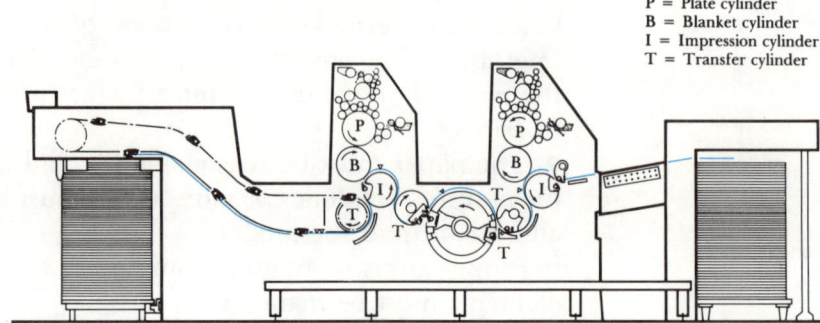

P = Plate cylinder
B = Blanket cylinder
I = Impression cylinder
T = Transfer cylinder

Stream Feeder

A stream feeder is better able to control the press sheet before its insertion into the first printing unit. Since each sheet of paper is traveling slower than the press, the sheets are easier to control and there is less sheet bounce.

The stream feeder, being more widely used, is discussed first. However, much of the information pertaining to the stream feeder is also applicable to the single-sheet feeder.

A feeder section of either basic type of feeder can be divided into several distinct segments that work together:

- **Pile table,** a raisable platform where the paper to be printed is loaded
- **Sheet-separation unit,** a device that uses both air and a vacuum to separate the top sheet from the pile

Feeder section of a
Miller TP104
sheetfed press

- **Feedboard,** or **feed table,** a platform or ramp on which the sheet to be printed is transported to registering devices that properly position the sheet and time its entry into the printing unit

Pile Table

Stock to be fed into a press must first be neatly fanned and loaded onto the pile table to prevent subsequent feeding problems. Variation in pile position from top to bottom—sometimes as much as an inch or more—may require the press operator to stop the press. Therefore, the press operator must keep the paper pile in the proper position.

Positioning the table. To initially position the pile table, the press operator lowers the table to its lowest position and aligns its center with the center of the feeder. To determine the position of the stock, the operator folds a sheet of stock exactly in half and places it on the pile table with the crease ¼ in. (6 mm) off center, toward the side opposite the device that laterally positions the sheet when it is on the feedboard. The pile guide, which must be perpendicular to the pile table, is securely positioned against the edge of the paper that is used for lateral positioning.

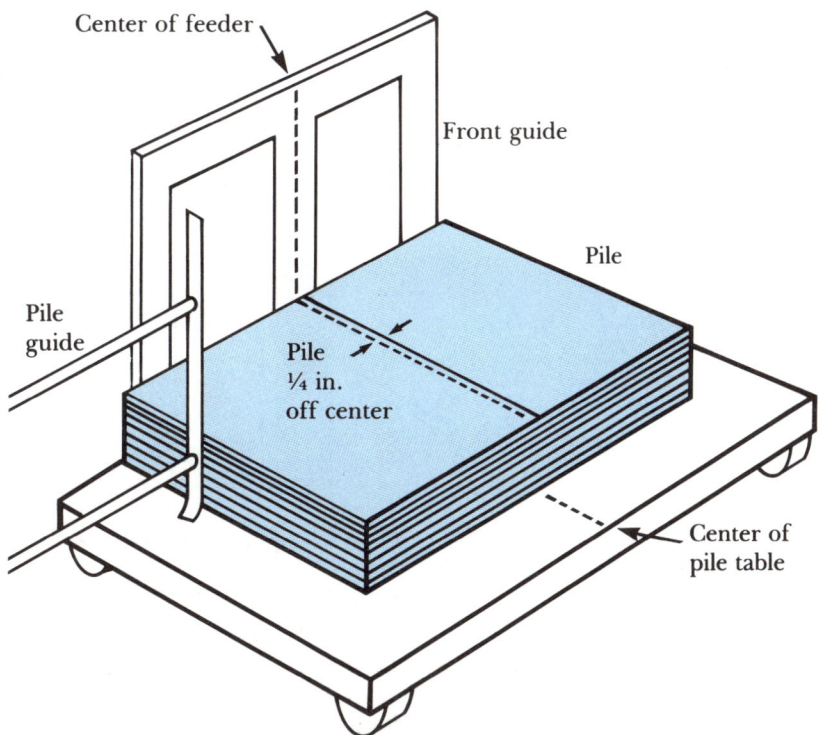

Pile positioned ¼ in. off center away from side guide being used

Checking stock. Before the pile is loaded, the stock must be checked against the job specifications. Some of these are size, color, weight, texture, moisture content, quantity, and grain direction. Also, all stock packet labels and ream markers should be removed and retained in case the final count is debatable. Occasionally, the paper supplier will indicate the preferred side-guide and gripper edges.

Stock should be preconditioned to the pressroom's relative humidity and temperature before the job is printed.

Loading the feeder. To load the feeder, each **lift** (a manageable amount of paper) is fanned and positioned against the front and side pile guides. Excess air is smoothed out after each lift. The side sheet steadiers are placed approximately 0.02 in. (0.5 mm) from the paper pile. Before the pile table is raised to feeding height, all ream markers are removed, and the edges and corners are checked to make sure none were bent during loading.

Bending your knees while keeping your back straight is a safe way to lift or load paper. Only as many sheets as can be easily handled should be lifted.

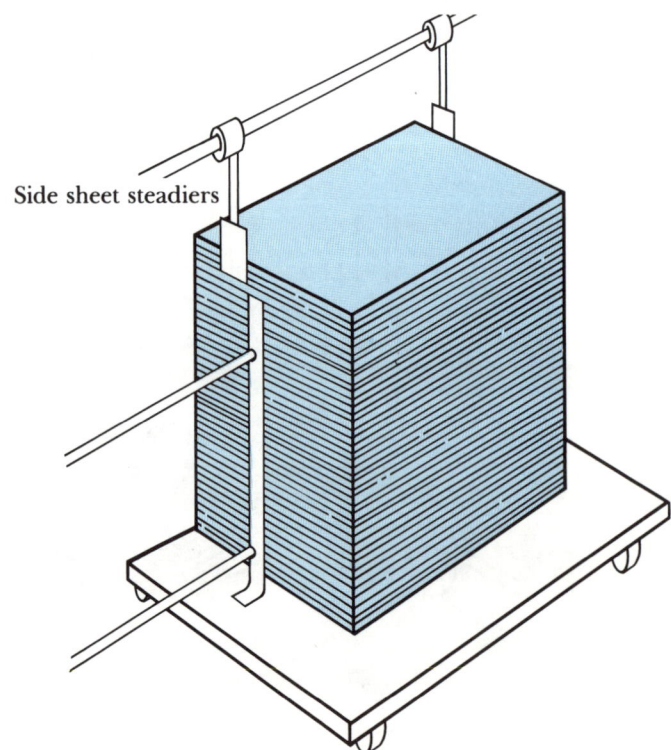

Positioning side sheet steadiers

Side sheet steadiers

Press operator fanning a lift of paper and positioning it against the front and side pile guides

Continuous feeder. Some feeders can be operated continuously, without the press being stopped so that the next pile of paper can be loaded. The exact means of reloading the pile without stopping the press varies, but typically either a secondary pile table attached to its own secondary pile hoist system or a series of rods, or swords, that fit through grooves is used.

In the system using swords, when all but a thousand or so sheets have been fed, the press operator inserts the swords into grooves that have been cut in top of the pile table. The swords are now under the remaining paper and rest on secondary hoist bars. Sheets continue to be fed and the pile continues to rise (supported by the swords) while the pile table is lowered and reloaded. When loading is complete, the reloaded pile table is raised until the top sheets of paper on it touch the swords. At this point, the swords can be removed.

Another type of continuous feeder uses a roll-on platform pile table instead of swords. This platform is at floor level. The skid is then trucked right onto the platform and dropped into approximate feeding position. The truck is withdrawn and the pile raised. This method is probably safer than the method requiring the use of swords.

The only precaution in the operation of a continuous feeder is to avoid changing the position or height of the top sheets during a pile change.

Another form of continuous feeder is the **roll sheeter,** a device that cuts paper on a roll into sheets and sends them to

Principle of roll sheeting

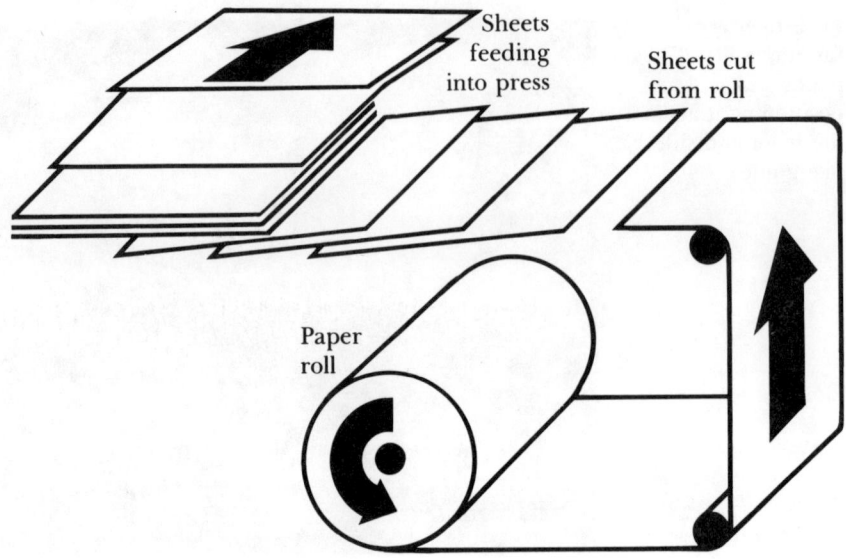

the press feeder. Roll sheeters are being used on an increasing number of presses, especially for long pressruns.

A roll sheeter saves the printer money because the most economically sized sheet is fed into the press. In addition, a roll sheeter combines the economies of roll stock with the quick makeready and low waste of sheetfed printing. Roll sheeting eliminates the need to stack paper piles.

Most roll sheeters are electronically synchronized to the press so that the press still runs at full speed. Usually, changeover from roll to sheet stock is quick and easy, taking less than 5 min. in some cases. Such a quick and easy changeover makes the press more flexible and less dependent on the availability of sheet stock. Most roll sheeters are accurate to within ±0.01 in. (±0.25 mm).

Many roll sheeters have a decurling rod to make the sheets flat so that they feed into the press easier.

A sheeter that feeds paper grain long into the press is preferable to one that feeds paper grain short (cross grain).

Roland-Mabeg roll sheeter
Courtesy Graphic Systems Div., Rockwell International

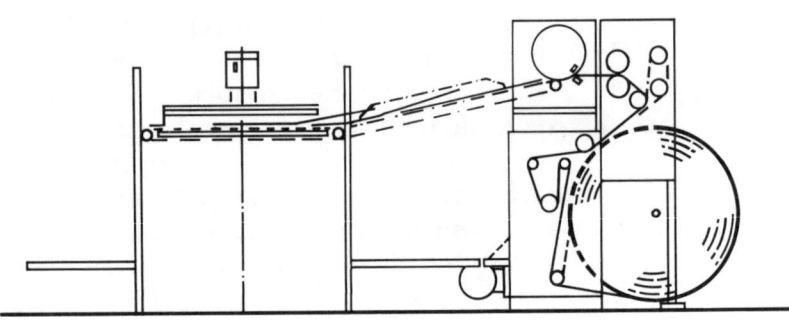

Sheet-Separation Unit

The sheet-separation unit consists of devices that separate the top sheet from the paper pile and forward the sheet to the feedboard.

Air-blast nozzles force air beneath the top five or six sheets of the pile. **Rear pickup suckers** then lift the top sheet. The feeder pressure foot drops down onto the pile, where it steadies the top sheets of the pile while the air-blast nozzles blow a cushion of air beneath the lifted sheet. **Forwarding pickup suckers** then transfer the sheet to the forwarding rollers. (On smaller presses, a single set of suckers is used to pick up and forward the sheet.) While this is happening, the rear pickup suckers are already lifting another sheet off the top of the pile. The overlapping, or feeding of sheets in a "stream," leads to the name *stream feeder*.

Sheet separation unit on a Miehle-Roland press

Both the vacuum for the suckers and the air for the air-blast nozzles can be regulated and should be set according to the size and type of stock and recommendations in the press manual. Some presses also have gauges that indicate air blast and vacuum pressure. The arrangement of holes in the suckers also varies according to stock used.

Pile height. A critical factor for trouble-free sheet feeding is correct pile height, which is usually 3/16 in. (5 mm) below the forwarding flaps at the front of the pile. If the pile height is

Principle of sheet separation on a stream feeder: (A) air-blast nozzles separate top sheets of pile, (B) rear pickup suckers lift top sheet while feeder pressure foot drops down onto pile, (C) pressure foot blows air beneath top sheet so that forwarding suckers can pick it up, (D) forwarding suckers transfer sheet to forwarding rollers, and (E) rear pickup suckers, pressure foot, and forwarding suckers work together to feed a stream of sheets

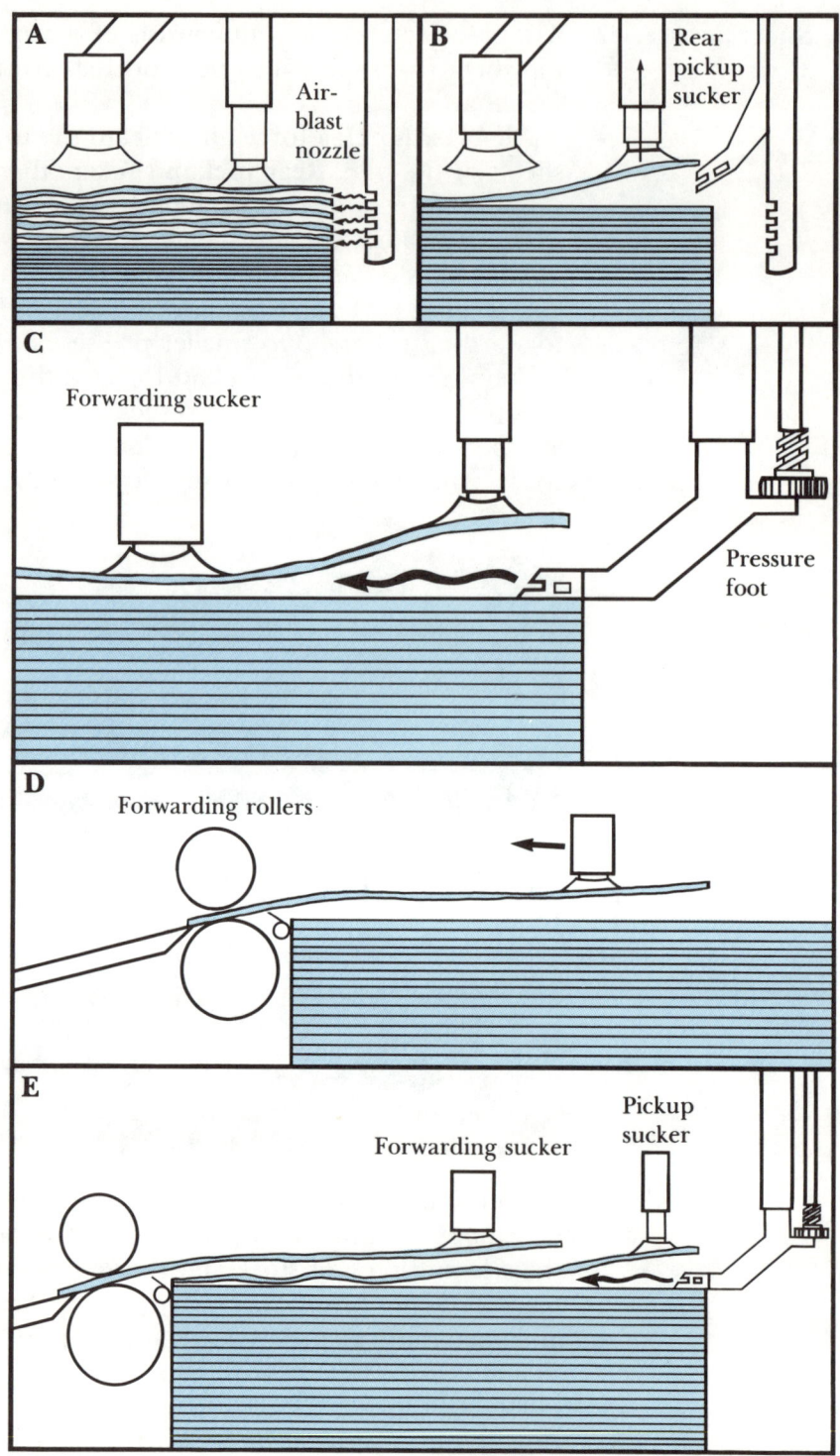

Sheet Control 109

Positioning the top of the pile ³⁄₁₆ in. (5 mm) below the top of the forwarding flap

not correct, the sheet-separation unit may not be able to separate the topmost sheet from the pile, or it may feed two or more sheets to the feedboard.

Three main methods are used to control pile height:
- Adjusting the feeder pressure foot up or down
- Tilting the separation unit
- Adjusting the separation unit up or down

The pressure foot's position is adjusted by means of a screw. Some presses do not have an adjustable foot, in which case the entire unit must be moved up or down to the desired height. On some presses, it is possible to pivot or tilt the separation unit. If the pressure foot is adjustable, this pivoting or tilting action compensates for uneven stock. If the pressure foot is not adjustable, the tilting action must be used to control pile height.

An adjustable pressure foot

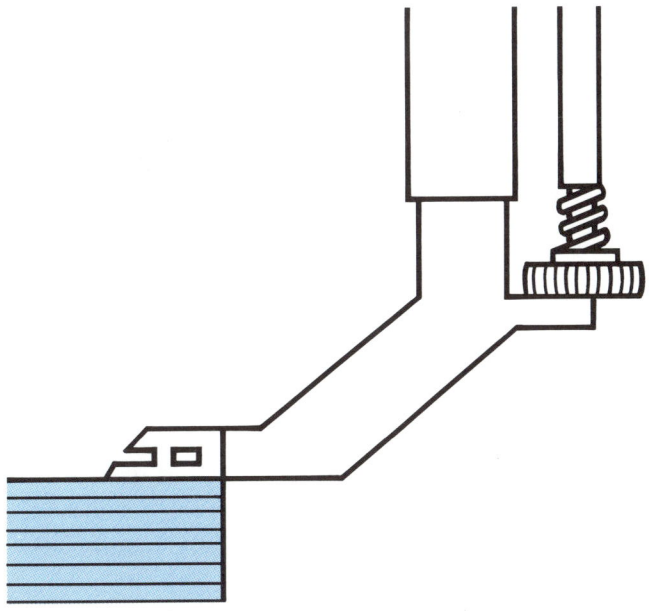

Sheet separation unit that can be moved up or down

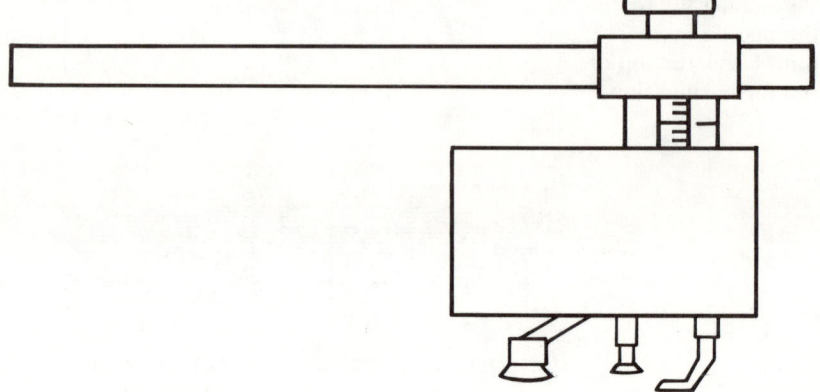

Use of the tilting ability of a sheet-separation unit to compensate for uneven stock

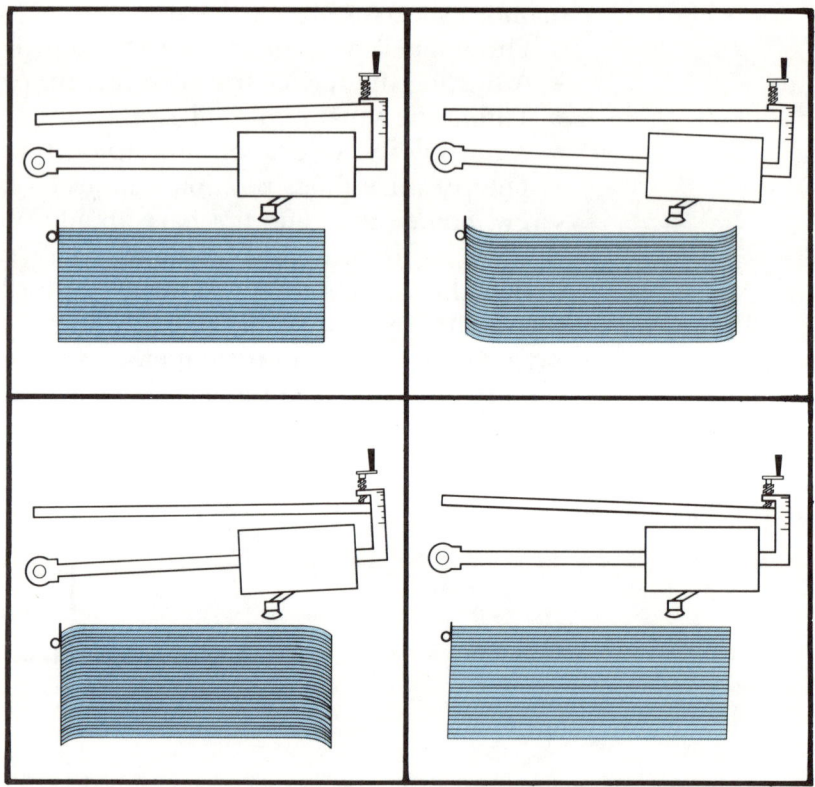

Sheet steadiers. Rear sheet steadiers are positioned at the outside quarters of the pile, with the weights riding freely on the pile. A sheet folded in four columns makes it easier to judge where the outside quarters are; the rear sheet steadiers are positioned on the outer creases. Side sheet steadiers are positioned so that they *almost* touch the pile edges, approximately 0.02 in. (0.5 mm) away.

Sheet Control 111

Positioning sheet steadiers

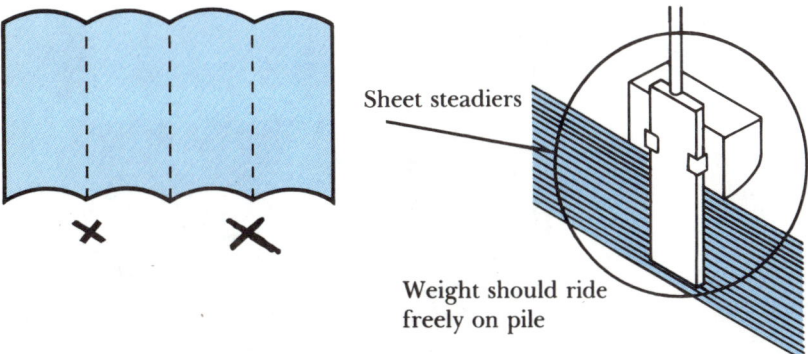

Sheet steadiers

Weight should ride freely on pile

Separator brushes and fingers. Separator brushes or fingers prevent the suckers from picking up more than one sheet at a time. They should be positioned about 3/16 in. (5 mm) in from the edge of the pile and 1/16 in. (2 mm) above it, or just touching it. Stock weight and caliper—thickness—affect the exact location of the brushes and fingers.

Positioning separator brushes and fingers approximately 3/16 in. (5 mm) into the pile

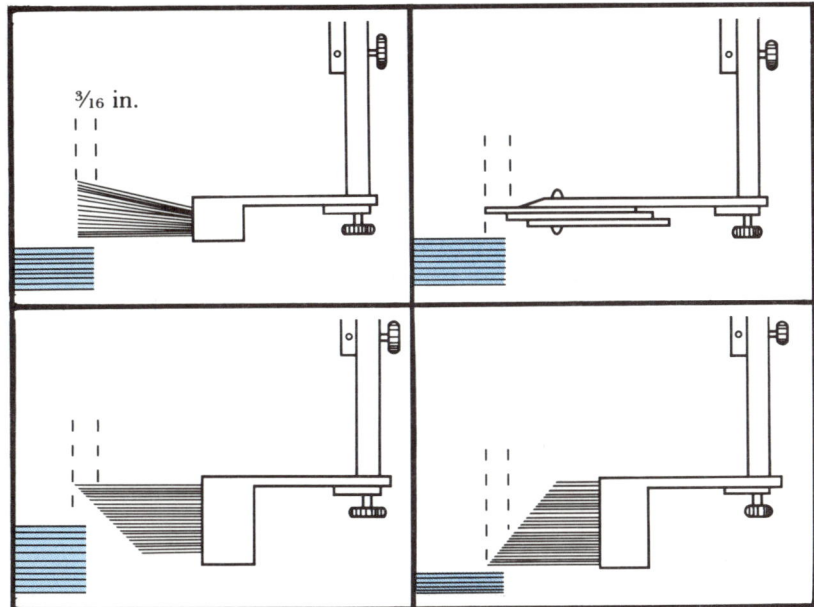

Rear pickup suckers. Also requiring adjustment are the pickup suckers, the devices that lift the top sheet off the pile. After being brought to their lowest position by turning the handwheel, they are adjusted so that they are parallel to the pile. On some presses, the pickup suckers tilt when they pick up a sheet. This tilting action helps prevent double sheets by slightly raising the back edge of the top sheet to permit air from the air-blast nozzles to better separate it from the sheet

Rear pickup suckers lifting the top sheet of paper from the pile

of paper just below it. Stock thickness also affects the angle of tilt that is required. In addition, stock thickness also affects the type of sucker and sucker holder that is used. The press manual should be checked to assist in the selection of the proper sucker and sucker holder for the material to be printed.

Forwarding suckers. The forwarding suckers, the suction devices that forward the sheet to the forwarding rollers, also require adjustment. They are brought to their lowest position by turning the feeder handwheel. For paper, the recommended minimum height for the suckers above the pile is $1/16$–$3/16$ in. (1–4 mm); if possible, the forwarding suckers should be angled inward to prevent sagging of the sheet. For board, the suckers should be just touching the pile or up to $1/16$ in. (1 mm) above it. They should be parallel to the pile, not angled inward. Some forwarding suckers are self-adjusting for height. Like the rear sheet steadiers, the forwarding suckers also are positioned on the outside quarters of the pile.

Air blast. The rear air-blast nozzles also require adjustment. Before the air flow is adjusted, the air pump is turned on, the feeder section engaged, the air to the separation unit turned on, and the feeder handwheel turned until the rear air-blast nozzles blow. Proper air flow will create an "air bulge" under the top 6–10 sheets of the pile. The air-blast

Sheet Control 113

nozzles can be adjusted up or down to separate the proper number of sheets.

When the rear pickup suckers first grasp a sheet of paper, the air blast through the feeder foot and/or the air-blast nozzles should provide an air cushion beneath the sheet. Properly adjusted air flow should separate the gripper edge of the sheet from the pile.

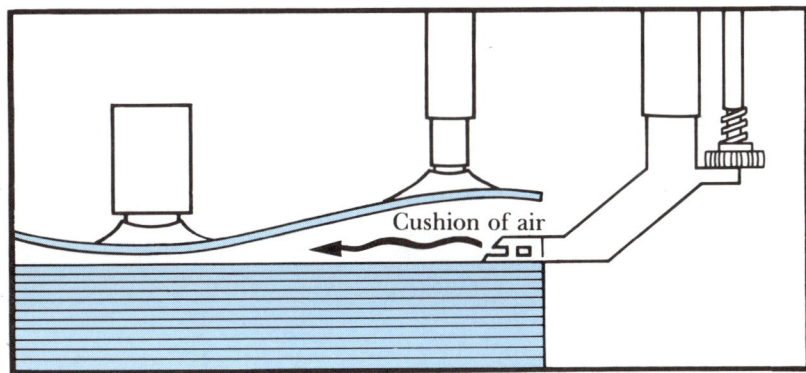

Feeder foot providing air cushion beneath the sheet

If all parts of the sheet-separation unit have been properly adjusted and the pile is at the proper height, the sheet of paper will be transferred to the forwarding rollers.

Ideally, the air compressors and vacuum pumps for the press should be located in a special room outside of the pressroom. This will lessen noise and, more importantly, dirt in the pressroom.

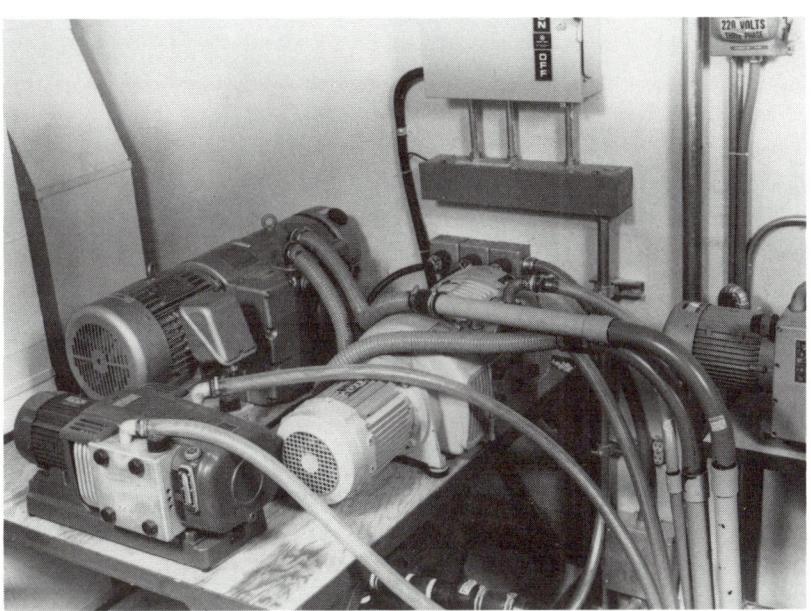

Air compressors and vacuum pumps in a special room outside of the pressroom

Feedboard

Once the forwarding rollers grasp the sheet of paper, the sheet of paper begins to be transferred to the feedboard.

If the sheet-separation unit is incorrectly adjusted, the suckers may pick up and forward two or more sheets of paper simultaneously. Therefore, located between the forwarding rollers is a **double-sheet detector,** or **two-sheet caliper,** a device that can be set to stop the feeding action of the sheet-separation unit if more than one sheet of paper is being forwarded.

Forwarding rollers and double-sheet detector

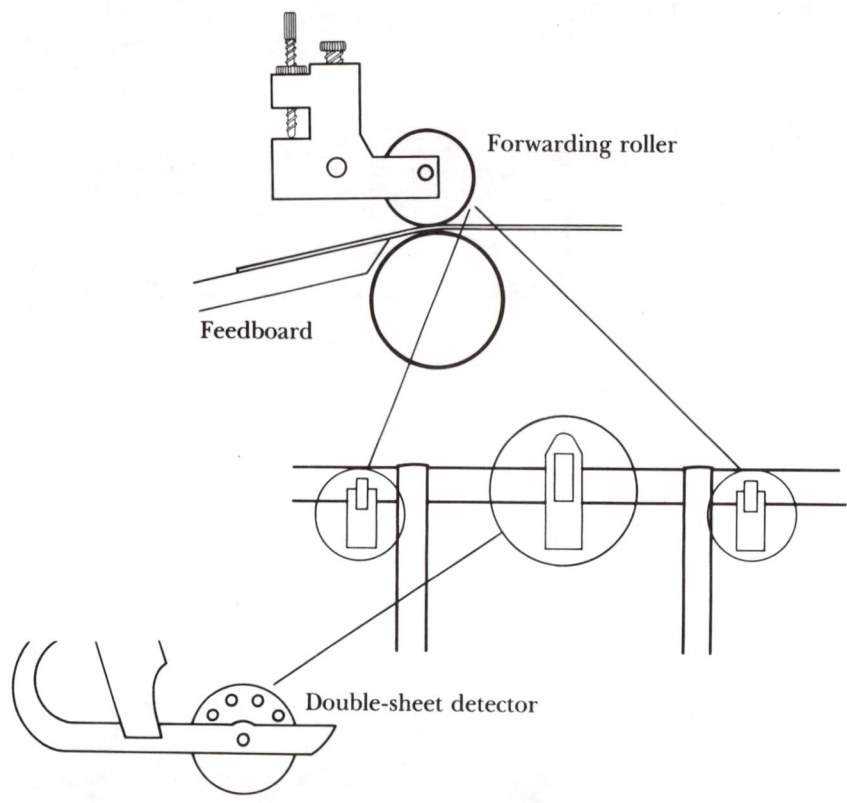

If the separation unit is functioning properly, a series of hold-down rollers, balls, rotary brushes, and/or flat brushes running on feed tapes transport each sheet down the feedboard. The sheet is driven and held against the **front guides,** a series of stops that halt the forward movement of the sheet on the feedboard. Then, a **side guide** pulls the sheet against a **register block,** which stops the sideways movement of the sheet. The front guides and the side guide position each sheet exactly, thus achieving lateral and circumferential register on the feedboard.

Feeder tapes, hold-down rollers, front guides, and side guide on the feedboard

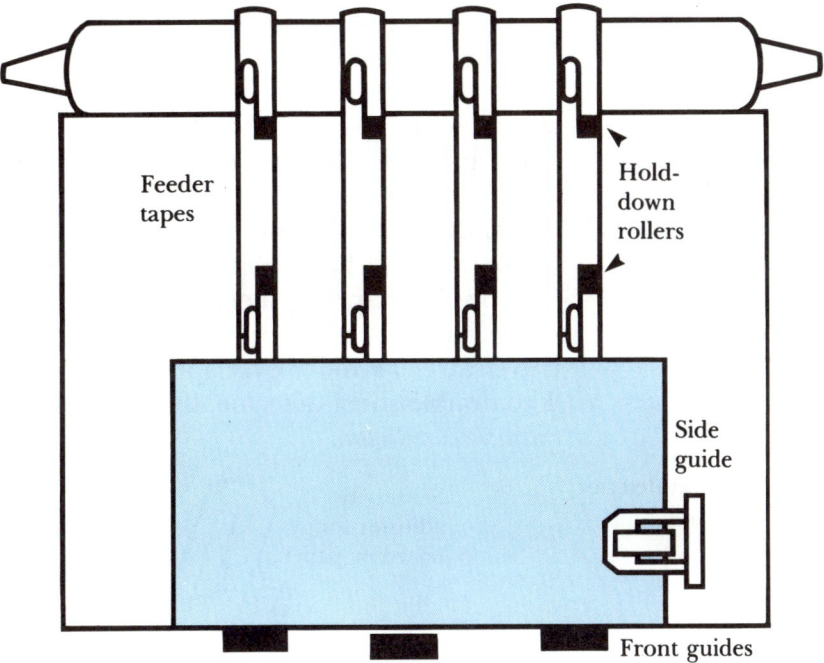

Forwarding rollers. Forwarding rollers must be accurately positioned. If the press has two forwarding rollers, they should be positioned on the outside quarters of the sheet. Folding a sheet of paper in four columns and positioning the forwarding rollers on the outside creases is a simple way to properly position the two forwarding rollers. If the press has four forwarding rollers, a sheet of paper should be folded into eight columns and the forwarding rollers positioned on the first, third, fifth, and seventh creases from the left side of the press sheet.

In addition to being properly positioned, the forwarding rollers should be properly tensioned. If necessary, the handwheel of the feeder is turned until the forwarding rollers drop onto the rear tape roller and begin to be driven. A strip of 0.004-in. (0.10-mm) paper is used to gauge the tension of the forwarding rollers. The strip is placed beneath the roller being set and then pulled sideways from under the roller. A light drag on the paper strip corresponds to the proper tension. Tension of all forwarding rollers should be the same—light and uniform. Poorly set rollers affect the timing of the sheet to the front guides. A feeler gauge is necessary to check the gap between the adjusting screw and wheel holder on some presses. Proper clearance is usually found in the press manual.

Double-sheet detector. The number of sheets passing beneath the caliper roller depends on the length of the stock being run. If a maximum sheet size is being printed, there are three overlapping sheets. If a minimum sheet size is being printed, there are two overlapping sheets. Hence, the term "double-sheet detector" when used in conjunction with a stream feeder is a misnomer. If a maximum sheet size is being printed, the double-sheet detector is set to trip if four or more overlapping sheets are passing under it. Similarly, if a minimum sheet size is being printed, the detector is set to trip if three or more overlapping sheets are passing under it. The double-sheet detector, then, could be described as an *extra-sheet detector*.

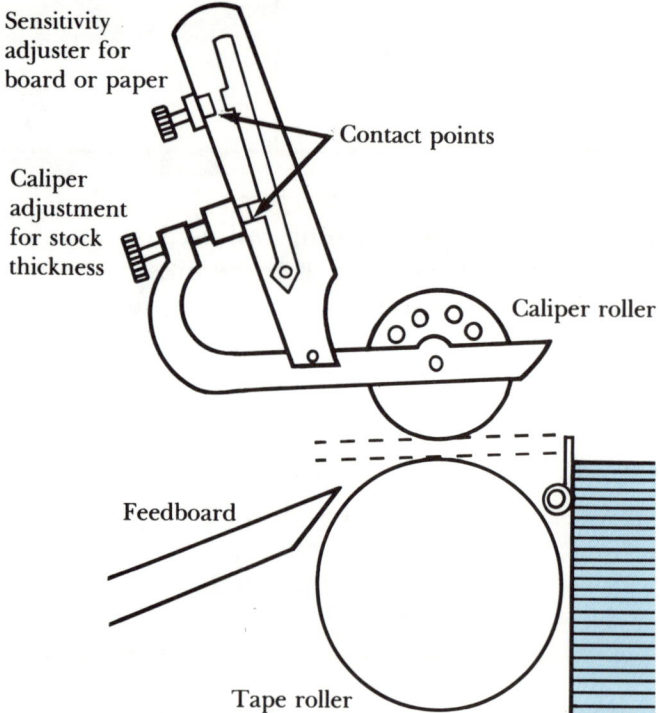

Double-sheet detector with electrical contacts

Clearance is also dependent on stock caliper (thickness). Consequently, the double-sheet detector is set using multiple strips of paper of the proper thickness. The number of strips of paper necessary is determined by feeding at least four sheets of paper to the feedboard and then counting the number of sheets of paper overlapping under the caliper roller.

- **Three-sheet clearance.** If three sheets overlap under the caliper roller, four 2×12-in. (50×300-mm) strips of the stock being printed are used to set the double-sheet detector. The caliper roller is adjusted to provide clearance for three overlapping sheets but to disengage if four sheets pass beneath it.

- **Two-sheet clearance.** If two sheets overlap under the caliper roller, three 2 × 12-in. (50 × 300-mm) strips of the stock being printed are used to set the unit. The caliper roller is adjusted to provide clearance for two overlapping sheets but to disengage if three sheets pass beneath it.

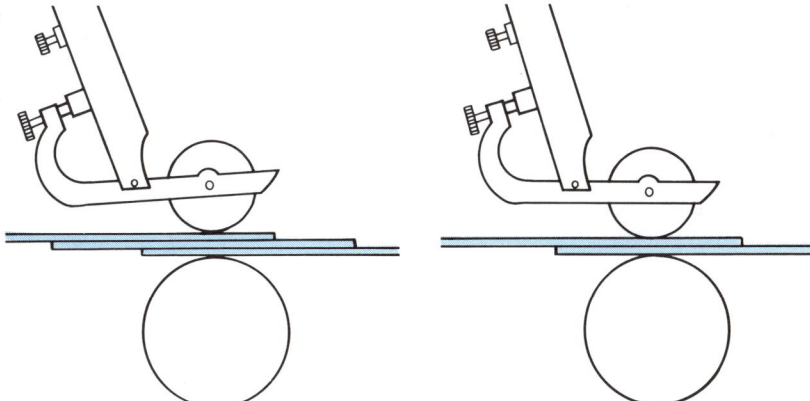

Double-sheet detector set for three-sheet clearance *(left)* and two-sheet clearance *(right)*

Detectors operate either electronically or mechanically. Some electronically operated detectors have a set of contacts that control the sensitivity to paper or board. False detection due to tail-end slap of board often occurs when the press operator changes from paper to board. Therefore, whenever the stock is changed, the detector must be adjusted accordingly.

Some mechanical detectors have a friction brake to prevent the caliper roller from turning too easily. This brake must not interfere with the roller when paper strips are being inserted. The sensitivity controls of an electronic detector serve the same purpose as the friction brake—to regulate the rotation of the caliper roller.

Many press operators feed sheets down the feedboard and then lower the sheet detector until the feeder trips. The sheet detector is then adjusted for clearance of the paper stream.

Feedboard devices to transport sheets to the front guides. After the press sheet is separated from the pile, it is transferred to the forwarding rollers and then to a series of devices on the feedboard that move the sheet to the front guides. The devices and their position on the feedboard vary from press to press. Depending on press manufacture, these devices may be rollers, balls, brushes, rods, bars, or wheels riding on tapes. Their function is to move a sheet of paper in a straight line until it is stopped by the front guides. In order for the paper to move in a straight line, the transport devices and the feed tapes on the feedboard must be properly adjusted. In addition, these devices must be kept clean, because ink buildup can cause the sheet to become cocked on the feedboard.

Sheet guide rods, or **hold-down rods,** are positioned so that they hold down the back corners of the sheet as it enters the feedboard. Properly positioned rods guide the sheet under the forwarding wheels and double-sheet detector.

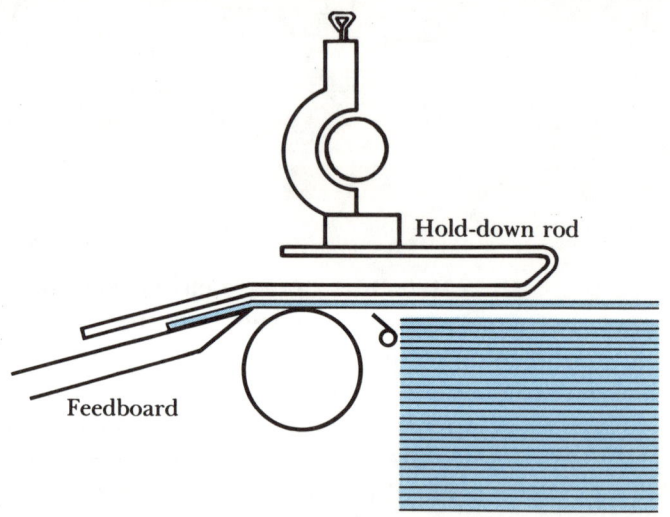

Positioning hold-down rods at the back corners of the sheet as it enters the feedboard

Feed tapes must be properly spaced and properly tensioned. In general, feed tapes are spaced approximately 4–6 in. (100–150 mm) apart. Spacing of tapes depends on the number of tapes on the press and the size of the sheet being printed. If a press has four feed tapes, a press sheet folded in four columns aids in positioning the tapes. The two inside tapes are positioned in the center of the inner quarter panels, and the two outside tapes are positioned almost in the center of the outside panels but a little closer to the outside of the sheet. If the press has six feed tapes, a press sheet folded in eight columns aids in positioning the tapes. One tape is positioned on each of the following creases of the press sheet (from the left): first, second, third, fifth, sixth, and seventh.

Sheet Control 119

Positioning and tensioning feed tapes

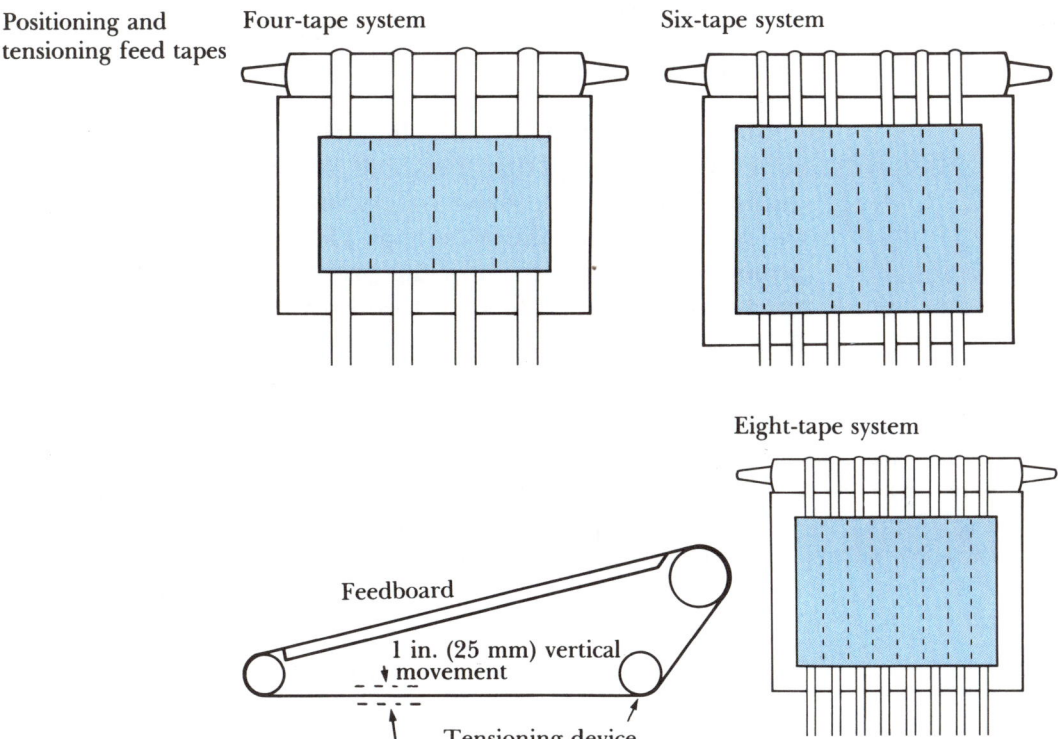

To properly transport a press sheet, the feed tapes must drive with a firm, uniform tension. As a general rule, vertical movement of the tapes should be limited to 0.5–1 in. (13–25 mm). Feed tapes should be kept clean, and worn tapes (e.g., frayed edges) should be replaced.

Before the hold-down rollers can be accurately set to the tail edge of the sheet, the front guides are set to their central or recommended (forward or back) position for correct gripper bite. (See the section discussing front guides for information on how to set them.) Once the front guides are set, the feeder is engaged, the air pump is turned on, and the feeder handwheel is turned until one sheet is picked up and forwarded. The sheet is transported along the feedboard until it is stopped against the front guides. Different procedures are used to set the feedboard for paper and board.

• **Setting the feedboard devices for paper.** Good register is the result of hold-down wheels and rotary brushes driving in line with a front guide. Good side-guide register is the result of hold-down rollers *not* driving the sheet when it is against the front guides; i.e., when the sheet is touching the front guides, the rollers must not be riding on the sheet.

Therefore, hold-down rollers are spaced so that they almost touch the tail edge of the sheet when it is against the front guides, but not so close that they impede with the side-guiding of the sheet. Flat brushes are positioned at the back edge of the sheet so that they hold it against the front guides. Rotary brushes and rollers run on the feed tapes and the rear quarter of the press sheet. Hold-down fingers are positioned near the front of the press sheet to guide it into the front guides and to keep the corners flat. Hold-down balls are adjusted to freely run on the feed tapes and the press sheet; lightweight balls (usually glass or plastic) are used for paper.

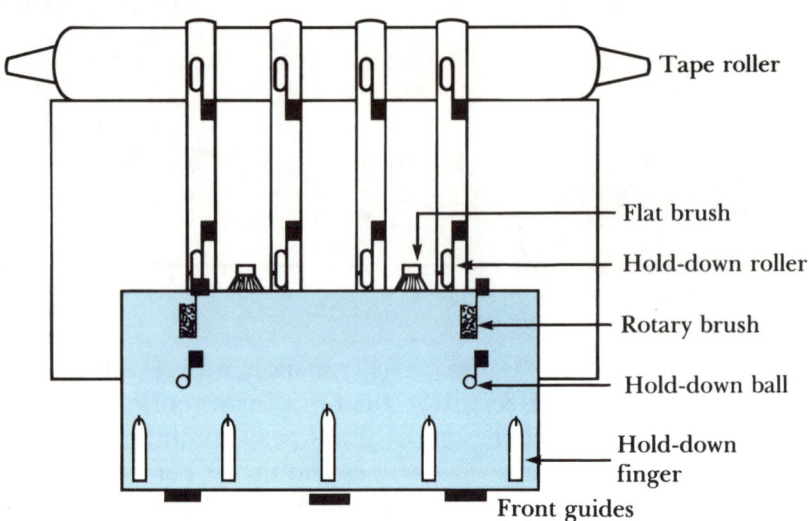

Setting the feedboard devices for paper

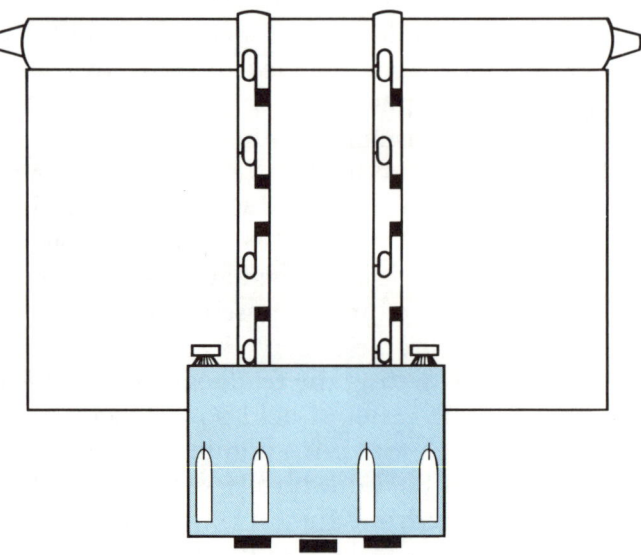

Relocation of hold-down rollers to transport minimum sheet size

Hold-down rollers, in addition to being positioned just back from the rear edge of the press sheet, must be properly tensioned. A simple way to set the hold-down rollers is to first decrease the tension on each roller until it stops turning and then to increase the tension until it just starts to turn positively on the tape.

- **Setting the feedboard devices for board.** Properly positioned rotary brushes just touch the tail edge of the board after it contacts the front guides. The brushes are adjusted by first releasing tension until they are no longer tape-driven and then increasing tension until they just begin to be tape-driven. Heavyweight balls are used as hold-down rollers. Flat brushes, hold-down rollers, guides, and fingers are positioned in the same way that they are for paper.

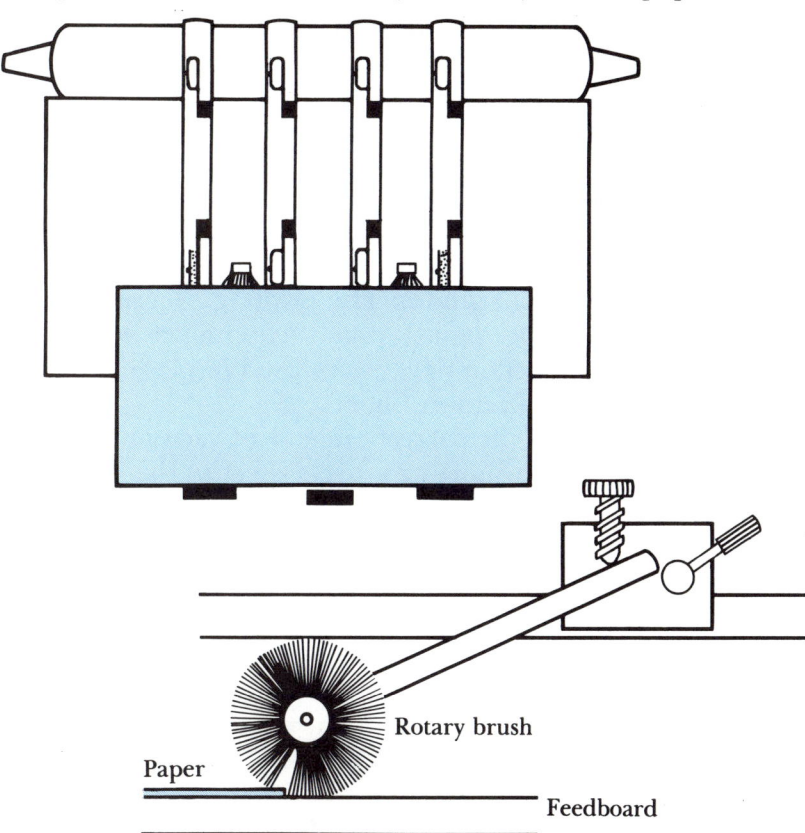

Setting the feedboard devices for board

Sheet bridges. Several evenly spaced sheet bridges are installed across the gap in the feedboard to prevent the stock from following the tape roller. One sheet bridge is positioned at each outside edge of the sheet, and two or more are positioned under the sheet, depending on its size.

Using sheet bridges to prevent the paper from following the tape roller

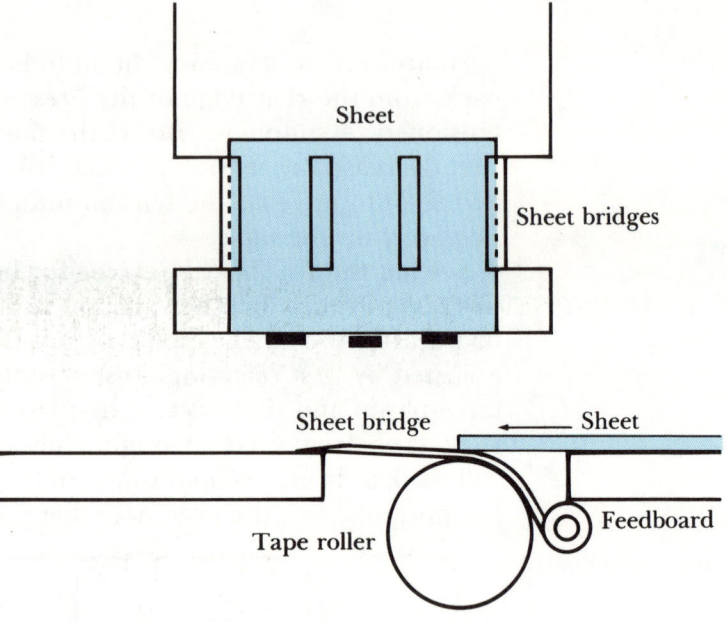

Suction devices. The feedboards of some presses are equipped with suction, or vacuum, devices. One type of device consists of a series of suction holes that hold the sheet flat when it is at the front guides. Another type consists of two or more nozzles that aid in transporting the sheet to the front guides. The printing of a small sheet requires the blocking off of all suction holes not covered by the sheet. Suction devices are used in place of, or in combination with, hold-down fingers.

The correct amount of vacuum is determined by transporting a press sheet to the front guides or moving it over the introducing nozzles, inching the press until the

Suction devices found on some feedboards

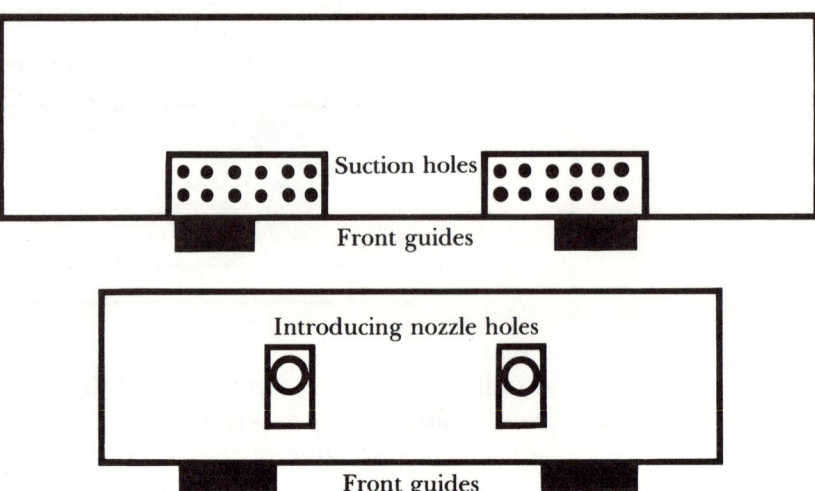

vacuum holds the sheet, increasing vacuum until the sheet becomes distorted, and then decreasing it until the distortion disappears.

Safety bar. Some presses have a **safety bar,** or **crash bar**—a device that detects foreign objects on the feedboard and prevents their passage into the printing unit. Foreign objects include wooden pile wedges and crumpled sheets of paper. Clearance between safety bar and feedboard, which is adjustable, varies from 0 to ⅜ in. (0 to 10 mm). In general, safety bar clearance equals the stock thickness plus ¼ in. (6 mm).

Early and late sheet detectors. In addition to the safety bar, most presses have a device that detects either the early or late arrival of sheets at the front guides. Four basic types of sheet detectors are used:
- **Mechanical type,** which detects late sheets. A sheet reaching the front guides at the proper time prevents a pin from entering a slot in the feedboard. However, if the sheet is late reaching the front guides, the pin drops into the slot, and the feeding action of the press stops. A mechanical detector is easily damaged due to paper-caused wear.
- **Electromechanical type,** which detects early sheets. The electromechanical detector consists of normally open electrical contacts. A sheet arriving too early at the front guides causes the contact points to close, and feeding action stops. An electromechanical sheet detector is also easily damaged due to paper-caused wear.
- **Photoelectric type,** which detects both early and late sheets. This type of detector consists of two photocells, one to detect early sheets and one to detect late sheets. Each photocell is paired with a lamp that does not shine on the photocell. If the front guides are up, an early sheet reflects light from the lamp of the "early detector" to its photocell, stopping press rotation and feeder operation. If the front guides are down and the sheet is late, no light reflects from the lamp of the "late detector" to its photocell, stopping feeding action. The operation of each photocell is timed to the position of the front guides. To operate properly, the photocells must be kept clean.
- **Pneumatic type,** which detects sheets located improperly at the front guide. Consisting of a series of vacuum nozzles, the device detects an improperly located sheet whenever air

Various types of early and late sheet detectors

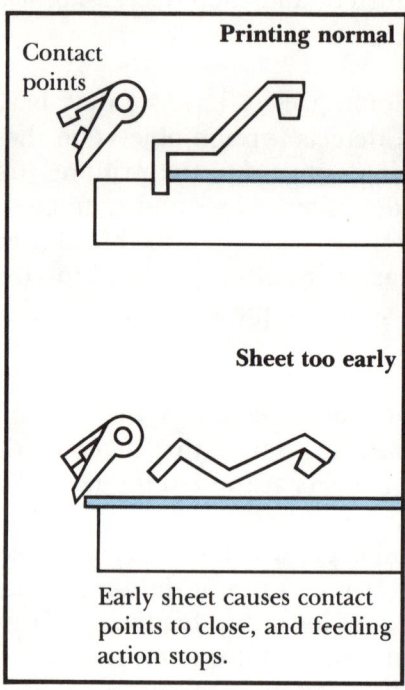

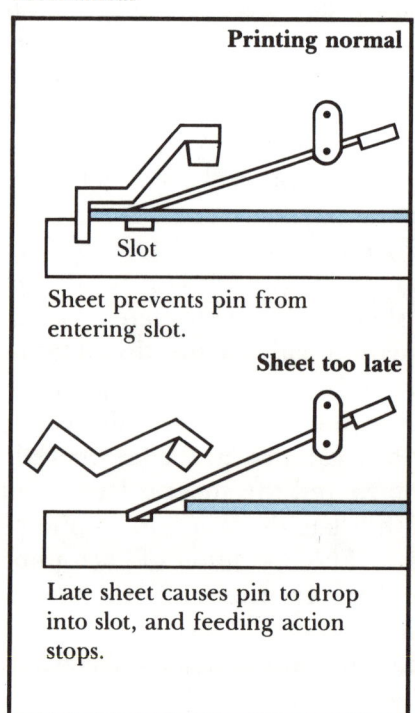

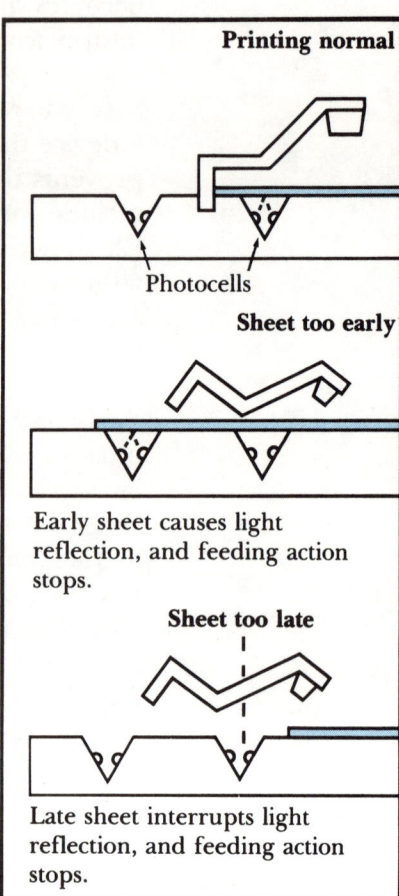

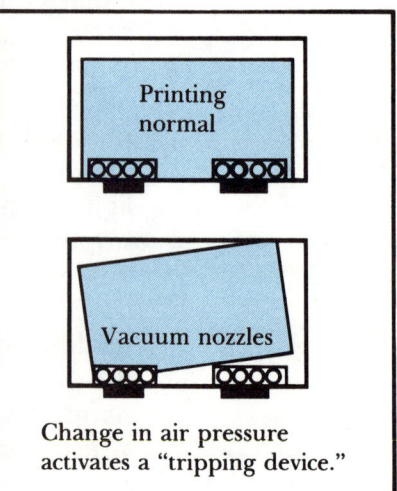

pressure changes. A change in air pressure activates a tripping device that stops feeding action. Porous stock may cause false detection.

No matter what type of detector is used, it must be cleaned daily. In addition, the detectors should be tested periodically. Testing usually involves the insertion of paper strips over the detectors to simulate an "early" or "late" sheet. The press manual usually contains information necessary to perform an accurate test.

Front guides. Front guides either pivot from above the feedboard or from below. They square the sheet in relation to the printing cylinders and determine the front margin. A consistent front margin contributes to the accurate and repeatable positioning of images on press sheets. The accurate positioning of images—either in relation to images on other press sheets or in relation to an image already printed on that press sheet—is called **register.** An inconsistent front margin contributes to **misregister,** incorrectly positioned printed images.

Front guides

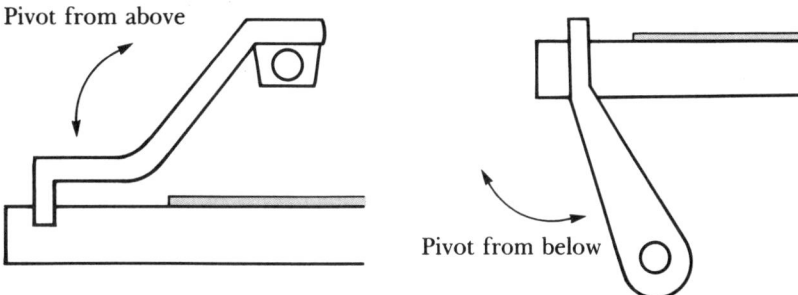

Sheet register on the feedboard requires three points to control the press sheet: two front guides and the side guide. Most presses have more than the two front guides required to register a sheet; the other guides are positioned in one of two ways:
• Slightly away from the sheet but close enough to maintain support
• As far away from the sheet as possible to avoid interfering with sheet register

The exact number of front guides on a press varies from manufacturer to manufacturer. However, factors affecting the number of front guides are the maximum sheet size and the thickness of the stock.

Placement of the front guides along the lead edge of the press sheet is critical. If the two front guides used for sheet register are too close together, the sheet often rests only on one of the two, resulting in a slightly twisted or cocked press sheet. If the front guides are too far apart, they inadequately support the center of the press sheet.

Lightweight stock under 30 in. (750 mm) in width and board stock require two front guides for register and perhaps one for maintaining support at the center. A press sheet folded in four columns aids the press operator in positioning the front guides. The front guides used for sheet register are positioned on the outside creases and are adjusted to their central position. If a guide is used to maintain sheet support, it is positioned on the center crease and adjusted so that it is 0.003 in. (0.08 mm) from the sheet; placing a sheet against the front guides aids in positioning the third guide slightly away from the sheet. Any remaining guides are positioned to their forward-most position; i.e., away from the paper. Whenever front guides are moved to compensate for changes in sheet size, they must align with the feed plate and infeed grippers. The front guides on some presses are not adjustable.

Lightweight stock over 30 in. (750 mm) requires two front guides for register and two for maintaining support of the center. A press sheet folded into eighths aids the press operator in positioning the front guides. The front guides used for sheet register are positioned on the outside creases and are adjusted to their central position. The two guides used to maintain sheet support are placed on the third and fifth creases from the left edge of the sheet; they are adjusted until they clear the sheet by 0.003 in. (0.08 mm). Any remaining guides are adjusted to their forward-most position.

Bite refers to the amount of sheet—margin—under the paper gripper of the impression cylinder. For tight-register work, gripper bite must be correct. Front guides in their central position provide the proper amount of bite. Front guides in the forward position result in maximum gripper bite but also tend to cause sheet transfer problems. Front guides in the back position result in minimum gripper bite, which often leads to a sheet tearing out of the grippers due to insufficient holding power.

Front guide height above the feedboard varies according to stock thickness. Regardless of whether the front guide incorporates a **smoother** (a device that helps to keep the sheet flat), the basic procedure for adjusting front guide height remains the same. For either a single-sheet or stream feeder, two 12 × 3-in. (300 × 80-mm) strips of the stock to be used are inserted under the front guide, which is then adjusted until it clears the two strips. A third strip is then inserted, with the front guide height adjusted until the third strip drags when pulled away from the front guide. For board stock, the front guide is set to clear the board plus two sheets of 0.004-in. (0.10-mm) paper.

Side guide. The third point of the three-pointed sheet-registering system is the side guide. Three basic methods of side-guiding predominate:
- Roller action
- Foot (plate) action
- Pneumatic (suction) action

Although the mechanisms vary, each pulls the sheet against the **register block,** or **register plate,** a device that stops the lateral (sideways) movement of the sheet. (The side guide for a single-sheet feeder *pushes* the sheet toward the center of the feedboard.)

Like the front guide, the side guide must be properly positioned to guarantee register of the press sheet. The register block of the side guide is reset to its zero or center

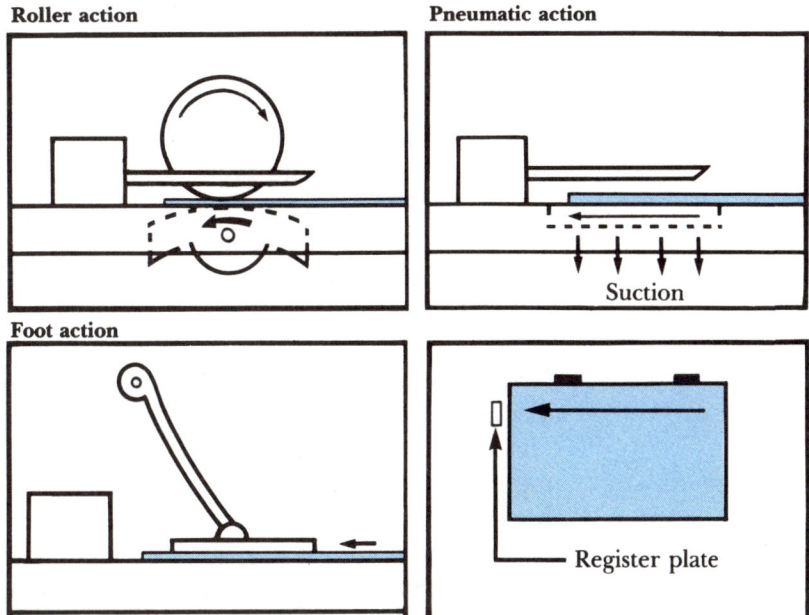

Basic methods of side-guiding: roller action *(upper left)*, foot action *(lower left)*, and pneumatic action *(upper right)*

All three methods pull the sheet against a register plate *(lower right)*

position using the micrometer-like side-guide adjustment. After a sheet is forwarded to the front guide, the register block is moved until it is ¼ in. (6 mm) from the sheet, and it is locked in that position.

The register block must be adjusted until it is parallel to the edge of the sheet. A new offset printing plate or a metal square aids in parallelling the register block to the sheet and in squaring the register block to the front guides.

The smoother attached to the register block must be adjusted to compensate for stock thickness. The press is inched until the smoother is at its lowest position. Two 12×3-in. (300×80-mm) strips of the stock being printed are inserted under the smoother plate, which is adjusted in height until it clears both strips. A third strip is then inserted, with the height being adjusted until the third strip drags when pulled away from the side guide. For board stock, the height is set to drag on one sheet of board and three strips of 0.004-in. (0.10-mm) paper. If the smoother is too high, a sheet may buckle when pulled against the register block, causing misregister.

Roller- and foot-action side guides. The puller roller and foot of the roller- and foot-action side guides need proper levels of tension. Too much spring tension applied to the puller roller or foot may cause the sheet to buckle against the register block. Tension, initially set to its lowest level, should be increased by one-half turn as each sheet passes the register block. When a sheet pulls over to the register block, tension is at its proper level. The tensioning device should then be locked in place.

In addition, the side-guide spring used must be appropriate for the thickness of the stock being printed:
- Lightweight stock requiring a lightweight spring
- Medium-weight stock requiring a medium spring
- Board and heavyweight stock requiring a heavy spring

Pneumatic-action (suction-action) side guide. A pneumatic-action, or suction-action, side guide has a **suction plate,** a device that holds the sheet by vacuum and then moves the paper against the register block. The suction plate used in this system must be appropriate for the stock being printed; e.g., a board-type sucker when board is being printed.

Proper levels of vacuum are necessary for the pneumatic side guide. Vacuum, initially set at its lowest level, is gradually increased as sheets pass the register block. When a sheet pulls over to the register block, the level of vacuum is correct.

Single-Sheet Feeder

Pile and Side Guide Positioning

Sheet control for a single-sheet, or successive-sheet, feeder is basically the same as for a stream feeder except in a few key areas.

The side guide for a single-sheet feeder is usually a push type. Therefore, the paper pile is positioned off-center 1/8–1/4 in. (3–5 mm) toward the side guide being used so that the sheet is pushed across the center of the feedboard as it is side-guided. Rear sheet steadiers are located on the outside quarters of the pile so that they just touch it.

Sheet-Separation Unit

With a single-sheet feeder, sheet separation occurs at the front (gripper) edge of the paper pile. Air is blown against the top several sheets of the pile, causing an air bulge that separates these sheets from the pile. Suckers located almost over the gripper edge of the sheet drop down and hold the top sheet due to vacuum. They move forward, putting the gripper edge of the sheet between some type of wheel/roller forwarding combination at the head of the feedboard. The entire sheet is forwarded onto the feedboard before the suckers remove the next sheet from the top of the pile.

Proper pile height—approximately 3/8 in. (10 mm) below the separating fingers—is critical to trouble-free feeding. The separating fingers are positioned 3/8 in. (10 mm) below the top of the air-blast nozzles when they are in their raised position.

Another critical adjustment factor is the air-blast nozzles. They are raised or lowered until they separate the top 6–10 sheets from the pile. Sufficient air blast creates a bulging of the sheets, making it easier for the pickup suckers to forward only one sheet to the feedboard.

The angling of the pickup suckers varies depending on the stock being printed. A greater angle is necessary for feeding paper than for feeding board. Angled pickup suckers help to minimize the feeding of double sheets. Therefore, the suckers are angled as much as possible while still maintaining positive pickup. Any suckers not being used to pick up the sheet are turned off.

Double-Sheet Detector

On a properly operating single-sheet feeder, only one sheet passes under the double-sheet detector at any time.

Consequently, the detector is set to prevent the passage of two sheets.

On some presses, a simple choke prevents the feeding of double sheets. The choke is set to jam two or more sheets against the feedboard. As a result, these sheets fail to reach the front guides, and the press subsequently trips off impression.

Infeed Section

After a press sheet is registered on the feedboard, it is moved in various ways from the feedboard to a set of grippers on the first impression cylinder. Then, the grippers on the impression cylinder close on the sheet and transport it through the first unit, where the sheet is printed. The front guides move aside to allow this transfer. The timing and adjustment of the devices in the infeed section are critical.

Four types of infeed are commonly encountered:

- **Direct system.** Front guides stop the sheet and move out of the way at the proper time. Impression-cylinder grippers tumble 180° to close on the sheet. No intermediate transfer device is used.
- **Swing-arm system.** Front guides stop the sheet and move out of the way at the proper time. Grippers on a swing-arm mechanism close on the sheet and transfer it to the impression-cylinder grippers.
- **Rotary-drum system.** Front guides stop the sheet and move out of the way at the proper time. Grippers on a rotating drum close on the sheet and transfer it to the impression-cylinder grippers.
- **Overfeed system.** Front guides on the feedboard pre-register the sheet and move out of the way at the proper time. Feed rolls or vacuum belts drive the sheet against stops (front guides) on the impression cylinder. The rolls or belts continue to drive the sheet, causing it to buckle. Grippers on the impression cylinder close on the sheet. The controlled buckling of the sheet ensures proper register.

Infeed Gripper Clearance

Infeed grippers that are noncompensating (unable to automatically adjust themselves for stock thickness changes) require a simple adjustment when stock thickness is being changed; e.g., from paper to board. This adjustment provides clearance between gripper pad and feedboard and varies for each type of press. The operator's manual typically includes the recommended clearance and method of adjustment.

Sheet Control

Principal types of infeeds

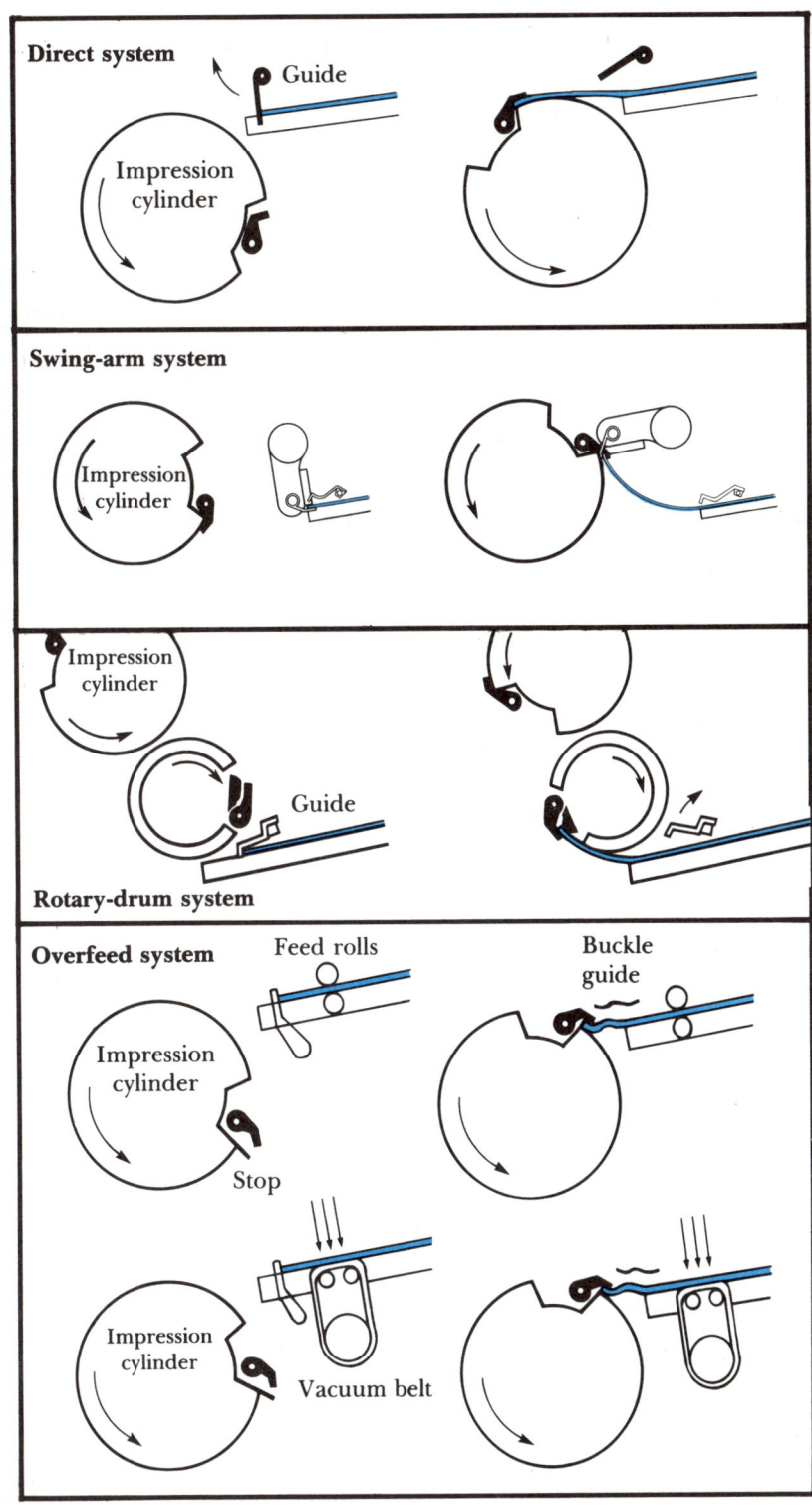

On one press, the recommended clearance between pad and the feedboard is 0.008 in. (0.20 mm) plus the stock thickness. If 0.004-in. (0.10-mm) paper is being printed, the clearance from gripper pad to feedboard is 0.012 in. (0.30 mm)—0.008 in. plus 0.004 in. (0.20 mm plus 0.10 mm).

Impression-Cylinder Stops

With the overfeed system only, the stops (front guides) on the impression cylinder are sometimes intentionally bowed to control distortion of the sheet, or **fan-out,** expansion of the sheet near the tail edge. Before the next pressrun is started, the stops are returned to their central position.

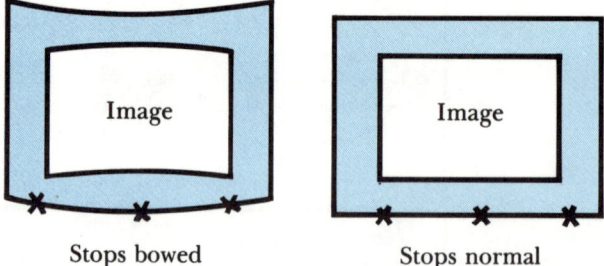

Effect of bowing the front guides (stops) on an overfeed system

Adjusting the stops on the impression cylinder permits depth of gripper bite to be increased or decreased slightly.

On a feed-roll overfeed system, changing to a very heavy caliper board requires adjustment of the tension between feed rolls. Textured stock that could crush also requires proper feed-roll tension. Improper tension between feed rolls often causes creases or wrinkles at the tail edge of the sheet.

Gripper Bowing

A gripper-bowing device compensates for the effects of fan-out by intentionally bowing the gripper bar as much as

Effects of fan-out

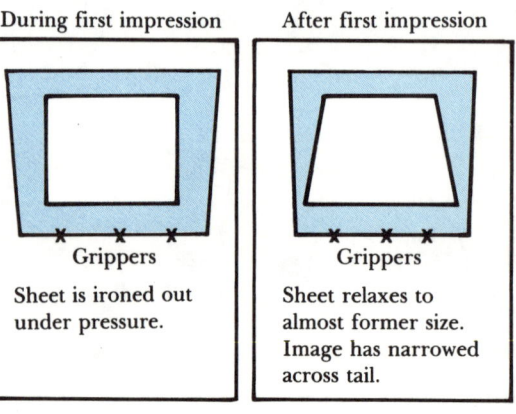
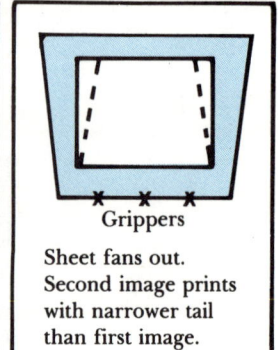

0.008 in. (0.020 mm) at its center. Such a device is usually part of an infeed drum, but some presses include the device throughout the transfer system.

Passing a sheet through the impression nip irons out the sheet, causing the sheet to fan out toward the tail corners. If the grippers are *not bowed,* the sheet relaxes to almost its former size after the first impression, resulting in an image narrowed across the tail. As the second impression is being printed, the sheet fans out again, but the second image prints with a narrower tail than the first image.

The use of a gripper-bowing device often minimizes the effects of fan-out. The gripper-bowing device is adjusted to bow the sheet gripper edge out, so that fan-out is exaggerated. This bowing, in turn, exaggerates the narrowing of the image at the tail of the sheet, compensating for further fan-out on the second impression and subsequent image narrowing at the tail of the sheet. During the first impression, the gripper pads are bowed out, resulting in a bowed-out sheet and exaggerated fan-out. After the first impression, the sheet relaxes and the image narrows more than usual at the tail. The grippers on the second impression are not bowed but are in their central position. During the second impression, the sheet still fans out, but the second image fits the first image because the first image is narrower than usual.

Bowing the gripper edge *in* is also possible. Bowing-in causes a widening of the image at the tail.

Gripper Bite

Impression-cylinder grippers that are too tight damage the lead edge of the paper and cause problems in the delivery. Wrinkling of the sheet often results when one gripper is set

Using a gripper bowing device to control fan-out

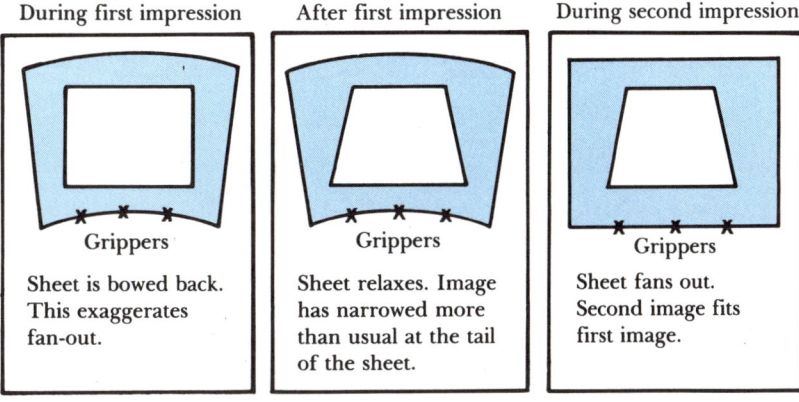

Bowing of the gripper bar of the first impression cylinder to compensate for a distorted sheet

Some gripper bars can be bowed in the center, moved forward or back, or angled.

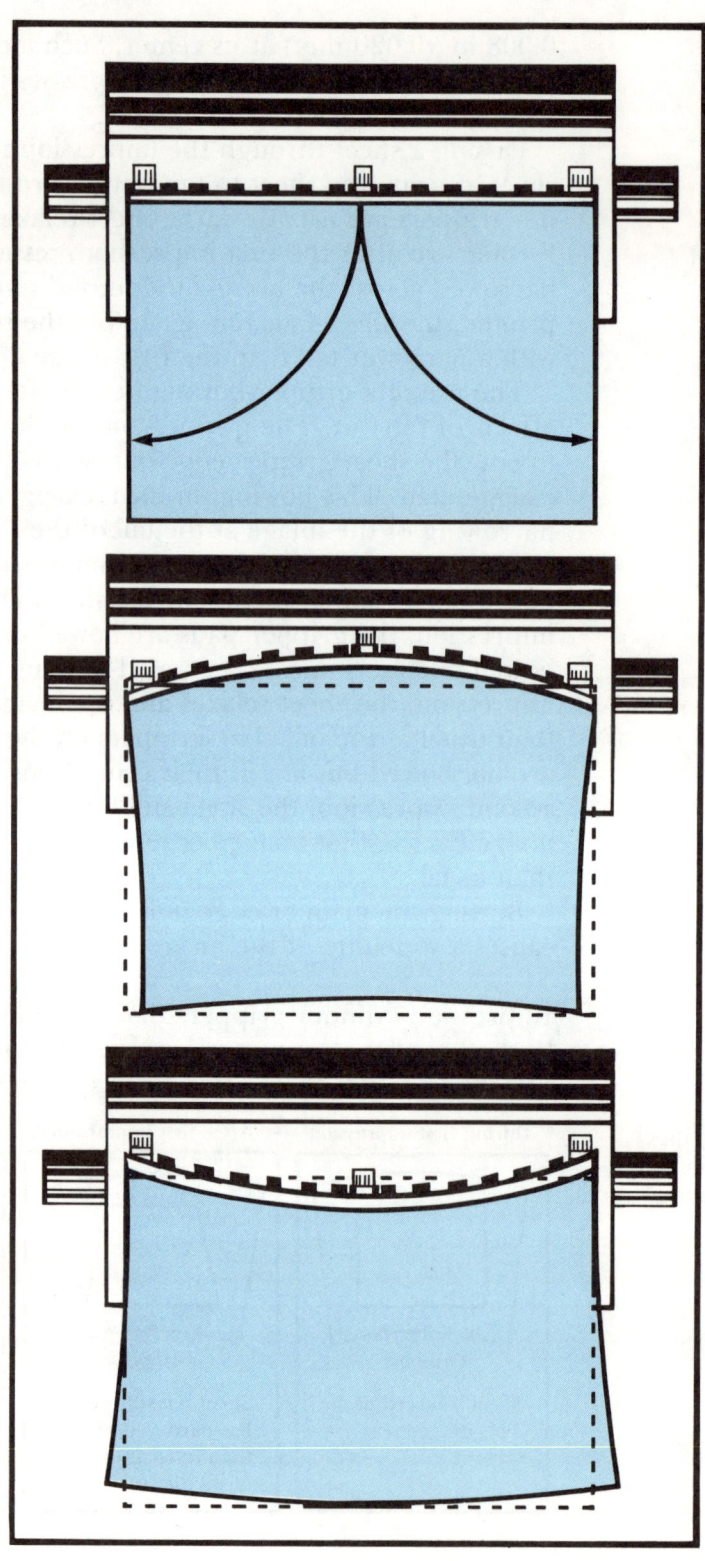

too tightly and the next one is set too loosely. Therefore, properly tensioned grippers are essential.

Sheet Transfer Section

The sheet transfer section transports the press sheet between the impression cylinders on a multicolor sheetfed press. Depending on the number of printing units, the number of sheet transfer sections varies. For example, a four-color press has three sheet transfer sections.

Three principal methods of sheet transfer are common:

- **Chain transfer,** where sets of grippers riding on a chain transport the sheet from one impression cylinder to the next. When the sheet is transferred from the chain grippers to the impression cylinder grippers, and vice versa, the sheet is held by both gripper systems for a short distance. Chain transfer lessens the chance of ink smearing because the paper contacts fewer surfaces. Specially designed metal shields minimize air turbulence in a chain transfer system.

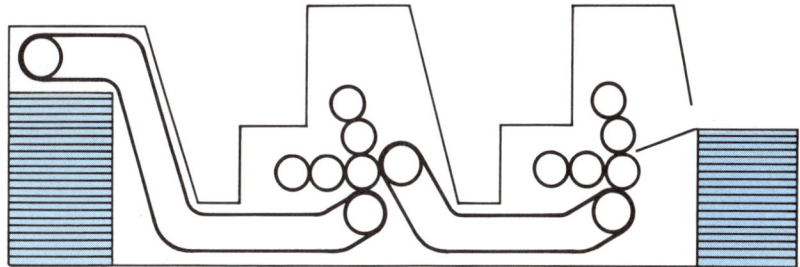

Chain transfer system with common impression cylinders

- **Single-drum transfer,** where a set of grippers on a large-diameter transfer cylinder transport the sheet from one impression cylinder to the next. The diameter of the transfer cylinder varies considerably with press design. For example, one press design has a common-impression cylinder three times the size of the plate or blanket cylinder and a transfer cylinder four times the size of the plate or blanket cylinder. (See also "Transfer Cylinder" in chapter two.)

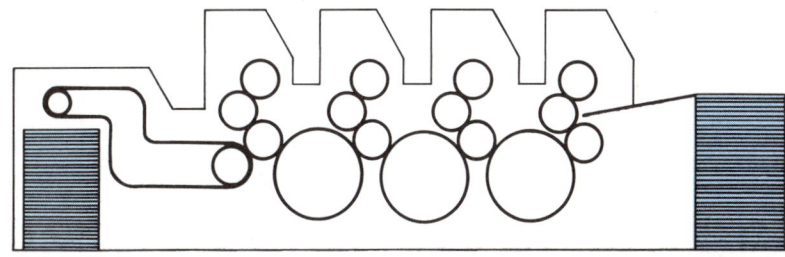

Single-drum transfer system

136 Sheetfed Offset Press Operating

- **Three-drum transfer,** where three transfer cylinders—are used to transport the sheet from one impression cylinder to the next. Each has a set of grippers.

Three-drum transfer system

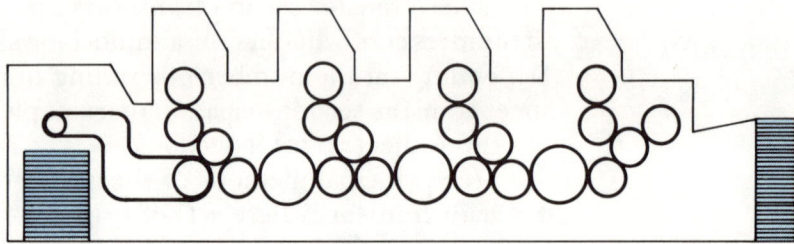

Antimarking devices are positioned in print margins of the press sheet. A special air-cushion drum on some presses can be used to float the sheet above the drum's surface without the tail edge fluttering, thus preventing marking of the printed image, or a special net-like covering can be attached to transfer cylinders that contact the wet side of the press sheet. (See "Transfer Cylinder" in chapter two.)

If the sheet transfer system has gripper-bowing devices, it is often necessary to reset them for a new job.

Delivery Section

The delivery section begins as the sheet leaves the final impression cylinder. Delivery grippers take the printed sheet from impression-cylinder grippers and transport it to the delivery pile, or table. The grippers typically travel on gripper bars. The grippers release the sheet onto the pile,

Delivery section

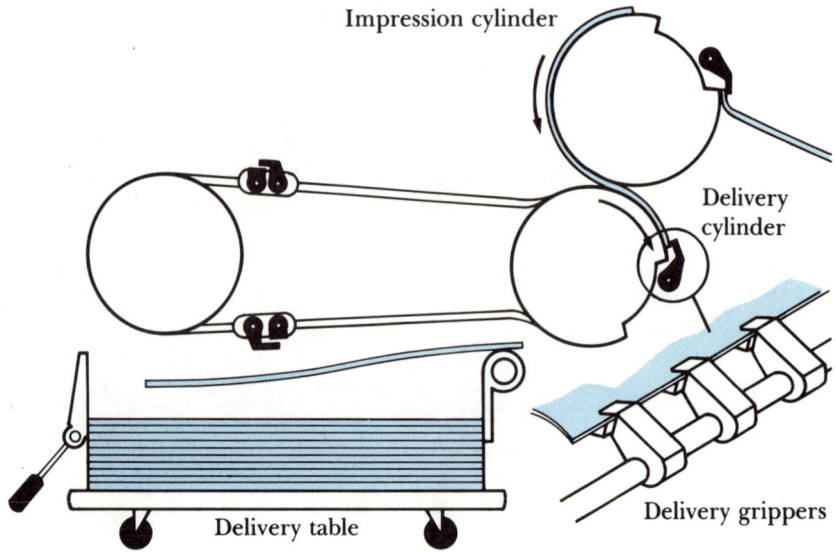

where various devices (joggers) arrange the sheets into a neat, uniform pile.

Often located between the last press unit and the delivery is a **sheet decurler,** a device that is designed to take troublesome curl out of press sheets.

Sheet decurler
Courtesy Baldwin Technology Corp.

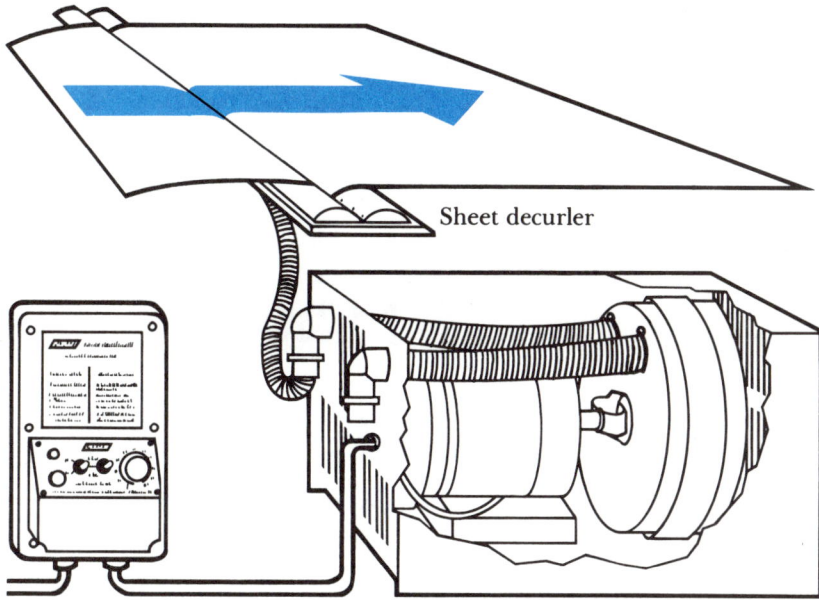

Baldwin sheet decurler installed on a sheetfed press

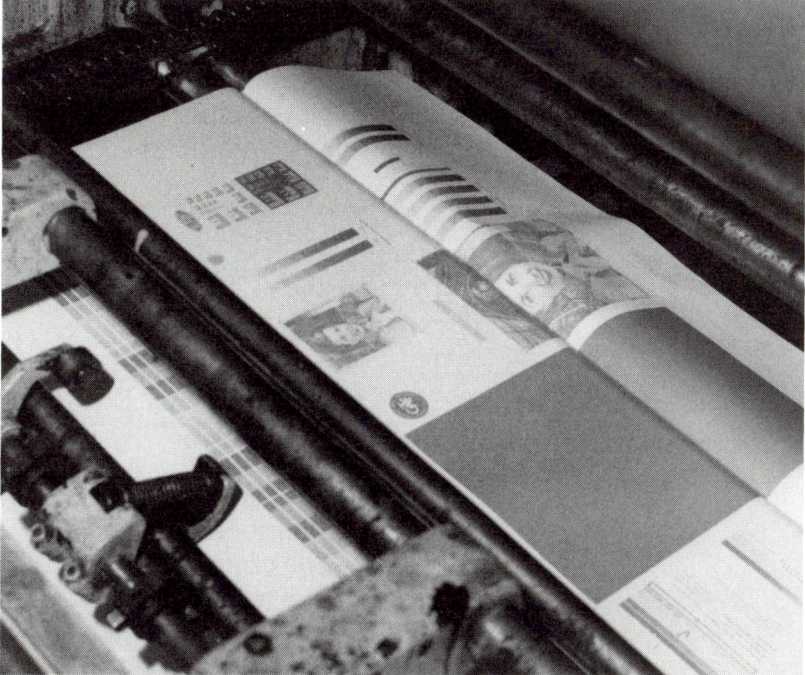

Jogging the Delivery Pile

Three movable devices (two side joggers and a rear sheet guide) and one fixed device (a front gate) jog the sheet into a pile, but the neatness of the pile depends on the proper positioning of the devices. Joggers are set to the exact size of the press sheet. An improperly set jogger—either with the side joggers set too close together or too far apart or with the

Setting the joggers in the delivery

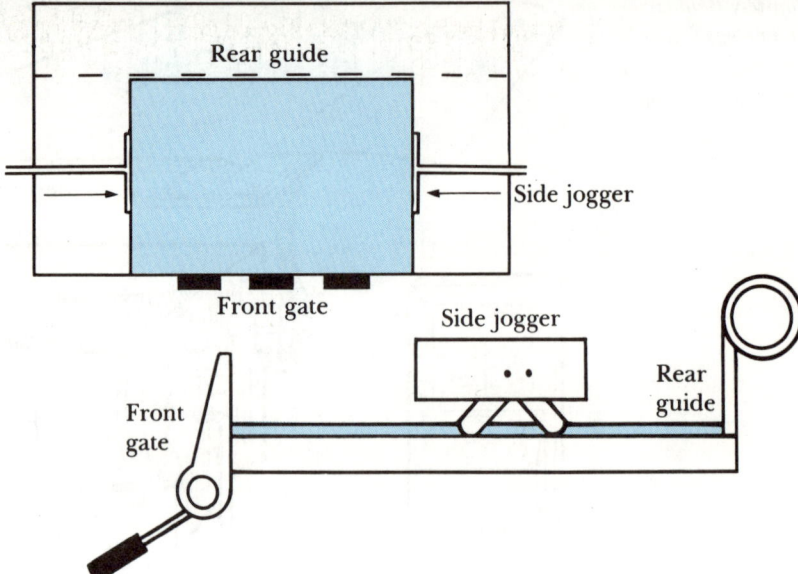

rear sheet guide set too far forward or too far back—results in an improperly stacked pile of sheets. A properly jogged pile helps to avoid errors in the trimming and finishing operations. Following is a procedure for setting the joggers:

1. Forward a sheet onto the feedboard using the feeder handwheel. Make sure that the impression control is in the "off" position.

2. Inch the press forward until the sheet just begins to be transferred from the impression cylinder grippers to the delivery grippers.

3. Move the side guide joggers to their outermost positions. Move the rear sheet guide to its rear-most position.

4. Inch the press forward until the sheet drops onto the delivery.

5. Inch the press forward until the joggers are at their innermost jogging position.

6. Put the press on "safe." Loosen the set screws of the rear guide and move it so that it holds the sheet against the front gate. Tighten the set screws.

Sheet Control

7. Loosen the set screws on each side jogger and move the joggers so that they touch the edge of the sheet. Tighten the set screws.

8. Inch the press forward, checking that the rear guide and side joggers are neatly boxing in the sheet.

Sheet-Guiding Devices

Several types of devices assist the grippers in moving the press sheet from the impression cylinder to the point just before the delivery gripper release. Common sheet guiding devices include skeleton wheels, star wheels, covered cylinders, and air-cushion drums, depending on the press.

Skeleton wheels are movable wheels that are positioned in nonprinting areas of the press sheet. Properly positioned skeleton wheels evenly support and help to peel the sheet from the last impression cylinder.

Positioning of sheet-guiding devices is usually done from under the feedboard or from the delivery. If counter guide rails are used, they are positioned to support the back of the sheet. Final location of sheet-guiding devices depends on the position of images on the printed sheet.

Positioning skeleton wheels to contact the nonimage areas of the sheet

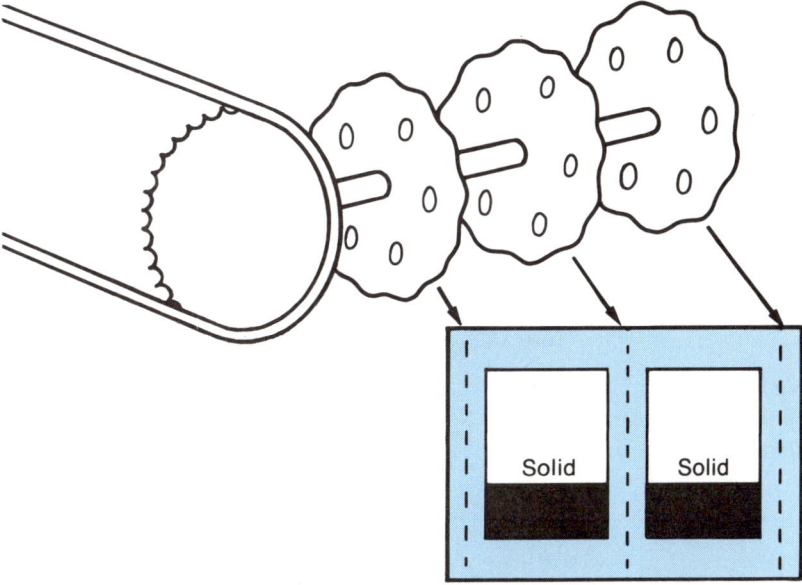

Delivery-Assist Devices

Several devices assist the joggers in neatly stacking the printed sheets. Commonly used devices include suction rollers, blow downs, and pile wedges.

Suction slow-down rollers. Suction rollers slow down and steady the sheet as it enters the delivery. They are usually positioned just behind the rear sheet guide and beneath the chain delivery. Only those suction rollers that the sheet passes over should be used, with all others being turned off. Test-running the press helps to determine the proper vacuum setting.

Blow-downs. Near the top of the delivery are the **blow-downs,** a series of air holes that assist in dropping the sheet onto the delivery table. Air is blown on the top side of the sheet, forcing it downward. Fans are also used for this purpose. The proper level of air depends on press speed and on the weight and type of stock. Test-running the press helps to determine the proper air pressure.

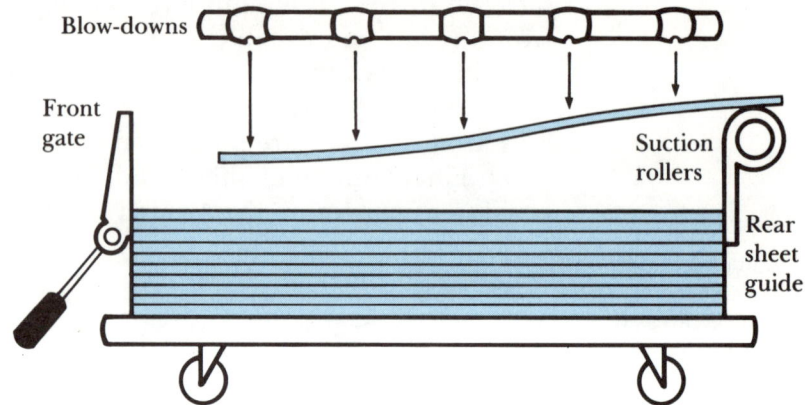

Sheet blow-downs and suction rollers, which assist in delivering the press sheet

Wedges. Wooden or plastic wedges are used at startup to produce a neat pile. By holding up the rear (trailing, or tail) edge of the sheets, wedges help to counter **tail-end hook** (a sharp curl at the back edge of the sheet). Edges can cause marking. Therefore, they must be carefully used.

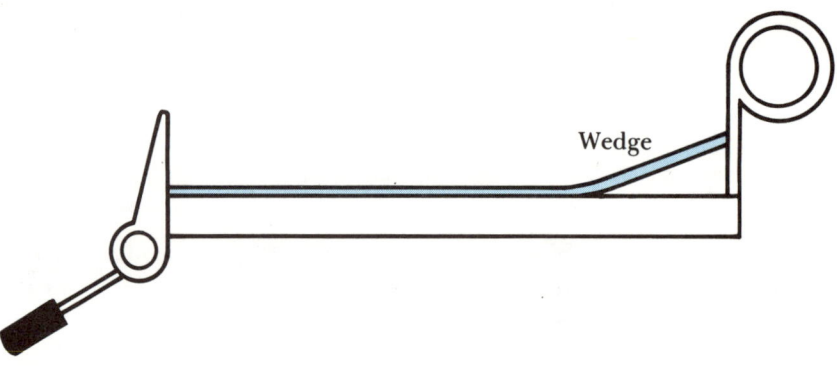

Wedge used to hold up the rear edge of the press sheet

6 Packing and Printing Pressures

There is one fundamental of printing unit operation: neither ink nor water will transfer without proper pressure between the transferring elements. The plate cylinder and blanket cylinder surfaces must run with pressure between them to effect ink transfer; running contact is not enough. There must also be adequate pressure between the blanket and the paper.

Pressure is more than essential in lithography; it is critical. Tolerances are small. The press operator's margin of error in squeeze is as little as 0.002–0.003 in.

The procedure for setting cylinder pressures is called **packing.** The noun "packing" also refers to the paper or plastic sheets that are put under the blanket and plate.

As discussed in chapter 2, the bodies of the plate and blanket cylinders are lower than the surface of the bearers. The exact difference in height—called the **cylinder undercut**—varies with the specifications agreed on by the manufacturer and the printing plant. Often, the amount of undercut is specified by the plant ordering the press. Knowing the exact amount of undercut on the plate and blanket cylinders is essential to setting proper pressures in the printing unit.

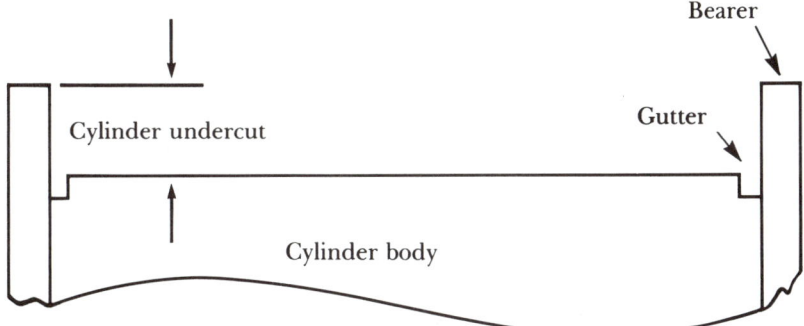

Cylinder undercut, the amount that the cylinder body is beneath the bearers

Packing sheets are put under the blanket and plate to increase the diameters of the cylinder bodies. (The true diameter of the cylinder is the same as the pitch diameter of the gears.) There are three primary reasons for altering cylinder diameters.

- **To compensate for different plate and blanket thicknesses.** Packing makes it possible to use a fairly wide range of plate and blanket thicknesses on one press. Packing sheets themselves are available in a variety of thicknesses.
- **To adjust the pressure between plate and blanket.** In order for ink to transfer from the plate to the blanket, either

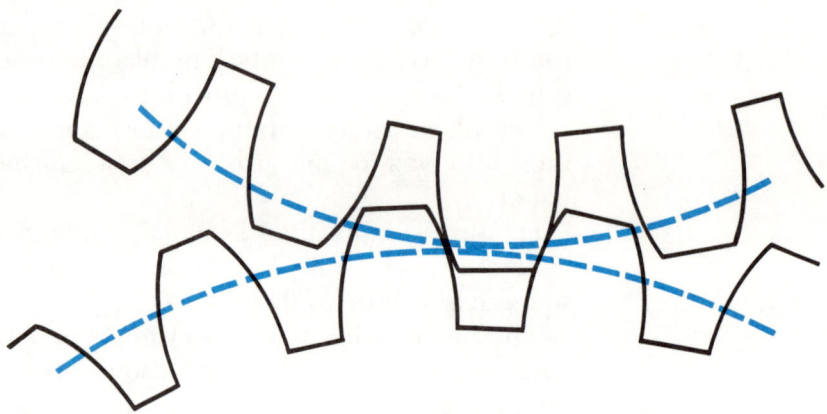

Gears of plate and blanket cylinders meshing at the pitch line diameter

the plate or blanket, or both, must be packed above bearer height. Pressure between plate and blanket is increased by adding packing sheets and decreased by removing packing sheets. The pressure between plate and blanket, and blanket and impression cylinder, is referred to as squeeze.

- **To compensate for paper growth, or stretch, during multicolor printing.** Paper stretches when it is printed. By changing the ratio of the plate and blanket cylinder diameters, a stretched print can be matched.

Packing Material

Any material having enough dimensional stability and uniformity of thickness to raise a plate or blanket to proper height and *keep it there* can be used for packing. In actual practice, few materials meet these requirements. Probably the most common material now in use is specially manufactured kraft paper. Kraft paper is a highly calendered, water-resistant paper with negligible compression. It is made in a variety of thicknesses so that the press operator, by choosing the right sheet or sheets, can create nearly any packed height that is required. Kraft packing paper is manufactured to reasonably close caliper tolerances, which is extremely important to the press operator.

Packing paper, however, does not offer the ultimate dimensional stability on the press. Mylar or similar plastic is much tougher and is coming into wide use as a packing material under plates—especially frosted Mylar. Mylar also has high resistance to lithographic chemicals. It is more expensive than kraft paper but, with reasonable care, can be reused. However, it should never be used under a blanket.

Press sheets or any other papers not designed for the purpose make poor packing materials. The thickness of the printing paper is not uniform enough to meet the critical standards required in press packing. It also compresses easily.

Packing sheets should be cut square and sized for the press, and stored according to caliper using a separate shelf for each thickness. Sheets of similar caliper should also be color-coded or stamped for ease of identification. If the press operator has to search for packing sheets, measure their thickness, and cut them to size while the press waits, makeready can be very costly.

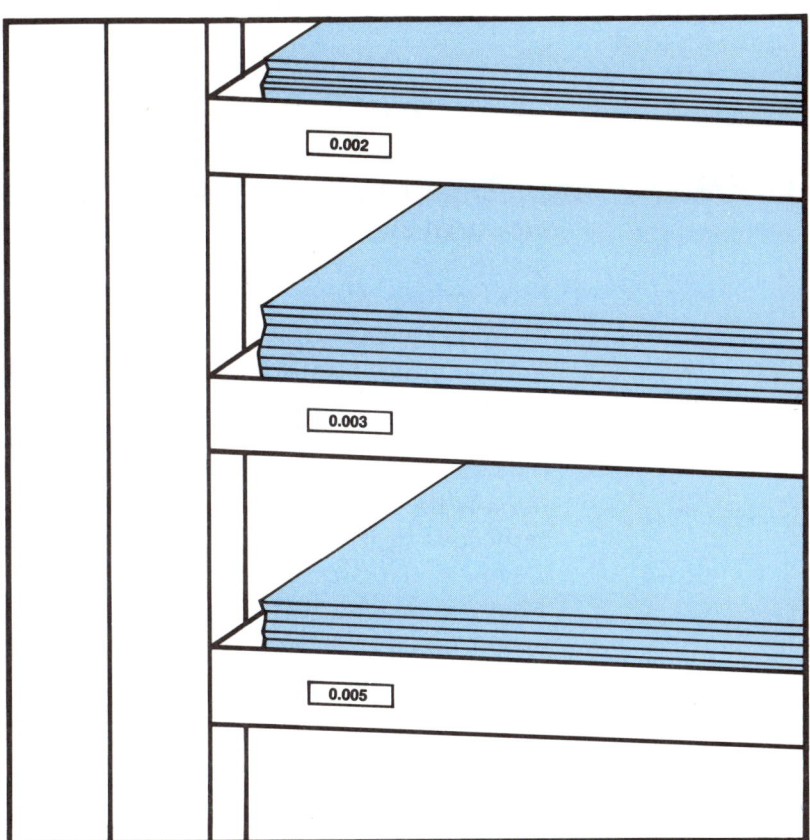

Storage of packing sheets according to caliper

Opinions vary regarding the optimum packing width. Some press operators prefer packing of the same width as the plate and blanket for easier alignment. Others like packing to be anywhere from 1/16 in. (2 mm) to 1/2 in. (13 mm) narrower than the plate or blanket, hoping that the dampening solution does not affect the packing sheets.

Water that gets under the edges of the plate and blanket soaks into the packing paper, causing it to swell. Thickness can increase by several thousandths of an inch (or hundredths of a millimeter) and raise the edge of both the blanket and the plate, increasing the pressure between them. Sometimes, fountain solution is wiped off the plate near the edges, and the quality of images close to the plate edges is lowered.

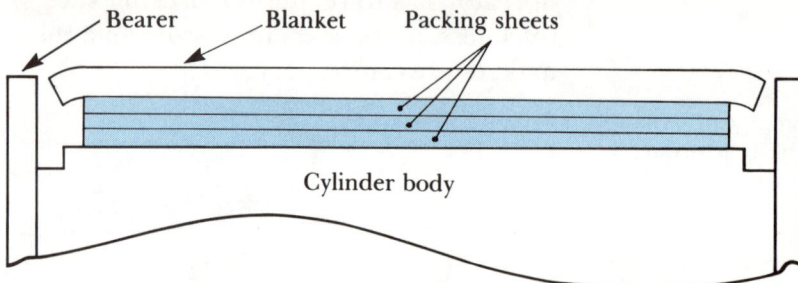

Packing cut slightly narrower than the blanket.

Notice that the blanket is packed above bearer height.

Cylinder Pressures

Unfortunately, pressures on a printing press are not measured and stated in pounds per square inch. No practical means has yet been found for measuring the pressure between two cylinders on a running press. As a result, pressures are described in the most convenient measure available: thousandths of an inch (or hundredths of a millimeter) of "squeeze." Squeeze on a bearer-contact press is the combined height of plate and blanket over their respective bearers, while squeeze on a non–bearer-contact press is the combined height of plate and blanket over their respective bearers *minus* the distance between the bearers.

How much pressure does a given amount of squeeze exert? That is difficult to say because pressure is not directly proportional to squeeze.

There is a simple principle behind the procedure used by the press operator to develop squeeze in the plate-to-blanket nip. Assume that an unpacked plate cylinder and unpacked blanket cylinder on a bearer-contact press are turning together with their bearers in firm contact with one another. Although the bearers are in contact, there is no pressure between the cylinder bodies because the bodies do not touch. The distance between the cylinder bodies is equal to the amount of undercut on the plate cylinder plus the amount of undercut on the blanket cylinder.

To develop plate-to-blanket squeeze, the press operator, in effect, increases the diameter of the cylinder bodies. The plate and its packing raise the height of the plate cylinder, and the blanket and its packing raise the height of the blanket cylinder. *The total thickness of the material that is put on both cylinders determines the amount of squeeze, assuming compression of neither materials nor cylinder bearers.*

Assume that the cylinders on a bearer-contact press are packed so that the plate and the blanket are exactly even with the surface of their respective cylinder bearers. How much squeeze is there? None, theoretically. The cylinders are *just* touching and there is no squeeze between them. *There is no pressure between the working surfaces until the press operator adds materials whose thickness is more than the total undercut of the two cylinders.* If, however, just one more sheet of 0.001-in. (0.025-mm) packing is added under the plate, the squeeze between the two cylinders is 0.001 in. If an identical sheet is added to the blanket cylinder, the squeeze becomes 0.002 in. (0.05 mm). The effective surface of each cylinder body is 0.001 in. above their respective cylinder bearers for a total of 0.002 in.

The squeeze at the printing nip is not just the amount that the blanket cylinder is packed in relation to the bearers. The actual squeeze also includes the thickness of the paper being printed and the pressure exerted by the impression cylinder. In calculating packing, the press operator starts by packing the plate and blanket cylinders according to the recommendations of the press manufacturer, or to the appropriate height for that press determined by experience. Depending on the thickness of the substrate being printed, the impression cylinder is positioned closer or farther away from the blanket cylinder to provide the proper amount of squeeze at the printing nip.

Squeeze between plate and blanket is less than that at the printing nip. The press operator's ultimate concern is with pressure and not squeeze, for it is pressure that determines the effectiveness of ink transfer. At the plate-to-blanket nip, a rigid surface (the plate) and a resilient surface (the blanket) are squeezed together. A given amount of squeeze at the plate-to-blanket nip exerts more pressure than the same amount of squeeze applied between the two resilient surfaces (the blanket and the paper) at the printing nip.

Determining the Proper Packing

What is the proper packing? The answer to this question is not simple. It is affected by ink, paper, blanket, bearer compression, and the quality vs. productivity requirements of the job.

Many manufacturers of conventional blankets specify a squeeze of 0.002–0.004 in. (0.05–0.10 mm), with a 0.003-in.

(0.08-mm) squeeze being the most common. The squeeze that provides highest-quality reproduction is the proper one. However, sometimes it is better to slightly overpack either cylinder by about 0.001 in. (0.025 mm) to compensate for the compression of the blanket that occurs during the pressrun.

Effect of Ink and Paper on Packing

Paper and ink tend to go together when considering their effect on proper packing. Probably the most important quality to be considered is the surface strength of the paper—that is, its ability to resist picking. In looking at a weak paper, such as newsprint, it is obvious that an ink with very low body must be used in order to minimize picking. Low-body inks require less pressure to transfer, and therefore the total plate-to-blanket squeeze required for sharp printing is relatively small. On the other hand, an ink designed for sharp printing on coated paper has considerable body.

Another consideration in determining proper packing is the roughness of the paper. Surface variations in rough paper make a uniform and continuous solid more difficult to achieve than with a smooth-surfaced paper. A rough paper requires more squeeze between blanket and impression cylinder so that the blanket contacts the low spots in the paper with sufficient pressure to transfer ink. For example, pebble-finish or embossed stocks require more impression cylinder pressure than coated papers.

Effect of Blanket on Packing

Another extremely important operating factor affecting packing and squeeze is the blanket. The type of blanket used—conventional or compressible—makes a difference. Compressible blankets make it possible to obtain good printing with considerably higher squeeze. This gives the press operator a little more margin for error in packing the press.

Compressible blankets do not all compress equally. The press operator should keep in mind that different compressible blankets can produce a great variety of printed results.

Packing is a means to control pressure. The squeeze-pressure relationships for different blankets can vary considerably. For example, let us assume that the minimum pressure required to transfer a certain ink is 200 lbs./in.^{2} (14 kg/cm^2). In examining the compression vs. pressure characteristics of different blankets, it can be demonstrated that to achieve 200 lbs./in.^{2} may require less than 0.003-in. (0.08-mm) squeeze on one blanket and as much as 0.007- or 0.008-in. (0.18- or 0.20-mm) squeeze on another blanket. The difference in compression produced by a given pressure depends upon the hardness and the compressibility of the blanket in question.

Effect of Bearer Compression on Packing

Another factor that affects the packing as measured on a bearer-contact press is bearer compression, or bearer deformation. Normally, press bearers that run in contact exert considerable pressure on each other. This pressure helps the press run more smoothly. Because it causes the bearers to compress at the nip, it creates problems when trying to predict the proper packing ratio for the press. For example, assume that the minimum squeeze between plate and blanket for present press conditions is 0.004 in. Assume also that the bearers compress 0.0005 in. each. If the plate and blanket are both packed exactly 0.002 in. over bearer, the actual compression between plate and blanket will be 0.005 in. rather than 0.004 in. The extra 0.001 in. of squeeze is due to the fact that the packing measurements are made relative to the uncompressed bearer. Bearer compression on newer presses is not excessive and probably runs in the range of 0.001 in. total compression for the two bearers involved. On older presses, however, bearer compression can run considerably higher, even as much as 0.002 in. compression per bearer. This would mean a total of 0.004 in. squeeze gained in a printing nip due to bearer compression.

The press operator uses the amount of undercut on the cylinders as a basis for calculating the amount of packing needed. The manufacturer's original specifications should be followed, and a packing gauge must be used to verify the packing of the cylinder.

When the press is put on impression and the bearers have been properly set, there is considerable pressure between them. These relationships can change, especially when press cylinders are small in diameter. For one thing, hard steel bearers do not remain perfectly circular, but deform under pressure. This changes the amount of undercut on the cylinders at the nip. The problem is greater on older, lightly built presses equipped with relatively small bearers.

Therefore, the press operator has to determine the effective cylinder undercut when the press is running under pressure. The procedure to determine effective undercut takes time but only has to be done once. The press is packed in normal fashion, and a plate that prints both solid and screened images is mounted on the plate cylinder. The press is run until ink and water are balanced. Then, packing is removed (starting under the plate), until the solids no longer print. At this point, the packing is reinserted, 0.001 in. (0.025 mm) at a time, until the press is again printing a good, full-strength solid. The press is now properly packed with minimum pressure.

The packed height is measured using a packing gauge. The indicated squeeze is the minimum for printing with the given paper, ink, and blanket combination, on the press in question, using the packing gauge normally used by the press operator. This figure automatically takes into account any bearer deformation occurring on the press.

The bearers on any press deform; the amount depends on the construction of the press cylinders. Change in the radius of the bearers is important because in effect it increases the amount of squeeze at the printing nip. The above procedure for determining squeeze automatically compensates for this problem.

The method described above also eliminates some potential difficulties inherent in using a packing gauge. The objective of the procedure is to adjust press packing until a visible standard of performance is achieved: a good, full-strength solid. The press operator then uses the packing gauge to measure the conditions on the press that yield this standard of performance. What do these measurements mean? The press operator's aim is to be able to reproduce those packing conditions at will. If the gauge is properly used, it indicates whether this has been done. The packing gauge used should be tested to see if its readings are sufficiently consistent to be used in the pressroom.

Effect of Quality and Production Factors on Packing

Another factor affecting the final packing ratios is the relationship between the quality requirements and the production requirements of the job. High-quality printing requires the correct amount of squeeze and, therefore, very tight control over packing. If emphasis is on production, however, overpacking is used to guarantee that a small decrease in the height of the blanket will still maintain ink transfer. As the emphasis shifts from quality to production, the tendency to overpack increases.

Packing and Printing Pressures

Measuring Packing Material Thickness

Packing a press is an important operation. It should never be done haphazardly. Every item of thickness should be checked carefully. There are many chances to make a mistake. Only by precisely measuring plate, blanket, and packing can the press operator be sure to obtain the proper squeeze. A dead-weight bench micrometer, such as a Cady gauge, is a good all-purpose measuring device for use in the pressroom.

Plate Thickness

Although plate thickness seldom varies to any appreciable amount from one plate to another, it is advisable to gauge several plates in a new shipment to determine if there is any deviation in plate gauge within the shipment. If any deviation is discovered, each plate in the shipment will have to be gauged before it is mounted on the press.

A preliminary check of plate thickness gives the press operator a known starting point when calculating packing requirements. Plate thickness, once determined, remains constant because plates are not affected by atmospheric or press moisture.

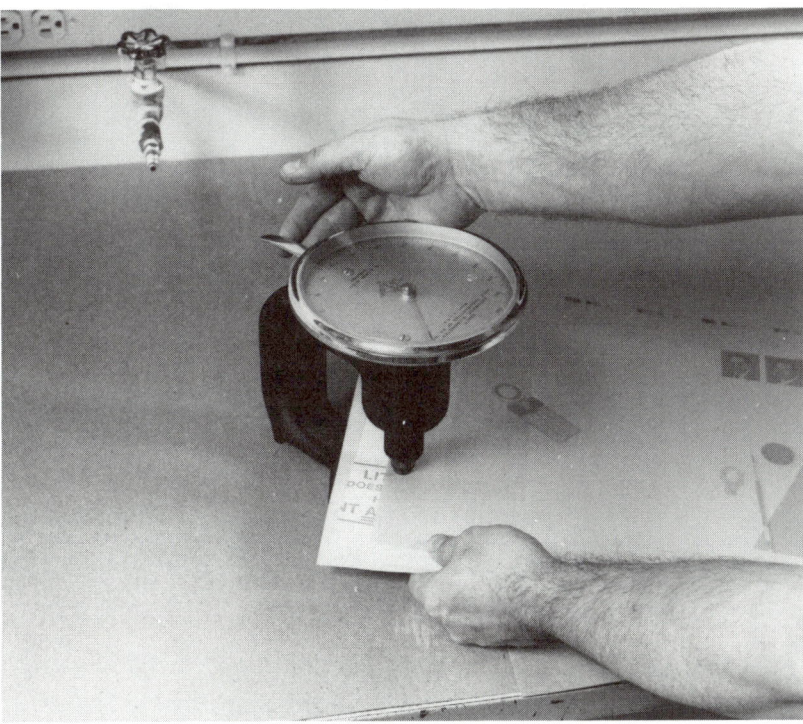

Press operator measuring the combined plate and packing thickness using a dead-weight bench micrometer from E. J. Cady & Co.

Blanket Thickness

Accurate measurements are needed just to give the press operator an idea of what is required. The thickness of everything used in packing should be checked, no matter how many times a particular brand of plate or blanket is used. This is especially true for blankets. *Each* blanket should be checked with a bench micrometer (a dead-weight gauge, such as the Cady gauge) and its average thickness marked on the back.

Thickness readings of a blanket should be taken in at least four places to get an average as well as to determine any deviation in the surface thickness of a single blanket.

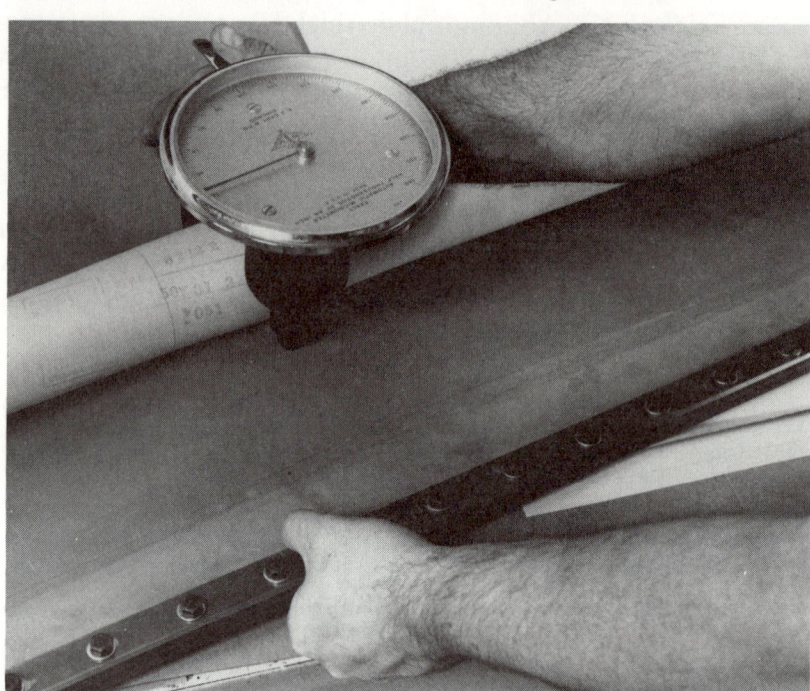

Press operator measuring blanket thickness using a Cady gauge

Packing Thickness

Packing sheets should be measured, even though the packing manufacturer indicates the caliper of the sheets. The best procedure to follow in measuring the thickness of packing sheets is to:

1. Open the package containing the packing sheets and permit the packing sheets to come into equilibrium with the temperature and relative humidity of the pressroom.

2. Measure the thickness of the packing sheets.

The higher-quality packing sheets are affected less by humidity.

Packing Gauge

In checking cylinder packing, there is no substitute for a good packing gauge designed for graphic arts use. The gauge gives the press operator an accurate reading of how far over or below bearers the cylinders are packed. This is

Packing and Printing Pressures

not to say the press operator shouldn't get accurate measurements on the materials used in packing the cylinders.

A packing gauge placed against the plate, with its base resting on the plate cylinder bearer, gives a reading of the height difference between the surface of the plate and the surface of the bearer. A reading should be taken from both ends of the plate cylinder. The height of the blanket in reference to the surface of the blanket cylinder bearers should also be measured using a packing gauge. The gauge manufacturer's instructions should be followed in order to properly zero the gauge in reference to the bearers.

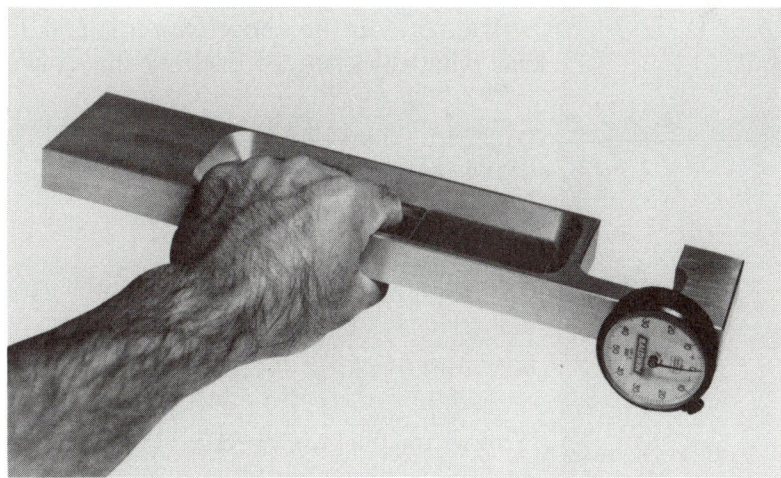

Baldwin packing gauge
Courtesy Baldwin-Gegenheimer

Arithmetic of Packing

Properly measuring the thicknesses of the various materials involved in packing is the first step toward successfully packing the press. Calculating the necessary amount of packing is the second step.

Plate-plus-Packing Height

The **plate-plus-packing height** is the total thickness of the plate and its packing. It is determined by (a) *adding* the plate height *above* bearers (as specified by the press manufacturer or determined through experience) to the cylinder undercut or (b) *subtracting* the plate height *below* bearers from the cylinder undercut.

The total thickness of the packing sheets needed is obtained by subtracting the plate thickness from the plate-plus-packing height.

For example, a press manufacturer specifies that the plate height above the bearers should be 0.003 in. (0.08 mm). The press manufacturer also indicates that the cylinder undercut is 0.019 in. (0.48 mm). What would be the plate-plus-packing height if the press is packed to the manufacturer's specifications?

```
  0.019 in.  Cylinder undercut
+ 0.003 in.  Height above bearers
  0.022 in.  Plate-plus-packing height


  0.48 mm   Cylinder undercut
+ 0.08 mm   Height above bearers
  0.56 mm   Plate-plus-packing height
```

If the plate in the above example is 0.014 in. (0.36 mm) thick, what thickness of packing sheets is necessary?

```
  0.022 in.  Plate-plus-packing height
- 0.014 in.  Plate thickness
  0.008 in.  Packing sheet thickness


  0.56 mm   Plate-plus-packing height
- 0.36 mm   Plate thickness
  0.20 mm   Packing sheet thickness
```

To reduce packing creeping, two 0.004-in. (0.10-mm) sheets of packing should be used, instead of one 0.008-in. (0.20-mm) sheet.

Blanket-plus-Packing Height

The **blanket-plus-packing height** is the total thickness of the blanket and its packing. It is determined by (a) *adding* the blanket height *above* bearers (as specified by the press manufacturer or determined through experience) to the cylinder undercut or (b) *subtracting* the blanket height *below* bearers from the cylinder undercut.

The thickness of the packing sheets necessary is obtained by subtracting the blanket thickness from the blanket-plus-packing height.

For example, a press manufacturer specifies that blanket height below the bearers should be 0.001 in. (0.02 mm). The press manufacturer also indicates that the cylinder undercut is 0.075 in. (1.91 mm). What would be the blanket-plus-packing height if the press is packed to the manufacturer's specifications?

Packing and Printing Pressures

  0.075 in. Cylinder undercut
−0.001 in. Height below bearers
  0.074 in. Blanket-plus-packing height

  1.91 mm Cylinder undercut
−0.02 mm Height below bearers
  1.89 mm Blanket-plus-packing height

If the blanket in the above example is 0.065 in. (1.65 mm) thick, what thickness of packing sheets is necessary?

  0.074 in. Blanket-plus-packing height
−0.065 in. Blanket thickness
  0.009 in. Packing sheet thickness

  1.89 mm Blanket-plus-packing height
−1.65 mm Blanket thickness
  0.24 mm Packing sheet thickness

Calculating Squeeze on a Bearer-Contact Press

Squeeze on a bearer-contact press is calculated by determining the height of the plate in relation to the plate cylinder bearers and the height of the blanket in relation to the blanket cylinder bearers. The two heights are added, with the resulting value being the squeeze.

  For example, a press manufacturer specifies that the plate height *above* bearers should be 0.003 in. and the blanket height *above* bearers should be 0.001 in. What is the squeeze?

  0.003 in. Height of plate above bearers
+0.001 in. Height of blanket above bearers
  0.004 in. Squeeze between plate and blanket

  For example, a press manufacturer specifies that the plate height *above* bearers should be 0.003 in. and the blanket height *below* bearers should be 0.001 in. What is the squeeze?

    0.003 in. Height of plate above bearers
+(−0.001) in. Height of blanket above bearers
    0.002 in. Squeeze between plate and blanket

  In the above example, since the blanket is packed below the bearer, its height is a negative number.

Calculating Squeeze on a Non–Bearer-Contact Press

Squeeze on a non–bearer-contact press is calculated by adding the height of the plate in relation to the plate cylinder bearers to the height of the blanket in relation to the blanket cylinder bearers and subtracting the distance between the plate cylinder and blanket cylinder bearers.

For example, a press manufacturer specifies that the plate height *above* bearers should be 0.007 in. and the blanket height *above* bearers should be 0.003 in. In addition, the distance between bearers is 0.008 in. and not adjustable by the press operator. What is the squeeze?

0.007 in.	Height of plate above bearers
+0.003 in.	Height of blanket above bearers
0.010 in.	Combined height of plate and blanket

0.010 in.	Combined height of plate and blanket
−0.008 in.	Distance between bearers
0.002 in.	Squeeze

With some non–bearer-contact presses, the distance between the plate cylinder bearers and the blanket cylinder bearers can be adjusted. Therefore, with such a press, follow the manufacturer's recommendations on adjustments and packing.

Problems Due to Improper Packing

A squeeze of 0.002–0.004 in. (0.05–0.10 mm) is all that is necessary to transfer ink from the plate to a conventional blanket to paper. When grainless plates, hard blankets, and coated paper are used, a squeeze of 0.002 in. is usually sufficient. With compressible blankets, a squeeze pressure between 0.005–0.008 in. (0.13–0.20 mm) is typical.

With a conventional blanket, excessive squeeze (typically any squeeze greater than 0.004 in.) results in a variety of problems. Similarly, if the squeeze is insufficient (typically any squeeze less than 0.002 in.), other problems arise. Excessive squeeze results in more serious problems: initial and often detectable dot gain, deterioration of print quality, and plate damage.

Note: Always follow the blanket manufacturer's instructions relating to proper squeeze pressure.

Excessive Squeeze

The press's tolerance to variation in packing is not great. Any squeeze between plate and a conventional blanket greater than 0.004 in. (0.10 mm) is usually considered excessive. Excessive squeeze causes premature plate wear. It is not the squeeze itself that causes this wear, but the fact that there is slippage between the plate and blanket at the point of contact. The slippage may result in a uniform dot gain in areas that carry enough ink to lubricate the surfaces. The visual effect on a 70% tint may be a slur. On lighter tints the slippage may be intermittent and cause streaks.

Excessive squeeze creates friction that wears plate images, breaks down the thin desensitizing film, and actually flattens the grain. On long pressruns, the plate may go blind and scum at the same time. Excessive squeeze between plate and blanket sometimes overcomes the traction between the bearers, causing the bearers to slip. Gear streaks then appear on the blanket and sometimes on the bearer surfaces.

Excessive squeeze between impression cylinder and blanket contributes to slur, paper curl, and picking. This pressure is independent of packing; there is a control on every press to adjust the impression.

Causes of excessive squeeze. Improper packing is the major cause of excessive squeeze between plate and blanket cylinders. The packing and blanket gauges must be read carefully when measuring the plate, blanket, and packing. Care must also be exercised when making packing calculations. Following a few precautions minimizes mistakes. One precaution is to post a sign over the work table of each press, simply recording the depth of the cylinder undercuts. The sign could read something like this:

> Plate .... 0.019 in.
> Blanket .... 0.075 in.

Another precaution against mistakes is to use sheets that are made expressly for packing. Putting each thickness of packing material on a separate shelf and color-coding similar thicknesses of packing material are two more ways to safeguard against errors.

Another common cause of excessive squeeze is inaccurate measuring of blanket thickness. It is almost impossible to find the true thickness of a blanket with the ordinary machinist's micrometer, which generally gives a reading of 0.002–0.003 in. (0.05–0.08 mm) less than the true thickness. This is enough to cause trouble. A special blanket thickness gauge has been developed for measuring blankets (see p. 150). Its use minimizes the chance of overpacking the blanket.

Perhaps the least suspected and yet the most dangerous cause of excessive squeeze is untrue cylinders. Cylinders that show no indication whatsoever of any surface damage may have low spots in them. These depressions are sometimes as deep as 0.005 in. (0.13 mm) without being discovered. A rag, sponge, or wad of paper passing between contacting cylinders can cause such depressions. If a cylinder has a depression, the packing can be increased in order to get the low spot to print. However, all other areas will have excess pressure.

The same thing is true when a blanket is slightly damaged. If a blanket is badly crushed, it is either repaired or discarded. But if the low spot is not easily noticeable, the press operator is apt to overpack it with one large sheet so that the low spot prints satisfactorily. However, all other areas will have excessive pressure.

Still another cause is unparallel cylinders. Misalignment causes light printing on one side of the press. Trying to correct this by adding all-over packing produces serious excess pressure on the other side.

Insufficient Squeeze

Squeeze less than 0.003 in. (0.08 mm) between the plate and blanket results initially in a light or faded print. There are several causes of insufficient squeeze:
- Inaccurate measuring of blanket
- Improper calculation of amount of packing needed
- Compression of blanket and packing during mounting
- Compression of blanket and packing during pressrun

The first cause of insufficient squeeze is easily avoided if correct measuring devices and techniques are used. The second cause is avoided if the press operator makes calculations carefully; press-mounted signs indicating proper packing thicknesses and a hand-held calculator are desirable aids. The use of a torque wrench when tightening a blanket compresses the blanket a uniform amount.

The fourth cause is the worst. When printing starts, the quality of the print is high, but as the pressrun continues, the quality deteriorates as the blanket and packing compress, reducing the squeeze to below 0.003 or 0.002 in. (0.08 or 0.05 mm). To compensate for the poor print, the press operator often increases the ink (and water) to the plate. The quality of the print might improve, but the problem of insufficient squeeze has not been solved. Insufficient squeeze reduces the amount of ink transferring to the blanket from the plate. The initial symptom of insufficient squeeze is that the ink density of the print becomes light and the solids and type appear grainy in spots. After the symptom appears and the incorrect increase of ink and dampening feed, further symptoms appear:

- Rough, fuzzy edges on halftone dots, type, and line images resulting from insufficient ink transfer pressure and an excessively thick ink film
- Snowflaky printing—tiny open holes in areas that should be solid, full-density ink—due to excessive amounts of water droplets (from dampening solution) in ink
- Dampening rollers dirtied by water picking up tiny ink particles resulting from running excess dampening solution

In addition to the above symptoms, there are numerous problems that result indirectly from improper squeeze and directly from either increased ink feed or increased water feed: stripped rollers, glazed rollers, blind images, slow ink drying, decreased ink tack, poor trapping, filled-in halftones and reverses, poor register, tinting on later units of a four-color press, coating piling, and paper curling.

All of the above problems would not occur if, instead of increasing ink and dampening feed, the press operator would stop the press and measure the height of the blanket using a packing gauge. Checking blanket height is the first thing that the press operator should do when the printing starts to look light after, say, 500 or 1,000 impressions. Adding the proper thickness of packing paper restores the squeeze to the proper level.

An incorrect remedy for light printing due to insufficient squeeze is to increase blanket-to-impression-cylinder pressure. This action, however, compresses the blanket still more, which further decreases the squeeze between plate and blanket. Excessive pressure is also placed between blanket cylinder and impression cylinder. Every time the gaps in the two cylinders meet, the excessive pressure is released, leading to vibrations throughout the cylinders. These vibrations, in turn, produce streaks.

Print Length Adjustment

Paper often stretches slightly between colors on a single-color or multicolor press. Consequently, the print must be made intentionally longer on the next color. On a sheetfed press, paper is run with the grain across the press. The paper stretches across the grain. Therefore, the stretch is around the cylinder. To match a stretched print, the press operator changes the diameter ratios of the cylinders. If the blanket diameter is larger than the plate diameter, the print will be longer. The reverse is also true: the higher the plate in relation to the blanket, the shorter the print. To match a stretched sheet on a bearer-contact press, then, it is only necessary to take packing from under the plate and put it under the blanket.

Print Length Adjustment on a Bearer-Contact Press

The following procedure is used to shorten print length on bearer-contact presses:

1. Increase plate height by adding packing.

2. Decrease blanket height by the amount of the packing change.

3. Increase the pressure between the blanket and impression cylinders by the amount of the packing change.

4. Decrease the inking and dampening roller setting to the plate by the amount of the packing change, if necessary.

The following procedure is used to increase print length on bearer-contact presses:

1. Decrease plate height by removing packing.

2. Increase blanket height by the amount of the packing change.

3. Decrease the pressure between the blanket and impression cylinders by the amount of the packing change.

4. Increase the inking and dampening roller settings to the plate by the amount of the packing change, if necessary.

Print Length Adjustment on a Non–Bearer-Contact Press

The following procedure is used to shorten print length on non–bearer-contact presses, assuming that the distance between the plate and blanket cylinders is adjustable:

1. Increase plate height by adding packing.

2. Decrease the pressure between the plate and blanket cylinders by the amount of the packing change.

3. Decrease the inking and dampening roller settings to the plate by twice the amount of the packing change, if necessary.

The following procedure is used to increase print length on non–bearer-contact presses, assuming that the distance between the plate and blanket cylinders is adjustable:

1. Decrease plate height by removing packing.

2. Increase the pressure between the plate and blanket cylinders by the amount of the packing change.

3. Increase the inking and dampening roller settings to the plate by twice the amount of the packing change, if necessary.

Note: No blanket cylinder packing change is necessary when adjusting the print length on a non–bearer-contact press.

Limits on Enlargement

How much enlargement is safe? Excessive transfer of packing from plate cylinder to blanket cylinder often results in slurring or doubling due to the variation in the surface speed of the two cylinders. Halftones also thicken, and the plate wears rapidly. Therefore, the question "How much enlargement is safe?" depends upon the packing conditions at the start of the pressrun. If initial plate packing conditions resulted in zero slippage, a packing shift of 0.004 in. (0.10 mm) would not cause excessive slippage. But, if initial packing conditions resulted in some slippage, the additional slippage caused by the 0.004-in. packing shift could easily exceed allowable slippage and could cause slurring, gear streaks, and false gear streaks.

No press manufacturer claims that presses must be packed at exactly one point and no other. Press manuals give the method of packing for which the press is designed. However, in color work, it is impossible to adhere to these specifications for each color and get good fit. Fortunately, there is a fairly wide tolerance permissible in the packing conditions, except for squeeze. Without this latitude, it would be very difficult for the press operator to fit multicolor images when the paper stretches.

A general recommendation: if the paper on a multicolor job is expected to stretch and it is being run on a one-color press, it is best to pack the press for a relatively short print on the first color; i.e., some packing would be shifted to the plate cylinder initially.

Calculating Print Length Gain for Different Substrates

The following procedure can be used to judge the print length for a given substrate, or paper stock:

1. On the sides of a flat plate, scribe two lines near the lead edge and two lines near the trailing edge. These lines should be scribed so that they print in the trim area of a press sheet.

2. Measure the distance between the lines.

3. Mount the plate on press and print several sheets.

4. Measure the distance between the lines on a press sheet.

Approximate position of scribed lines in the trim area

Trailing edge

Lead edge

5. Subtract the distance between lines on the plate from the distance between lines on the press sheet. Divide this number by the distance between lines on the plate. The answer will be the average print length gain per inch for that substrate.

This test can be repeated for other substrates to determine how to pack the press to compensate for print length gain. Through experience, the press operator will be able to predict print length gain and be able to make the necessary changes in packing to correct for it.

7 Blankets

Blankets cause many problems, but they have the one redeeming feature that has made offset lithography what it is: blankets have the ability to transfer ink to paper with high fidelity. They can transfer an image to fairly rough paper, and they can transfer good solids and very fine dots.

The blanket's importance is often overlooked, but it is as important as any other part of the printing system. Because it is the last image transfer point, it directly affects the quality of the printed job.

Blanket Manufacture

The use of rubber for offset blankets goes back to the invention of the modern offset press by Ira Rubel in 1909. Rubel knew of the excellent image-transfer capability of rubber surfaces, and he made this capability the central design feature of the first offset press.

The first commercially used offset blankets were made of natural rubber, which was somewhat less than ideal in this application. These blankets had a tendency to swell, stretch, blister, and become tacky. They had poor resistance to solvents and oils. In addition, rubber—being a naturally occurring substance—could not be produced to uniform specifications and close tolerances.

The development of synthetic rubbers in the 1930s made it possible to overcome the disadvantages of poor solvent and oil resistance associated with natural rubber blankets. The use of synthetic rubbers also made it possible to control formulations and to produce close-tolerance blankets in uniform batches.

The synthetic rubbers most commonly used today are Buna-N and, to a lesser extent, neoprene. The specific formula used is generally kept secret by the blanket manufacturer. In addition to the basic rubber compound, the formula contains additives to toughen and reinforce the blanket surface. Softeners and plasticizers are also added to give the blanket resiliency. Finally, a vulcanizing agent, usually sulfur, is included to cause the molecules of the rubber compound to cross-link during the vulcanizing process.

Manufacture begins with the weaving of the fabric backing. The material used is a very high grade of long-staple cotton. The tolerances on the finished fabric are extremely rigid (especially in terms of thickness and strength).

Before the rubber is applied, the fabric backing is stretched in the same direction as the tension to be applied when the blanket is mounted on the press. Prestretching minimizes the amount that the blanket stretches when it is mounted on the press. The backing fabric is woven to be much stronger lengthwise (around the cylinder) than across its width. Colored threads are woven into the backing to indicate the direction of greatest strength. (The direction of maximum strength is called the **warp;** the direction of minimum strength is called the **weft.**) On the press, blanket strength is needed in the around-the-cylinder, or warp, direction, and the warp threads should always run from leading to trailing edge. If they run from side to side, the blanket stretches beyond recovery and runs loosely, causing doubling and slurring.

Warp threads on the fabric side of a blanket

The prestretched fabric is coated with a thin layer of adhesive cement, and another layer of prestretched fabric is placed on top of the first. A three-ply blanket has three such fabric layers. Most offset blankets are three- or four-ply, although two-ply blankets are also made. Three-ply blankets are usually between 0.062 in. (1.57 mm) and 0.066 in. (1.68 mm) thick. Four-ply blankets generally fall in the 0.072-in. (1.83-mm) to 0.076-in. (1.93-mm) thickness range.

After the fabric layers have been cemented together, the rubber surface is applied to the backing in sixty to eighty individual coats, each carefully laid down. The entire operation is carried out in a temperature-controlled, dust-free atmosphere. Conditioned air is necessary in meeting thickness tolerances. Standard tolerance on blanket thicknesses is about ±0.0005 in. (±0.013 mm).

The blanket is then powdered, festooned, and cured (vulcanized). This last operation causes rubber molecules to cross-link, giving the finished blanket its strength and dimensional stability. A good blanket stretches less than 2.5% in the around-the-cylinder direction and has a tensile strength of about 300 lb./in. Because of this very high tensile strength, excessive tension from end to end is not nearly as much of a problem in mounting blankets as is uniform tension across the blanket width.

Performance Requirements

Sheet Release

A "good" blanket—like a good ink and a good paper—is the result of tradeoffs between a number of opposing characteristics.

Release is the readiness of the blanket to give up the paper after it leaves the nip. The smoothness of the blanket surface is a factor; very smooth blankets tend to have poor release. Even so, it is clear from research that smoothness is not the only factor that contributes to blanket release.

Press operators agree almost universally that a hard blanket gives the best release. Whatever theoretical justification there is for this contention has not yet been supported by research findings. One stumbling block has been finding a reliable means of measuring hardness that allows comparison between blankets. Durometers require a sample thickness many times greater than the thickness of the rubber surface layer on blankets. This makes the value of blanket durometer readings questionable.

The blanket is just one of several factors affecting sheet release. Press speed, ink tack, printing pressures, and paper surface also affect sheet release. The increasing use of lightweight paper, faster press speeds, and higher tack inks makes the importance of a blanket with good sheet release characteristics all the more critical.

Resilience and Durability

Resilience and durability are two other important qualities. **Resilience** is the ability of a blanket to return to its original thickness after pressure on its surface has been removed. Resilience is usually most important to the press operator as **smash-resistance,** the ability of a blanket to *recover* from being momentarily subjected to excessively high pressure. **Durability,** on the other hand, is the blanket's ability to withstand the pressure, tension, and physical abuse it continually undergoes on the press.

Surface Smoothness

Surface smoothness is another important quality. The nature of blanket manufacture creates microscopic contours on the rubber surface. Some have suggested that this graining is important in removing water from the plate. Others argue that optimum blanket performance is obtained with a polished, grainless surface. In any event, nearly all blankets sold commercially have a slightly grained surface. It is important that the grain is not so great that it affects printing, especially in solids. Grain is another reason why a light washing of the blanket surface is inadequate for keeping the surface clean. The surface should be free from pinholes, pits, or other defects.

Solvent Resistance

A blanket must have an affinity for ink but should be resistant to the ink vehicles and the solvents used to clean it. To perform satisfactorily, the blanket must not swell when contacted by a solvent. Solvent-resistance properties vary considerably, which means that only solvents compatible with the blanket are suitable for cleaning it.

Stretch and Tensile Strength

A blanket should undergo minimum stretch on the press. However, it is normal for a newly mounted blanket to stretch slightly. As a result, the initial blanket tension decreases and the blanket becomes slightly loose. Therefore, it is not uncommon that the blanket has to be "taken up" (retightened) after the first 3,000 or 4,000 impressions. After that, the blanket should remain dimensionally stable (i.e., not stretch) on the press for the rest of its run life, assuming that it has been properly mounted. The blanket with the least tendency to stretch after the initial stretch has been taken up is the one most satisfactory from the standpoint of maintaining uniform conditions during the pressrun. If it is necessary to retighten a blanket at regular intervals, printing pressure may be excessive, lockup tension may be insufficient, or the blanket may be stretching excessively.

Compressible Blanket

Use of the compressible blanket has become widespread in recent years. Like a conventional blanket, a compressible blanket has a surface of synthetic rubber and a fabric backing of several plies. But in addition to the fabric layers, the backing includes one or more layers of a compressible

Compressible blanket

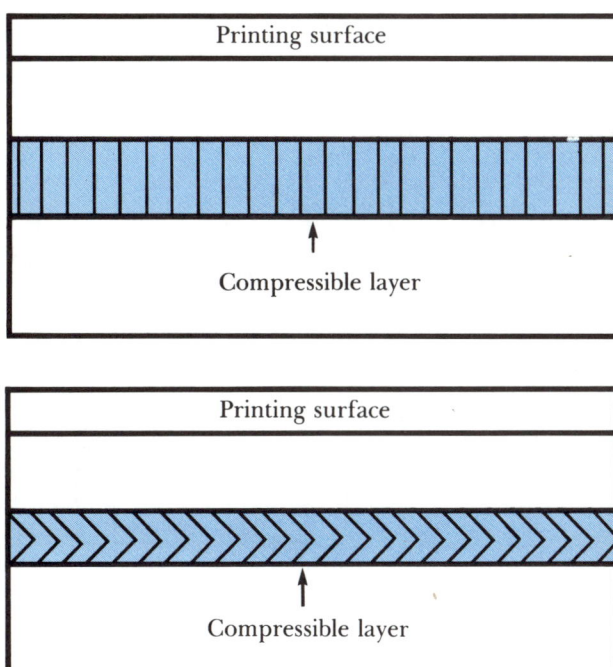

material, such as adhesive–foam rubber, cork, or nonwoven fibers.

One advantage of a compressible blanket is its wider packing latitude. With either type of blanket, an increase in packing also increases pressure. However, with a compressible blanket, the pressure increase is not as great. In effect, over a given range, a change in packing produces a relatively small change in pressure. Consequently, the press operator has somewhat wider packing tolerances. This is important because improper pressure can lead to a host of process problems: plate wear, dot spread, ink film graininess, mottle, dot slur, gear marks, blanket low spots, changes in image length, and paper pick. Although packing latitude is greater with a compressible blanket, it is not recommended that the blanket be overpacked by more than 0.002 in. (0.05 mm).

Reduced slippage at the nip is a second advantage of a compressible blanket. (**True rolling** is a term often used to describe the condition of no slip in the printing nip.) With a conventional rubber blanket, bulges form on either or both sides of the nip. Because the blanket deforms, its surface speed through the nip is different from the surface speed of the plate. In other words, there is usually slippage between the plate and a conventional blanket, which can lead to

The results of tests conducted by a blanket manufacturer on how blankets react to pressure

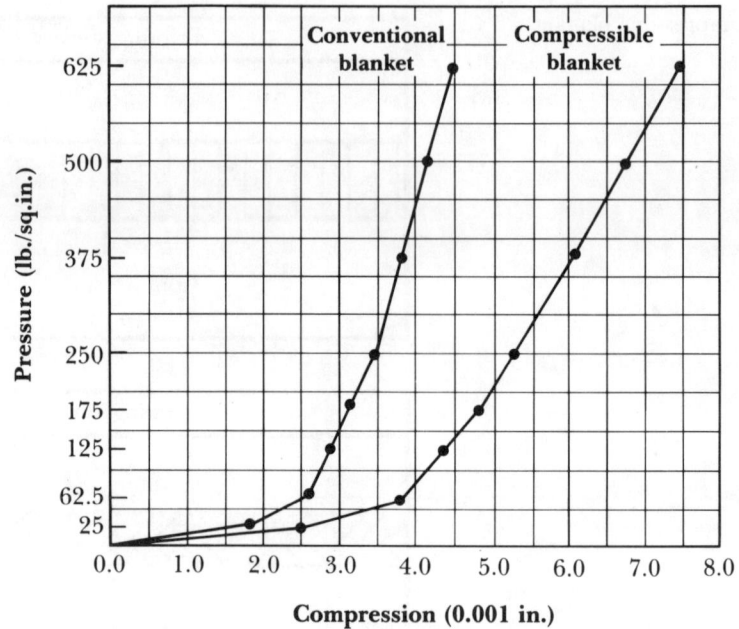

slurring. A compressible blanket does not deform in the same way. Less rubber is displaced, and the bulges on either side of the nip are smaller. The speed differential between plate and blanket is considerably reduced.

The deformation of compressible and conventional blankets at the nip between between the plate and blanket

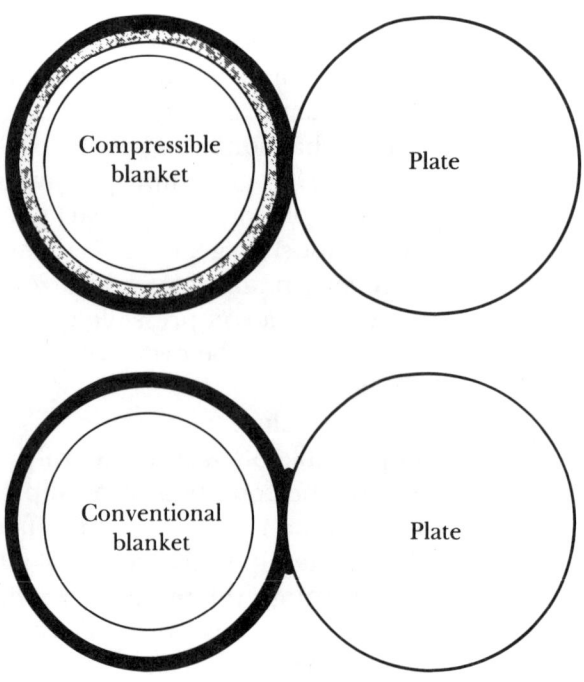

Some manufacturers say that using a compressible blanket leads to longer plate life. Reducing slippage between plate and blanket means that the polishing action of the blanket against the plate is reduced.

Whenever a solid object goes through the press, a **smash,** or undesired localized compression of the blanket's surface, results. A compressible blanket resists smashing better because of its ability to compress. Smash recovery, depending upon the severity of the smash, may be within 2–10 sheets. **Compression set** is the permanent reduction in thickness of any of the blanket's component parts.

Another advantage of a compressible blanket is that any thickness variation tends to "even out" in the blanket-to-plate-cylinder and blanket-to-impression-cylinder nips.

Compressible vs. conventional blankets

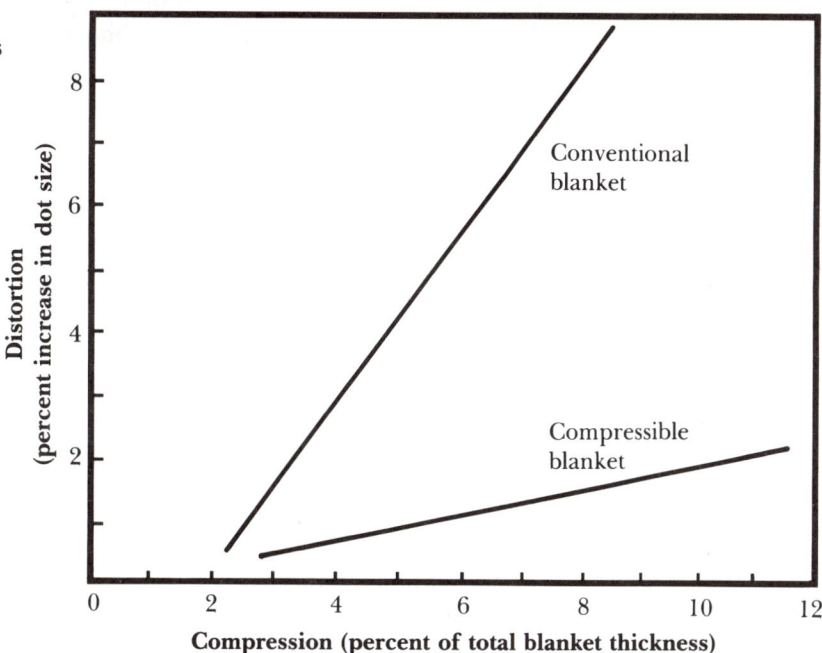

Compressible blankets usually produce sharper halftones, better register, less paper distortion, and fewer washups.

Perhaps the only disadvantage of the compressible blanket is that it does not print on rough or textured surfaces as well as a conventional blanket does, particularly in solids.

Blanket Selection

In choosing a blanket, the press operator should select a thickness that minimizes the amount of packing needed. The blanket should also be wide enough to run from gutter to gutter. This helps to prevent chemicals and other contaminants from working their way under the blanket during the pressrun.

Color Coding

Blankets come in different colors. At one time, the blanket's color indicated its hardness. This is no longer true.

Blanket Hardness

Many blanket manufacturers now question the usefulness of thinking in terms of blanket "hardness." Durometer tests provide inadequate measures of blanket hardness because the rubber layer is too thin to make accurate measurements. Also, the readings are affected by the relative compressibility of backing materials.

Quick-Release Properties

Many blankets are sold today as "quick-release" blankets. The quick-release properties of a blanket are probably associated with the surface roughness of the blanket. The rougher the surface, the less tendency there is for the paper to adhere to the blanket. However, as the roughness of the surface increases, the blanket's ability to reproduce fine dots and smooth solids decreases.

Blanket Thickness

Today's blankets usually have their thickness marked on the back. This figure may be accurate, but it does not convey enough information about the blanket to the printer.

One of the problems with depending on these figures is that the printer does not know which instrument was used to make the measurement. Due to different instruments and different measuring techniques, it is quite reasonable to assume that a measurement of 0.065 in. (1.65 mm) by one manufacturer may not agree with the same measurement by another manufacturer.

A single figure stamped on the back of a blanket does not ensure uniformity. Each printer should have an agreement with the blanket supplier regarding acceptable **nonuniformity,** or overall variation, of a given blanket. Although blanket manufacturers talk in terms of uniformity of ± 0.001 in. or ± 0.002 in. (± 0.025 mm or ± 0.05 mm), such a figure actually refers to the uniformity of an entire shipment of blankets. The printer's problem is nonuniformity within a given blanket, which can produce a problem that the printer cannot resolve.

Checking each blanket's thickness necessitates a standard procedure. This procedure involves making a fixed number of measurements at the center and edges for each blanket received, using a dead-weight micrometer, such as a Cady gauge. The average reading of all measurements should be marked on the blanket back to enable accurate computations of required packing thickness. The difference between the highest and the lowest readings should also be noted, and if this difference exceeds the agreed-upon tolerance, the blanket should be returned to the supplier.

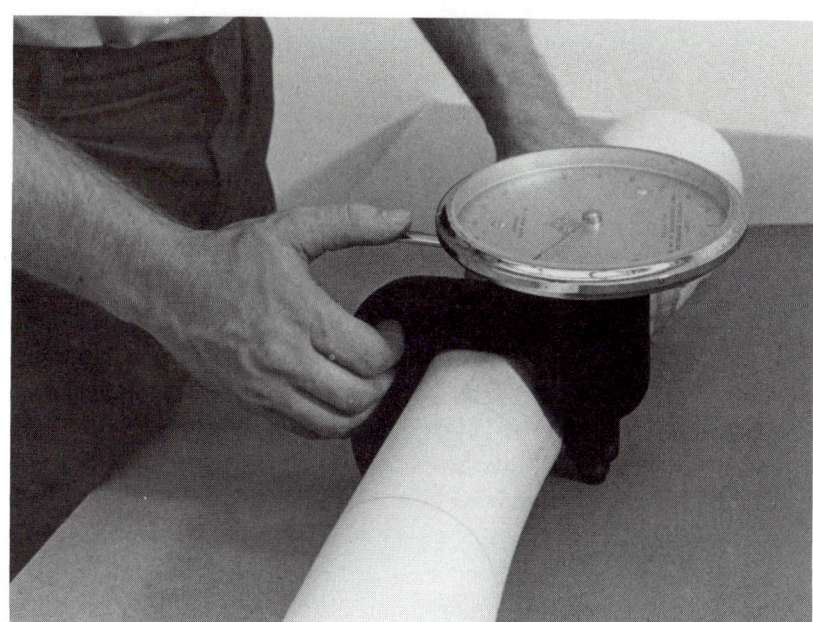

Press operator using a dead-weight bench micrometer from E. J. Cady & Co. to measure blanket thickness

Proper Care of Blankets

Today's blankets perform very well under press-related stresses and pressures. They also resist well the chemicals applied to their surface: ink, solvent, water, acids, gums, and salts, for example. However, they must be cared for properly.

The blanket should be rolled up carefully when being transported. It must not be folded, because the crease will permanently damage the blanket's face.

Blanket Storage

Off-press abuse—even of a seemingly minor kind—can ruin a blanket.

Exposure to light is a good example of off-press abuse. Directly exposing a blanket to sunlight will, over a period of time, crack and craze the rubber surface, making it unusable. Fluorescent light and heat can have a similar effect. Blankets should be stored in a dark, dry, cool place.

The tube in which a blanket is shipped is a good storage place. The tube should be stored on end. The press operator should never put too many blankets in a single tube, however. The innermost blanket will be very tightly wound, and prolonged storage under high stress may ruin the fabric backing.

Blankets can be stored flat. If they are, they should be stored so that rubber contacts rubber and fabric contacts fabric. Prolonged contact between a rubber surface and a fabric backing can cause the fabric pattern to emboss on the adjacent rubber surface.

Some manufacturers recommend flat face-to-face storage, and others recommend standing tube storage.

Blanket Solvents The press operator must make sure that the solvents used to clean the blanket are compatible with the ink *and* blankets. The ideal solvent should have a high solvency power for ink and the other compounds that frequently find their way onto the blanket during printing. It should have no damaging effects on the resiliency or printability of rubber. It should be nontoxic and have a flash point above room temperature, yet not so high that it takes a long time to evaporate.

Many commercial solvents come close to filling this bill. Any solvent should be approved by the blanket manufacturer to make sure that it is compatible with the materials in the

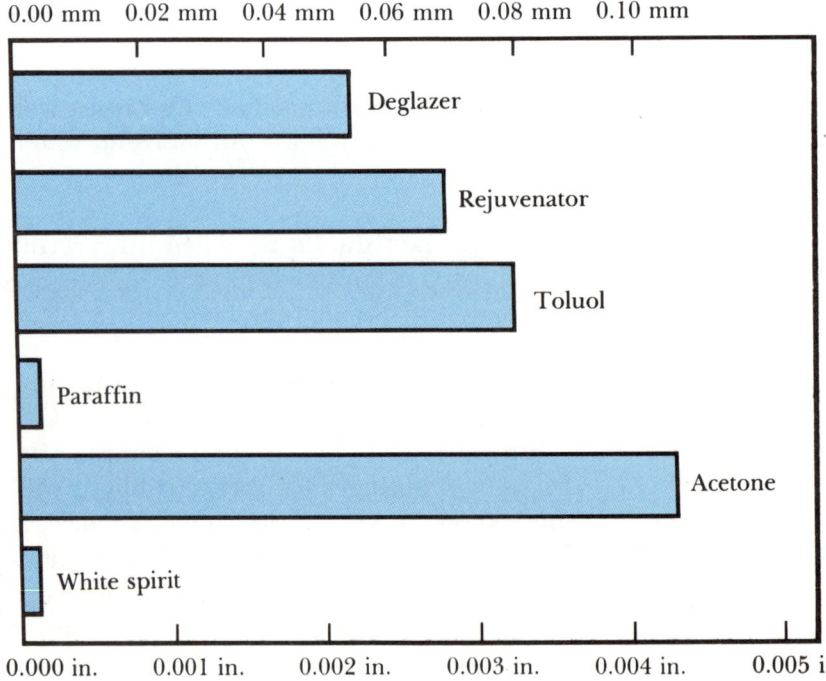

Swelling of a blanket caused by exposure to various solvents for a period of 5 min.

blanket and does not cause swelling or premature aging. Roller and plate suppliers should also be consulted before using a new solvent. Some press operators still use mineral spirits, but when they do, they sweep the solvent across the blanket with a rag in one hand, and *immediately* wipe it off with a rag in the other hand.

Repeated use of a solvent easily absorbed by the rubber causes deterioration. Washes with high kauri-butanol (KB) solvents should be avoided. A solvent with a high KB number is more easily absorbed by the rubber and evaporates more slowly. Rate of evaporation is important. A low rate forces delays in reinking after a blanket wash. Retained solvent increases the tackiness and frictional coefficient of the blanket.

Solvents containing benzol or toluol damage natural rubber, making it softer, tackier, and gummier. They should not be used. The use of solvents like kerosene and mineral spirits, which have a high boiling point and take a long time to dry, should be avoided.

Some substances that swell blankets include chlorinated and coal tar solvents, ketones, and esters. Aromatic solvents like toluene, xylol, turpentine, and pine oil also cause swelling. Benzene, perchloroethylene, trichloroethylene, carbon disulfide, and carbon tetrachloride should not be used because of their high toxicity and ability to dissolve rubber. All chlorinated solvents are toxic.

The previous discussion concerning matching the KB of the blanket wash to the blanket also applies to the ink itself. Sending an ink sample along with a blanket order ensures compatibility.

Material Safety Data Sheets should be on file for all pressroom solvents.

Washing and Reconditioning the Blanket Surface

A clean blanket is essential to high-quality printing. Scrubbing a blanket removes the hardened surface left on the blanket by the various gum and ink vehicles used during printing. Scrubbing also diffuses the oils and driers just below the blanket's surface, greatly increasing the life of the blanket.

When washing blankets, the press operator should be careful not to splash solvent along the blanket edges, because they may not be sealed. The top layer of the blanket is probably solvent-resistant; the under layers are probably not. Excess solvent attacks the adhesive that bonds the fabric plies

Press operator cleaning the blanket with solvent on a wadded rag

Notice that the press operator is wearing rubber gloves as protection against the solvent.

Press operator using a clean lint-free cloth to dry the blanket

together. Cutting blanket packing to less than full blanket width makes it difficult for excess ink to build up at the edges in the first place. It is important that the solvent-treated portion of the blanket be wiped dry with a clean lint-free cloth as soon as possible.

Proper reconditioning of a blanket requires some work as well as attention over a period of time. The first step is ink removal by means of a solvent. Once ink is off, the blanket is washed with water to remove gum residue. At this point, the blanket is usually removed from the press and placed on a table for scrubbing. (Pumice should not be used to clean the blanket's surface, because it could produce scratches.) The blanket surface is scrubbed vigorously until it has the velvety feel of live rubber. A hand blanket scrubber, such as a pocket-shaped scrubbing pad containing a cellulose sponge, is used.

Hand blanket scrubber

The back of the cleaned blanket is then soaked for a day or so to restore the fibers, and the blanket is hung up to dry. A mixture of one part glycerine to four parts water generally restores blankets better than plain water. Never return a blanket to the press until it is *absolutely dry*.

174 Sheetfed Offset Press Operating

Blanket Mounting Bars

In many instances, blankets can be ordered with mounting bars attached. Otherwise, the press operator must square the blanket, punch holes in it, and mount a bar to it.

The blanket must be evenly tensioned when it is stretched on the cylinder. The first step toward ensuring uniform tensioning is to make sure that the blanket is perfectly square. Usually, blankets are properly cut and squared before being shipped, but it is a good idea to check squareness anyway. The sides of the blanket should be parallel to the warp threads, which run in the direction of the arrow printed on the back of the blanket. (The warp threads on some blankets are colored for easier

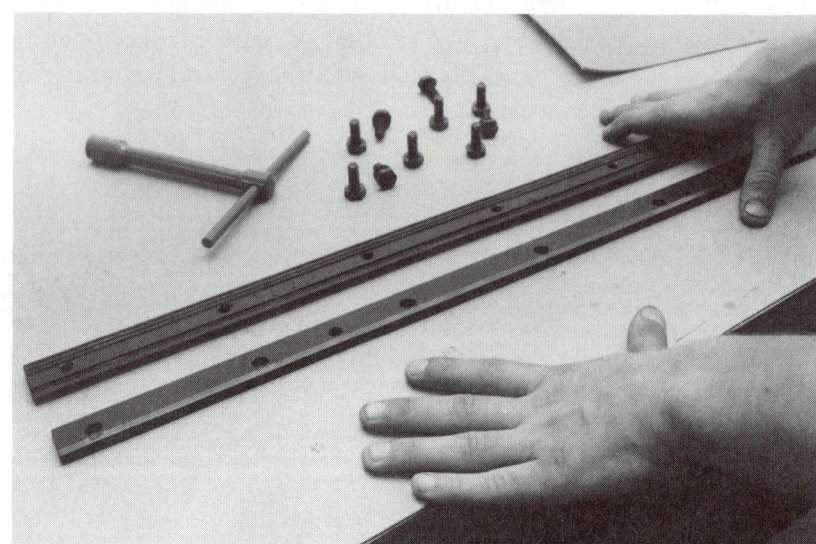

The blanket bars, bolts, and T wrench used to attach the bars to a blanket

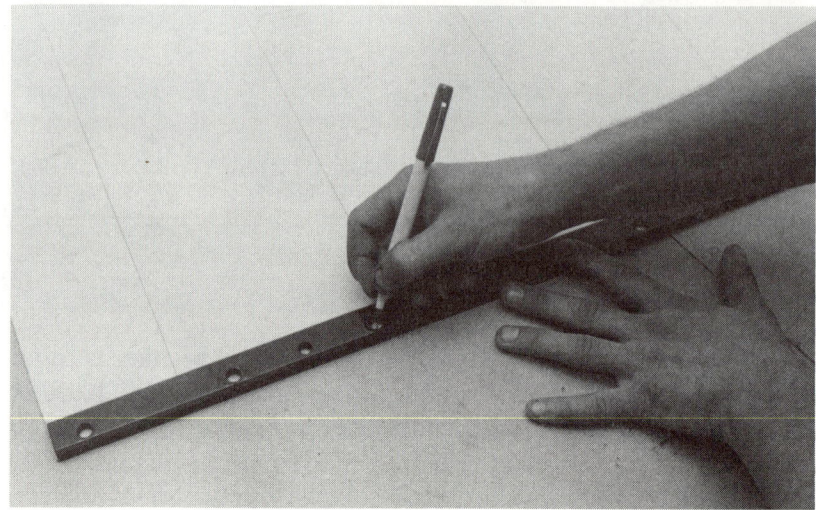

The holes for the bolts being marked on the fabric side of the blanket

The blanket bar is being used as a template

identification.) If the sides are not parallel, the blanket should be carefully trimmed. The ends of the blanket have to be perpendicular to the warp threads and sides. A large carpenter's square can be used. If the ends are not perpendicular, they should be carefully trimmed.

An unsquare blanket probably will be mounted to bars in an unsquare manner. If the ends of the bars are closer together on the right side than the left (because the warp threads are not perpendicular to the bars), the blanket will have more tension on the right side when on the press and, more importantly, will be pulled thinner on that side. For the

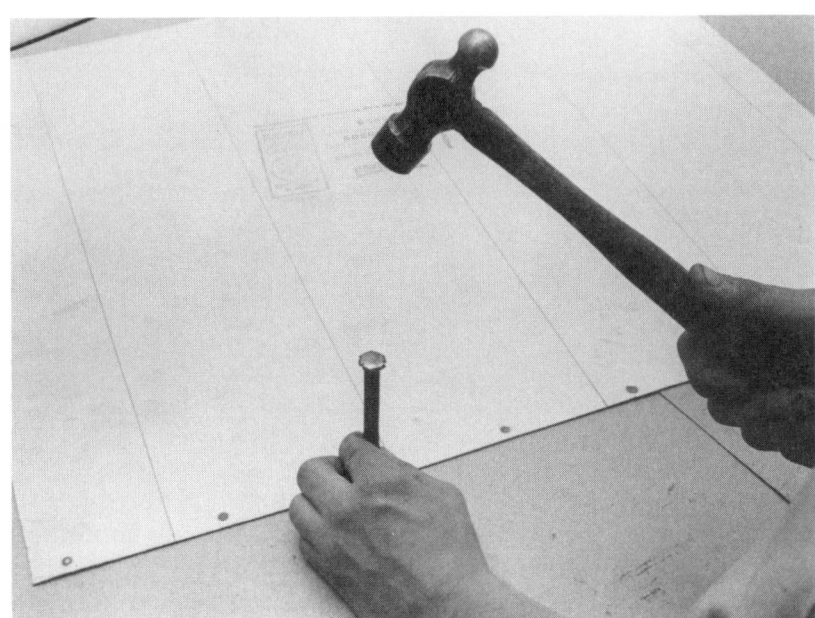

Holes being punched in a blanket using a hammer and a punch that is the same size as the blanket bar holes

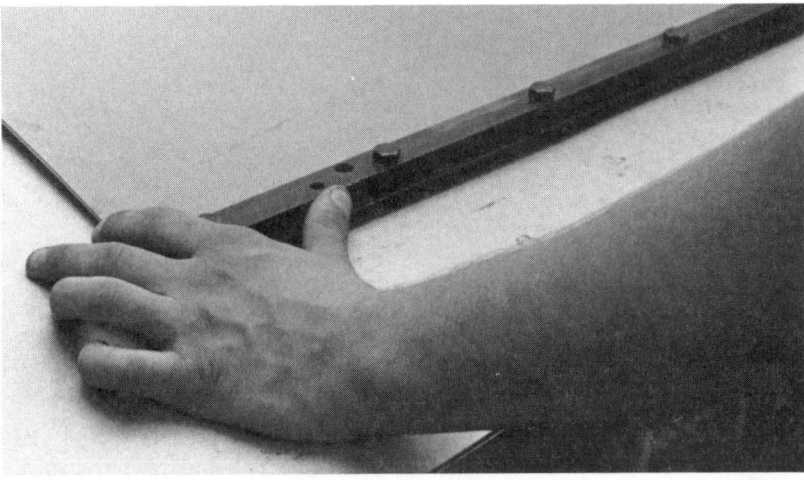

Blanket bars being fastened by aligning the holes in both bars with the holes in the blanket and then inserting the bolts

right side to print under this condition, the left side must print with excessive pressure, resulting in poor print quality and worn plates. It is a part of the press operator's job to see that the blankets are square.

Every press should be equipped with one or two blankets, mounted on bars, ready to be put into the press at an instant's notice.

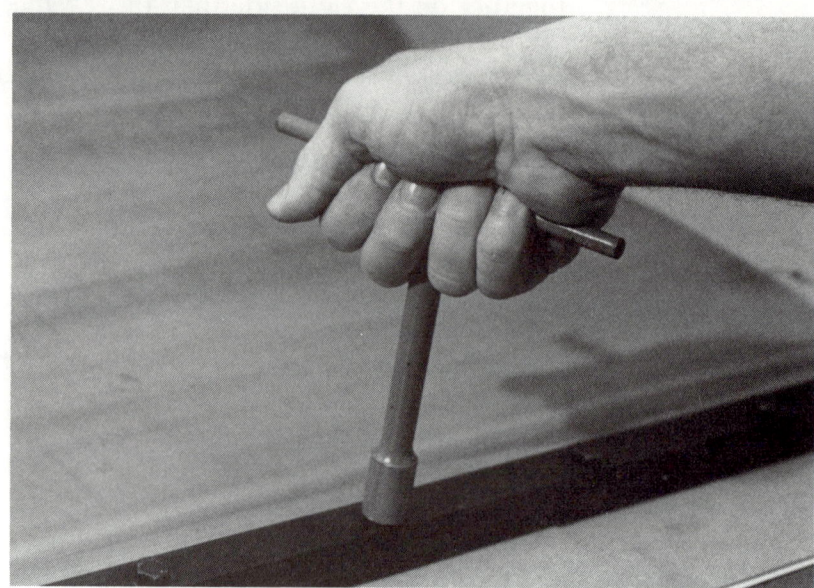

T wrench being used to tighten the bolts starting from the center and working towards the ends

Blanket Mounting

Blankets are usually three- or four-ply for commercial work. Three-ply blankets are generally mounted on blanket cylinders with undercuts of 0.075 in. (1.9 mm) or less. Four-ply blankets have an extra layer of fabric backing for greater strength and are mounted on larger presses with undercuts of more than 0.075 in. Three-ply blankets generally are not mounted on cylinders with undercuts designed to accommodate a four-ply blanket. A three-ply blanket mounted on such a cylinder requires an extra 0.010 in. (0.25 mm) or so of packing. On the deeper-undercut cylinders, most press operators prefer using a four-ply blanket and less packing to avoid the problem of packing creep.

The previous chapter of this book discusses packing in detail. Only packing paper is used under a blanket; Mylar causes numerous problems when used as a blanket-cylinder packing material. (Some press manufacturers specify the use of a special "underlay" blanket in addition to packing sheets.) Press operators typically attach the packing to the cylinder body and then mount the blanket instead of attaching the packing to the back of the blanket. Before packing is attached, the cylinder body and bearers should be cleaned, and any rust should be removed.

Blanket packing should *always* extend all the way from leading edge to trailing edge. This practice ensures good plate-to-blanket and blanket-to-impression-cylinder contact all around the cylinder and maximizes the printing area on the form. Blanket packing should be cut about 1/16–1/8 in. (2–3 mm) narrower than the blanket to prevent packing swelling. Blanket packing is allowed to extend slightly into the cylinder gap so that the blanket helps to hold the packing in place and to prevent it from creeping while the press is running.

Many press operators use paint to indicate the exact center of the blanket cylinder to aid in placing blankets and packing. By marking the exact center of the blankets and packing, the press operator can match the cylinder, blanket, and packing marks and accurately center blankets and packing with minimal effort.

The blanket bars mounted at the leading and trailing edges of the blanket are inserted into the blanket lockup mechanism. However, the elasticity of a blanket makes blanket mounting difficult because mounting tension is critical. When tightening the lockup at the trailing edge, the

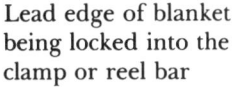
Lead edge of blanket being locked into the clamp or reel bar

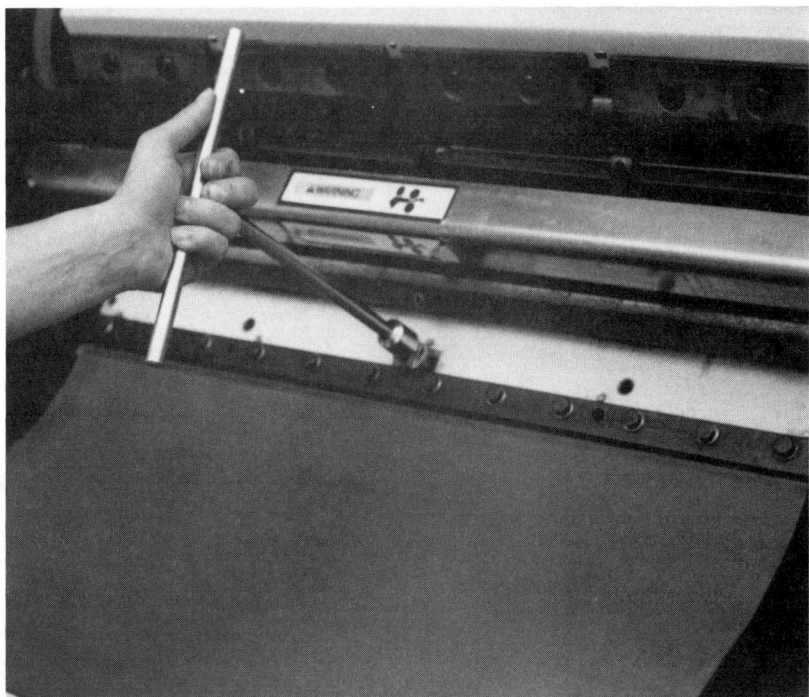

press operator should take care not to pull the blanket thin at one spot or another. One factor is the strength of the press operator. Another is the blanket itself; blanket A may stretch lengthwise and therefore decrease in thickness 0.001 in. (0.025 mm), whereas blanket B might decrease 0.002 in. (0.05 mm). These factors make it difficult to properly mount a blanket. Doing it right is something that comes only with

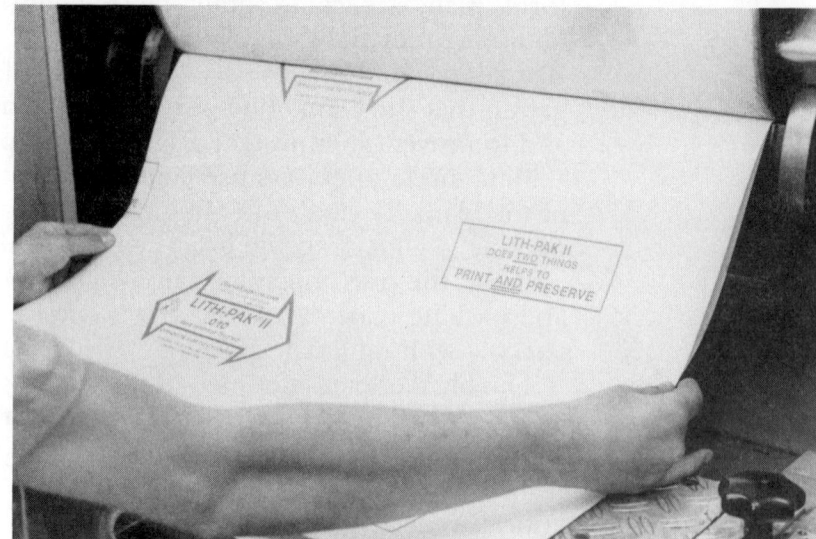

Proper thickness of packing being applied to back of blanket

Press operator holding the blanket and packing together while slowly inching the press until the trailing edge reel bar is accessible

Trailing edge of blanket being inserted into reel bar

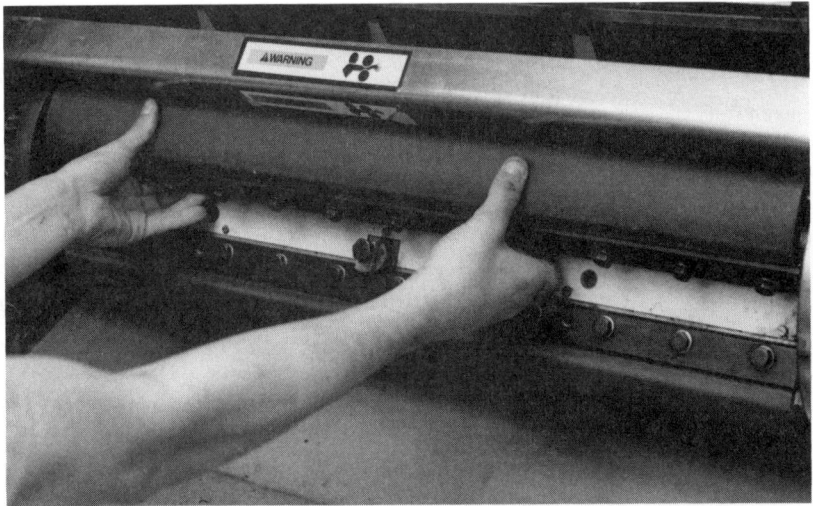

experience, although using mechanical aids is helpful. A high-quality micrometer-adjustable torque-sensing wrench applies a known amount of tension to the mounted blanket. The torque wrench can be set to a specific torque value, and the wrench will click when the press operator tightens the blanket to the preset torque value.

Torque wrench, adjusted to recommended tension, being used to tighten the trailing edge reel bar

Overtensioning a blanket damages it. A procedure recommended for properly tensioning a new compressible blanket follows:

1. Overpack the blanket by 0.002 in. (0.05 mm).

2. Print approximately 500 sheets and retighten the blanket using a torque wrench.

3. Print another 500 sheets and again retighten the blanket. A quality compressible blanket should require no more tightening during a pressrun.

Micrometer-adjustable torque-sensing wrench

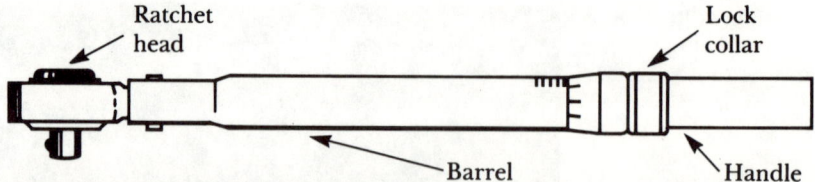

Some manufacturers provide recommended torque values for blanket tensioning. However, in most cases, the press operator should determine the value by using a press-mounted blanket that is producing high-quality printing as the standard for that press/blanket combination. Following is a simple procedure for determining the torque value of a properly mounted blanket:

1. Adjust the torque wrench to its lowest reading.
2. Place the wrench on the blanket reel, and apply pressure to the wrench as if tightening the blanket.
3. If the wrench *does not* make a clicking sound when pressure is applied, the torque exerted on the blanket will be indicated by the setting of the torque wrench. If the *wrench* does make a clicking sound, increase the setting of the torque wrench by the smallest increment possible.
4. Repeat steps 2 and 3 until the torque value of the blanket is determined. This value should be recorded. All press units should receive the same amount of tensioning.

Recovering from a Blanket Smash

In some plants, a routine procedure is followed for keeping blankets in good repair. In these plants, the supervisors not only insist upon thorough, frequent scrubbing but also have a routine for handling damaged blankets. If a blanket receives a smash during a run, no time is wasted on repairing it at that time. It is quicker and easier to install a spare blanket on the press. If the printing surface of the blanket is cut or damaged, the blanket should be replaced. However, slightly damaged or slightly cut blankets can be used when scoring or perforating on the press.

If a blanket is smashed but the surface is not cut, soaking the back side of the blanket often saves the blanket. When a blanket is smashed, most of the damage is done to the cloth fabric under the rubber. The rubber returns to its original thickness, but the cloth fibers remain compressed. The cure is to bring fabric fibers back to their original size.

1. Remove the blanket from the press and scrub the back thoroughly.
2. Place the entire blanket in a container of water, and

soak it for a day or so. (A little wetting agent, such as glycerine, helps.)

3. After the soaking, hang the blanket by the clamp bar and let it dry thoroughly. (Some blankets become wavy after being soaked, but they usually smooth out when stretched around the blanket cylinder.)

If the blanket is too big for any available container, an alternative procedure is used:

1. Clean off the back of the blanket, and hang it up by the clamp bar.

2. Use a sponge to soak the back with water. Rewet the blanket every hour or so. Rewet the damaged areas especially. Continue this periodic rewetting for a couple of days depending on the condition of the blanket.

Either of these treatments restores the original thickness of the blanket in practically all of the smashed areas. Just how successful these treatments are depends on how badly the blanket was smashed. *These treatments do not work if the rubber is cut or the cloth fabric under the rubber is torn or shredded.*

Use of Slightly Damaged Blankets

In most cases, if the printing surface of the blanket is damaged—e.g., cut—the blanket should be discarded. However, at least one slightly damaged blanket should be keep on hand whenever scoring or perforating is done on the press. The scoring or perforating dies would damage a new blanket, but since no printing occurs on that blanket, the use of an old blanket is acceptable.

The scoring or perforating dies are self-adhesive tapes designed to be attached to the surface of the impression cylinder. Usually, an image is printed on the last impression cylinder, and the dies are attached to that cylinder using the printed image as a guide. Another method involves attaching the dies to a printed sheet of paper, which is later attached to the printing cylinder:

1. Attach (tape) the die(s) to a printed press sheet.

2. With impression off, feed the sheet through the press until its lead edge is in the grippers of the last impression cylinder.

3. Lift the trailing edge of the sheet, and apply rubber cement to the back side of the press sheet so that the sheet becomes cemented to the surface of the impression cylinder.

4. Inch the press until the grippers open on the press sheet. Remove the portion of the sheet that is held by the grippers, and then rubber-cement the lead edge of the press sheet to the impression cylinder.

5. Run the printed press sheets through the press. The perforations and scores will be in register.

6. After scoring and perforating is completed, remove the press sheet from the cylinder surface. **Caution:** Wear rubber gloves when handling rubber cement and its thinner.

8 Plates

The lithographic press operator is concerned with plates in two ways. One is the physical action of mounting, adjusting, and removing the plates. The other is assuring that the delicate chemical separation of image and nonimage areas is completely maintained during the pressrun. This requires more careful attention in lithography than in any other printing process. In rotogravure, the image areas are cut into a metal surface. In letterpress, they stand out solidly above the surface. But the level surface of the lithographic plate requires a chemical distinction between image and nonimage areas. The press operator does not need to know all the techniques required to make a plate, but understanding the nature of the lithographic plate and how it carries its image is helpful in maintaining the image satisfactorily.

Types of Plates

There are several types of photolithographic plates, but they share one key feature: during platemaking, a photochemical process divides the plate surface into areas with two different chemical properties. **Image areas**—the parts that are to print—are made oil-receptive **(oleophilic)** and water-repellent **(hydrophobic). Nonimage areas**—the parts that are not to print—are made water-receptive **(hydrophilic)** and oil-repellent **(oleophobic).** Therefore, when the plate is contacted by the dampening rollers, only the nonimage areas accept the water-based dampening solution and become wet. When the dampened plate is contacted by the inking form rollers, only the image areas accept the oily lithographic ink.

The objective of the platemaker is to make the image areas as ink-receptive and water-repellent as possible and to make the nonimage areas as water-receptive and ink-repellent as possible. The press operator must try to keep them that way.

Lithographic plates are made of various base materials, but most of them are made of grained aluminum, usually anodized and then silicated to create a durable water-receptive surface. Most of them are **surface plates,** in which an ink-receptive light-sensitive coating applied to the plate surface remains on the plate in the image areas after processing, while in the nonimage areas coating is removed from the water-receptive layer.

Plates are usually imaged by exposure through a photographic film (although some are exposed by laser directly from information output by computers). In the United States, most plates are exposed through a negative; such plates are called **negative-working,** or **negative, plates.**

In a negative-working plate, the light that strikes the plate forms the image areas; therefore, laser-imaged plates are negative-working.

When a negative-working surface plate is exposed through a negative, the light-sensitive coating hardens and becomes insoluble in the image areas. During development, only the unexposed, unhardened coating over the nonimage areas dissolves, leaving the water-receptive aluminum uncovered. In the usual kind of negative-working surface plate, called **subtractive,** the exposed coating is very tough and durable on press. This material remains on the plate as the image areas but is removed ("subtracted") from the nonimage areas when the coating is dissolved away. However, the bared aluminum in the nonimage areas, although it is already water-receptive, must be made even more so. This **desensitization** is accomplished by **gumming,** the application of a thin, uniform coating of a gum arabic or similar solution that protects the surface from oxidation and makes the surface very water-receptive. The kind of negative-working surface plate that requires the addition of an image-reinforcing material during development is called **additive.** Although most of these additive plates are **wipe-on** plates that are coated by the platemaker, presensitized additive plates are also available.

It may be useful for a press operator to know something about certain other types of plates besides the more commonly used ones described above. A plate exposed through a positive is called **positive-working.** Presensitized positive-working plates are very similar to subtractive negative-working plates except that the insoluble image areas are unexposed while the nonimage areas become soluble during exposure and are then removed during development. Positive-working plates are always subtractive. Many of these plates can be thermally cured at high temperatures to harden the image areas for better press life.

Very durable positive- and negative-working surface plates that last for more than 1,000,000 impressions under normal conditions are available. For even longer pressruns, multimetal plates are available. They are made of two or even three laminated metals. One of the metals—usually electroplated copper because of its ability to accept ink—provides the image areas. Another metal—aluminum, stainless steel, or chromium, because of the ease with which they accept water—forms the nonimage areas. If a third

General processing sequence for a negative-working multimetal plate

1. Electroplate image metal on nonimage metal plate.

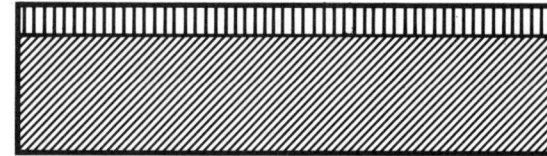

2. Coat image metal with light-sensitive material and expose through a negative.

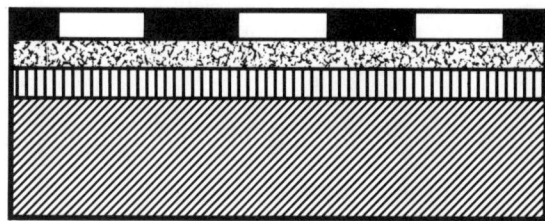

3. Dissolve unhardened coating in nonimage areas.

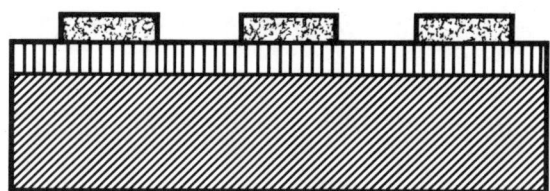

4. Etch through image metal in nonimage areas.

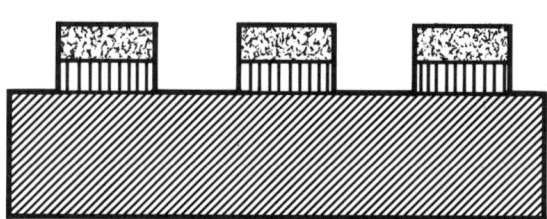

5. Remove hardened coating from surface of image.

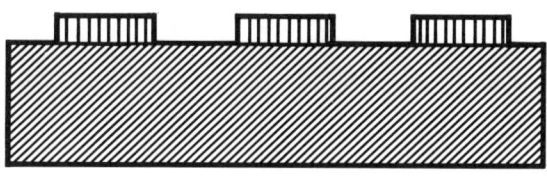

 Light-sensitive coating

 Film negative

 Nonimage base metal

 Electroplated image metal

General processing sequence for a positive-working trimetal plate

1. Electroplate a non-image metal over an image metal that is bonded to a base metal.

2. Coat with light-sensitive material and expose through positive.

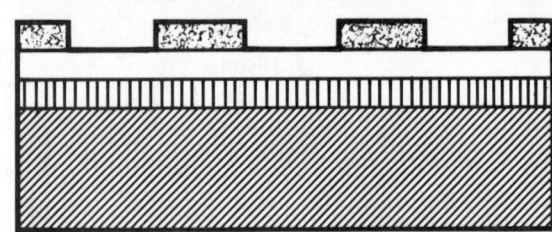

3. Dissolve and remove unhardened coating from image areas.

4. Etch through non-image metal in image areas.

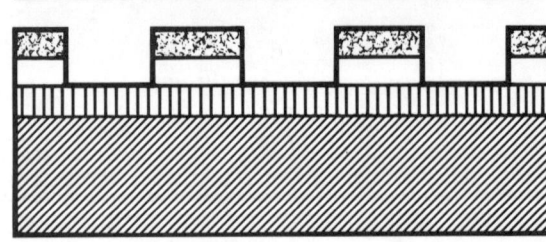

5. Remove hardened coating from non-image areas.

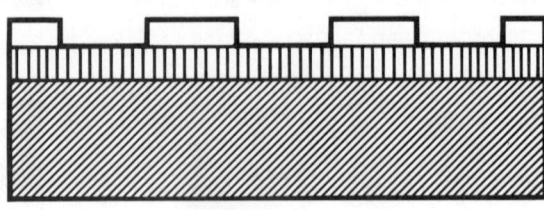

 Base metal

 Film positive

 Electroplated image metal

 Electroplated nonimage metal

 Light-sensitive coating

metal is used, it serves simply as a base metal to support the two top metals. Multimetal plates can be either negative- or positive-working. The top metal carries the coating of photosensitive material.

Negative-working multimetal plates are usually **bimetal:** copper electroplated on a nonimage metal. Exposure light penetrates the transparent image areas of the negative and hardens the photosensitive coating. During processing, the unhardened coating of the nonimage area dissolves, baring the copper. Then an etch removes the copper from the nonimage metal—aluminum or stainless steel.

Most positive-working multimetal plates are exactly like the negative-working multimetal plates except that the coating becomes soluble when exposed to light. During development, the exposed coating is dissolved away to uncover the copper. Then, the copper is etched away leaving the water-receptive aluminum or stainless steel as the nonimage area.

But whatever the type of plate and however it is made, its action on the press is very much the same. For best results, follow the manufacturer's instructions and use only recommended products and chemicals. The type of plate will be mentioned subsequently only if it affects troubleshooting or other matters of plate handling on the press.

Preparing for Plate Mounting

Before plates are mounted, presized and calipered packing material should already be stored in a rack. Litho packing or Mylar is used instead of printing paper, which compresses easily and absorbs too much moisture. Packing width should be exactly the same as the plate width or slightly narrower (e.g., 1/16–1/8 in., or 2–3 mm); wider packing absorbs dampening solution from the dampening rollers. If packing has to be cut down, an old plate can serve as a guide.

Handling and Inspecting the Plate

Whenever a plate is handled, it should be held at the gripper and tail edges to avoid damaging the gum protecting the nonimage areas. The plate should be placed on a clean, dry, flat surface to check it against the instruction ticket and copy. It should be inspected for defects, such as scratches and unwanted images. Minor deletions are made following the manufacturer's recommendations, and then etch and gum are applied to the erased area. Sometimes, minor image-area additions can be made by scratching the plate and then applying ink or tusche. A new plate should be made for any major correction.

188 Sheetfed Offset Press Operating

Press operator holding the plate at the gripper and tail edges

Notice the paper protecting the image area from scratches.

Determining Packing Requirements

To determine the total thickness of packing that will be needed, the thickness of the plate must be measured. A dead-weight bench micrometer, mounted flush with the bench surface, is recommended for the pressroom because it can be used to measure both compressible and non-compressible materials. If the pressroom is not equipped with one, a paper micrometer is preferred over a machinist's micrometer because its anvil has a larger area, which measures compressible materials more accurately.

With the plate on a flat surface, its thickness is measured in at least three places, and its average thickness is calculated. If a machinist's or paper micrometer is used, it must be held firmly and flat on the plate when measurements are being made.

Total packing thickness required is determined from the measured plate thickness in the following way. The press specification plate or press handbook indicates the **cylinder undercut** (the difference between cylinder body radius and bearer radius) and the **height above bearers** (the height the surface of the plate should be above the surface of the bearers with proper packing). The sum of these two figures equals the combined thicknesses of the plate and the proper packing. If the cylinder undercut is added to the height above bearers and the plate thickness subtracted from that sum, the difference is the proper total packing thickness:

$$\begin{array}{r}\text{Cylinder undercut}\\ +\ \text{Height above bearers}\\ -\ \underline{\text{Plate thickness}}\\ \text{Packing thickness}\end{array}$$

Preparing the Plate Cylinder

Most sheetfed presses have plate cylinders that can be moved circumferentially (around the cylinder) and plate clamps that can be adjusted in one or more directions. Therefore, before the plate is mounted, the plate cylinder and plate clamps are returned to their "zero" positions. In addition, the cylinder body must be cleaned.

Preparatory to plate mounting, the plate cylinder bolts for circumferential register are loosened and the plate cylinder is moved to its zero position, in accordance with operating manual instructions. All bolts must be retightened carefully.

The trailing edge (tail) plate clamp is zeroed by being placed in its lowest position (toward the cylinder body). It is then centered between the cylinder bearers, and its side bolts are finger-tightened. If the press is of the kind that has the tail plate clamp split into two or three sections, each section is zeroed according to operating manual instructions.

The lead clamp is zeroed according to the press operating manual procedure. This action properly positions the start-of-print line. The lead clamp is centered, and its side bolts are finger-tightened.

Plate cylinder equipped with a pin register system

Cleaning the cylinder body with a solvent helps to remove dried ink, gum, or old packing particles. Any rust should also be removed. A light application of oil to the cylinder helps to prevent rust and holds the packing in place.

Plate Mounting

Procedures explained in the press operating manual are used to mount the plate. The following is a typical procedure:

1. Lock off the inking and dampening rollers to prevent them from contacting the plate during mounting. Put the press "on impression" and inch it for two complete revolutions to ensure the pressure.

2. Insert the gripper edge of the plate into the leading clamp. If the press has a pin system, push the plate holes over the pins; if not, line up the plate centerline with the clamp centerline. Tighten the clamp bolts from the center outward.

Press operator inserting gripper edge of plate into the leading clamp

3. Insert the calculated amount of packing behind the plate, making sure that no edge is bent over or extends beyond the side edge of the plate. Line up the scribe marks on the plate with the preregister marks on the plate cylinder by adjusting the leading clamp tensioning bolts.

4. While holding the plate and packing with one hand and keeping tension on the plate, inch the press forward until you can insert the plate tail into the trailing clamp. The

Plates 191

Press operator inserting packing behind plate

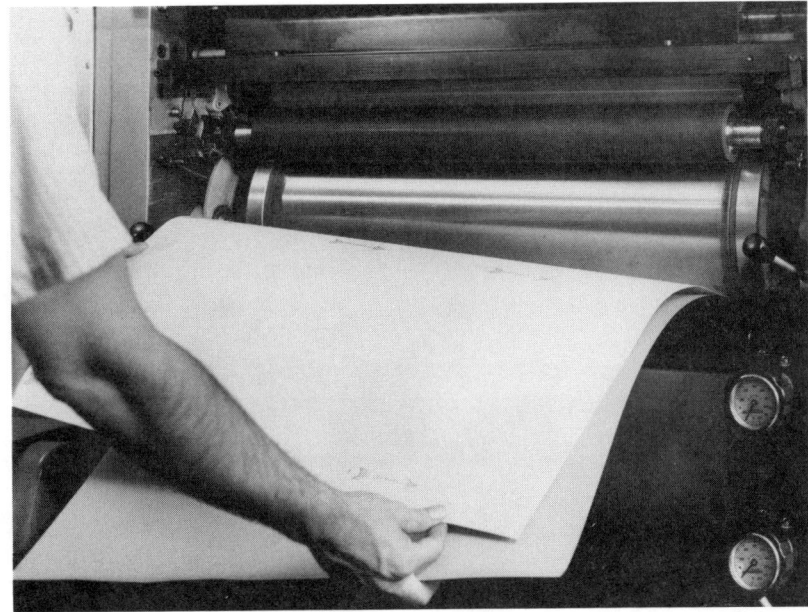

Press operator inching the press while keeping tension on the plate and packing

pressure between plate and blanket cylinder should be "on" to help roll out the plate as it goes around the cylinder. *The primary objective is to get the plate to fit snuggly against the cylinder.*

5. After inserting the plate tail into the trailing clamp, close the clamps; but before tightening them, slowly inch the press forward to a point just *before* the point of contact between the plate and blanket surfaces. This action seats the

Press operator inserting the tail edge of the plate into the trailing clamp

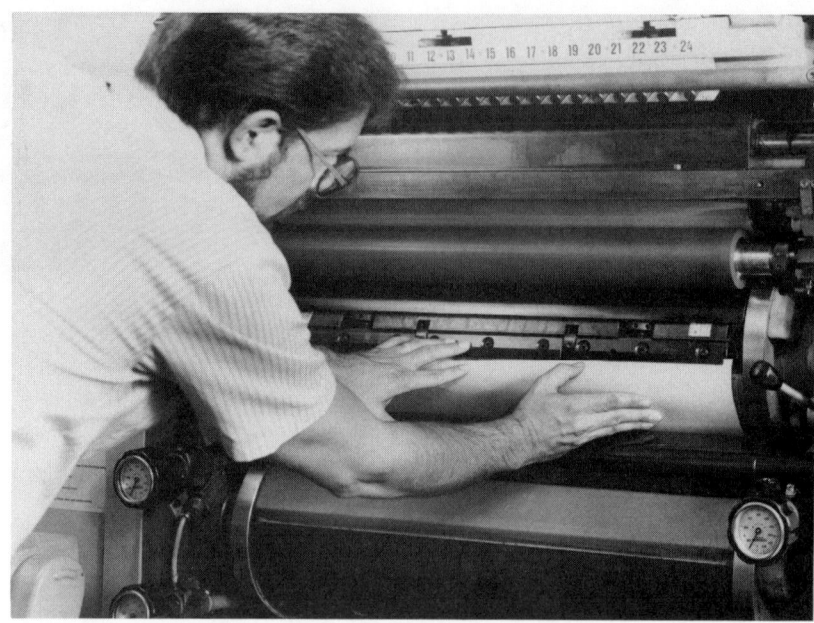

plate into the clamp and minimizes sideways movement of the plate tail clamp. Tighten the trailing clamp bolts, working from the center bolts to the outside bolts. If the press is equipped with speed clamps, which have quick-throw eccentrics, adjust them to bite hard onto the plate. Check the press operating manual for proper adjustment procedures.

Press operator tightening trailing clamp

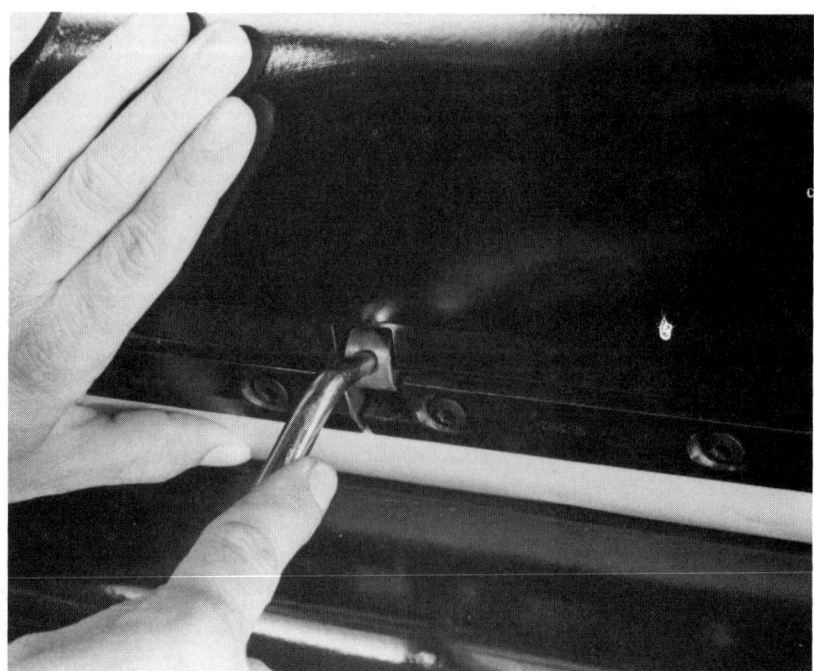

6. Draw up the plate as squarely as possible with the center tensioning screws. Tighten the tension bolts, not fully, but until a crease forms on the plate as it pulls around the edge of the cylinder gap.

7. Tap the plate with your knuckles or fingernails near the lip of the cylinder. If the plate is not snug on the cylinder, it will sound hollow. If it does, continue tapping on the plate while simultaneously applying additional tension on the trailing clamp bolts until the plate and packing are tight against the cylinder body. Be careful not to overtighten the plate. Then put the press "off impression" and inch it forward two revolutions.

If a bulge is noticeable on either side of the plate, it is not squarely seated. Try relaxing some of the tension on the trailing clamp side bolts and moving the trailing clamps to push the plate tail to the center of the press. Then draw up tension on the trailing clamp. If this doesn't work, take the plate off and remount it.

When a plate must be removed, whatever the reason, loosen the securing bolts or quick-action eccentrics of the trailing-edge plate clamp. Ease the plate out of the clamp. Reverse-inch the press while keeping a firm tension on the plate tail and packing to avoid any scratching. Loosen the plate clamp bolts or quick-action eccentrics of the leading plate clamp and remove plate and packing.

Measuring the Height of a Mounted Plate

After a plate has been mounted, the height of its surface above the bearers should be measured even though the amount of packing to make it the correct height was calculated. A hand-held packing gauge is needed to make this measurement. Such a gauge may have a magnetic or nonmagnetic body.

Before using the a packing gauge, clean the bearers thoroughly, being sure to remove any gum or ink particles. To avoid scratching or damaging the plate, place a single sheet of lightweight paper over it.

Follow this procedure to use a magnetic packing gauge:

1. Place the gauge base onto the paper that is protecting the plate on the cylinder and move the ends back and forth until the base seems to be solidly seated on the cylinder.

2. Place the indicator bar into the base slots with the feeler foot on the plate.

3. Check if the base is seated properly by adjusting the packing gauge dial to indicate a zero reading, then turning

Press operator zeroing a magnetic-base packing gauge on the plate

the feeler foot around and checking for a zero reading from the other side. If it does not show a zero reading, reset the base. Repeat until the reading from both sides of the base is zero.

4. Slide the indicator bar over and onto the bearer. A positive reading on the dial indicates how far the plate surface is above the bearer height. (A negative reading indicates how far the plate surface is *below* the bearer height.)

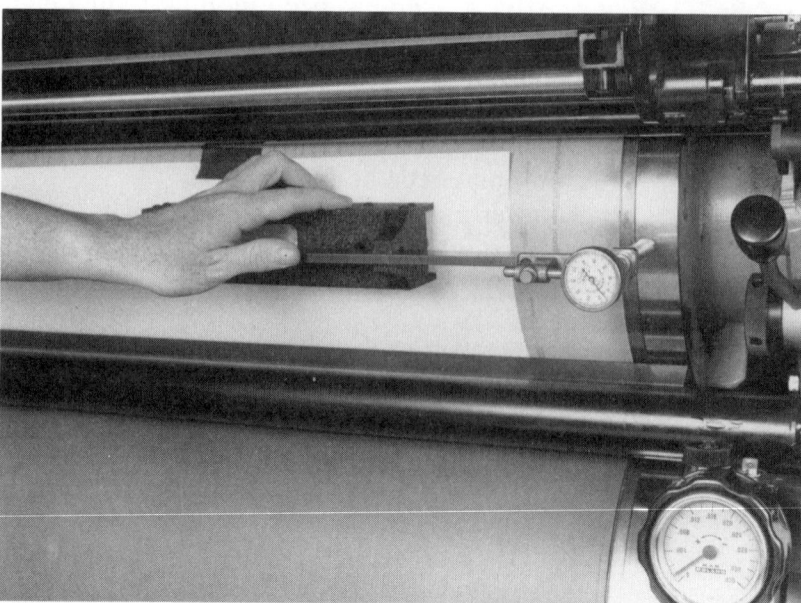

Press operator measuring the height of the plate surface in relation to the bearer

Prepare for the use of the nonmagnetic packing gauge in the same manner as for the magnetic gauge, and then follow this procedure:

1. Place the packing gauge body and feeler foot onto the plate and turn the dial until it reads zero.

Press operator zeroing the nonmagnetic-base packing gauge on the plate

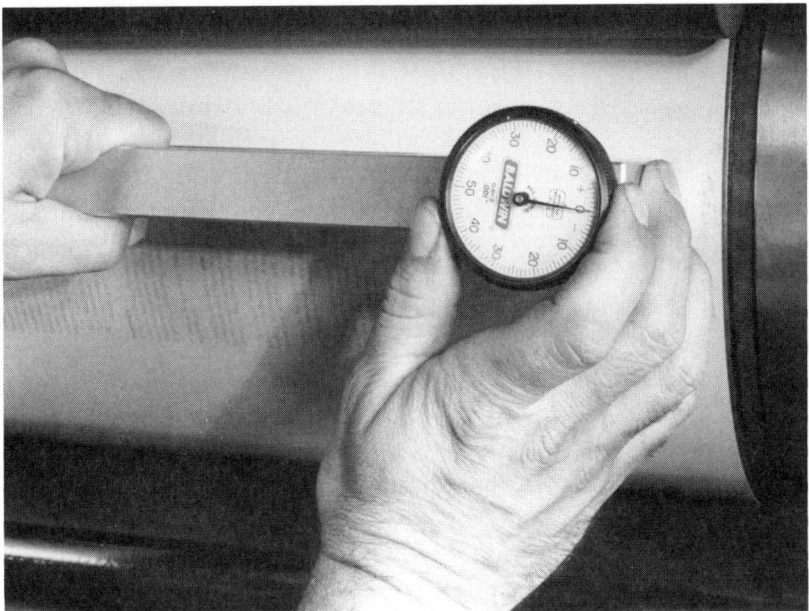

2. Move the gauge over so the feeler foot rests on the bearer. A positive reading on the dial indicates how far the plate surface is above the bearer height. (A negative reading indicates how far the plate surface is *below* bearer height.)

Press operator measuring the height of the plate surface in relation to the bearer

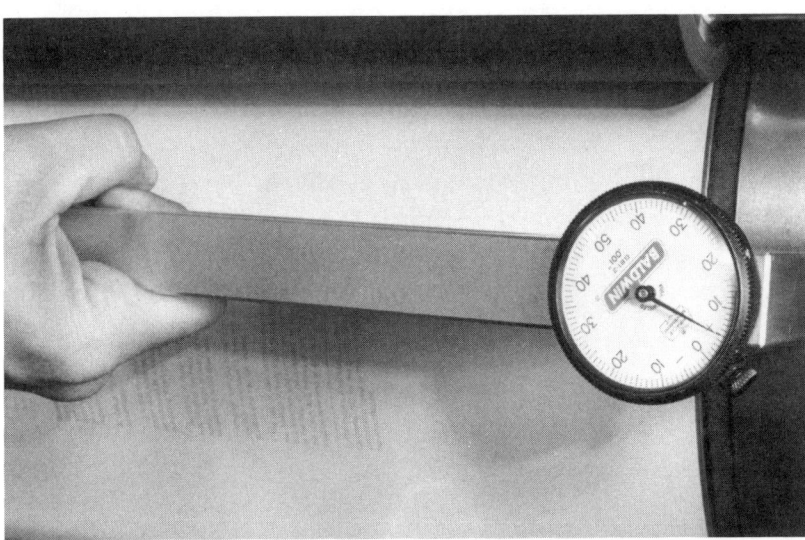

Making and Keeping the Plate Runnable

When the press operator receives the plate, the nonimage areas are coated with gum. After the plate has been mounted, the gum should be washed off the nonimage areas with water. Image areas on most plates as received are so ink-receptive and water-repellent that no protection is needed. Then the plates should be rolled (inked) up, and the **lay** (position of the printed image on the sheet) determined.

The printed image must be exactly square in relation to the paper or previously printed colors. Sometimes the plate may need to be repositioned by tilting or cocking the plate cylinder clamps. Repositioning the plate is preferable to adjusting the front sheet guides, which alters the amount of "gripper bite" and thus may cause register problems.

The following procedure can be used to reposition the plate:

1. With a pencil or marking pen, rule a line that extends from near the side edges of the plate onto the cylinder body (or use the preregister marks if they are on your press).

2. Rule another line on one side of the cylinder body that indicates how far the plate is to be moved.

3. Release the trailing clamp tension bolts so the plate can be pulled forward on the desired side.

4. Push the clamp sideways one-third the distance the plate needs to be drawn forward, using the trailing clamp side bolt. Make sure that the other side bolt is clear of the bearer. The plate should now be loose and bulging on the desired side.

5. Tighten the leading clamp tension bolts to draw the marks into alignment. If the plate does not pull forward easily (excessive force will split the plate), decrease the tension of the trailing clamp further and push it a little more sideways.

6. Draw up the tension at the trailing clamp when the marks line up satisfactorily. Tap-test the edges of the plate to make sure it is snug on the cylinder.

Once good plates are properly running, the image and nonimage areas are protected by the printing process itself. But when the press is stopped more than one hour, the plates should be gummed and the image areas left inked up. For longer stops, including overnight shutdowns, ink drying must be prevented by either washing the ink off with a suitable solvent or using a finisher recommended by the plate manufacturer. Ink remaining on the plate can dry so hard that it will not accept ink, thus blinding the plate.

A commonly used finisher is an asphaltum-gum etch (AGE), which deposits a film of protective gum arabic on the nonimage areas and asphaltum on the image areas. Asphaltum, which is somewhat greasy, preserves the ink-receptivity of the image areas for a long period. When the plates are ready to be run again, they are washed off with water. This removes gum from the nonimage areas while leaving asphaltum on the image areas, so they will readily accept ink.

Caution: Use only the finisher recommended by the plate manufacturer. AGE, for example, could cause gum blinding in the image areas of certain brands of plate.

9 Paper

Manufacture

One of the costliest printing materials used by the press operator is paper. An understanding of its manufacture, although not essential, helps the press operator to interpret paper behavior on press.

Raw Materials

Fiber. The principal raw material used in papermaking is wood fiber obtained from trees or from recycled paper. Other plants, such as sugar cane or bamboo, are also used as fiber sources. A fiber with a hollow tubular or quill-shaped structure is required for papermaking. Nonwood plants provide a minor source of fiber for papermaking, but many of the nonwood fibers are important to the manufacture of specialty papers.

Trees are abundant, replenishable, easily harvested, and easily transportable, making them the ideal source of cellulose in papermaking. Cellulose fibers have a very high tensile strength and a great affinity for water, meaning that the fibers can be bonded together strongly in a network to form paper. The size and shape of fibers, which vary with type of tree and even within a given tree, have an important influence on paper properties.

Nonfibrous materials. In addition to a fiber that can network with other fibers to form a sheet, a wide variety of nonfibrous substances are added during papermaking to alter the properties of paper.

Fillers (finely divided, relatively insoluble inorganic materials or minerals) are added prior to sheet formation for a variety of reasons, such as to increase opacity and brightness, reduce ink strike-through, and decrease the harshness of the papers. The addition of fillers also improves softness, reduces bulk, increases smoothness, makes paper more uniformly receptive to printing inks, improves printability, and contributes to greater dimensional stability. Clay (from refined natural kaolin clay), titanium dioxide, and calcium carbonate are the most commonly used fillers.

Paper often has internal sizing added to it to retard the penetration of water or other fluids. Rosin and papermakers' alum are two materials commonly used for internal sizing. Paper may also be sized by coating it with a solution of starch.

The addition of starches, gums, and synthetic polymers to the paper prior to sheet formation enhances fiber adhesion, dry strength, and filler retention.

Dyes and colored pigments tint white papers and produce colored papers.

Pulping Methods Pulping permits papermaking fibers to be separated from wood. Several methods are used; the three basic methods are mechanical pulping, chemical pulping, and semichemical pulping (a combination of mechanical and chemical pulping treatments). Each method produces pulp that imparts different properties to paper.

The principal types of mechanical pulp are **groundwood,** produced by forcing pulpwood against a revolving, abrasive grinding stone; **refiner mechanical pulp (RMP),** produced by passing wood chips through a disk refiner instead of pressing the wood against the grinding stone; and **thermomechanical pulp (TMP),** produced by preheating wood chips with steam prior to passing them through a disk refiner. The heat generated by disk refining and preheating the wood chips softens the lignin that holds the fibers together, permitting fiber separation with little fiber damage. Each of the mechanical pulping methods gives a high yield of pulp because the lignin and other materials are retained.

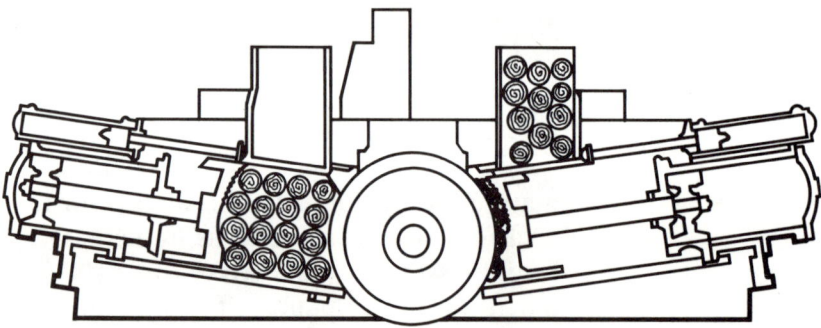

Two-pocket grinder for manufacturing groundwood pulp
Courtesy Montague Machine Co.

Debarked logs are pressed against a revolving pulp stone in the presence of water.

Chemical pulping liberates the cellulose fibers from the lignin that bonds them together. During chemical pulping, chemicals dissolve the lignin and hemicellulose in wood to free cellulose fibers from the wood. The bleaching of chemical pulp removes residual lignin and hemicellulose. Chemical pulping has a yield of 45–55%, compared to the yield of 90% or more common with mechanical pulping methods. Chemical pulping processes use acids, such as sulfurous acid, and alkalis, such as lye (caustic soda).

Semichemical pulps are produced by first mildly cooking wood chips with chemicals, most commonly sodium sulfite or a small amount of an alkaline salt, such as sodium carbonate, bicarbonate, or hydroxide. The cooking partially removes and softens the lignin, weakening the bond between fibers. After cooking, the chips are passed through one or two disk refining steps for fiberizing. A wash removes the chemicals. Semichemical pulping retains a considerable amount of lignin, and consequently, yields are typically 60–80%. Bleaching reduces the yield, as it does with any pulping method.

Bleaching of Pulp

Unbleached wood pulp ranges in color from cream to dark brown; a brown paper bag is made of unbleached pulp. Bleaching removes residual lignin in the pulp without causing severe chemical damage to the cellulose fibers. Bleaching a pulp makes the resulting paper whiter, which improves printing contrast. Whiter pulps produce colored papers that are more brilliant.

Stock Preparation and Refining

The fibers obtained by pulping must receive further treatment before they can be used to make high-quality paper. This treatment is called **stock preparation,** and it entails fiber refining and the mixing of fibers with nonfibrous materials to produce a paper of the desired properties. Paper is formed on the papermaking machine, but many of the characteristics of paper are determined during stock preparation.

During refining, beaters, conical-type refiners (jordan), or disk refiners are used to subject the fibers to varying degrees of brushing, cutting, fraying, and shortening actions depending on the properties desired in the paper. As a result, the fibers swell and soften and their surfaces develop fine hairs, all of which promote bonding to make a stronger paper.

Conical-type (jordan) continuous refiner
Courtesy Black Clawson Co.

Fibers are refined as they pass between the refining bars of the rotating plug and the stationary bars of its surrounding shell.

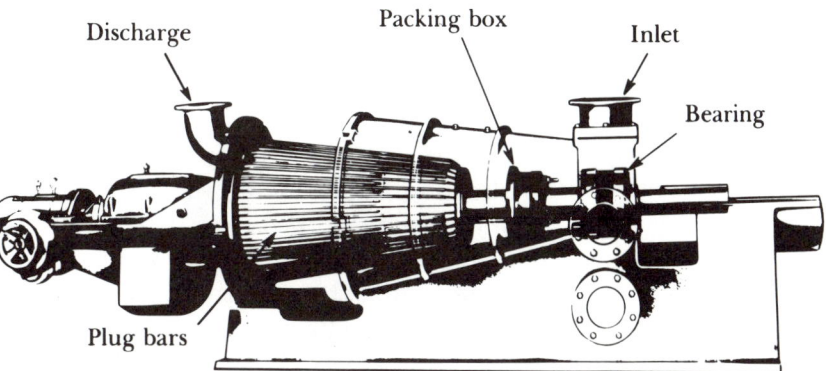

During stock preparation, the cellulose fibers are mixed with fillers, internal sizing, dyes and colored pigments, and other additives that impart properties to paper.

Paper Machine

The paper machine converts the papermaking **furnish**—the mixture of fibrous and nonfibrous materials created during stock preparation—into paper.

In the **wet** or **forming section** of the paper machine, the diluted furnish is formed into a mat of fibers, from which most of the water is removed by gravity or vacuum. In a fourdrinier paper machine, one side (the bottom) of the fiber mat is in contact with a wire (a finely woven mesh of bronze or plastic material) and is called the **wire side.** The top side of the fiber mat is called the **felt side.** The felt side has shorter fibers, more fines, and more fillers, contributing to the two-sidedness of paper produced on a fourdrinier machine. In a twin-wire paper machine, the paper is formed between two converging wires, with water being drained through both sides of the sheet. As a result, the paper does not exhibit two-sidedness. With a cylinder machine, the paper is formed on a wire-covered cylinder. When the fiber mat reaches the top of the rotating cylinder, it is transferred to the underside of a felt.

Paper machines also have a **press section,** where as much water as possible is removed from the web by pressing and suction, and a **drying section,** where the remaining water is removed, this time by evaporation caused by hot drying cylinders. Paper leaving the dryer has a moisture level from 2 to 8%, depending on its desired end use.

A paper machine also has a **calender,** a series of all-metal rollers running in contact that evens out the thickness of the paper, increases its density, and makes it smoother.

Finishing

Finishing, in a discussion of papermaking, refers to operations that begin at the paper machine reel and end when the paper is packaged for shipment. The finishing operations that are of particular interest to press operators are sheeting, supercalendering, and embossing.

Some sheetfed offset presses are equipped with a roll sheeter. However, most paper reaching the pressroom has been sheeted at the papermill. Rolls are converted to sheets on the sheeter, which has a rotary cutting unit. The single rotary cutter has a fixed-position bedknife and a second knife mounted on a rotating cylinder, and the double rotary cutter has two knives mounted in cylinders that rotate in sychronization. Sheet length depends on both the speed of rotation of the rotary cutter and the speed of the web.

Supercalendering is another finishing operation. Unlike the paper machine calender, the supercalender has both metal and soft, resilient rolls. The hard metal rolls press into the resilient rolls at the nip, producing a polishing action that imparts varying degrees of smoothness and gloss to the paper.

The supercalender

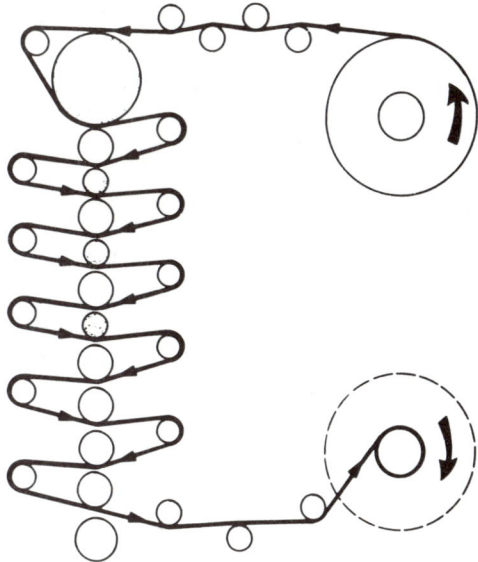

Embossing gives paper a pattern finish. Like a supercalender, the embosser consists of a metal roll that rolls against a soft-surfaced roll. Unlike the supercalender, the metal roll carries an embossed pattern, which is imparted on the soft-surfaced roll through direct running. Paper passing through the nip between these two rolls receives the embossed pattern.

Coating

The press operator often uses the printing press to put a varnish coating on the paper after it has been printed, usually for protective or aesthetic purposes. However, the papermaker also may apply a coating to the surface of paper to make the paper more suitable to its end use. A pigment coating, for example, improves the paper by filling voids in its surface. Coating increases the paper whiteness, paper opacity, ink holdout, water resistance, gloss, and pick resistance.

Paper Weight

The weight of paper is designated as basis weight or grammage.

Basis weight is the weight, in pounds, of a ream of paper cut to its basic size, in inches. With few exceptions, a **ream** of paper is 500 sheets. **Basic size** is the sheet size in inches of a particular type of paper. Each basic size has been adopted because of widespread practice and usage. Following are four common basic sizes:

Paper type	U.S. sheet size	Metric sheet size
Bond and writing	17 × 22 in.	432 × 559 mm
Cover	20 × 26	508 × 660
Newsprint	24 × 36	610 × 914
Book	25 × 38	635 × 965

Basis weight is sometimes specified per 1,000 sheets. If so, the basic weight is typically followed by a capital M, representing 1,000 sheets. For example, a particular bond paper having a basis weight of 20 lb. would be designated "40M," indicating that 1,000 sheets weigh 40 lb. The weight of paperboard is per 1,000 sq. ft.

In the metric system, grammage is the word used to express the weight of paper. **Grammage** is the weight in grams of a single sheet of paper having an area of 1 m². Grammage is abbreviated as g/m². (One pound contains 454 g, and one meter equals 39.37 in.) Conversion factors are used to convert basis weight to grammage, and vice versa.

Factors to convert basis weight to grammage, and vice versa

Basic ream size	To convert from grammage to lb./ream, multiply g/m² by:	To convert from lb. to g/m², multiply lb./ream by:
17 × 22 in.	0.266	3.76
20 × 26	0.370	2.70
20 × 30	0.427	2.34
22 × 38	0.438	2.28
22½ × 28½	0.456	2.19
25½ × 30½	0.553	1.81
23 × 35	0.573	1.74
24 × 36	0.614	1.62
25 × 38	0.675	1.48

Paper Requirements for Sheetfed Lithography

Paper for lithography must meet certain requirements:
- **High surface and internal bonding strength,** to withstand the tackier ink films of lithography
- **Good, but not excessive, water resistance,** to prevent softening and weakening of the paper surface (which can result in picking and fiber or coating transfer to the blanket) and to prevent excessive moisture pickup from the dampening system (which causes curl and paper dimension changes)
- **An exceptionally clean and strongly bonded surface,** to counteract the tendency of the blanket to collect loosely bonded material from the paper's surface
- **Compatibility with the chemistry of the ink and dampening system,** to prevent any active materials in the paper from reacting unfavorably
- **Ability to withstand repeated separation from an inked and moistened blanket,** to prevent stretching, curling, and releasing of surface material

Paper must be accurately trimmed and square. It must not have bowed edges, which can cause misregister and wrinkling on the press and inaccurate trimming.

Paper Properties

Several paper properties are particularly important to the press operator. Among these are gloss, opacity, grain direction, ink absorbency, moisture content, dimensional stability, and surface strength.

Gloss

Gloss is the high reflectance of light from a smooth surface. Paper with high gloss increases the gloss of the printed ink film. Brilliance and intensity of color are similarly enhanced. Paper absorbency and ink holdout can affect the gloss of an ink film. Therefore, for color to remain uniform throughout a pressrun, the paper must have minimal variations in gloss, which is the responsibility of the knowledgeable papermaker.

GATF Research Project Report 6060, *A New Method of Rating the Efficiency of Paper for Color Reproduction,* discusses the effect of gloss and absorbency on print color. Variations in gloss and absorbency, as well as texture, opacity, brightness, and color neutrality, affect the appearance of the color of the same ink on different papers. Differences in gloss and absorptivity of paper are major factors in variations of printed ink color. Differences in them can shift the hue or grayness of the primary ink (cyan, magenta, and yellow), cause a hue shift of secondary overprinted colors (red, green, blue), and require changes in the amount of color correction needed. As a result, color reproduction depends on properly prepared color separations, ink, and paper.

Opacity

Opacity is the extent to which light transmission is obstructed. Like gloss, it is an important consideration in a printing paper. Insufficient opacity causes excessive show-through, which reduces printing contrast and lowers print quality.

Grain Direction

Grain direction in paper results from water-suspended fibers flowing onto the moving paper machine wire. In referring to the grain of paper on a printing press, the terms "grain long" and "grain short" are used. With **grain-long paper,** the grain parallels the long dimension of the press sheet. With **grain-short paper,** the grain parallels the short dimension.

Grain-long paper is preferred for printing register. However, grain-short paper has greater stiffness, better blanket release, and less tendency to develop embossing and tail-end hook. Heavier-weight paper conforms better to the curvature of the cylinders if it is run with the grain parallel to the press cylinder axis.

Binding considerations also affect the preferred grain direction. Grain parallel to the bound edge of a book is preferred. Grain perpendicular to the bound edge can cause buckling and distortions at the spine and make the pages stiffer and more difficult to turn. However, with paper used in a loose-leaf binder, having the grain perpendicular to the binding edge results in a paper that has greater strength and stiffness for turning.

Paper folds more easily with the grain and tends to crack less. However, the strength at the fold is greater if the paper is folded across the grain. For right-angle folds, the more difficult fold should be made with the grain.

The preferred grain direction for printing register is often different than that preferred for folding and finishing. Consequently, the various considerations have to be compared to determine the grain direction.

If the grain direction of a sheet of paper is unknown, a square sample cut from the sheet can be placed in water or moistened on one side. The axis of curl is parallel to the grain direction. It is helpful to indicate on the square which side parallels the long dimension of the sheet and which side parallels the short dimension.

Curl test of paper grain

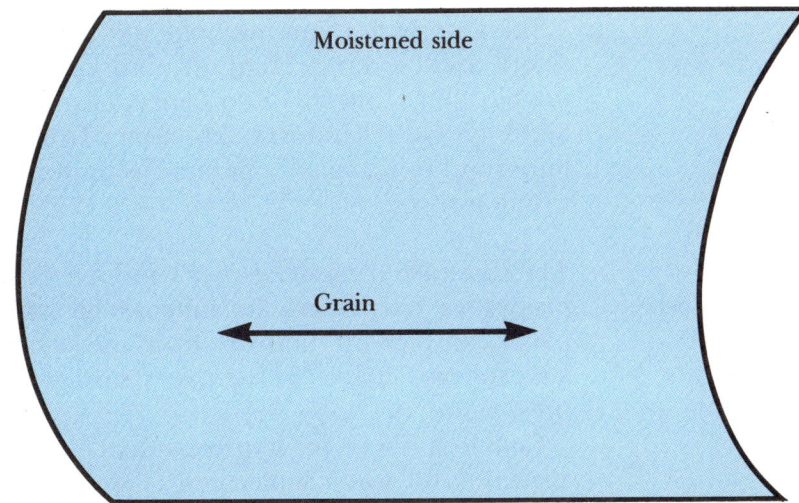

Another way to determine grain direction requires two strips of paper, ½ × 6 in. (13 × 150 mm). The sheets are cut at right angles to each other and parallel to the sheet's edges. The strips are aligned at one end and then alternately placed one on top of the other. The strip cut grain short bends more easily and, consequently, falls away from the other strip when placed on the bottom. Grain direction of the press sheet is determined from the grain direction of the strips.

Flex test of paper grain

Since paper is stiffer across the grain, two strips of the same width cut at right angles from a sheet can show grain direction.

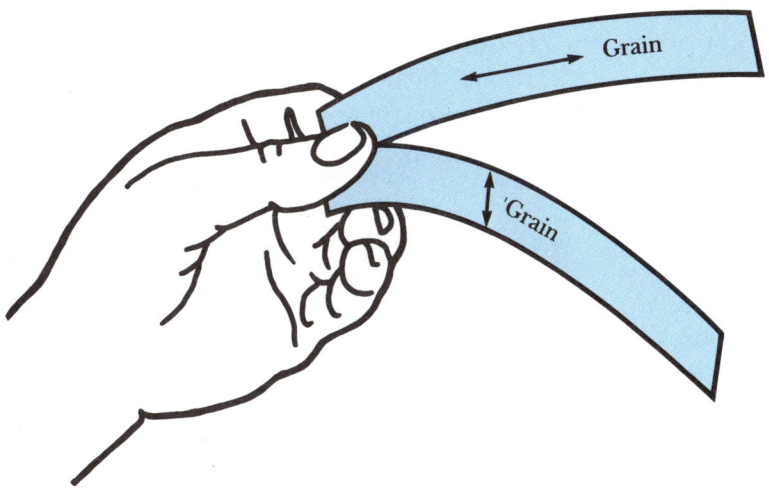

Ink Absorbency

Ink absorbency determines at what rate and in what amount printed ink penetrates the paper. Ink vehicle penetrates into the voids, capillaries, and pores, depending on the absorbency of the paper. Ink holdout, related to ink absorbency, is the extent to which paper resists or retards the penetration of the freshly printed ink film.

Ink absorbency and ink holdout influence ink drying, ink setoff, and blocking. High ink absorbency prevents setoff and ink blocking. Low ink absorbency means high ink holdout and high gloss. Uniform absorbency from sheet to sheet is as important to the press operator as uniform absorbency within a sheet.

Moisture Content and Relative Humidity

The moisture content of paper influences numerous paper properties, particularly its dimensional stability. In addition, paper can pick up moisture from the surrounding atmosphere, such as in the paper storage area and the pressroom.

Cellulose fibers are **hygroscopic,** i.e., they have a strong attraction for water molecules. Fibers become larger upon absorbing moisture and become smaller upon giving up moisture. Therefore, a change in moisture content of paper results in dimensional changes. Consequently, a major cause of register problems, curl, and paper distortion during printing is a change in the moisture content of paper.

The moisture content of the paper should be in equilibrium with the relative humidity of the pressroom. However, for multicolor and multipass printing, a moisture content slightly higher than its equilibrium value minimizes dimension changes between printings.

If the moisture content is too low, the paper tends to be hard and brittle, decreasing resiliency and smoothness under printing impression. Paper having optimum moisture content

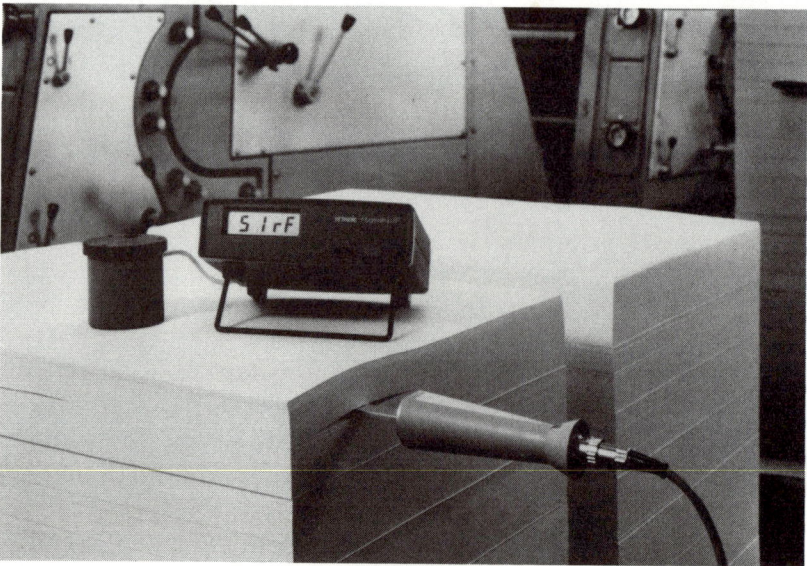

Rotronic Hygroskop sword probe
Courtesy Kaymont Instrument Corp.

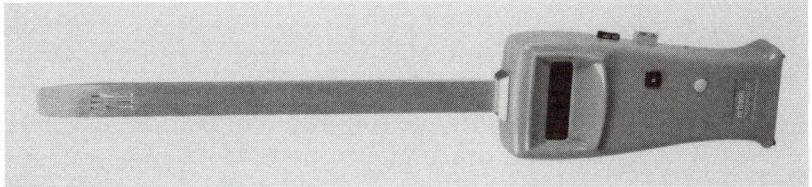

Sword probe with Hygromer sensor
Courtesy Kaymont Instrument Corp.

prints better because the moisture increases the paper's resiliency, which helps it to flatten out and conform to the printing surface under impression.

Dimensional Stability

Dimensional stability refers to the ability of a sheet to maintain its dimensions with changes in its moisture content or applied stress. All cellulosic papers expand or shrink with changes in their moisture content. Papers with little refining, high porosity, or large amounts of fillers tend to have good dimensional stability. Tightly bonded, strong sheets have less. Since sheetfed printing exposes paper to moisture from both blanket and atmosphere, dimensional stability is an important consideration when a paper is printed. The best R.H. to maintain dimensional stability of the paper is 35–50%.

Surface Strength

The surface of a printing paper is exposed to numerous forces during printing. A paper with high surface strength is necessary to resist these forces. **Surface strength,** or **pick resistance,** is the ability of a paper to resist a force applied perpendicularly, such as that in the splitting of an ink film, to its surface before picking or rupturing occurs. **Picking** is the removal of surface fibers and coating in the printing nip. Picking usually appears as the complete removal of a piece of paper or coating from the surface. **Wet picking** results when a surface's strength is reduced due to dampening.

Paper Handling

Not only must paper be handled carefully during shipment but it must also be handled carefully in the plant.

Paper must be brought to pressroom temperature before opening so that it does not curl due to the gain or loss of moisture. Paper should remain tightly wrapped until it is ready for the press, and it should be wrapped tightly after printing to keep the press sheets from developing tight or wavy edges.

Temperature Conditioning

Temperature conditioning means that the paper is not unwrapped until it reaches the same temperature as the pressroom where it will be used.

In some printing plants, paper is stored in the pressroom. Consequently, it is at pressroom temperature when it goes to press. Because the paper is stored in the pressroom, temperature conditioning is unnecessary.

In other plants, however, paper is kept in a warehouse or separate storage area. Paper is brought to the pressroom only as needed. Temperature conditioning is necessary because the temperature of the storage room is usually different from that of the pressroom.

Temperature changes, which occur when paper from a cold warehouse or truck is delivered to a warm pressroom, cause trouble even if the paper is wrapped and sealed to protect it from humidity changes. When cold paper is unwrapped in the pressroom, moisture condenses on the edges of the paper. As a result, the exposed edges of the paper absorb moisture and become wavy; the paper is often referred to as **wavy-edged paper.**

If the temperature of the paper is higher than the temperature of the pressroom when unwrapped, the surrounding air becomes warmer and its relative humidity is lowered. The paper's exposed edges lose moisture to the

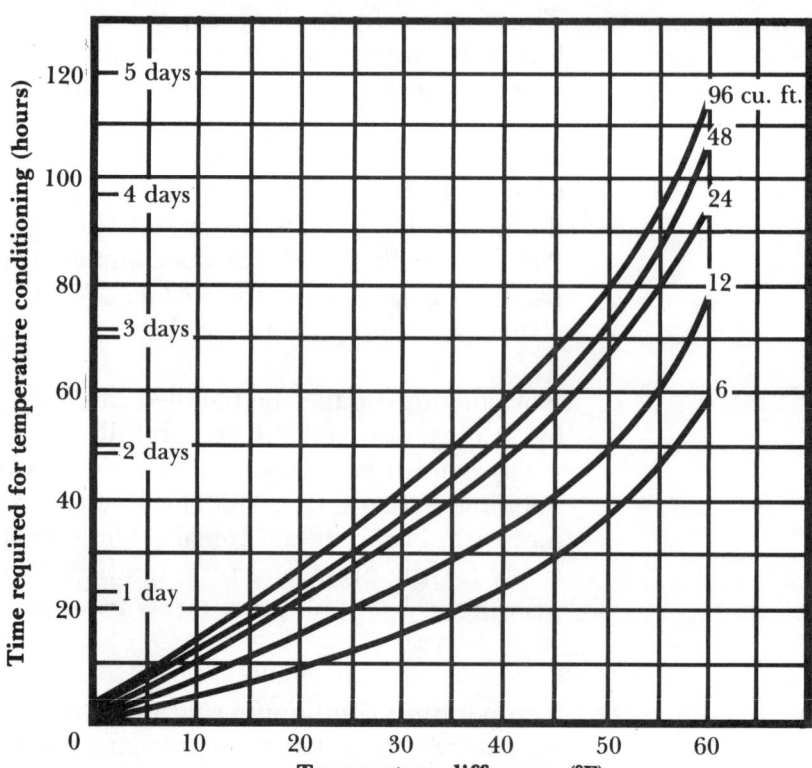

Temperature conditioning chart for paper (American units)

Temperature conditioning chart for paper (metric units)

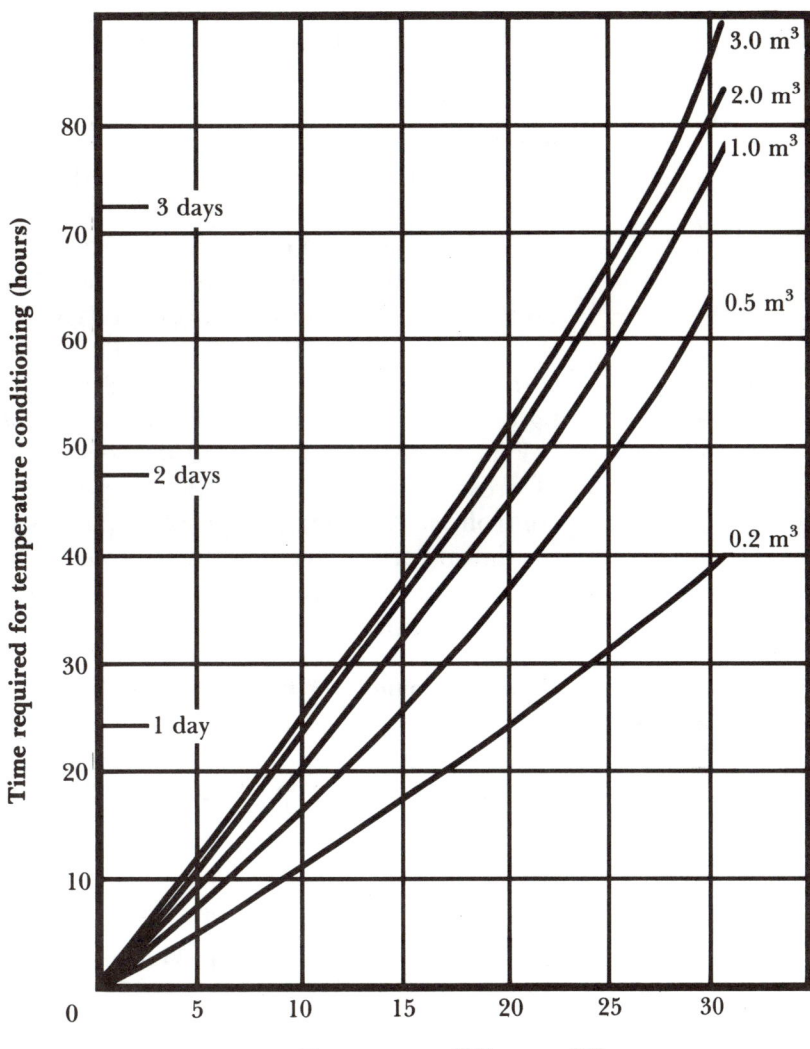

atmosphere and shrink; the paper is often referred to as **tight-edged paper.**

Chilling the air with an air cooling unit dries the air and creates tight edges in the paper. Air conditioning requires control of both temperature and humidity.

Air Conditioning

Paper is manufactured so that it stays flat and does not develop wavy or tight edges before or during printing in a normal pressroom atmosphere. An air-conditioned pressroom greatly reduces moisture problems.

If the pressroom R.H. (and temperature) is kept at a constant level, the printer can order paper that is in reasonable balance with a specified relative humidity.

The R.H. of most paper manufactured in the United States and Canada is in the range of 35–50%. The R.H. of an air-conditioned pressroom should be maintained at a selected value within this range.

Paper with an R.H. 5–8% higher than the pressroom R.H. is desirable for high-quality, close-register printing requiring more than one pass through the press. Paper with this R.H. loses moisture to the pressroom atmosphere at about the same rate that it picks up moisture from the press, assuming that the pressroom R.H. is controlled. Since moisture change is minimal between successive printings, the printing of tight-register work is more easily accomplished.

Paper cannot be produced to meet the R.H. requirements of pressrooms in which the R.H. and temperature are not controlled. Papermakers produce papers that meet the R.H. conditions of the average pressroom. If the pressroom is not temperature- and humidity-controlled, the paper should still be temperature-conditioned.

Guide for decision on printing sheetfed paper, assuming paper at 45% R.H.	Nature of printing	Pressroom R.H. (%)	Recommendation
	No register, danger of wrinkles only	33–53	OK to print
		Less than 33 or more than 53	Change pressroom R.H.
	Loose register (2–3 rows of dots)—printing on two- or four-color press	37–53	OK to print
		33–36 or 54–55	Marginal
		Less than 33 or more than 55	Change pressroom R.H.
	Close register (one row of dots)—single printing on two- or four-color press	40–53	OK to print
		35–39	Marginal
		Less than 35 or more than 53	Change pressroom R.H.
	Loose register (2–3 rows of dots)—two or more printings	41–53	OK to print
		37–40	Marginal
		Less than 37 or more than 53	Change pressroom R.H.
	Close register (one row of dots)—two or more printings	45–53	OK to print
		40–44	Marginal
		Less than 40 or more than 53	Change pressroom R.H.

Storage

To ensure that paper is received in proper condition, all deliveries should be checked upon arrival. Wrappings or cartons having minor tears should be repaired. Skids with punctures, tears, or breaks in the protective wrapping should be rejected. The truck driver or train man should note the damage on the way bill and initial it. Printers should photograph damaged skids and cartons before they are removed from trucks or railroad boxcars. The photograph acts as proof of the paper condition upon arrival. In addition to protecting the printer, the photograph helps the papermill track down the causes of damaged paper. If paper wrappings must be removed for sampling or testing purposes, the wrapped paper should be brought into temperature balance before opening and then rewrapped immediately. Careful handling of paper minimizes unloading damage.

Ideal warehouse and storage conditions minimize the movement and rehandling of paper from the time it is received by the printer until it arrives at the press. Each time paper is moved, either to gain access to other skids of paper or to be transported to the press, the likelihood of handling damage is increased.

Paper must not contact concrete or damp basement floors. The moisture damages and distorts the paper. Consequently, platforms or racks that elevate the paper above the floor are recommended. Papers should be stored *away* from any object (such as a radiator) that heats the paper, but warehouses should be heated in winter.

After paper is printed, protective plastic covers should be placed tightly over the pile to minimize changes in R.H.

Reusable plastic skid cover, available from Poly-Kleen Co.

Paper Problems

Lithographic paper problems can be classified broadly into three groups: register problems, printability problems, and runnability problems. Close register, so essential to multicolor work, is obtained only by close control of the moisture in the paper. Preconditioning paper to pressroom conditions and controlling pressroom relative humidity and temperature reduce register problems. Printability problems include hickeys, piling, ghosting, back-edge curl, and surface rupture.

Runnability problems include curl, sheet defects, and static electricity. Sheet decurlers installed in the delivery minimize curl. Many sheet defects that affect runnability are relatively uncommon: sheets with turned-over corners, sheets stuck together, sheets with edges that are crimped together due to a dull cutting knife, and out-of-square sheets. Static, however, is a common problem. Static electricity causes sheets to cling tightly to each other or to parts of the press. Consequently, static electricity interferes with sheet pickup and forwarding, prevents proper sheet transport on the feedboard, causes variations in positioning at the grippers and side guide, and results in jogging problems at the delivery. Proper control of humidity eliminates most static problems. Use of a static eliminator in the delivery is also helpful.

Aereon antistatic bar, which uses an air stream and ionization to remove dirt and static charges
Courtesy Cumming Corporation

Register Problems

Misregister problems occur if the paper's moisture content changes during a pressrun. A moisture change causes the paper to change its dimensions in both directions, although more so across the grain. Misregister due to moisture change is an unlikely problem with single-pass printing on a multicolor press. However, where two or more passes per side are involved, dimensional change due to moisture change between successive printings can be serious. Therefore, use as little dampening solution as possible, or use alcohol in the dampening solution to reduce the amount of water needed to keep the plate clean, and run the paper grain-long.

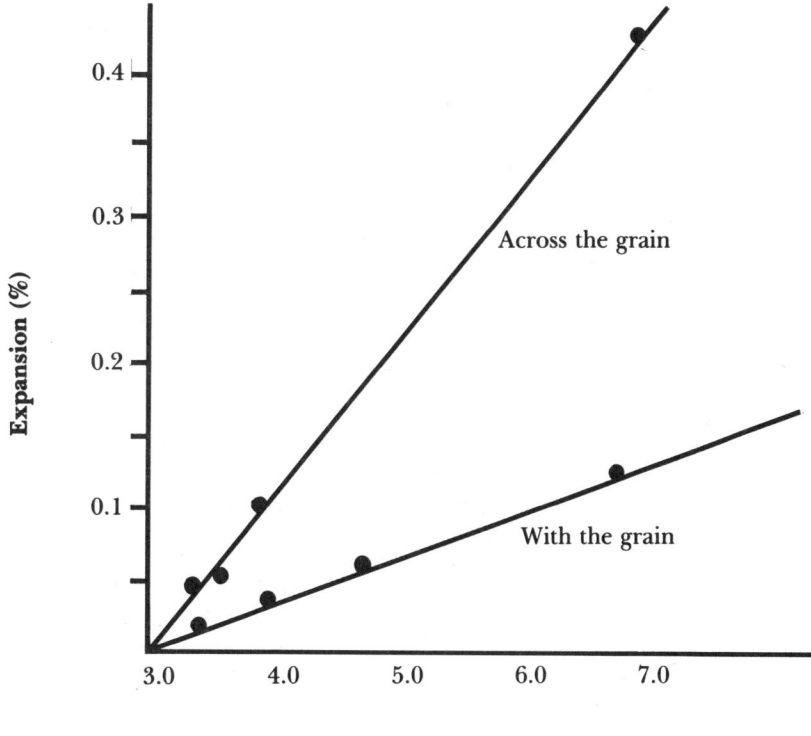

Expansion of paper with and across the grain as moisture content increases

In offset printing, the mechanical forces of the press tend to stretch the paper in the direction of its travel. The following four recommendations help to minimize sheet stretching:
- Reduce the pressure between impression and blanket cylinders to the minimum required for acceptable printing.
- Reduce the tack of inks as much as possible if large solid areas are being printed.
- Use blankets that have good release properties, to avoid overstretching the paper.
- Print solids close to the gripper edge.

If some subjects on a press sheet register and others do not, or if the misregister varies from sheet to sheet, the problem is called **random misregister.** This condition usually occurs when printing heavily embossed papers or papers with a puckered or cockle surface. Reducing the blanket-to-impression cylinder pressure helps lessen the misregister but the transfer of ink to the paper may be incomplete. A solution to this problem is to run heavily textured papers through the press once without printing.

Misregister along the back edge of the press sheet is usually caused by tight- or wavy-edged paper, so proper handling of the paper *before* printing helps to eliminate register problems *during* printing.

Hickeys

A hickey is an imperfection in printing due to a particle on the blanket or, sometimes, the plate.

Hickeys are of two types. The first, a **doughnut hickey,** consists of a small, solid printed area surrounded by a white halo, or nonprinted area. The other, a **void hickey,** is a white, unprinted spot surrounded by printing.

Doughnut hickeys are caused by ink-receptive, solid particles on the plate or blanket. Ink skin is a common cause of a doughnut hickeys.

Blanket contamination from paper usually produces void hickeys. Occasionally, coating debris accepts ink and produces doughnut hickeys. However, repeated dampening causes the particle to become water-receptive, and the doughnut hickey eventually changes to a void hickey.

Water-receptive particles on the plate or blanket produce void hickeys. Because of their thickness, they prevent the plate or blanket from receiving ink in their immediate surrounding area.

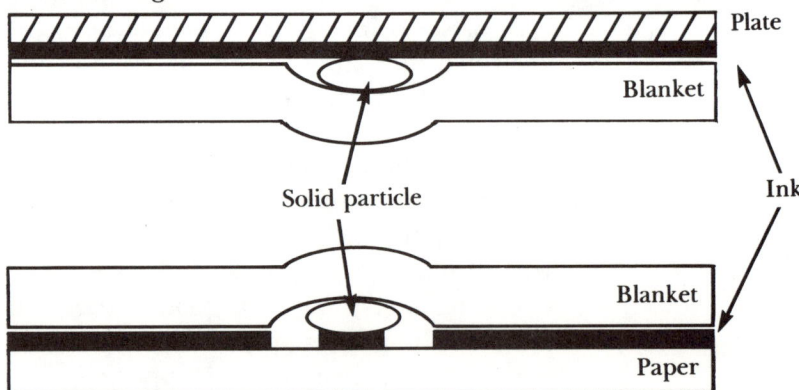

A solid particle (such as dirt), enlarged, on the blanket, producing a hickey on the printed sheet

Piling

The accumulation of material on the blanket in such quantity that it interferes with print quality is called **piling.** Piling in the nonimage areas is often caused by fillers and coating particles that become attached to the blanket. Improper ink and water balance can also cause nonimage area piling.

Back-Edge Curl

Back-edge curl, or **tail-end hook,** is a curl in the paper at the back edge of a press sheet as a result of printing heavy solids close to the back edge during offset printing. The heavy solid causes the sheet to stick to the blanket. Back-edge curl is avoided if large solid areas are printed on the front half of the sheet. The use of quick-release blankets and sheet decurlers lessens the problem of back-edge curl.

Surface Rupture

Picking, plucking, tearing, and similar problems occur when paper or coating is not strong enough to withstand the pull of the inked blanket. The principal causes are insufficient bonding strength in the paper or excessive ink tack.

Picking is the removal of pieces of paper surface by the ink. They stick to the blanket or plate, causing spots in the printing.

Tearing occurs when the ink pulls a continuous strip of the paper surface, leaving a delaminated area in the press sheet. (The term "delamination" is reserved for a phenomenon that occurs on blanket-to-blanket web presses.)

Splitting occurs when large areas of the paper surface are torn loose from the press sheet and stick to the offset blanket. Splitting usually starts in a solid printed area and continues to the trailing edge of the sheet. It sometimes develops into a V-shaped tear.

The following recommendations eliminate or minimize the problems of surface rupture:

- Reduce the ink tack.
- Change to a blanket with better release properties or with a rougher surface.
- Decrease press speed.
- Decrease the pressure between the impression and blanket cylinders.

10 Ink

Unlike flexography and letterpress, which print from a raised or "relief" surface, and rotogravure, which prints from an engraved or "intaglio" surface, lithography uses a planographic plate to separate the image from the nonimage areas. The image area of the plate is preferentially wet by ink, and the nonimage area is preferentially wet by water. Therefore, unlike other inks, lithographic ink must be formulated to work with water. In offset lithography the ink on the plate is transferred to a blanket. In direct lithography, sometimes used to print newspapers, the ink is transferred directly from the plate to the paper.

Ink is a complex mixture of pigment, varnish or vehicle, and modifier or additives. The important properties of ink are drying properties, color, color strength, opacity or transparency, and body or working properties. All of these properties must be selected to suit the particular job and, most importantly, the paper or other material being printed.

Ink is discussed comprehensively in GATF's book *What the Printer Should Know about Ink,* and ink problems are discussed comprehensively in GATF's book *Solving Offset Ink Problems.*

Inkmaking

The actual manufacturing of ink is relatively simple, but formulation is a complex problem and involves advanced science. When dry pigments are used, varnish and pigment or pigments are weighed and stirred together in a tub using high-speed dispersion equipment to mix the pigments with the varnish. This mixing operation, wetting the pigment and mixing the ink ingredients thoroughly, saves subsequent milling time. Most sheetfed inks are now made from "flushes" in which the pigment is dispersed during manufacture.

Next, the mixture is ground on a three-roll mill where it is sheared as it passes between rollers. As can be seen by examining the illustration, the rollers of the three-roll mill,

Three-roll mill

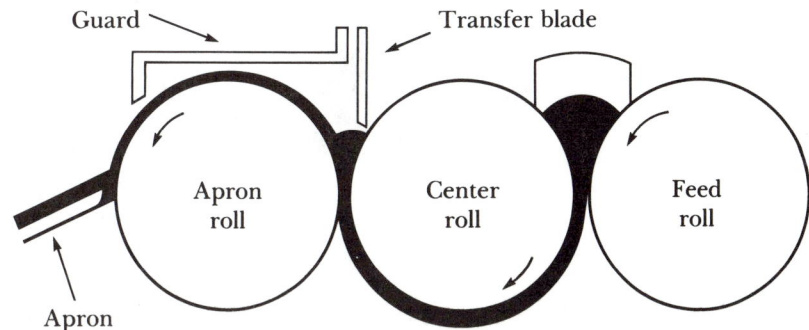

which turn at different speeds and in different directions, shear the ink film between them. This shearing breaks up the pigment agglomerates into microscopic particles so that each becomes completely surrounded and wet by the varnish. Milling also "classifies" the pigment, permitting finely dispersed pigment to flow through the mill and retaining or holding back coarser pigment particles. Ground ink is taken off the high-speed roll by a blade, as shown in the illustration. A thorough job of grinding may require as many as three passes through the mill, depending on whether the pigment is soft or hard and how easily it is wet by the varnish.

Milling is a costly procedure, and inks can be cheapened by reducing the amount of milling. This causes several problems including lower color strength and larger pigment size. Large pigment particles in the ink can cause problems such as scratches and plate wear. Since the pigment is the

Bead mill
Courtesy Buhler-Miag, Inc.

most expensive part of the ink, and uniform dispersion is accomplished by extensive milling, the better inks become more expensive.

Progress in recent years has resulted in the production of inks that have good stability in the can. However, it is still a good practice to make sure that new inks arriving in the ink room are not placed on the front of the shelf and used first. Rather, a system of "first-in, first-out" should be used to ensure that the oldest inks are used first. This prevents inks from becoming so old during storage that they must be discarded.

Ingredients of Inks

Since formulation of inks is the ink manufacturer's responsibility, the subject is presented only briefly here.

A sheetfed lithographic ink contains the following materials:
- Pigment: carbon black, phthalo blue, rubine, or other
- Varnish: long-oil alkyd, phenolic, or urethane litho varnish
- Drier: cobalt and manganese salts
- Solvent: heatset oil, 535°F (280°C)
- Modifier: wax compound for rub resistance

These standard inks dry primarily by a chemical reaction, a polymerization reaction initiated by oxygen and catalyzed by cobalt and manganese ions from the drier.

Pigments

A **pigment** is a finely divided solid material that gives an ink color. Lithographic ink pigments vary widely in chemical composition, their principal requirements being that they (1) do not dissolve or bleed in the press dampening solution, (2) are unchanged in color or tinctorial strength by chemicals in the dampening solution, (3) produce inks that are not broken down by the plate moisture, and (4) do not possess abrasive properties that would damage printing plates. These requirements narrow the field of acceptable pigments.

They can be either opaque or transparent. The body and working properties of an ink depend not only on the type of vehicle and its viscosity but also on the nature and amount of pigment it contains. In addition to color and opacity, important pigment characteristics include particle size, specific gravity, refractive index, texture, wettability, and free surface energy.

The **particle size** of pigments suitable for inks ranges from about 0.01 to 0.5 microns. Since one micron is approximately 0.00004 in. (10^{-6} m), this corresponds to a range of

0.000004–0.00002 in. (0.0001–0.0005 mm). Among the process colors, carbon blacks are the finest and chrome yellow particles are the coarsest, one of several reasons that diarylide yellows are preferred. In general, pigments of fine particle size work best and, with the exception of blacks, produce the more transparent inks. Coarser pigments not only produce more opaque inks but also tend to pile on the ink rollers, plate, and blanket. Special formulation is often required to make such inks transfer properly. Large pigment particle size causes fairly rapid plate wear.

The **specific gravity** of a pigment is the ratio of the weight of one of its particles to the weight of an equal volume of water. Heavy pigments generally require less varnish per pound than light pigments, and the volume and mileage of a pound of their inks are less.

Refractive index is a measure of the ability of a pigment particle to bend or refract light rays. If the pigment and vehicle have the same refractive index (vehicles also have a refractive index), the film is transparent. If the refractive indexes are different, the light rays are bent and scattered and the film is opaque. The greater this difference, the more opaque the film is. Pigments vary in refractive index much more than vehicles. Opaque pigments like titanium dioxide and chrome yellows have high refractive indexes.

Texture is the hardness or softness of a pigment in its dry form. If it rubs out easily to an extremely fine powder between finger and thumb, it is soft. If much pressure is needed, or if the powder feels gritty, it is hard. Texture determines the ease of grinding or dispersing a pigment in its vehicle—in other words, the number of passes through the mill necessary to produce a good ink. Recent research indicates that sharp or gritty pigment particles can greatly accelerate plate wear. This can be true even for particles that are acceptably small.

Wettability is the ease with which a pigment can be completely wet by the *ink vehicle*. In offset inks particularly, complete pigment wetting by the ink vehicle is necessary to prevent breakdown and dispersion in the dampening solution. At least one press problem can be traceable to poor pigment wettability. In waterlogging, water begins to wet the surface of pigment particles, and as a result, the pigment and vehicle separate, often leaving pigment caked on the rollers.

Free surface energy involves the molecular forces at the surface of the pigment particle. These forces determine whether the particle "prefers" to be wet by oil or by water. Pigment surface forces probably play a part in determining whether a pigment will grind to a short or a long body in an oily vehicle.

Because pigments vary much in particle size, specific gravity, wettability, and free surface energy, each pigment poses a different problem in ink formulation. The inkmaker requires many varieties of ink vehicles, extenders, and modifiers in order to produce good working inks in all colors.

There are two broad classes of pigments: organic and inorganic. The term **organic** means "derived from living organisms." Organic pigments contain hydrogen and carbon and usually one or more of the following chemical elements: oxygen, nitrogen, sulfur, and chlorine. Organic pigments include furnace black, lampblack, and channel black for black inks, diarylide yellows and Hansa yellows for yellow inks, phthalocyanine for cyan inks, rubine for red-shade magenta inks, rhodamine for blue-shade magenta inks, and red lake C in red inks. Inorganic pigments include titanium dioxide, chrome yellow, molybdate orange, cadmium yellow and cadmium red, iron blue, and ultramarine blue.

Vehicles

Pigment particles are dispersed in a complex liquid mixture known as the **ink vehicle.** The nature of the vehicle determines most of the working properties of the ink and some of its optical qualities as well. The vehicle disperses the pigment and, after drying, bonds the pigment particles to the paper. A variety of substances including synthetic resins and modifications of natural rosin are used in ink vehicles.

Additives

The inkmaker adds various materials to the ink to make it press-ready for sheetfed lithographic printing.

One additive is a **slip compound** that improves scuff resistance of the printed ink film. Waxes are used in the compound, which is either a micronized dry powder or a fine dispersion of several waxes in an appropriate oil vehicle.

Also added to many inks are **wetting agents,** which promote the dispersion of pigments in the vehicle. The wetting agent selected by the inkmaker must be carefully chosen, to avoid excessive emulsification of dampening solution into the ink and other problems.

Setoff is controlled by the addition of **antisetoff compounds,** which prevent setoff either by protecting the ink surface or by shortening the ink (decreasing its gelling time). Compounds containing wax or grease shorten the ink, which decreases its setting time.

Shortening compounds reduce ink flying, or misting. The addition of a wax compound shortens the ink. Press operators should not add such materials to an ink except on the advice of the inkmaker because they can interfere with the proper flow on the press.

Reducers, such as kerosene or other petroleum solvents, are occasionally added to an ink to soften it and reduce its tack. Light varnish, such as #0000 litho varnish, boiled linseed oil, or a light linseed isophthalic alkyd, also reduce the tack of an ink. It is much easier to reduce tack than increase it.

Stiffening agents, such as body gum (#8, #9, and #10 linseed varnish) stiffen an ink that is too soupy and that fails to print cleanly and sharply. It lessens the tendency of an ink to cause scumming or tinting and helps to prevent chalking on coated stocks.

Antiskinning agents are antioxidants that counteract the drying of sheetfed inks so that they do not skin over in the can.

The printer should make every effort to obtain inks that are press-ready direct from the can. Not only is altering the ink a nuisance, but it often causes more problems than it cures. If it becomes necessary to add anything to the ink, it should be done only on advice of the inkmaker.

Drying Agents, or Driers

An additive omitted from the previous section is the drying agent. Most printing inks benefit from the addition of a **drying agent,** or **drier,** which acts as a catalyst to convert a wet ink film to a dry ink film. Drying agents are, most frequently, salts of cobalt and manganese. Mixed driers are more effective than single driers. For years, the conventional drier has been a three-way type composed of cobalt, lead, and manganese salts. Due to environmental regulations concerning the use of lead, two-way driers using cobalt and manganese or three-way driers using zirconium instead of lead are being used increasingly.

Cobalt, a very active drier, is referred to as a **top drier** since it gives a very hard surface to the ink. Manganese, less active than cobalt, is referred to as a **through drier** since it dries the ink film throughout and does not form a hard surface.

If metal salts are suspended in liquids such as petroleum solvent, the resulting driers are referred to as **liquid driers.** The largest class of printing ink driers currently used consists of soluble drier containing resins and plasticizers to achieve the desired body or viscosity; these are referred to as **paste driers.**

Although drying agents are already included in the ink by the manufacturer, extra driers can be added by the printer. When driers are added at the printing stage, it is important not to exceed the manufacturer's recommendations for each ink. Using too much drier will not improve the drying rate of the ink greatly and, in some instances, may actually slow the drying.

Drying of Sheetfed Inks

The **drying** of a sheetfed ink is the process by which it is transformed from an original semifluid or plastic to a solid. On paper, drying takes place in two stages that, though separate and distinct, occur to some extent simultaneously. These stages are (1) setting by absorption and (2) solidification of the liquid vehicle by oxidation and polymerization.

An ink film setting on uncoated paper

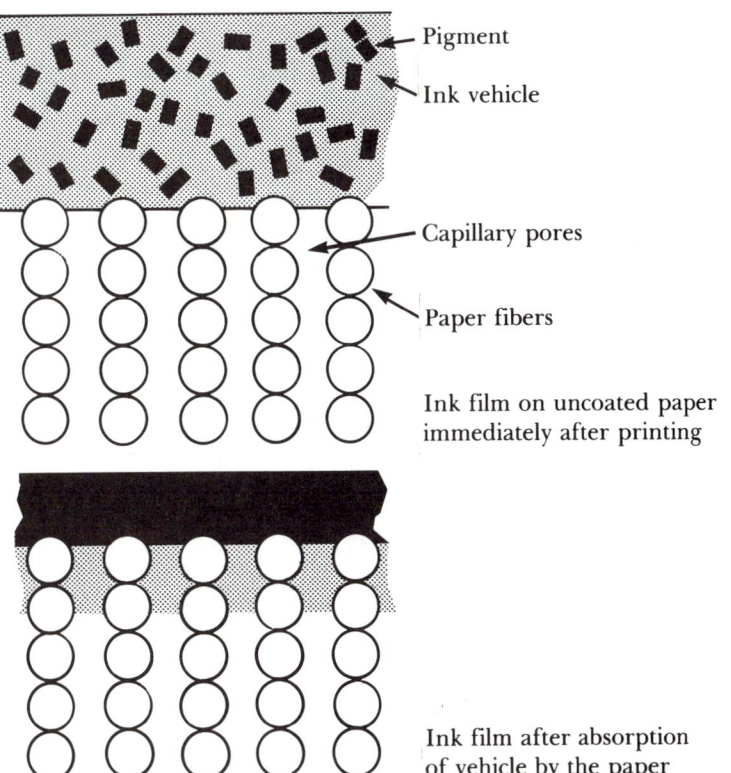

Pigment

Ink vehicle

Capillary pores

Paper fibers

Ink film on uncoated paper immediately after printing

Ink film after absorption of vehicle by the paper

226 Sheetfed Offset Press Operating

Setting   Proper setting of ink is dependent on a correct relationship between absorbency of the paper and body of the ink vehicle. If the ink vehicle is too fluid or the paper too absorptive, or both, the pigment remains on the paper surface with insufficient binder, and the print "chalks." On the other hand, if the ink vehicle is too viscous or the paper insufficiently absorptive, or both, the ink does not set

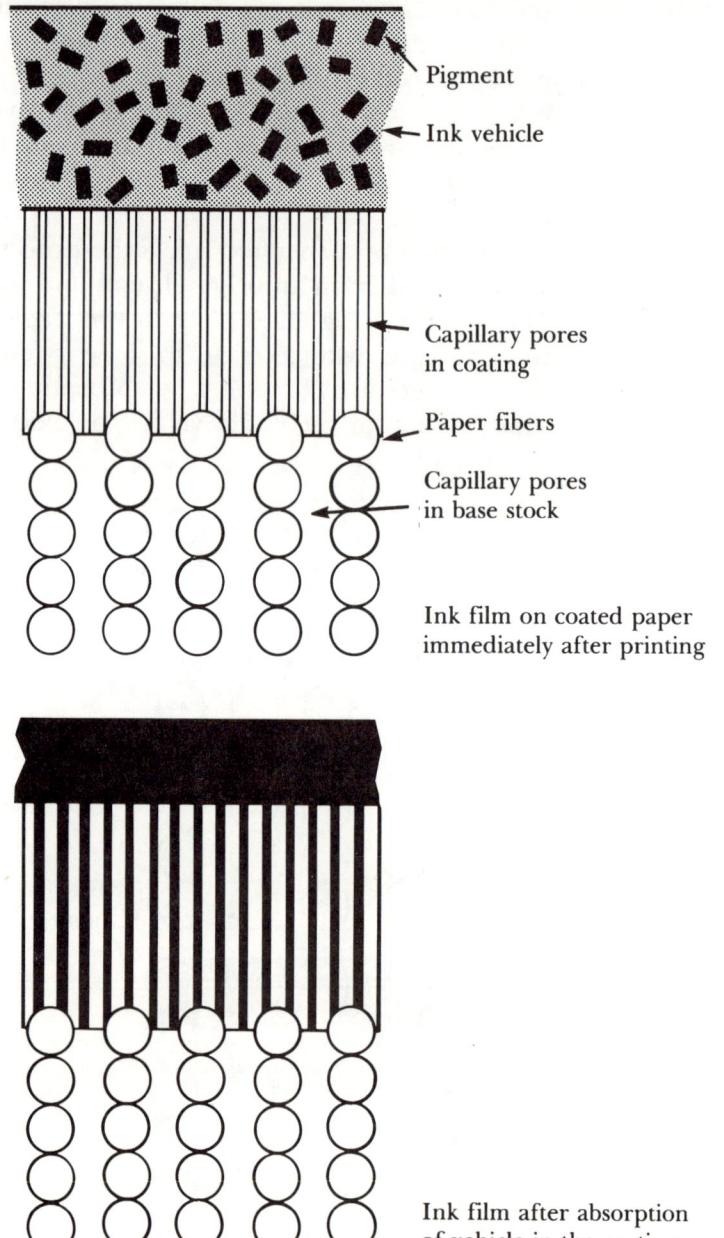

An ink film setting on coated paper

Pigment

Ink vehicle

Capillary pores in coating

Paper fibers

Capillary pores in base stock

Ink film on coated paper immediately after printing

Ink film after absorption of vehicle in the coating

properly, and the result is setoff, sticking, or, in extreme cases, "blocking." Ordinarily the paper is selected on the basis of requirements of the printed product, and the ink is adjusted to the paper.

Drying by Oxidation and Polymerization

The principle of polymerization is illustrated in the accompanying diagram. Those varnishes that are derived from drying oils, such as linseed oil, chinawood oil, or soya oil, react with oxygen in the air to form a chemical called a hydroperoxide. In the presence of a cobalt or manganese salt, called an initiator or a catalyst (a drier), the hydroperoxide reacts with another oil molecule, forming a molecular chain that continues to grow. As the chain gets longer and longer, it flows less and less readily until, after 2–4 hr., enough chains are formed to prevent ink flow. It will not smear when it is rubbed; it is dry.

Polymerization

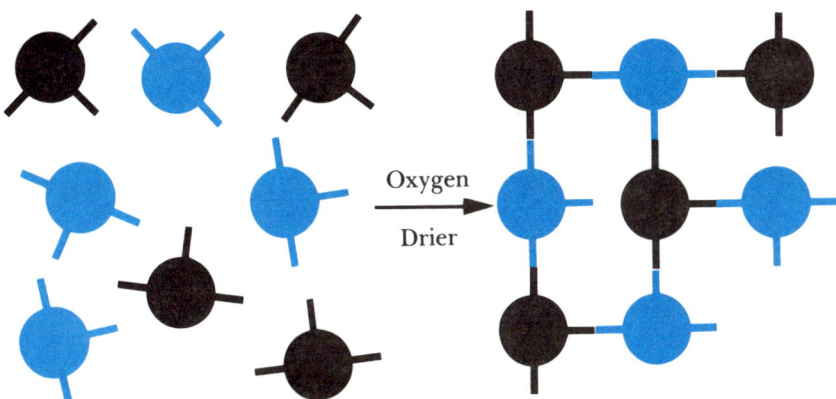

Factors Affecting the Ink Drying Rate

Several factors affect the drying rate of inks containing drying-oil varnishes. Among these factors are the nature of ink pigment and other ingredients, nature of paper, temperature, amount of moisture present, acidity of dampening solution, availability of oxygen for drying, and ink film thickness.

If an ink does not dry in a reasonable length of time, the ink is often blamed. However, not only the ink but also the paper, the press, and the atmosphere are involved.

The major factors related to *ink components* that affect the drying rate are:

- **Pigments.** Some pigments themselves help drying, while others absorb drier and remove it from the reaction.
- **Varnishes.** Some varnishes dry much faster and harder than others.

- **Type of drier.** Cobalt, manganese, and zirconium compounds are used. They are not equally efficient as driers.
- **Amount of drier.** More drier is not necessarily better. It is important to have the correct amount of drier in the ink, and this amount is best determined by the inkmaker.

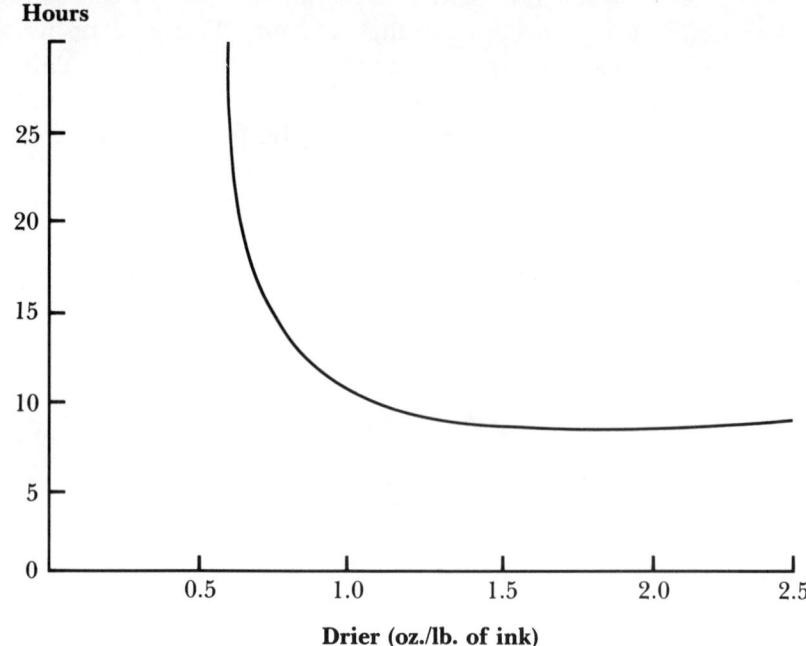

Effect of drier content on drying time of ink

- **Drier dissipation.** The drying rate of an old ink should be checked before the ink is used on a job. A drier may become dissipated, or inactive, if the ink has been on the shelf for more than one year.

Some *paper characteristics* affecting ink drying are:
- **Absorbency of the sheet.** Absorbency of the paper does not affect real drying. However, the more absorbent the paper, the faster inks printed on it will set.
- **Paper or coating pH.** The more acid an uncoated paper is, the slower the printed ink dries. The more alkaline a coating is, the faster the ink dries. The coating on coated paper can also be responsible for the chalking of inks.
- **Moisture in the paper.** The more moisture there is in a paper, the slower the printed ink dries.

The method of controlling a press is particularly important in lithographic printing. It is necessary to have good ink/water balance for best printing conditions: enough ink should be used to get full color, with only enough water to keep the plate running clean. Important *press factors* are:

- **Acid level of dampening solution.** Excess acid (pH too low) is the most common cause of ink drying problems. As the dampening solution is made more acid, inks with drying-oil varnishes take longer to dry because the acid reacts with the drier, destroying its effectiveness. The pH is best maintained between 4.5 and 5.5.
- **Water in ink.** The more water that becomes emulsified in the ink, the slower the ink dries.
- **Kind of form.** Heavy solids cause more drying problems than light line work or halftones.

Temperature and relative humidity also affect the ink drying rate. The higher the temperature at which sheets are stored after printing, the faster the ink dries. An ink that requires 12 hr. to dry at 68°F (20°C) may dry in about 6 hr. at 80°F (27°C). On the other hand, excessive warmth generates blocking, dot gain, and other problems. As the relative humidity of the air increases, inks dry more slowly.

Effect of temperature on ink drying time

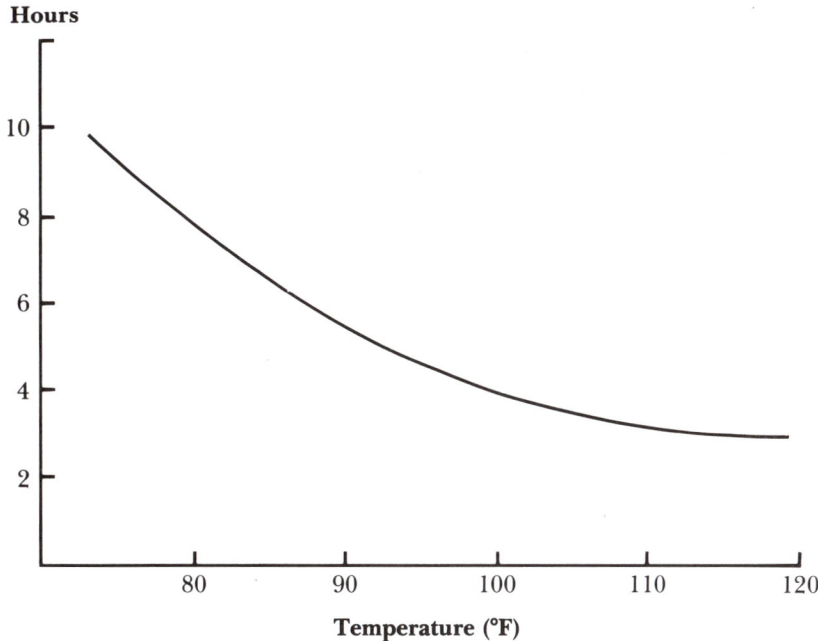

Acceleration of Drying Using Radiation

Some inks used in sheetfed printing use ultraviolet (UV), infrared (IR), or electron-beam (EB) radiation to accelerate the drying process.

The UV ink drying system involves specially formulated inks *and* a series of special lamps that emit ultraviolet radiation. When UV inks are exposed to UV radiation, the polymerization reaction speeds up to a point where it is

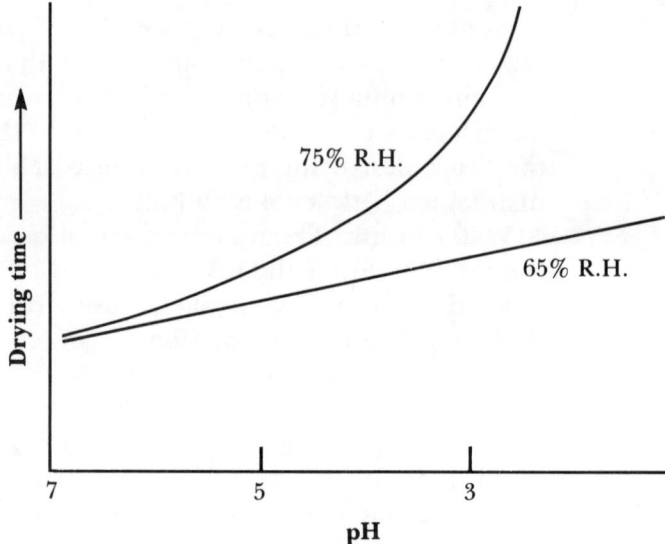

Effect of constant relative humidity (R.H.) and changing pH on drying time

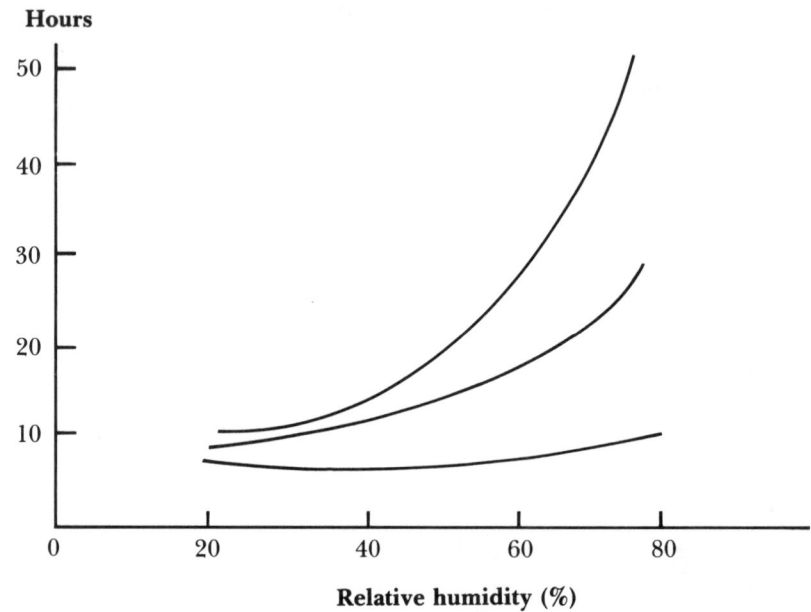

Effect of relative humidity on the drying times of three inks

virtually instantaneous and complete. Some describe UV drying as "curing." These inks contain no solvent, so solvent-fume emission from the press is eliminated. One of the difficulties in formulating UV inks has been the successful use of the photoinitiators required to trigger the polymerization in UV inks. These photoinitiators are expensive and difficult to use.

The EB drying system uses inks similar to those used for UV drying with the exception that photoinitiators are not required. A stream of electrons bombard the ink film and accelerate polymerization.

Infrared radiation does not usually cure inks. As commonly used, infrared radiators increase the setting speed of inks. When infrared radiation is used with quickset inks, the speed of setting is very fast. Special quickset infrared inks permit backing up a pile of prints 15 min. after they have been printed. Less spray powder is used with IR dryers, but the system must be kept under control to avoid embrittling the sheet or blocking the prints.

Quickset Inks

Quickset inks are formulated with a quickset varnish. A quickset varnish contains a low-viscosity, high-boiling-point hydrocarbon oil. When the ink is printed, the hydrocarbon oil is absorbed by the paper coating, and the viscosity of the printed ink film rises rapidly; that is, the ink sets.

Sheets printed with quickset inks can be handled more quickly than those printed with a nonquickset ink. In addition, quickset ink can set rapidly enough to increase the tack of the printed ink between units on the press. If they set sufficiently between units, it is possible to print process colors using four **unitack** inks; i.e., inks that have the same tack rating. This means that the printer can use one set of process colors in any printing sequence desired. However, better trap and color uniformity are achieved if the normal tack sequence is used (tack is highest on the first unit and decreases on subsequent units) and the printer uses only one color sequence or a different set of inks for each color sequence. When a normal tack sequence is printed, the ink film is usually thinnest on the first unit and increases in thickness with each succeeding unit, provided the inks are properly formulated and nothing has been added to the ink in the pressroom.

Optical Properties of Ink

The impression of color is a personal experience. It is received as light that is reflected, transmitted, or radiated from an object to our eyes. Light stimulates the nerve cells in our eyes and our brain to create the sensation of color. Being a personal experience, color identification varies between individuals, as well as the state of our health, our physical surroundings, and other physiological factors. The eye is sensitive to three colors, red, green, and blue. All of the various colors that we perceive are combinations of these three frequencies of light. In printing, the reflection of these three colors (red, green, and blue) from the surface of the paper are respectively controlled by application of the transparent inks known as cyan, magenta, and yellow.

Color

It is common to think of color as a property of objects and materials. Nothing, however, appears colored unless it is either illuminated or emits light. Pigments appear colored in white light because they absorb certain wavelengths and reflect or transmit others. They appear to change color if the spectral composition of the light is varied.

The three process color inks—cyan, yellow, and magenta—are transparent. Ideally each absorbs light from one-third of the spectrum and transmits light from the remaining two-thirds. Cyan has its characteristic color because it transmits blue and green light while absorbing (or filtering out) red light. Yellow transmits red and green light and absorbs the blue. Magenta absorbs green light and transmits the red and blue. Because process inks are transparent, one process color can be overprinted by another without changing the way each absorbs or transmits light. For example, magenta overprinted by cyan will produce blue because magenta filters out green light and cyan filters out the red.

Ordinary nonprocess inks are opaque and work in a slightly different manner. An opaque yellow ink, for example, reflects (rather than transmits) red and green light and absorbs blue light. When opaque inks are overprinted, the top color hides the bottom color, making them unsuitable for process color printing.

Printed ink films exhibit both masstone and undertone. **Masstone** is the color of a thick film of the ink. It is the color of light reflected by the pigment. **Undertone** is the color of a thin film of ink. It is the color of light reflected by the paper and transmitted through the ink film. In order to judge these two ink properties, the following procedure is followed:

1. Place two small samples of two different inks side by side on a piece of paper.

2. Use a drawdown knife to draw the samples down to adjoining films, first lightly for about 1½–2 in. (40–50 mm), then with heavy pressure for another 2 in.

3. Determine the relative masstone of the two inks by comparing the thick films and the undertone by comparing the thin films.

Ink 233

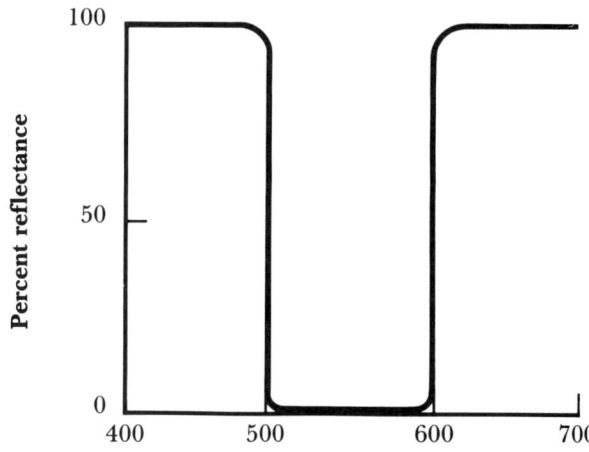

Spectral reflectance curve of a "perfect" magenta

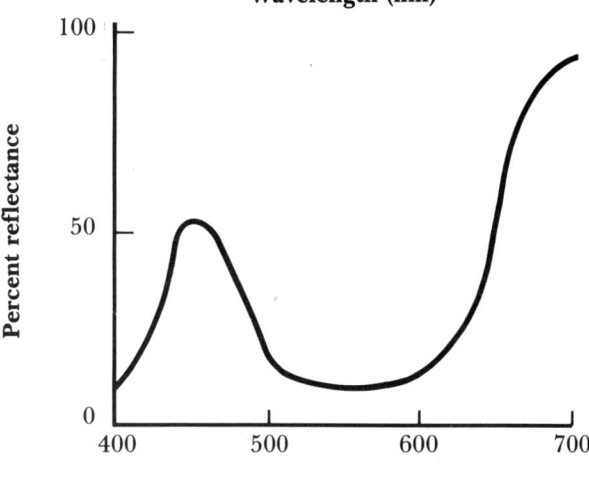

Spectral reflectance curve of a typical magenta ink

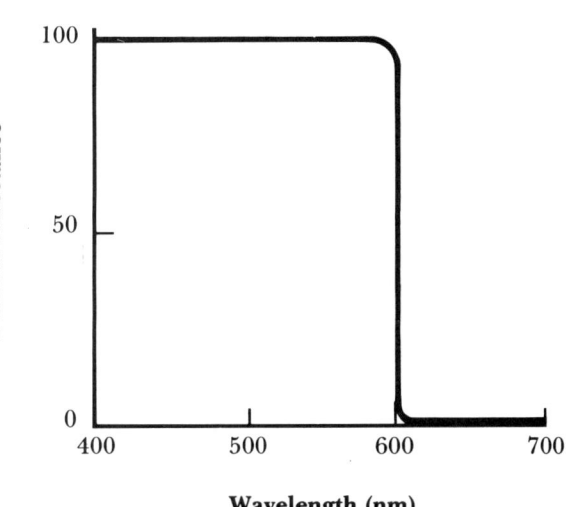

Spectral reflectance curve of a "perfect" cyan

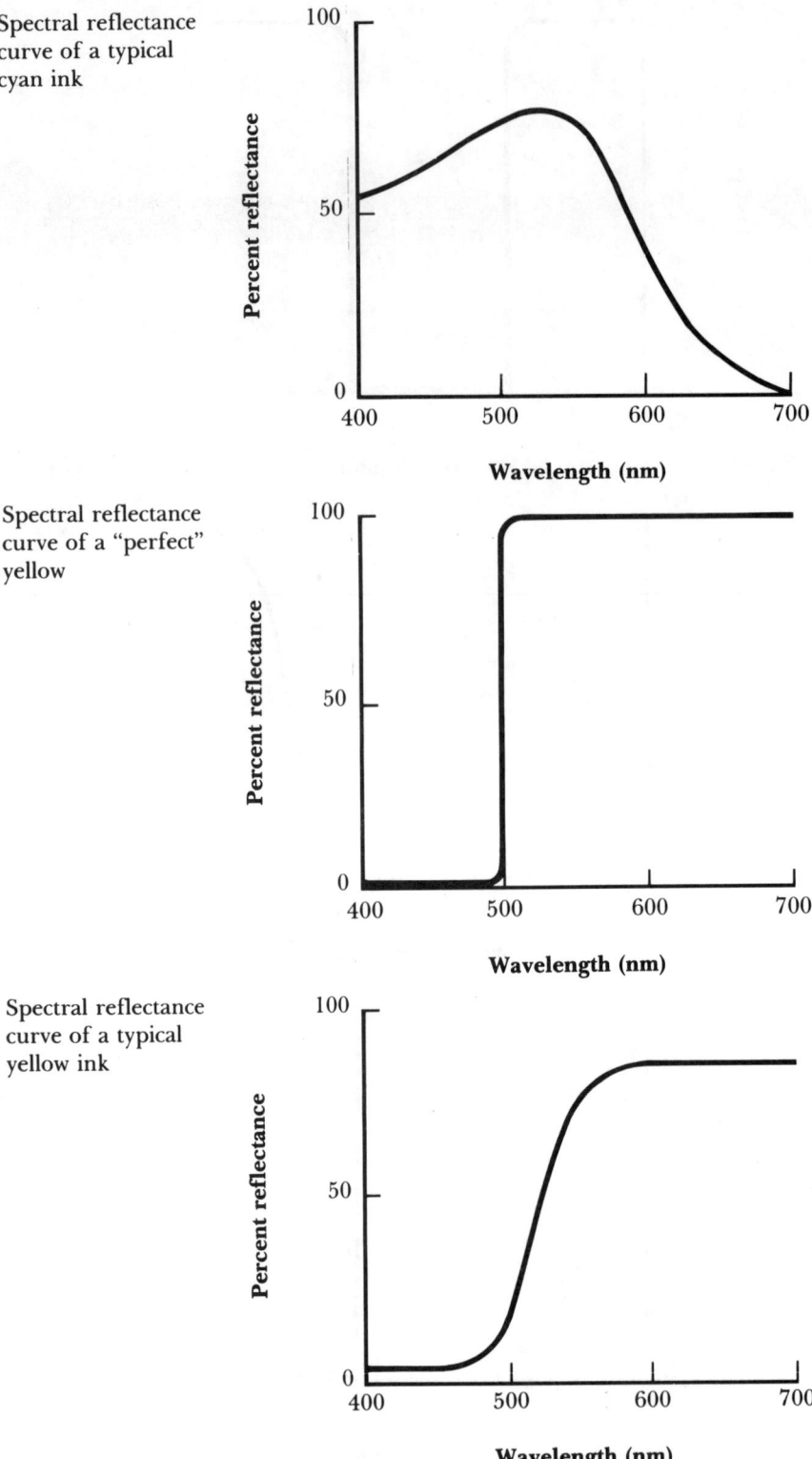

Spectral reflectance curve of a typical cyan ink

Spectral reflectance curve of a "perfect" yellow

Spectral reflectance curve of a typical yellow ink

The difference between masstone and undertone applies to ink films as printed. For example, if an ink film is thick, the resulting color tends towards masstone. But if the ink film is thin, the undertone becomes predominant. A red ink with a bluish undertone may print a warm red if run with normal thickness but go to cold pink if run very thin. Such an apparent color change can cause problems on the press.

Color Strength

The **color strength** of an ink is its coloring power and is determined by pigment concentration. Color strength determines the value of an ink and the amount of ink required to produce the desired color. Cheap inks contain less color, and the printer must run more ink—creating emulsification and drying problems, dot gain, and other problems. In lithographic inks, color strength must be great enough to produce the desired color in a printed ink film of normal thickness. Determination of color strength of an ink is a difficult procedure best left to the expert. A printer can often get the inkmaker to test a pair of inks of the same hue to determine which has the greater strength, or the ink can be sent to a testing laboratory.

Opacity

Opacity is the hiding power of an ink—the ability of its printed film to hide what is underneath. Some pigments have high opacity while others, particularly process ink pigments, are much more transparent. Two pigment qualities, refractive index and particle size, largely determine the opacity or transparency of ink. Opacity can be determined by making drawdowns over black or a contrasting color.

Even minor opacity in a process ink affects the way process colors reproduce. An opaque yellow run on the third unit can blank out much of the visual effect of cyan and magenta, and opaque inks should be avoided in printing process color.

Gloss

Although most of today's high-quality printing is done with high-gloss inks, gloss is largely a matter of taste and preference.

Gloss is largely related to the varnish used in the ink, but high gloss is obtained when the resins in the ink film dry. Coarsely ground pigments can interfere.

Working Properties

Many common liquids like water, alcohol, and petroleum solvents are true "Newtonian" liquids. That is to say that any force applied to them will produce flow, and their rate of flow is directly proportional to that force. But other viscous materials, lithographic inks included, will not flow until a definite force is exceeded. The ink chemist describes this force as the "yield stress" or "yield value."

Offset inks are viscous fluid materials. They are called **viscoelastic** because they behave both like fluids and like elastic solids. While it is not easy to separate these two types of behavior, the science of the subject forces us to shift from one type to another to explain why inks behave as they do on the press.

Body, length, tack, and thixotropy are ink properties that strongly affect how the ink feeds from the fountain, how it transfers and distributes on the rollers, and how it prints from the blanket.

Body

The term **body** means consistency. It is a rather loose, overall term referring mainly to stiffness or softness of the ink, although it often implies other things including length and thixotropy. **Thixotropy** is the characteristic of a material that causes it to change consistency on being worked. Working an ink on a slab with a spatula reduces its body and viscosity. After standing a while, the ink will regain its original viscosity.

Length

Ink must possess a certain degree of length in order to feed properly and transfer without piling. Too much length, however, may cause an ink to fly or mist. The ink formulator may test length by placing an amount of ink on a tilted slab. After 15 min., the ink's flow down the slab is measured.

More commonly, length is observed by tapping out a small sample of ink on a slab or dish. A short ink breaks after forming a short string, while a long ink forms a long string.

Short inks are sensitive to water pickup and have a tendency to become waterlogged. They also transfer poorly and tend to pile on the plate or blanket. Inks in this condition do not transfer properly and make color control difficult.

Thixotropy

As explained above, working an ink reduces its viscosity, and when the work is discontinued, the ink regains its original body or viscosity. This means that an ink becomes more fluid while it is on the press and sets up when it is on the sheet. This behavior is called thixotropy.

Effect of Temperature on Viscosity

The viscosity of all liquids changes rapidly with the temperature. The temperature coefficient of viscosity for inks may be −5% per degree Fahrenheit (about −9% to −10% per degree Celsius) or even greater. This means that a temperature increase of 10°F (5.5°C) can reduce the viscosity of the ink by 50% or more. (Raising the temperature 20°F reduces the viscosity by around 75%.)

The high negative temperature coefficient of viscosity has several implications for the printer. In the first place, if a multicolor press is not warmed to working temperature before printing starts, the color changes as the press warms up. Furthermore, should the temperature on one of the units change, owing to environmental conditions, the flow of ink changes on that unit, changing the color of the print.

In lithographic printing, if the press is cold when the paper is fed to it, the highly viscous ink may cause picking of the paper. The press and the pressroom must be up to temperature before attempting to feed paper into the press.

Tack

Tack is the resistance of a liquid to splitting. It is measured by determining the force required to split an ink film between two surfaces. Tack is an important property of an ink film because it can determine whether or not an ink will pick the paper surface or trap properly in multicolor printing, and it at least partially determines how sharp the printed image is.

In multicolor work involving the successive overprinting of wet ink films, it is necessary that the tack of ink films on the paper be higher than the tack of ink on the blanket. It is important to understand that the tack referred to is *tack at the printing nip*. The tack of fresh ink will in all probability bear little relationship to its tack at the printing nip of a lithographic press. *A number of on-press factors can either increase or decrease an ink's tack.*

The most important factors affecting tack are viscosity, press speed, and ink film thickness. In general, tack increases with viscosity and press speed. A high-viscosity ink run on a high-speed press will have a very high tack and can create problems such as picking of the paper surface. In this case, the picking may disappear by simply reducing press speed. Inkmakers have responded to the increased operating speeds of today's presses by formulating inks with lower tack.

The thinner an ink film, the more it will resist splitting. A thin film of ink has a higher tack than a thick film. Thus, when running process work, effective ink tack at the printing nip varies until the press operator establishes the required printed color densities by arriving at the proper ink film thickness. It is important to remember that the press operator varies ink film thickness to achieve the desired color. Thus, the ink film thickness on the press is related to color strength of the ink.

Emulsification also affects the tack of ink. Water works its way back into the roller train in the form of tiny droplets, which are milled into the ink films on the roller surfaces. Inks can sometimes pick up 20% or more water in this way and run with no problems. But a 20% pickup will significantly lower tack because a film of water has a much lower tack than an ink film. The amount of water picked up by the ink depends on the nature of the ink and the condition of the ink/water balance.

Finally, solvent evaporation can also increase ink tack. Heat generated by friction in the printing units, pressroom temperature, and air flow can cause the solvents in heatset inks to evaporate before they reach the dryer. The result, of course, is that the ink begins to set, the extent depending on the rate of solvent evaporation. Tack increases as more solvent evaporates. It should be kept in mind that an increase in temperature without a loss of solvent results in a lowering of tack.

These are the factors that influence ink tack on the press: the tack of the ink when fresh, press speed, ink film thickness, water pickup (emulsification), thixotropy, solvent evaporation, and the temperature of the ink. When faced with a tack-related problem on the press, the press operator should check these factors immediately.

The tack numbers displayed on the ink can by the manufacturer are based on Inkometer readings taken in the laboratory. The press system exerts a strong effect on these ratings. Generally, a new ink having the same tack number as the old will perform in roughly the same way as the old ink if the press system is not changed. On the other hand, tack number should not be relied on as an indicator of ink performance in cases involving changes in press, speed, plates, paper, etc.

Color Matching

Many times, a customer requests a specific color other than black, cyan, yellow, or magenta. Depending on the amount of the ink required, the printer either orders the specific color from the inkmaker or mixes it in the printing plant. Obtaining the ink from the inkmaker is preferred if the color is a shelf ink or if the amount required is large. Small amounts of a particular ink can be mixed in the plant. Color charts from an inkmaker are extremely helpful.

In plants where a great deal of color matching is done, the press operator seldom mixes the ink. A better way—both economically and from a quality control standpoint—is to have a special person assigned the responsibility to do color matching.

The simple rule of good color matching is to use the formula method. Every mixed color that is used in the plant should have each ingredient carefully weighed and recorded. This includes additives like driers. A small, accurate scale is convenient for mixing small samples.

When the proper shade is found, a large batch is mixed, following the formula. After the color is printed on the job, a small sample from the printed sheet is saved, and the formula and date are marked on the back. A sample should not be kept too long, perhaps one year for lightfast colors. In addition, the name and/or number of the job should be put on the sample in case of a reprint. The inks are then listed, with brand, name, number, and weight indicated.

Ink samples can be drawn out with a spatula, rolled out with a Quickpeek tester, or printed using a proof press and allowed to dry. Exposing one sample to atmospheric conditions overnight and enclosing the other in a book gives an indication of the drying behavior of the ink.

Sometimes, two or three small color samples are mixed if the color is expected to change during drying. For example, if a green made from a certain blue and yellow is expected to dry toward the blue side, a second sample would be made with less blue in it. The one drying closest to the desired color is used. If the color desired falls between two samples, a new sample can be mixed, using the formulas from the first two samples as the basis for the new formula.

A tint of a color is produced by adding an **extender,** a white transparent tinting medium, to a colored ink. The simplest form of color matching, as performed by the printer, is mixing an ink to obtain a required shade. The stronger color should always be added to the lighter colored ink in order to obtain a match more quickly and economically. The color should be viewed under different light sources to check for **metamerism**—the phenomenon of colors that match under one light but do not under a different light.

Without a knowledge of color theory and without perfect color perception, an individual will resort to trial-and-error color matching. Fortunately, color matching systems are available that take the trial and error out of color matching.

Ink Handling on Press

Handling ink on an offset press is one of the press operator's most important skills. It seems simple to set an inking fountain to satisfy the demands of a plate. Apparently, all that fountain setting consists of is to open up the keys that feed underinked areas and close down on keys that feed overinked areas.

It is not as simple as it appears. An area may seem to require more ink, while the fact is that the area is overdampened. The effect looks about the same. Under a strong glass the difference can be seen, but it takes a little practice. The same thing is true regarding overinked areas. The amount of dampening has a more marked effect than the amount of ink. Usually, when tones start filling up, the press operator's first reaction is that dampening is excessive or the acid level in the dampening solution is incorrect. Often, the trouble is too much ink.

The first thing to be sure of, when manipulating the ink feed, is that the amount of dampening is correct. Dampening should be reduced to the point where the entire plate appears dry. Some plates require more dampening than others to keep them clean. Knowing how dry a plate can be and still run safely on the press is another skill acquired with experience.

Probably the worst thing that can occur on press, regarding ink, is too much dampening solution. The water in the dampening solution is worked into the ink (emulsified) and changes its characteristics. All inks emulsify water to some degree. Excessive emulsification causes problems, such as the caking of ink on rollers. Several conditions contribute to the emulsification of too much water in an ink:

- Too much dampening solution being fed to the plate
- Too much acid and gum in the dampening solution
- Too little ink on the ink rollers
- The nature of the ink itself

A water-in-ink emulsification

Once dampening is set at the proper level, the ink feed demands are set. Using a densitometer to measure the density of color patches on the press sheet helps in determining the proper amount of ink.

Too little ink on the plate is dangerous to the image, which requires ink to protect it from the acid and gum. Too much ink is dangerous to nonimage areas because it overcomes the desensitizing film and causes the plate to scum. The proper range of inking is small.

In handling ink, the press operator should take every precaution to avoid its contamination. Special care should be taken to prevent mixing dried ink (ink skin) into the fountain ink. To remove ink skin from a can, first cut around the edge with an ink knife and remove the oiled paper cover. Then scrape off any ink skin formed around the edges. Use a broad knife to remove ink evenly from the surface rather than digging deeply into the can. When the required amount of ink has been taken out, smooth the surface with a broad knife and either replace the old oiled paper circle (the "skin sheet") or apply a new one. Press it into uniform contact with the remaining ink to prevent entrapping air bubbles. Ink that has been improperly stored should be discarded—not put onto the press where it can ruin print quality and press performance.

Be sure that the press is clean before inking up, especially if a light color or tint is to be run. Traces of a previous ink remaining on inking or dampening rollers can alter the hue or cleanliness of an ink. To avoid this condition, ink up the press with a light-colored ink or a transparent white ink and run it for several minutes. Then, scrape some of the ink off one of the drums to see how much its color has changed. Wash up the press and repeat until the ink is no longer contaminated.

A number of suitable press washup solvents are available. Strong solvents effectively remove ink but also swell rollers and blankets. Incorporation of a good detergent helps to remove ink without swelling the rubber. Formulation of a good press wash requires knowledge and experience, as does everything else. In addition to being a good ink solvent, it should also be safe from the standpoint of fire hazard and toxicity. Petroleum solvents, which are commonly used, should have flash points of at least 100°F (38°C) in order to meet underwriters' requirements. There are also two- and three-solution washup systems that remove not only ink but also residues of gum arabic, which tend to cause stripping of rollers. Properly used, these and other proprietary washup solutions are more efficient cleaners than petroleum solvents. They reduce makeready times, wasted paper, and wasted ink.

Problems with Lithographic Inks

The most aggravating problems in lithography are often interaction problems, which arise when there is more than one deficiency among the paper, ink, press, and press operation factors. Consequently, adjusting the press may solve the problem temporarily, only to have it recur later or to have it pop up as a "different" problem.

Even if the ink is not the primary cause of the problem, making adjustments to the ink is usually more practical than changing the paper or changing the form to be printed. Thus, a picking problem caused primarily by too much ink on a marginally suitable paper will often be treated by softening the ink rather than by changing the paper or reducing the solids in the print.

The greatest number of ink-related problems are probably due to (1) ink that is not suited to the paper and (2) excessive acidity or dampening. Excessive acidity and dampening destroy or reduce the drier in the ink, and excessive acidity causes tinting and plate blinding.

Ink in the Nonimage Area

Ink in the nonimage area involves a variety of problems, some of which are easily confused.

Dot growth, slur, and doubling increase the area of paper that is printed and, in the printing of process colors, change the color of the print. Except for dot growth resulting from applying too much ink or ink that is too soft, these are not normally considered to be ink problems.

Catch-up, tinting, toning, and scumming are ink/plate/dampening problems that are often correctable on the press. **Catch-up,** or **dry-up,** is the name applied to ink appearing in the nonimage area because of insufficient dampening of the plate. **Tinting** or **toning** results from ink emulsified in the fountain solution, while **scumming** is a permanent image—usually spots—in the nonimage area. To distinguish toning, scumming, and catch-up, the wet-thumb test is useful.

Scumming can arise from a number of sources, including the ink. Several possible causes can occur simultaneously. Scumming can be caused by film and film processing, plates and plate processing, dampening solution, lighting, press adjustment, paper, or ink.

Ink can cause scumming for several reasons. Addition of oleic acid to the ink can create a scummy plate. Uncontrolled or unexpected changes in the pigment or the resin treatment

Ink in the nonimage area

Problem	Cause	Wet-Thumb Effect	Solution
Catch-up	Plate too dry	Removes ink	• Increase dampening
Scumming	Poor plate	Does not remove ink	• Increase dampening • Replace plate • Clean up plate
Toning	Ink emulsification	Removes ink	• Decrease dampening • Avoid detergents • Change inks • Check roller pressure
Tinting	Plate/paper problem	Does not remove ink	• Decrease dampening • Change paper • Use better plates
Ink dot scum	Plate corrosion	Does not remove ink	• Dry plates rapidly

can also cause printing problems. Improper grinding that leaves grit in the ink will accelerate wear of the plate and result in scumming and/or plate blinding.

Piling

Piling is the accumulation of ink pigment or coating from the paper onto the blanket or plate. The major cause of image area piling is the shortness of ink caused by emulsification with water and dilution with dust, pigment, or other debris from the paper.

As an ink becomes emulsified it becomes short. Poorly ground or gritty ink tends to be short. Addition of pigment or dust from the paper aggravates the problem. Water is mixed into the ink at the form rollers, while paper dust and debris may be added at the blanket, and it is at the blanket that piling becomes worst.

In addition to ink and paper, the blanket plays an important role in piling. If the surface of the blanket is very smooth, it forms a tight bond with the paper, pulling dust and pigment from the surface. Changing to a rougher blanket may help, but addition of a nonpiling additive (a glycol or a wax emulsion) to the dampening solution will also improve blanket release and often solve the piling problem. Dampening solution additives should be purchased from printers' suppliers.

The table on page 245 shows the many factors that contribute to piling. At first glance it may seem impossible to print a job without serious piling, but further consideration suggests that it should be possible to find several factors that can be adjusted or modified to cure a piling problem without contributing to other problems.

Linting

Removal of lint from the surface of uncoated paper is generally considered to be a paper problem, but it can often be solved by manipulating the ink. Decreasing the ink tack and increasing the flow of dampening solution are two of the ways to reduce linting.

Trapping

Variations in trapping result in color variation in lithography. Causes of trapping problems when attempting to trap on wet ink are entirely different than those when attempting to trap on dry ink. **Wet trapping** is the ability of a wet ink film to accept another wet ink film printed over it, while **dry trapping** is the ability of a dry film to accept a wet film printed over it. Chapter 13 discusses the procedure for

Sources of piling

Ink
- Poor selection of varnish promotes emulsification.
- Poor grinding results in gritty pigment.
- Excessive tack picks or causes linting or dusting of paper.
- Improper formulation promotes emulsification.
- Excessive pigment promotes shortness.
- Loss of ink solvent increases tack.

Paper
- Dusty or linty paper adds solids to ink.
- Insufficient binder or insolubilization of binder increases paper coating in the ink.

Dampening Solution
- Detergent or soap promotes ink emulsification.
- Excessive gum makes blanket sticky, promoting linting or dusting.
- Alcohol promotes precipitation of gum.

Blanket Wash
- Excess detergent can work its way into dampening solution, emulsifying the ink.
- Aggressive solvent creates tacky blanket that attacks paper.

Blanket
- Tacky blanket pulls dust out of paper.
- Excessively smooth blanket pulls dust out of paper.

Press
- Increasing press speed increases force on paper surface.
- Increasing back cylinder squeeze increases dusting of paper.
- Reducing ink film thickness increases forces removing dust from paper.
- Heated roller system evaporates ink solvents, increasing ink tack.
- Low temperature increases tackiness of ink.

measuring trapping using overprints of magenta, cyan, and yellow.

Wet trap. To assure good wet trap, two things must be kept under control: ink tack and ink film thickness. GATF has always recommended that inks vary by one or two tack units on multiunit presses. A thin ink film will not trap properly over a thick ink film, so that even if ink tack is properly controlled, ink film thickness must still be controlled (lighter forms should be run before heavy forms, and the color strength of the ink must be controlled).

Inkmakers often offer process inks all of the same tack. These can be made to work satisfactorily if ink film thickness is properly controlled, but even better results are achieved if the recommended tack sequence is observed. The inkmaker can then help his customers by varying the pigmentation level of the ink so that the operator must use the proper ink film thickness on press.

Dry trap. Some inks, notably the quick-, hard-drying inks based on chinawood or tung oil, dry to form a hard, impervious surface; the process is commonly called **crystallization.** High drier content is also believed to promote crystallization. Addition of hard waxes (for example, carnauba wax), which give a scratch- and abrasion-resistant surface to the dried ink, also interferes with dry trapping; thus, the inkmaker usually avoids their use.

If excessive drier is added to the ink, the nondrying oil in which the drier is dissolved can rise to the surface and produce a nonimage area on the dried ink film, an area in which ink will not trap.

As with all ink-drying problems, dry-trap problems are more easily prevented than cured. Getting the right ink in the first place is the best prevention. Some inks trap better than others, and if the printer is faced with a dry-trap problem, the inkmaker should be consulted.

Hickeys

Hickeys (small solid areas, sharply defined and surrounded by white halos) are sometimes referred to as ink skin hickeys, but any source of dirt (the press, the pressroom, raw materials, crew) can cause hickeys. In addition to common sources of dirt, there are many unusual sources, and the solution to a hickey problem often involves a careful, lengthy search. Paint, spray powder, and other materials falling from the ceiling frequently cause hickeys.

Gloss Ghosting

Gloss ghosting is also referred to as fuming ghosting or chemical ghosting. It is the transfer of a printed image (but not by setoff) from the front of one sheet to the back of another, not through the sheet. This type of ghosting results from one printed ink film altering the drying of a printed ink film on the adjacent sheet in the pile. It can be seen on metal that is printed on two sides, but slipsheeting the pile eliminates it. The ghost image is always the image of the other side of the page. There are several theories concerning the cause of gloss ghosting; all are complex, all supported by good evidence. Gloss ghosting may, indeed, arise from several different causes. As with other ink-drying problems, it is easier to prevent than to cure.

Gloss ghosting is not a very frequent problem, but it can be a very expensive one. In fact, gloss ghosting is very difficult to create in the laboratory. Although ink is involved, ink alone cannot be the cause, because ghosting often appears on some but not all prints of the same job. Paper, printing sequence, design, and level of gloss are also involved in ghosting.

Gloss ghosting is most apt to arise in quick-turnaround, high-quality jobs, which may explain the apparent increase in its frequency. It is seen only on highly glossy jobs; the human eye does not detect small differences in gloss at low levels of gloss. Work at GATF and elsewhere shows that the sooner sheets are backed up after printing the first-down side, the more severe the ghosting. It is recommended that production personnel schedule at least 24 hours of drying before backing up jobs that appear to be troublesome. The printer's salespeople may not favor this approach, but it is far faster than reprinting the job.

Regardless of the mechanism of its origin, the cure and prevention of gloss ghosting are the same. First of all, the printer should have the inkmaker supply an ink suitable for the paper to be run, and the printer should carefully follow good pressroom procedures. If the heavier form is printed first, ghosting will be reduced or eliminated. The ghost of a large solid is not visible in lines and alphanumeric characters.

It has also been shown that adding cobalt drier aggravates gloss ghosting. Printers and inkmakers often add cobalt when the job must be rushed. There is no evidence that infrared heaters cause gloss ghosting, but they do make it possible to back the job up sooner. Quickset inks also make it possible to back the job up faster, and evidence from Switzerland suggests that quickset inks may contribute directly to gloss ghosting.

Although application of a varnish or a lacquer over a ghost usually does not make it disappear and often makes it worse, if five clear varnishes of widely differing bodies are applied to a sample of the ghost on the workbench, it is often found that one of them will mask or obliterate the ghost. This varnish is a good choice for overprinting the ghosted sheets.

If a suitable gloss varnish cannot be found, the technique of applying and drying a matte or nongloss varnish and then following that with a gloss varnish has been found to be successful in overcoming ghosting.

Mechanical Ghosting

Mechanical ghosting includes ink-starvation ghosting and "repeat" ghosting. The ghost image is always carried on the same side of the sheet. Mechanical ghosting results from inadequacies of the inking systems found in lithographic presses. Some forms are almost impossible to print on lithographic equipment, and salespeople should help customers avoid such artwork.

When ink is removed from a form roller by a heavy form on the plate, the ink is not completely replaced by the ink splitting between the ink form roller and the oscillating roller. Differences in ink film thickness on the roller result in differences in ink film thickness on the paper and cause color differences.

Emulsification of the ink with water is equivalent to printing a thinner film of ink, which aggravates ghosting. Using alcohol in the dampening solution is helpful.

Ghost areas that run around the cylinder can often be reduced by increasing the travel (or side-to-side motion) of the oscillating roller. If mechanical ghosting is caused by improper diameter of the form rollers, these should be replaced by rollers of the diameter specified by the press manufacturer. It goes without saying that a press with four or five form rollers is capable of better ink distribution than one with two or three. Some printing characteristics are already established when the press is purchased.

The following recommendations help to overcome mechanical ghosting:
- Reduce water (add alcohol or wetting agent).
- Use an opaque ink.
- Increase ink film thickness.
- Increase pitch of the vibrator.
- Check diameter and hardness of form rollers.
- Be sure all ink rollers are adjusted and operating properly.
- Go to another press.

Mottle

Mottle is irregular and unwanted variation in color or gloss caused by uneven absorbency of the paper. It can usually be overcome by increasing or decreasing the body of the ink so that all of the ink is held out by the sheet or so that all of it is absorbed by the sheet. It is only when the ink body is just right to show differences in sheet absorbency that mottle becomes a problem.

In general, the heavier the paper, the greater the variation in absorbency. Mottle is seldom found on uncoated book paper, only occasionally on cover stock, and frequently on carton board.

Variations in binder migration in paper coatings sometimes create mottle on coated papers. Like the ink, the binder detects differences in paper formation or absorbency and exaggerates small differences in the base stock.

Overprint Varnishes

An overprint varnish, used for protection as well as gloss, contains the following materials:
- Pigment: none; sometimes clay for viscosity control
- Varnish: linseed, tung oil alkyd, phenolic resin
- Drier: cobalt and manganese
- Modifier: wax

Overprint varnishes are inks without any pigment. The ideal overprint varnish is colorless and transparent, yielding good gloss and scuff resistance when dry. Overprint varnishes also must be stable on the press, dry rapidly, and adhere well to the print.

Water-based varnishes, or coatings, may be applied on the last unit of a multicolor sheetfed press. To apply the coating, the inking system is disconnected and the varnish is applied directly to the blanket from a coater, a specially designed dampening system is used, or a roller coater is attached to the delivery end of the press. These water-based varnishes consist of emulsions of acrylic resins. They form films very rapidly after they are applied to the print, and varnished pieces can be cut or folded a few minutes after printing.

Varnishes for ultraviolet drying can be applied similarly, then dried with an ultraviolet lamp to give a surface that is resistant to scuffing, water, and most solvents.

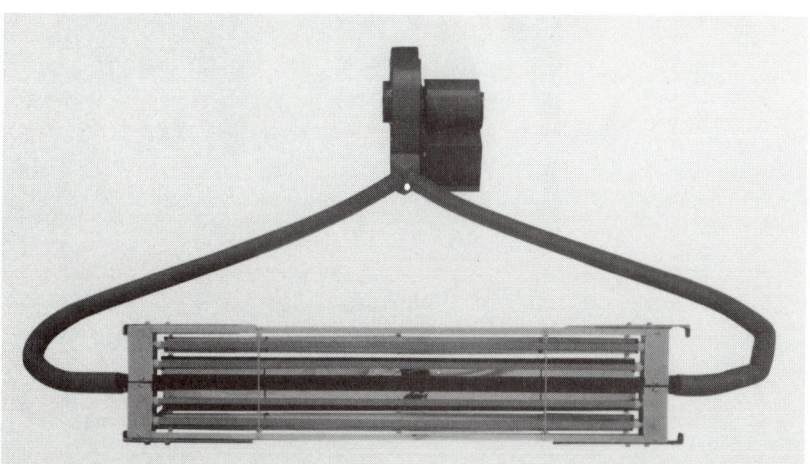

An infrared dryer
Courtesy AMJO, Incorporated

If an ink will be overprinted with a varnish, the inkmaker must be informed so that the ink can be formulated to be varnish-resistant. If it is not, the ink could bleed through the varnish.

Tower coater/perfector located between the last printing unit and the delivery on a Miehle-Roland sheetfed press
Courtesy Graphic Systems Div., Rockwell International

A Cotordry coating unit on a Miller TP-104 sheetfed press

11 Premakeready

Premakeready encompasses more than just those procedures that are performed to shorten makeready time and prevent downtime on the press. It also includes seemingly unrelated tasks that contribute to a press crew's productivity. Layout, tools, materials, teamwork, training, and inking and dampening system washup are the principal features of premakeready.

Printing Plant Layout

The layout of the printing plant, although apparently not related to premakeready, helps to reduce downtime and increases efficiency.

Space Allocation

When a printing plant is constructed or remodeled, several layout problems challenge management. Every operational station, including printing presses, must be properly positioned in the plant, with its location determined by its position in the sequence of normal operations. Each operational area must be allocated the proper amount of space, depending on the size of the equipment, the work area needed, and the amount of supplies stored in the area.

The space provided for a press depends on the type of press, the type of work to be printed, the pressroom turnover, the amount of paper that must be stored near the press, and several other factors.

Three-dimensional plant layout system
Courtesy Harris Corporation

Accessibility of Tools

Convenience is an important consideration in laying out a pressroom. Each press station should have a complete set of small tools, instruments, parts, and supplies that are not shared with any other station. Although sharing expensive items that are only used occasionally is practical, small often-used tools must be within easy reach. Operators should never have to walk two or three stations away to obtain the necessary tool.

Floor Layout and Aisles

Aisles between presses must be wide enough to permit a forklift truck to move paper from the storeroom to the feeder section of the press, and to move printed paper from the delivery to the bindery or shipping dock if it is going to an outside bindery.

Floor space is expensive and must be used efficiently. Access requirements, including room for efficient truck operation, and the floor load rating, which is stated in pounds per square foot (or metric units), should also be considered when allotting floor space.

Using a standard, single-size paper pallet permits the standardization of material handling equipment and makes better use of floor space. Safety and efficient stock retrieval are two other considerations in plant layout. Once available storage spaces and aisles have been determined, a good, long-wearing paint or tape should be used to clearly mark these areas. Trucks should be confined to aisles that are wide enough for maneuvering. Well-defined aisles and storage spaces make housekeeping easier.

Tools

Tools and measuring instruments that are needed for the next pressrun should be gathered while the present pressrun is still in progress, *not* during makeready. Often, crew members are idle at certain points during a pressrun. When not needed at the press, they can start gathering the tools and materials for the next job. This decreases downtime during makeready.

The numerous tools and measuring instruments required for makeready should be stored near the press. Some of the more important ones are listed below:

- Torque wrench, for tightening the blanket
- Assorted wrenches, for making press adjustments
- Dead-weight micrometer, for measuring packing, plates, and blankets
- Packing gauge, for measuring plate and blanket heights on the press
- Magnifiers, for checking dot structure
- Densitometer, for measuring the density of the ink

During premakeready, the packing, plates, and blankets can be measured with the dead-weight micrometer.

Materials

Stock Control

If stock control is poor or if the purchasing procedure is poor, the pressroom may run out of many small items from time to time. Each time, however, the press sits idle. Unfortunately, these missing items are not discovered until makeready, and an hour or two of press time is lost. As a consequence, the schedule is upset and overtime is necessary to get back on schedule.

Paper

Paper handling plays an important role in reducing press downtime. Preconditioning paper to the conditions in the pressroom is a part of premakeready.

Paper must arrive in the pressroom early enough to become temperature-conditioned. The press crew should not have to try out a pile of paper on the press to find out if it works. On multicolor or close-register jobs, the crew can spend hours of makeready time trying to get a poor sheet to fit. This generally happens when the paper goes through the press the second time, and the first-down color has fanned out across the back. It is too late to do anything about the paper then.

The moisture content of paper can be tested with a sword hygroscope. The pressroom should be air-conditioned, and its relative humidity controlled.

The paper must be inspected and tested before makeready begins. Wavy-edged paper can be detected as soon as the skid is unwrapped. The pH of the coating could be measured, and the straightness of the gripper edge checked.

Inks

There is no economy in purchasing inexpensive inks if they cause problems on the press. An ink that lacks color strength has to be printed in such a thick ink film that dampening and plate problems occur. Inks should be tested, adjusted, and color-matched long before makeready time.

Blankets, Dampeners, and Rollers

Spare blankets, dampeners, and at least one spare roller set should be on hand at the press at all times. The spare blankets should be prepunched, if needed, and premounted in bars. The spare dampeners should be washed or re-covered; i.e., press-ready. The condition of press rollers should be monitored continually.

The way blankets are handled has a marked effect on press downtime. Blankets should be alternated so that one can rest while another is used. When a bad smash occurs, it is easier and faster to replace the blanket than to repair it. A moderately smashed blanket can usually be salvaged by soaking the fabric side of the blanket in water for several hours or days.

Blankets must be cleaned and deglazed every time they are removed from the press. Only the washup solution recommended by the blanket manufacturer should be used to ensure chemical compatibility and blanket longevity.

Packing

Packing sheets should be hard, smooth, water-resistant, easy-handling, and cut to the size of the plate. They should be kept separate according to caliper (thickness); a separate shelf for each thickness is desirable. If the press crew has to look around the pressroom for packing sheets, determine their caliper, and cut them to size while the press waits, makereadies will be very costly.

Soft, limp papers should not to be used. They contain so much air that accurate packing is impossible because the sheets compress excessively. Only specially produced packing sheets or Mylar®-like plastics should be used to pack a printing press.

Material Testing and Reporting

The practice of material testing and reporting is not as far removed from premakeready as it may appear. For example, a plate that performs poorly during the start of a job can cause considerable press downtime.

Manufacturers test materials, but press operators must also test these products to determine if they perform in accordance with their own standards. A product may work fine in plant A but fail miserably the first time it is tried in plant B. The personnel in plant B may have to reuse the product several times to find out why it failed. This type of problem occurred when paper dampener covers were introduced and when presensitized plates were introduced. This problem probably occurs, to varying degrees, whenever a new product is introduced.

When something is new, it is usually different in some way and probably requires a change in handling technique. Therefore, a period of training, learning, and experimenting is needed. However, retraining or experimenting should not be done on production jobs.

Many large plants have established quality control laboratories for testing incoming inks, paper, and other materials. Quality control personnel also monitor jobs in progress, the performance of new materials, and the performance of equipment. Sometimes, small presses have been installed in the quality control laboratory for testing, because even a small offset press can yield valuable product-performance information.

Pretesting as a part of premakeready. The pretesting of new materials is recommended. Any pretesting of materials constitutes premakeready because of the potential reduction of press downtime. Pretesting, whether performed on a small press or by some other means, provides information about the performance of plates, paper, ink, blankets, blanket cleaners, washup materials, and various other printing materials. All testing and experimenting should be done where and when it is inexpensive, which means that production should not be interrupted.

Controlling the quality of materials. GATF's Technical Services Report 7227, *Controlling the Quality of Pressroom Materials,* gives printers a variety of recommendations on how to reduce variation and defects in purchased materials by controlling plate, blankets, rollers, paper, ink, solvents, and lubricants. Control must be exercised in selection and purchase; receiving, handling, and inspection; proper storage; and proper use, including an accurate record of performance. The real differences between a testing laboratory and a production floor atmosphere must be recognized.

According to the Technical Services Report, there are five basics of quality control for management:

- **Standardization.** Management should standardize on a few suppliers and select materials on the basis of performance, delivery, and cost.
- **Specifications.** Specifications should be established for materials before an order is placed, and these specifications must be communicated to the supplier.
- **Inspection.** Inspection of incoming materials for verification of size, quantity, and/or weight and the detection of external damage is necessary. Some inspecting and testing are performed in the pressroom.
- **Proper handling and storage.** A first-in, first-out inventory system should be used, to prevent newer materials from being used before older, dated material such as inks and plates. Remember also that careless handling ruins materials.

- **Recordkeeping.** Records should be kept on the conditions and performance of materials. This is essential in providing feedback to suppliers. Records not only help the printer confirm the existence of defects and deviations from specifications but also help the supplier resolve problems in the manufacture of the material.

Inking and Dampening System Washup

The washup belongs to and is charged to the job that dirtied the press. But a *good* washup is considered a part of premakeready. A poor washup causes glazed rollers and other printing problems. A poor washup can mean that a makeready has to be stopped just to wash up a press unit again.

Rollers do not transfer ink properly if they are glazed. Controlling inking and dampening is troublesome. Obtaining a quality OK sheet is difficult—and maintaining the quality is even harder.

A good method of washup keeps rollers in a like new condition for a long time. A good washup is also a clean washup so that fresh color will not be contaminated by old ink left on the rollers. Fortunately, on four-color presses, there is seldom a change in color on any one unit, but that is no reason to get careless with washups.

A good washup not only lessens the buildup of glaze on rollers but also prevents hickeys caused by dried ink particles. These particles come from the ink fountain, roller ends where dried ink has built up, and small cracks in a glazed roller's surface. Good washup techniques eliminate most hickey problems of this type.

The same general idea holds for the dampening system. It is easier, safer, and less time-consuming to keep the dampening system in good order than to wait until a problem occurs.

Teamwork

The operative word in the term "press crew" is "crew." Like the pit crew in racing, each member of a press crew should have certain clearly defined responsibilities and the necessary training to perform these responsibilities efficiently and effectively.

Downtime is reduced if each crew member is assigned specific duties. They must know exactly what to do, how to do it, and, just as importantly, when to do it. Any duties that can be performed during running time should be done then. These duties then become a part of premakeready.

Such duties as policing the workstation, getting supplies, and replenishing all receptacles are important but are not done during the time periods reserved for makeready or washup. Putting away makeready and washup equipment and supplies is most efficiently performed during running time. Preparing new blankets, checking stock, transporting stock to the pressroom, adjusting ink, mixing dampening solution, cleaning platforms, and reracking tools are only a few of the things that can be done while the press is running. The greater the number of duties that are performed while the press is running, the more systematic the washup and makeready are.

Training

Press crew training is a part of premakeready. Print quality is a function of the overall quality of the press crew; it is no better than that of the poorest trained crew member. Each crew member must become thoroughly familiar with his or her specific duties and the proper timing for these duties.

Any method of handling a press crew so that the crew works efficiently is a good method. The head press operator should assign specific duties and responsibilities to each crew member in writing. In addition, the head press operator specifies when to perform each duty. Thus, each crew member is aware of the "what" and "when" of efficient press operation.

New crew members may have learned press operating in school or on a small offset press. However, they cannot be expected to function smoothly immediately upon becoming part of a crew for a large sheetfed offset press. Each crew member below the rating of first press operator can be considered as a worker in training, with the head press operator functioning as an instructor. The head press operator does not have to be responsible for all instruction but must supervise. The second person in command learns from the head press operator and teaches the third in command. In turn, the third in command instructs the person in the fourth position, and so on until all crew members are trained in performing their duties. In other words, each crew member is coached by the person immediately superior.

New crew members are encouraged to read the press operating manual. It is also beneficial for new crew members to attend in-plant or school training courses. Reading articles in trade magazines and books on press operating helps to prepare the individual for the next job position. Learning about ink, paper, plates, and other materials makes the crew member a better problem-solver, if and when a problem occurs on press.

Scheduling

Proper scheduling of jobs is an important factor in plant efficiency. Without proper scheduling, time is lost all through the plant, but especially in the high hourly-rate pressroom.

The schedule should start in the control office and carry right through to shipping. Every department then knows what is coming, when it will arrive, and when it should be completed.

Most important of all, proper scheduling ensures the procurement of paper and ink for each job in time for the press to be made ready. It ensures ample time for paper inspection, cutting, and conditioning. It provides time for ink matching and testing and for arrival at the plant. It ensures that all plates will be ready when needed. Proper scheduling may even eliminate some press washups if the press operators know which ink is to be used on the next printing job.

The time to think about the next job is while the press is running for the current one. The head press operator or a designated crew member should check the next job and find out the following:

- What the job order says
- What the next job number is
- If the plates are ready
- If the paper has been conditioned and piled
- If the ink is ready to be used
- If there are any waste sheets that can be used to set up the press
- If there is a spare blanket available and ready to use
- If the packing supply is sufficient to pack the press for the next job

Summary

Work smarter, not harder. Premakeready operations reduce downtime. Practically all preparatory steps taken in the pressroom help to reduce downtime if the press is running. These include getting all supplies from the storeroom and replenishing workstation cabinets, taking care of waste sheets that can be used on future jobs, and checking tools and equipment that will be used on the next washup and makeready.

With a little thought, the head press operator can make a list that includes many more things than those that have been mentioned here. Everything from the finishing of one job to obtaining an OK on the next job should be listed. The list can be enlarged to include all pressroom work. It may take a week or two and the cooperation of the press crew to get a complete list, but once the list is prepared, it is a great help in writing job descriptions, assigning duties to the crew, arranging a training program, and separating makeready steps from premakeready operations.

12 Makeready

Makeready is the series of operations that changes the press over from one job to the next. Makeready ends when acceptable press sheets enter the delivery of the sheetfed press.

The press crew's responsibilities during makeready differ from plant to plant. Efficient makeready requires that materials for the next job are already on hand when the previous job ends. Following a premakeready program, as described in Chapter 11, is the only way this can occur.

Good preparation for makeready means having all necessary materials at the printing units at the time they are needed. Plates should be packed, blankets laid out and ready to go on the press, and packing cut and ready to go under the blankets. Paper, ink, and dampening solution should be ready. If a need for a color change arises, washup materials should be waiting at the press.

The key to efficient makeready is a press crew that knows its job and works together as a team. Each member of the crew should be fully occupied during makeready. Responsibility for this rests with the head press operator, who must know how to organize and supervise the crew. Each member of a well-organized crew should know what to do and when to do it. For example, two persons might work as a team in changing plates and blankets, a procedure made even more efficient if another crew member can hand the plates, blankets, and packing to the two persons working in the unit.

What Is Makeready?

Makeready is a term describing all of the operations necessary to get the press ready for the present job. Once acceptable printed sheets are being produced, makeready ends. During this period, paper is being "wasted" out of necessity. Therefore, waste can be minimized by completing the makeready as quickly as possible. The press is then raised to running speed in a series of steps—and the actual pressrun begins.

Types of Makeready

Makeready can be divided into three categories: simple makeready, partial makeready, and full makeready.

Simple makeready occurs most often when printing books or forms on a single-color press. It consists of just a plate change. Other variables such as the ink, ink fountain settings, dampening system settings, and type and size of paper are unchanged.

Partial makeready occurs on single- and two-color presses that are printing four-color work. After the first two colors are printed, the press is stopped, and inking systems are cleaned. New plates are installed; blankets and packing may or may not be changed. The delivery is unloaded and the feeder is loaded, but feeder, guide, or delivery settings are not changed. The inking system is washed up, and the ink fountain is refilled and reset for the new color.

The most common type of makeready is the full makeready, which consists of all steps necessary to start an entirely new job. On single- and two-color presses, the entire press is washed up; a washup of the inking system on a four-color press is usually unnecessary if the same four inks will be used in the same color sequence. (A press/inking system washup is usually chargeable to the previous job.) Plates and packing are changed, and blankets are washed. Feeder, guide, and delivery settings are usually changed. The feeder is reloaded, and the delivery is emptied.

Makeready Procedures

The order in which a makeready progresses is largely dependent on the press crew's preferences. However, developing and following an established makeready procedure is strongly advised. In any analysis of pressrun time versus downtime (makeready, scheduled preventive maintenance, and unscheduled delays), the productivity of the press can be improved only if press downtimes are shortened; pressrun time cannot be shortened if the press is already operating at the maximum speed that produces prints of the desired quality. Therefore, better planning, improved preventive maintenance, precise control of all prepress operations, and coordinated use of the press crew reduce press downtime and improve productivity.

Of the four methods for reducing downtime, only better planning and coordinated use of the press crew are controlled by the press crew. This is where the "pit stop" concept of makeready comes into focus—like the pit crew for a racing car, the operating crew of a press must be prepared to service the machine as quickly and efficiently as possible. In the first case, the improved efficiency gets the racing car back on the track quicker; in the second case, it gets the press operating at full speed quicker. With the "pit stop" concept of press makeready, each crew member has specific, clearly identified responsibilities.

Makeready consists of the following steps:
1. Prepare the press for the new pressrun.
2. Check copy, plates, paper, and ink against instructions.
3. Set sheet-handling mechanisms.
4. Pack and mount the plates.
5. Check and prepare new blankets (if necessary).
6. Prepare the dampening system.
7. Prepare the inking system.
8. Prepare the makeready "books" for printing.
9. Make trial impressions.
10. Examine the trial impressions.
11. Make necessary adjustments to image position/register, impression quality, and color.

Steps 9–11 are repeated until a press sheet that is acceptable to the customer is produced. This press sheet is usually called the **okay,** or **OK, sheet.**

Many of the procedures followed during makeready are covered in detail in earlier chapters of this book.

Preparing the Press for the New Pressrun

Before makeready begins, the press is prepared for the new pressrun. The paper from the previous job is removed from the delivery, and plates are removed and stored for possible reuse. Damaged blankets are also removed. If there are any color changes, the inking system is also washed up. The dampening system may also have to be cleaned.

Inking system washup. Routine washups usually involve a two-step solution. The first solvent is water-miscible and removes contaminants, gum, and alcohol substitutes; the second solvent flushes away the first solvent, leaving the rollers with no solvent residue. Special attention should be given to roller ends, where ink builds up and cakes during running. **Caution:** *Do not clean roller ends or any part of the inking system by hand while the press is operating.* A good reconditioning washup will make it possible to change from black to yellow with no problem of residual color. The roller manufacturer can recommend suitable two-step washup solutions. Make sure the manufacturer supplies a Material Safety Data Sheet (MSDS) with each chemical solution purchased; an MSDS provides detailed information on use, handling, and storage of chemicals.

Although the actual solvents vary, two-step washup solutions perform the same functions. One solution cuts the dried ink and liquefies the wet ink, causing pigment particles

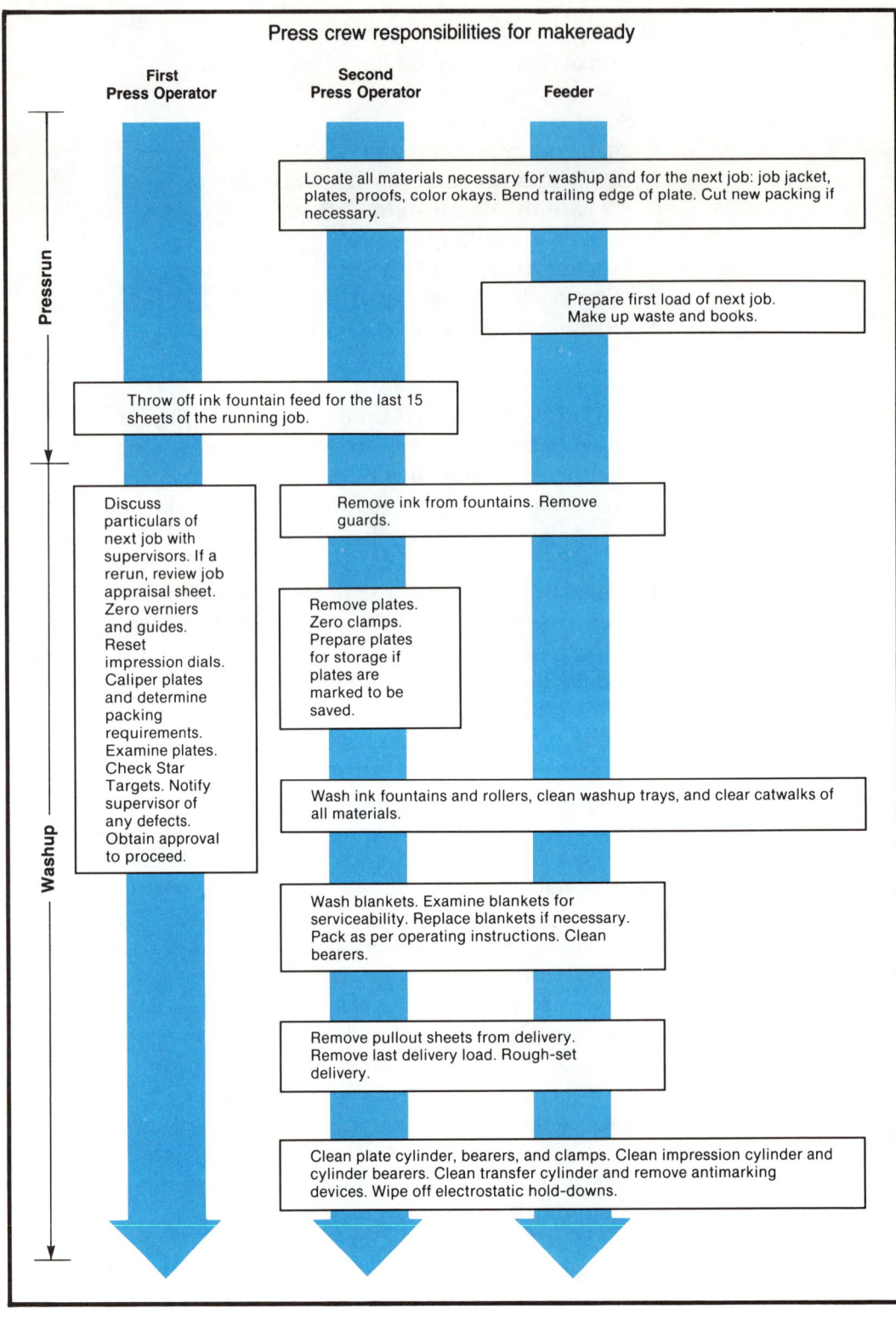

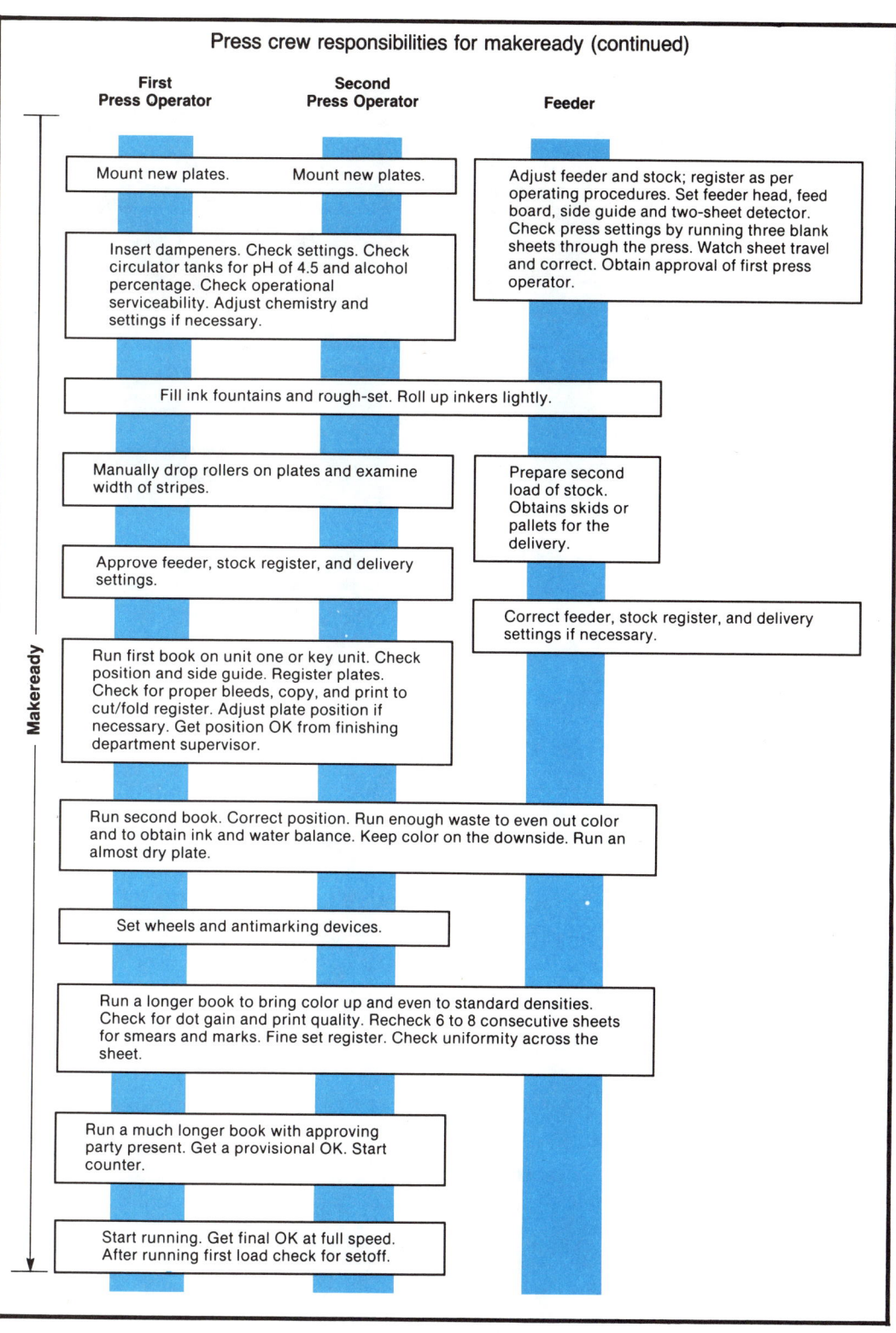

266 Sheetfed Offset Press Operating

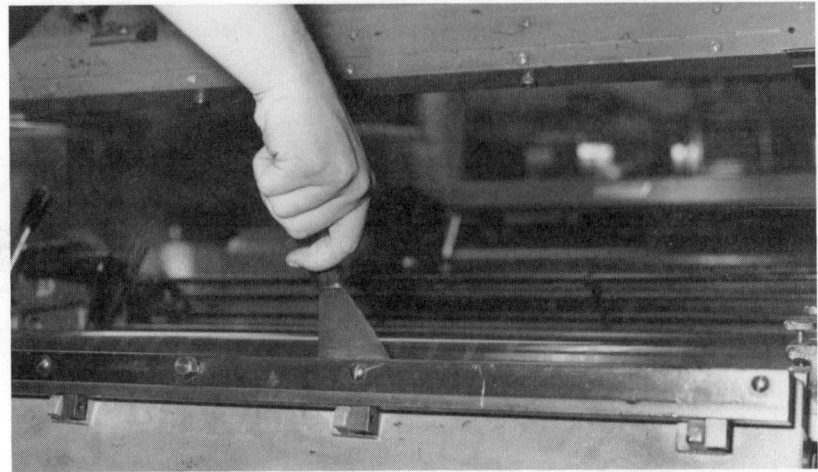

Press operator using an ink knife to remove ink from the ink fountain

Unused ink being returned to ink can

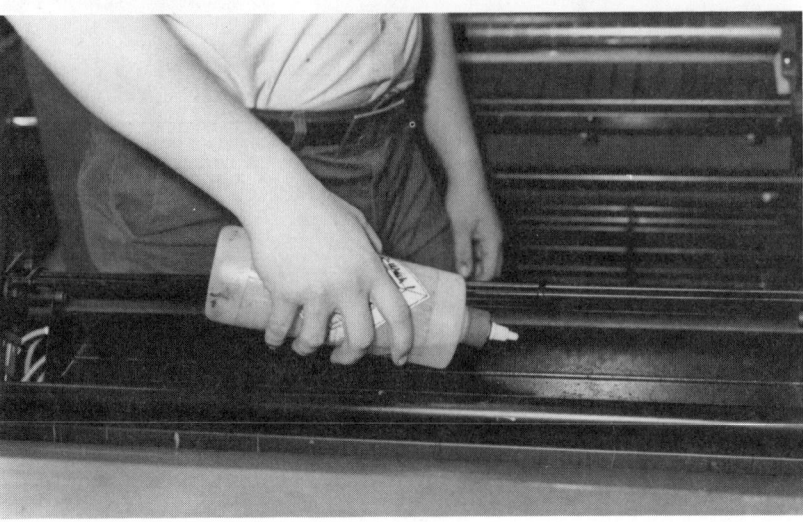

Press operator squirting washup solvent on the surface of the ink fountain roller

to dissolve. These particles are carried down through the rollers to the washup machine. Water is then used to remove dried gum. Between each step, or in a separate final step, the inking system is rinsed to remove all traces of these solutions.

The solvents in a two-step washup solution must be used in their correct order because they are designed to work in a specific sequence. Never substitute solvents when using a two-step washup solution.

To remove ink, the press operator attaches a washup machine to the press. After use, the blade and pan of the washup machine are thoroughly cleaned. A washup machine does a thorough job of cleaning the rollers, but the press operator must learn the difference between rollers that look clean and rollers that are clean.

On most presses, at one end of the ink fountain is a throw-off handle that raises the fountain roller away from the blade (or drops the fountain and blade away from the roller) and holds them apart for easy cleaning. A rag soaked with solvent is used to remove the remaining ink in the fountain. All parts of the fountain coming into contact with the ink should be thoroughly cleaned. A good washup routine includes cleaning the edge and as much of the underside of the blade as can be reached.

The copperizing of steel inking rollers is often made part of the reconditioning washup. Copperizing solutions deposit a thin layer of copper on the roller and make the roller more resistant to stripping. Copperizing requires that the roller be very clean, so the most appropriate time to do it is during the reconditioning washup.

The durometer of rollers should be checked regularly (once a month). The information is used to determine whether the rollers need to be reconditioned or replaced. If the maximum recommended durometer has been exceeded, the roller should be removed from the press and placed in a reconditioning wash. If the roller still exceeds the maximum, it should be reground or re-covered.

Cleaning the dampening system. Ordinarily, ink solvents are not used to clean the dampening system, though they can be used to clean some types of paper coverings. Cloth covers, which retain ink solvents, should only be cleaned with suitable detergents, then thoroughly rinsed.

Changing cloth covers is so time-consuming that the crew should have an extra set ready to go on the press at all times.

The dirty rollers can be cleaned and changed during the pressrun. Cloth covers must be carefully mounted. If the cover has a seam, it should be straight. The cover should be uniformly tight along the roller length, and there should be equal amounts of overhang at each end. When tied, the ends should be flat—not rounded off.

Whenever a roller is removed from the press, it should be reinstalled with the ends in the same direction. Reversing the ends of the roller causes the roller to rotate in the opposite direction and causes a paper sleeve or cloth cover to creep.

Regardless of the type of cover used, changing dampener covers changes the running diameter of the rollers. Consequently, roller settings should be rechecked and adjustments made where necessary.

Preparing plates for storage. With some types of plates, any press shutdown longer than a few minutes requires that the plates be gummed. A gum arabic coating prevents the surface of the plate from oxidizing, which can lead to scumming. A gummed plate generally starts up more rapidly than an untreated plate. Gumming a plate for storage while it is still mounted on the plate cylinder is difficult because of the restricted work space on most presses. By giving the mounted plate a quick gumming, the crew can finish gumming the plate later (e.g., during the next pressrun) by placing the plate on a large worktable.

The plate manufacturer can recommend suitable materials for cleaning and preserving the plate. Combinations of gum, asphaltum, and solvent are commercially available as plate washout solutions. Gum arabic in an 8–10° Bé solution is used to make nonprinting areas on the plate water-receptive. The solvent removes ink from the image, and the asphaltum provides a nonhardening ink-receptive surface on the image.

Usually, the press-mounted plate is first wiped with a sponge that has been dampened with gum in a water solution. The entire surface of the plate should then be rubbed down evenly with a soft, damp cloth. When the gum is applied in reasonable amounts, it does not cover the greasy image areas of the plate still carrying ink. When overapplied, the gum adheres to image areas in such a thick coating that it becomes impervious to solvent.

Once the gum has dried into a thin, even film, the plate is wiped with a solvent to remove ink from image areas and is covered with paper to protect it from scratches.

Checking Instructions

The copy, plates, paper, and ink are checked against the instructions written on the work order. Any differences must be immediately brought to the pressroom supervisor's attention. Usually, the instructions should be checked before the previous pressrun ends as part of the premakeready procedure.

Setting Sheet-Handling Mechanisms

Setting the sheet-handling mechanisms is a time-consuming operation. If paper size and thickness have changed, practically all settings are adjusted. The nature of the work also influences the adjustments required. Chapter 5, "Sheet Control," discusses these adjustments in detail. The following sequence is representative of the steps involved in setting the sheet-handling mechanisms when paper stock has changed:

1. Position the feed table and load paper stock onto the press.

2. Adjust the various components of the sheet-separation unit: pile height regulator, sheet steadiers, separator brushes and fingers, rear pickup suckers, forwarding suckers, and air-blast nozzles.

3. Adjust the various components of the feedboard: forwarding rollers, double-sheet detector, feedboard devices that transport the sheets to the front guides (e.g., hold-down rollers, feed tapes, and brushes), suction devices, and early and late sheet detectors.

4. Adjust front guides and side guides.

5. Set infeed grippers and impression-cylinder stops.
If necessary, compensate for fan-out of images on the press sheet by following the press manufacturer's recommendations.

6. Set the impression cylinder pressure relative to the stock thickness.

7. Feed a sheet through the press and set the sheet joggers, delivery-assist devices (sheet slow-downs), and gripper release timing.

These steps are repeated until the sheet passes through the press smoothly. Additional minor adjustments to the side guide and feeder pile position are necessary to get image register, which occurs later.

Installing the Plate

Procedures used to mount the plates vary considerably, depending on the size of the press crew. In many cases, one crew member hands plates to another who is stationed between printing units mounting them. No matter which procedure is used, all members of the crew must know how to safely use the **inch** controls of the press.

The basic operations (most of which are discussed in detail in chapter 8, "Plates") are as follows:

1. Check the work order for the proper plates to be mounted.

2. Inspect the plate for quality and proper copy.

3. Measure the plate caliper (or thickness) with a micrometer, determine packing requirements, and prepare the packing. (If a print length adjustment is required, make the necessary compensation in packing. Chapter 6, "Packing and Printing Pressures," discusses print length.)

4. Check that the plate cylinder and the back of the plate are clean. Adjust the plate cylinder and plate clamps to their starting or zero positions.

5. Mount plate and packing on the press, following the procedure in Chapter 8.

These three things must be remembered when mounting plates:

- Insert the correct packing.
- Make sure that the tension on all screws is set uniformly and that the plate conforms to the cylinder.
- Align the plate with any preregister marks.

Occasionally, it is necessary to reposition a mounted plate to a predetermined position by twisting or cocking it. If the printed image is not exactly square in relation to the paper or previously printed colors, the plate must be repositioned. It is always better to reposition the plate than to adjust the front guides. The basic procedure of cocking a printing plate follows:

1. If the press does not have preregister marks, extend a pencil line from the plate to the cylinder body or gutter.

2. Determine how much the plate must be cocked to make the image square on the press sheet. Draw a new mark on the cylinder body or gutter. **Caution:** Cocking a plate excessively could damage the plate.

3. Release the trailing clamp tension bolts so that the plate can be pulled forward on the desired side.

4. Use the side bolts to push the trailing clamp sideways one-third the distance that the plate needs to be drawn forward.

5. Tighten the leading clamp tension bolts to draw the positioning marks into alignment.

6. Tighten the trailing clamp tension bolts.

Preparing New Blankets

Changing blankets and packing is not required on all makereadies. But, on a long-run, four-color job or any job demanding high quality, it can be a costly mistake to start up with damaged blankets on the press.

Blankets contaminated with ink must be scrubbed until they are immaculate. If any low spots have developed during the previous pressrun, the blanket should be replaced. A good time to determine if a blanket has any low spots is after the previous job is completed but before the inking system has been washed up. Simply gum and dry the plate, and then roll it up solid and print to paper. Depressions will be immediately noticeable.

Chapter 7, "Blankets," discusses blankets, blanket care, and mounting procedures in detail. Following is a summary of those procedures:

1. After removing the old blanket, clean the body of the cylinder and wipe off the bearers.

2. Lock the leading edge of the blanket into place, and insert the calculated amount of packing beneath the blanket. Work the packing slightly into the cylinder gap to prevent it from creeping while the press is running.

3. Slowly inch the press until the trailing edge can be locked in the trailing clamps. While the press is inching, maintain tension on the blanket. Lock the trailing edge into the trailing clamps, and use a torque wrench to tighten the reel mechanism to provide proper blanket tension.

Preparing the Dampening System

The following sequence is representative of the steps involved in preparing the conventional dampening system during makeready. The sequence varies somewhat with continuous-flow dampening systems.

1. Install clean roller covers where required.

2. Measure and adjust the dampener roller pressures, if necessary.

3. Prepare the dampening solution according to the manufacturer's directions.

4. Measure dampening solution pH and conductivity levels, and adjust the dampening solution until the proper operating levels are obtained. The proper pH and conductivity levels depend on plate, paper, and ink variables. The water used to prepare the dampening solution has a major impact on the solution's pH and conductivity.

5. Turn on the circulating pumps, and fill the fountain pan or circulating tanks with dampening solution.

6. Adjust the dwell of the ductor roller on the fountain roller to govern the amount of water transferred to the oscillator.

7. Set ductor and fountain roller controls for the pressrun. (These are only initial settings.)

With a continuous-flow dampening system, a typical procedure might include the following steps. However, since each manufacturer's dampening system starts up differently, refer to the manufacturer's instructions.

1. Mix fountain solution in a separate container. Add isopropyl alcohol in the minimum percentage necessary for the system to operate properly. Fill the circulating tanks with the solution, and turn on the circulating pumps to fill the fountain pan.

2. Turn on the system's drive motors. Check that the metering roller is engaging with its drive gear. Adjust each printing unit's dampening control to the normal operating speed.

3. Make preliminary adjustments to the metering roller. Adjust the metering roller until it almost touches the chrome roller on each end. Tighten the adjustment screws on the gear and operator's sides until the heavy film of water disappears, and then tighten the screws an additional one-half or three-quarters turn. The metering roller must be parallel to adjust the overall feed evenly. Some metering rollers can be skewed to adjust dampening; therefore, refer to the press manual for initial setting of such a roller.

4. Adjust the speed of the chrome roller, which controls the amount of water delivered to the plate. The speed of this roller is adjusted during the pressrun to compensate for temperature changes, humidity variations, alcohol evaporation, and ink drying problems.

Preparing the Inking System

Chapter 3, "The Inking System," discusses the inking system, roller settings, inking problems, maintenance, and a basic operating procedure, which consists of the following principal steps:

1. Check the work order for the proper ink to be used. Mix ink to customer's specifications, if necessary.

2. Supply ink to ink fountain, and adjust ink flow from the fountain roller to the ductor roller. With the ductor roller and fountain roller contacting, rotate the fountain roller several times. Adjust the ink fountain keys to deposit a light, even film of ink on the ductor roller.

3. Ink the rollers in the ink train by starting the press. Use the image on the plate to determine how much ink should print across the press sheet, and adjust individual inking keys accordingly.

4. Set the swing (amount of rotation) to a 50% stroke, and set the speed of the fountain roller.

A large number of presses are now equipped with remote control consoles. If the press is also equipped with a plate scanner, the plate is scanned, and the readings obtained directly for the plate are used to automatically preset the inking fountain keys. If the press does not have a plate scanner, place the printing plate on the console, estimate the inking requirements at each point across the plate, and set the inking accordingly. Always keep the keys of a segmented blade open a little, even if the plate requires no inking in that area. A minimum ink flow is required to adequately lubricate the ink fountain roller.

The most common color sequence on a multicolor press, according to a recent survey by a major supplier, is black-cyan-magenta-yellow (KCMY), which is used over 80% of the time. CMYK is used 7% of the time, and YCMK is used 4% of the time.

Preparing the Makeready Book

The **makeready book** is a pile of press sheets consisting of both waste sheets (previously printed sheets) and clean, unprinted sheets. The ratio of clean sheets to waste sheets is typically 1:5. To make the book, cut the waste sheets to the same size as the clean, unprinted sheets. Insert 10 clean sheets between every 50 waste sheets. The completed book will have approximately 1,100 sheets; this number will vary depending on the complexity of the makeready. The makeready book is then placed on the feeder pile.

Making Trial Impressions

The press crew can now make the first trial impressions. The following is a general procedure:

1. Open the plate(s) with water to remove the gum, and turn on the press at a slow speed.

2. Turn on the dampening system, and check for even dampening on the printing plate.

3. Ink the printing plate. On a multicolor press without a preregister system, ink up only one plate at this time. Select a color other than yellow, because yellow is difficult to see on a white press sheet. If the press is equipped with a preregister system, all plates are inked up simultaneously.

4. Start the feeder. Put the press on impression and continue printing until the first trial press sheet ("unprinted sheet") exits the delivery. Inspect for proper sheet feeding, forwarding, and delivery.

5. Stop feeder, take press off impression, and disengage dampening system.

Sheets being removed from delivery for inspection

Examining the Trial Impressions

The trial impressions are inspected on a slightly inclined, flat surface. Examine for the following points in sequence:
- Position and/or register of image
- Quality of print
- Ink/water balance
- Color of print

The major point to inspect with the first trial impression is the position of the image, because the inking and dampening systems are not yet balanced.

Image register and position. The first trial impression is checked for image position. If only one color appears on this press sheet, the image is registered to the paper. Make sure that the image is positioned properly and squarely on the page. If the image is not properly positioned sideways, adjust the side guide and the pile position. If the image must be moved toward or away from the gripper edge, adjust the plate cylinder accordingly.

When the next trial impressions are made, one or more of the other printing units are put on impression. These images are registered to each other, not to the paper as was done with the first trial impression. All colors are registered to the image made by the color that was also used for the first trial impression. The side guide can no longer be adjusted to get image register. Therefore, all position changes must be made by moving the printing cylinders or cocking the printing plate, if the images are not square with each other. Packing may have to be transferred from plate to blanket to get image fit if image length has changed.

If all colors are printed on the first trial sheet, the colors are registered to each other and to the paper.

Quality of print. The quality of the impression on the earlier trials is unlikely to be correct. The two principal quality defects that can be identified from these early trial impressions are an **overall weak print,** due to excessive dampening or insufficient ink, and a **heavy print,** due to excessive inking. Other problems include scumming and filling in of halftones, mottling, grainy prints, sheets that stick to the blanket, and excessive sheet curl in the delivery. Most of these problems have a common cause—incorrect inking and dampening. Therefore, the press operator must identify the proper cause and adjust the inking and dampening accordingly, while attempting to obtain ink/water balance at the lowest possible level. If the image is not transferring properly from the blanket, the squeeze pressures between blanket and impression cylinder must be rechecked and adjusted as necessary.

Color of print. Once images are properly positioned and the impression quality is acceptable, the press operator must adjust the inking system until the color of the print is acceptable.

The press sheet must be viewed under standard lighting conditions (5,000 K). The color proof supplied with the job guides the press operator in making adjustments to the inking system. (An improperly prepared color proof will be impossible to match on the press.)

All multicolor jobs should have a color control bar, such as the GATF Compact Color Test Strip, printed in the trim area along the trailing edge of the press sheet. The press operator uses a densitometer to measure the densities of the solid process-color patches. (The two- and three-color overprint solids can be used to check trapping of the last-down ink over the previous-down ink.) Most printing companies have established standard ink densities for the pressroom, such as yellow, 0.95 ± 0.05, magenta, 1.30 ± 0.05, cyan, 1.30 ± 0.05, and black 1.60 ± 0.10 for coated paper. (These densities, measured using a wide-band densitometer, are for example only; they should not be assumed to be applicable to all printing presses and all ink sets.) Setting ink fountains according to established reference values by means of a reflection densitometer enables achieving faster fine adjustment of ink using fewer sheets. When a computer-controlled scanning densitometer or plate scanner is used, the color OK can occur quicker because these devices indicate the relative amounts of inking required across the press sheet.

Since each horizontal position across the press sheet has different inking needs, the inking keys must be set according to those ink needs. In other words, the press operator must open up the keys in areas requiring additional ink and close the keys in areas requiring less ink. A graph (or profile) of inking across a press sheet has high points (indicating areas of great ink demand) and low points (indicating areas of little or no ink demand, such as the unprinted trim areas of the press sheet).

Press operator adjusting inking from a remote control console (Heidelberg CPC1)

Side-Guide Marks

A side-guide mark, fine vertical and horizontal lines about 6 in. (150 mm) back from the paper's gripper edge, allows the press operator to fan a series of sheets to determine if the side guide is properly functioning, overpulling, or underpulling. If the vertical line is on the edge of the sheet, the guide is functioning properly. If the line is in slightly from the edge, the guide is overpulling the paper. If the line is missing completely, the guide is underpulling.

The horizontal line of the side-guide mark allows the press operator to check the consistency of circumferential (gripper-to-tail) register. A similar horizontal line should be positioned on the opposite side of the press sheet to monitor gripper-to-tail register on that side of the sheet. Any misregister, caused by sheets bouncing out of the front guides, will show as a jagged line.

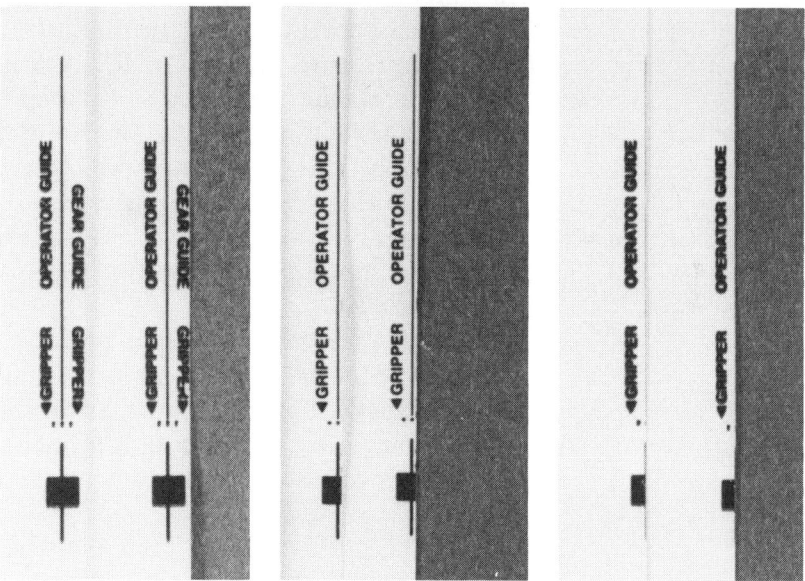

GATF Side-Guide Marks on a series of press sheets: excessive underpulling *(left)*, slight underpulling and circumferential misregister *(middle)*, and proper positioning on the edge of the sheet *(right)*

Usually, the side-guide mark is added to the printing plate during platemaking. However, if necessary, the press operator can scribe a side-guide mark on the plate after the completion of makeready.

The GATF Side-Guide Mark, one of four image control marks marketed by GATF, is available as a film negative or positive. The mark is a vertical line approximately ⅞ in. (22 mm) long with a 3/16-in. (5-mm) horizontal line. In film assembly, the side-guide mark is attached to the master marks flat (key sheet) so that it will print at the guide edge of the press sheet, and the plate is then exposed. During press makeready, the press operator adjusts the side guide until the vertical mark is positioned on the sheet edge so that half of the mark is bleeding off. By jogging several sheets on a square surface and then fanning them, the press operator can determine if the side guide is properly functioning.

If the printing plate does not have a side-guide mark, a mark can be scribed on the plate. The following method is one way of putting the mark on the plate:

1. After the image is in proper position on the sheet (i.e., makeready is complete), tap ink on the side edges of the paper about 6 in. away from the gripper edge. (This distance corresponds to the typical placement of the side guide in relation to the front guides.)

2. Place this inked sheet on the feeder pile and put six sheets of paper on top of it. Lock off the dampening and ink form rollers.

3. Run ten sheets of paper through the press under impression pressure. The ink marks will transfer from the paper to the blanket and then to the plate in exact register.

4. Align a plastic straightedge with the ink marks on the plate, and scribe a vertical line and a horizontal line on the guide side of the sheet and another horizontal line on the opposite side.

Another commonly used method for putting the mark on the plate follows:

1. After the image is in proper position on the sheet (i.e., makeready is complete), cut out a pie-shaped wedge on each side of the sheet about 6 in. away from the gripper edge. The wedge must be large enough to include at least an inch of image area to make it easier to register the press sheet to the plate.

2. Inch the press until the image on the plate is accessible. Tape the press sheet from step 1 in register over the plate.

3. Align a plastic straightedge with the edges of the taped press sheet, and scribe a vertical line and a horizontal line on the guide side of the sheet and another horizontal line on the opposite side.

13 The Pressrun

Once the pressrun starts, the press operator periodically removes press sheets from the press and compares them against the OK sheet and inspects them for various print defects, such as hickeys. In addition, the press operator double-checks the functioning of the press. For example, the press operator may have to make adjustments to the feeder during the pressrun. Perhaps, the pile is not rising fast enough, or the air flow that separates the top sheet from the rest of the pile is insufficient.

Inspection of Press Sheets

Periodically during the pressrun, the press operator removes—**pulls**—the most recently printed press sheets from the press delivery. Typically, one inspection sheet is pulled for each set of delivery grippers. For example, if the press has 10 sets of delivery grippers, 10 inspection sheets are pulled. Inspections are required every 10 min. or more frequently, depending on whether the printing is single-color or multicolor and the quality level.

In order to remove the set of inspection sheets, the press operator reaches into the delivery end of the operating press. Therefore, for obvious safety reasons, the press operator must be prohibited from wearing loose long hair, watches, rings, bracelets, or long-sleeved shirts. With most presses, whenever the front gate of the delivery is opened, a set of metal fingers extends into the delivery and catches the press sheet before it falls on the pile. This system allows the press operator to easily remove the required number of sheets from the top of the pile. When the front gate is closed, the fingers retract, allowing the printed sheets to drop on top of the paper pile again.

The set of pulled sheets are inspected either at the remote control console of the press or in a standard viewing booth where they are compared to the OK sheet and to each other. A reflection densitometer equipped with red, green, and blue filters; a $10\times-20\times$ magnifying glass for general work; and an illuminated $50\times$ magnifier for critical inspection of halftone dots are the three principal tools used during inspection.

It is not necessary to use the densitometer to measure ink densities on every set of inspection sheets; using the densitometer once for every 1,000 sheets is more common. A quality control color strip cut from an OK sheet is useful for visual comparison. Among the items checked during inspection are the following:

Press operator comparing an inspection sheet with the OK sheet

• **Positioning of side-guide marks** from one inspection sheet to the next. Fanning the sheets easily shows if the positioning is inconsistent. If the side guiding varies, the side guide mechanism and, perhaps, the paper pile may have to be adjusted.

• **Register and fit of the individual printed ink films.** If the problem is **misregister,** the side guide and plate cylinder may have to be adjusted. Most high-quality printers attempt to maintain register within one dot on a 150-line halftone. Even if the press is side-guiding properly, paper conditions such as tight or wavy edges, improper moisture balance, or poor paper trimming can cause misregister. A light table and a T square or a line-up table should be used to make sure that the images are straight. If the problem is **image fit,** packing must be transferred from the plate cylinder to the blanket cylinder, or vice versa, to compensate for dimensional changes in the paper. Unfortunately, fit problems can also be caused by platemaking and stripping errors, in which case the press superintendent must be consulted to determine if a new plate must be made.

• **Plugging of halftones.** Inking must be reduced.

• **Dry-up of the plate in nonimage area.** Dry-up occurs more frequently on the gear side of the press because that side is warmer. Dampening must be increased.

• **Excessive inking.** The finger rub test is an easy way to determine if inking is excessive. Lightly draw a finger over the wet ink on the inspection sheet. The drag of the ink on the finger and the amount of smudging are compared to that experienced on the wet OK sheet.

- **Presence of printing defects.** The most common printing defect is the hickey. The press may have to be stopped in order to remove the cause of the hickey from the plate, blanket, or inking form rollers. Additional print quality problems include dot doubling, excessive dot gain, and slur. Several film quality control devices, discussed later in this chapter, are available to monitor for the presence of these factors. Unwanted images in the nonimage area of the printing plate can be corrected using a deletion pen; defects in the image area usually require a new printing plate. GATF's *Solving Sheetfed Offset Press Problems* and *Solving Offset Ink Problems* textbooks offer remedies for various printing problems occurring in sheetfed printing.
- **Consistency of color, compared to the OK sheet.** Visually compare the colors in the corresponding blocks of the color control bar and corresponding image areas. Remember, however, that adjacent colors can affect how a certain color is

Tag inserted into pile to indicate start of makeready, start of pressrun, and sheets having defects

	Tail	
Color Off	**M K**	**C Y**
Too Light ☐	Too Dark ☐	Dry-up ☐
Setoff ☐	Wrinkled ☐	Misregister ☐
Scratch ☐	Tracking ☐	Hickey ☐
	Gripper	

(Gear — left side; Operator — right side)

Comments _____

_____

_____

☐ Other   ☐ Here Up   ☐ Here Down

perceived. Periodically measure the densities of the inks printed in the cyan, magenta, and yellow solid patches of the color control guide. The densities should remain within the tolerance limits set for the inks being used. Inking can be adjusted either *locally,* by opening or closing individual ink fountain keys, or *overall,* by increasing or decreasing the rotation of the ink fountain roller or dwell of the ink ductor roller. Ink/water balance must be maintained at all times. Several times during the pressrun, check the trapping of secondary colors, hue error, and grayness, especially of the yellow ink.

Tickets or tags are inserted into the paper pile to indicate start of makeready, start of pressrun, and sheets that have defects. If the tag is not color-coded, a simple explanation of the problem is written on it.

Control of Press Functions during Pressrun

Maintaining the Inking System

Consistent color is a primary objective during the pressrun. The ink fountain ratchet should be set halfway between the minimum and maximum strokes. Color will remain consistent only if the ink fountain is always at least half full. The ink in the fountain exerts pressure on the fountain blade. If the ink level is too low, the gap between fountain blade and fountain roller closes slightly, and less ink transfers to the ductor roller. As a result, the press operator increases the ink feed. Eventually, the press operator notices that the ink fountain level is too low and refills the fountain. When the fountain is refilled, the weight of the ink increases the gap between fountain roller and blade, resulting in a surplus of ink being fed to the ductor roller. The ink feed must now be reduced, and maintaining consistent color has become impossible.

Scratching a mark at the halfway point on the cheek or side of the fountain is one of the best ways to ensure that the ink level never drops below one-half.

The ink in the fountain must be periodically agitated. Agitation, either manual or automatic, prevents the ink from skinning (a major cause of hickeys). In addition, agitation lessens an ink's natural tendency to back away from the fountain blade. An automatic ink agitator is a recommended accessory for any press. However, if manual agitation is required, a good rule of thumb is to stir the ink once every 1,000 impressions.

Ink/water balance, discussed extensively in GATF Research Project Report 6113, must be maintained during the pressrun. Inking is adjusted to obtain the proper densities on the printed sheet, and the dampening is adjusted according to the inking level. Press operators often use the glossiness of the plate surface and the thickness of the ink film as visual clues to ink/water balance. Additional clues are the dot quality and types of patterns or marks in the image and nonimage areas of the press sheet. It is necessary in any given pressrun for the balance between ink and water to be achieved by trial-and-error adjustments of their feed rates. Enough water must be fed to keep nonimage areas clean and fine shadow dots open, but not so much that the water causes snowflake patterns in the ink film. The choice of initial settings for ink and water fountains are usually based on the press operator's experience with the type of press and its dampening system. After makeready, the ink film thickness and reflection density are generally close to the required standard and the water feed is near a satisfactory balance. Fine adjustments in either feed rate during the pressrun may require a corresponding adjustment in the other rate. After each adjustment, several inspection sheets should be pulled and checked after the press has reached a new equilibrium balance. Among the problems encountered in controlling the balance point is differentiating normal sample-to-sample random print variations from those due to longer drifts that occur during the pressrun. Minor variations are inherent in press operation.

The press operator must make sure that all covered rollers remain clean and that the ink does not bleed into the dampening fountain.

Experienced press operators judge ink/water balance by inspecting the appearance of the *scum line* that occurs at the lead edge of the plate. A sharp, even line indicates perfect balance. If the line is indistinct and fuzzy, the plate is too dry. If the line is broken, the plate is too wet.

Maintaining the Dampening Solution

Like the inking level, maintaining a satisfactory level of dampening solution in the fountain is extremely important. Insufficient dampening leads to plate dry-up in the non-image areas of the plate.

Periodically during the pressrun, the dampening solution's pH, conductivity, specific gravity, and temperature must be measured. Depending on the meters and hydrometers used, the measurements are made either in the dampening fountain (preferred) or in the supply tank. If a ball hydrometer is being used in the supply tank, wait until the air bubbles subside before reading it. If any measurement falls outside predetermined limits, immediate corrective action is required. For example, if the alcohol concentration falls below a certain percentage, additional alcohol is added to bring the concentration to normal operating levels.

Operating the Feeder

Like all press subsystems, minor adjustments are necessary during the pressrun. Vacuum and air often have to be adjusted to separate more or fewer sheets from the paper pile, depending on what feeding problems are encountered. Wedges may be required if the paper develops a curl. Pile height, sheet separation, and sheet transfer mechanisms may also require minor adjustment during the pressrun.

One commonly overlooked cause of a sheet transfer problem on the feedboard is glazed feedboard tapes. If they become glazed, they lose traction. They should be deglazed once every six months.

With a conventional feeder, the press must be stopped to change to a new paper pile. With a continuous feeder, the new pile is built below the expiring pile.

Operating the Delivery

If the press has a conventional delivery, it is stopped to unload the paper. If the press has a continuous delivery, some type of mechanism permits the press operator to unload the pile while a new one is building in the delivery. Recommended skid height in the delivery varies with ink coverage, spray powder usage, and the possibility of setoff.

If a paper jam occurs in the delivery (or feeder), the press is stopped immediately and the jammed sheets are manually removed. Once the press is restarted, monitor the first few sheets to make sure that the problem has been solved.

Adjusting the delivery joggers is seldom necessary once makeready is finished. However, adjusting spray powder levels is extremely common. Spray powder, discussed extensively in GATF Technical Services Report 7220, *Cutting Down on Spray Powder,* is one means of reducing **setoff,** the transfer of ink from the surface of the printed sheet to the back of the sheet on top of it. Excessive spray powder causes several problems:
- Quality problems, such as reduced gloss and scratches
- Maintenance problems, such as clogged filters in the ventilating system, worn bearings, and dust specks on plate and film in the stripping and camera areas

Exhaust hood over the delivery to remove antisetoff spray powder from the air

- Health problems, if the microscopic powder particles enter the worker's lungs
- Explosion potential in the pressroom if the concentration in the atmosphere exceeds about 0.04 oz./cu.ft. (42 g/M^3)

Therefore, a minimum of spray powder should be run. The amount required is easily determined by conducting the following test:

1. At the start of the pressrun, reduce the spray powder discharge until it is just visible, and then reduce it slightly more. Spray levels will be enough for most jobs.

2. Near the start of the pressrun, reduce the spray powder discharge even more.

3. Print ten sheets at this reduced level, and tag them accordingly.

4. Inspect the sheets the next morning. If setoff did not occur, the spray level can be reduced even more.

Repeating this test several times will give the press operator a basis for controlling the levels of spray powder used.

If the press operator has a choice of running excessive spray powder or stacking the printed sheets in small lifts to lessen setoff, stacking the sheets is preferred—although it causes the press operator additional work.

Racking can be used to stack several small lifts of paper. In racking, one lift of paper is placed on the delivery board, two L-shaped legs are placed at opposite corners of the paper pile, and a piece of plywood (cut to the same size as the delivery board) is placed on top of the legs. A second level is then built on top of the first piece of plywood, and a third level is then built on top of the second piece, and so on.

Use of L-shaped legs to stack small lifts of paper on multiple levels

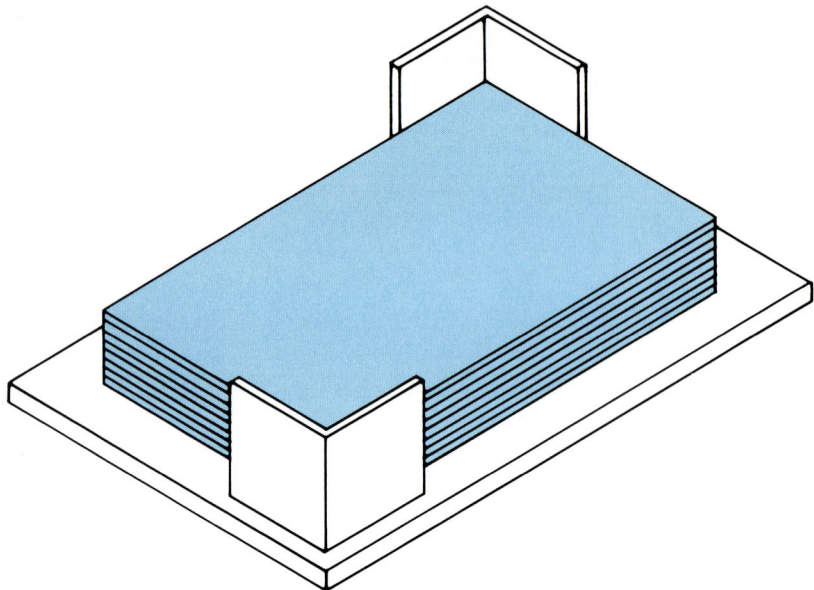

Quality Control during the Pressrun

Perception of color varies from person to person and from time to time by the same person. People cannot remember colors with any great degree of precision. Furthermore, control of production to reduce variation in color requires objective control that can be obtained only with instrumental measurement. On the other hand, the human eye is an excellent device for comparing two adjacent color samples and for detecting defects in print quality. Consequently, quality control has both visual and instrumental components.

Densitometry

The reflection densitometer is an indispensable quality control device. It can easily detect changes during a pressrun and indicate density variation between inspection press sheets and the OK sheet. Although some companies house the densitometer in quality control areas for periodic inspection at a central site, most densitometers are conveniently located at the press inspection area. Many modern presses have

Pressmate™ 3
reflection
densitometer
*Courtesy Cosar
Corporation*

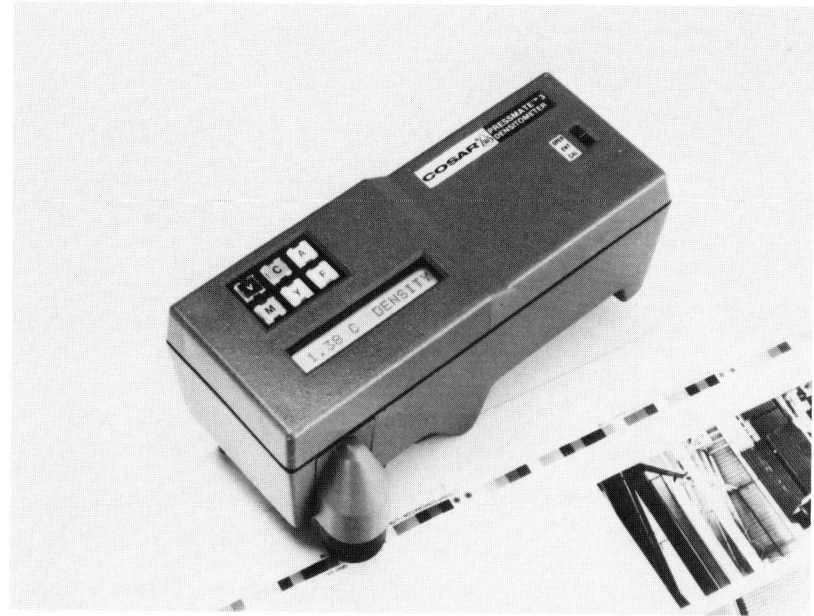

Model B318
reflection
densitometer
*Courtesy X-Rite
Company*

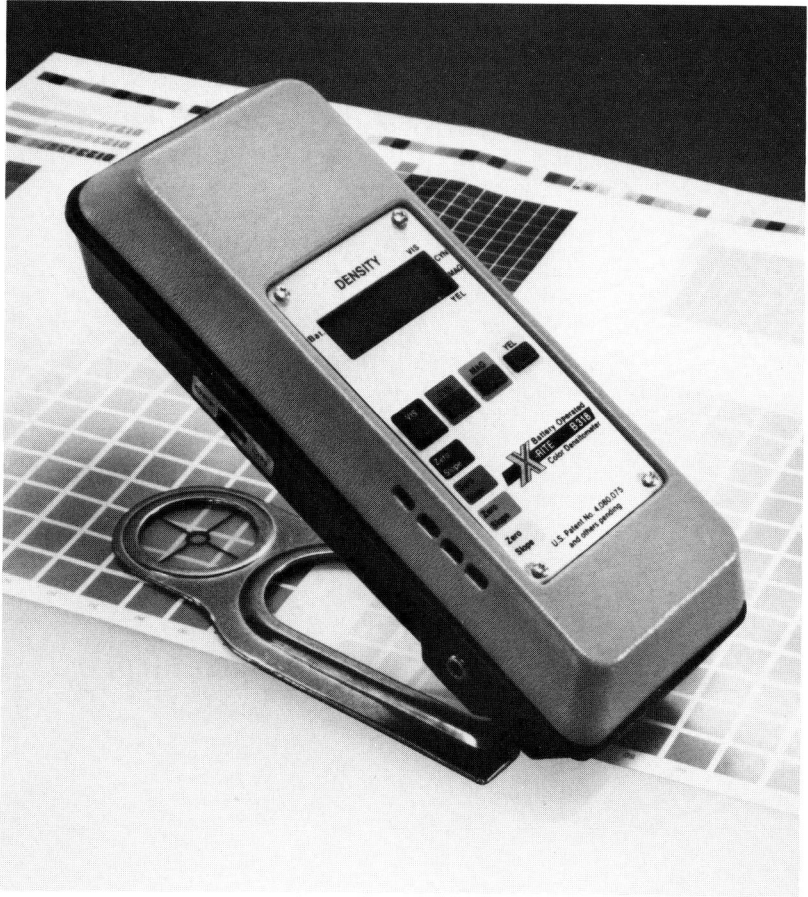

Model D 152
reflection
densitometer
Courtesy Gretag

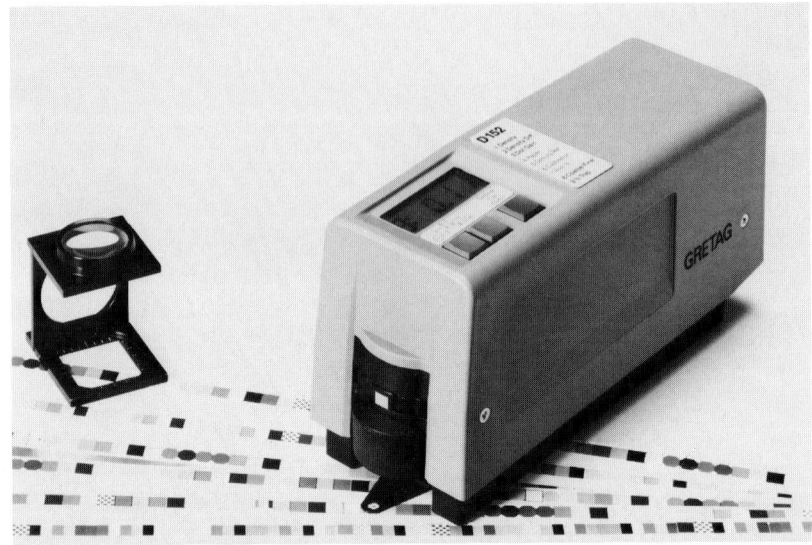

built-in densitometers. Stand-alone scanning densitometers, appropriate for any press, provide density readings on solid patches of color bars as well as critical halftone or solid image areas.

A program should be established to determine the optical density tolerances of each job. Density tolerances for each pressrun should be determined from density measurements taken on an approved press sheet *before* the pressrun begins.

Model RCX
reflection
densitometer
*Courtesy Tobias
Associates, Inc.*

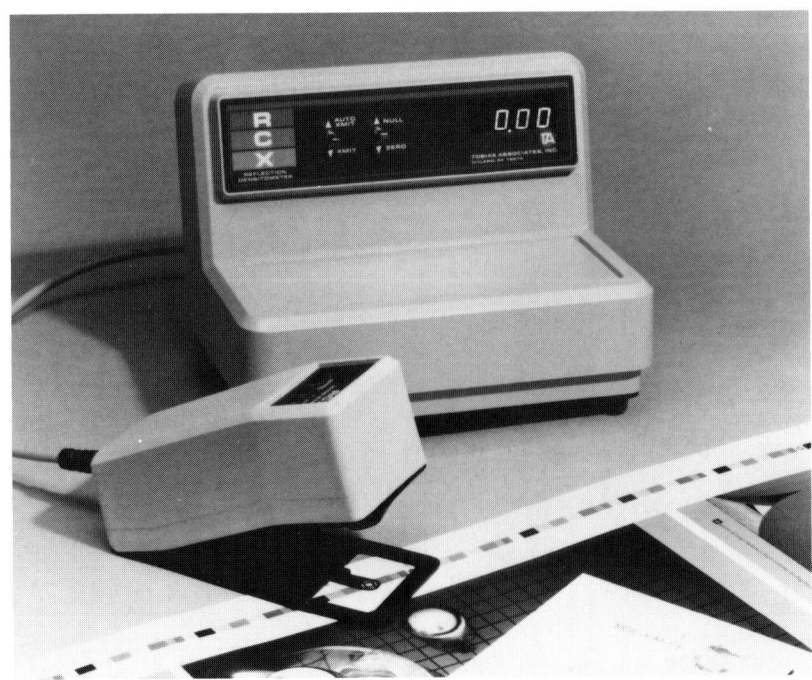

These measurements should be manually recorded or stored in computerized press densitometers or stand-alone densitometers.

If tolerances are established by a central quality control department, one of the approved sheets should be returned to the press on which printing will take place. It then becomes the press operator's responsibility to maintain color both numerically (using a densitometer) and visually (by comparing the inspection sheet with the OK sheet).

Periodically measuring the densities of an inspection sheet indicates whether or not the press operator is maintaining the original numerical tolerances established on the OK sheet.

Color Control Bars

Density monitoring programs require the use of color control bars. The GATF Compact Color Test Strip is one example of such a bar. The strip not only supplies information on the consistency of ink density from sheet to sheet, but it also provides information on ink trapping, dot gain or sharpening, slurring or doubling tendencies, and gray balance of the inks being used.

Commercially available color bars, such as the Compact Color Test Strip and the FOGRA PMS Print Control Strip, usually include overprints of two- and three-color solids and tints, in addition to solid and tint blocks for cyan, magenta, yellow, and black. Most also include additional aids to monitor other printing variables. The Test Strip, for example, also includes GATF Star Targets (also available separately), which visually indicate dot gain or sharpening, slur, and doubling.

Another GATF Q.C. device is the GATF Six-Color Control Bar, which is a 150-line/in. (5.9-line/mm) two-tiered press control bar for use on sheetfed presses. Designed for presses that are capable of printing up to six colors, the bar contains all of the elements from which ink densities, dot gain, trapping, and print contrast are measured. Elements are also included in the bar to allow the press operator to visually evaluate slur, doubling, and dot gain. The top tier of the bar contains twelve repeats of the six solid single colors and ten repeats of the green, blue, and red solid overprints. The lower tier contains four repeats of the GATF Star Targets for each of the six colors; four repeats of 25%, 50%, and 75% tint patches of the magenta, cyan, yellow, and black; four repeats of the GATF Dot Gain Scale-II© for each of the

One segment of the GATF Compact Color Test Strip

One portion of the FOGRA PMS Print Control Strip, which is available from GATF

One portion of the GATF Six-Color Control Bar

GATF QC strip: 10× enlargement *(left)* and actual size *(right)*

GATF Star Target: positive *(left)* and negative *(right)*

GATF Dot Gain Scale and Slur Gauge: sharpened image *(top)*, dot gain without slur *(middle)*, and dot gain caused by slur *(bottom)*

six colors; two sets of green, blue, and red 50% tint patches; and four repeats of three-color grays.

Color control bars are placed in the trim area across the tail end of the press sheet.

Other production Q.C. devices from GATF. The GATF Dot Gain Scale-II© was designed to visually indicate dot gain in the middletone area of a halftone, which is the area most sensitive to dot gain and the area so critical to color balance and critical quality. The scale visually shows dot gain in seven increments (1%, 2%, 5%, 10%, 15%, 20%, and 30%).

The GATF Quality Control Strip was also designed to be a visual aid for the press operator. The strip on the OK sheet is placed alongside the strip on the inspection sheet, and the two strips are compared. Any difference between them alerts the press operator to look for the cause of the difference in press conditions. Ink film thickness, ink/water balance, and dot quality can be visually controlled with the Quality Control Strip.

The GATF Dot Gain and Slur Gauge visually indicates dot area changes and slurring or doubling on press. The dot gain portion of the device consists of a series of numbers created by finely spaced horizontal lines of differing thicknesses on a coarse-dot background. A change in the position of the number that blends into the background indicates that dot gain or sharpening has occurred. The slur portion of the device consists of the word "slur" created by finely spaced horizontal lines on a background of finely spaced vertical lines. The occurrence of slur or doubling causes either the word "slur" or the background to become predominant.

The GATF Dot Gain Scale-II© showing seven individual targets (approximately 11× enlargement)

Controlling Color during the Pressrun

The problem of controlling and maintaining color during the pressrun involves controlling the thickness of the ink film, the ink trap in overprints, halftone tint values, and dot gain. Consequently, the ink film thickness is controlled by observing color changes and density differences that occur as the thickness varies. A densitometer provides numerical feedback to changes in halftone tint values, and a dot gain scale visually indicates changes in dot gain and, usually, slurring and doubling. The color and reflection density of a halftone area is more sensitive to changes in dot size than to changes in ink film thickness. A densitometer equipped with red, green, and blue filters is necessary to measure the reflection densities of the magenta, cyan, and yellow inks and their overprints. The use of a densitometer allows trapping, hue error, grayness, and print contrast to be calculated. Many densitometers measure these directly.

Trapping. The reflection densities of magenta, cyan, yellow, and their two-color overprints are used in the following formula to determine percent trapping.

$$\text{Percent trap} = \frac{D_{OP} - D_1}{D_2} \times 100$$

In this equation, D_1 is the reflection density of the first-down ink, D_2 is the reflection density of the second-down ink, and D_{OP} is the reflection density of the overprint. These density readings are taken with the filter normally used for the second-down ink. This equation indicates *apparent trap*, because effects such as changes in gloss between single- and two-layer ink films could influence the percentage.

In printing, the amount of ink film transferred to a previously printed ink film can be more than, equal to, or less than that transferred to paper. The amount of transfer is referred to as **trap.** In printing, wet trap seldom exceeds 90% in red and blue, although trap exceeding 90% occurs often with green; 80–90% trap values are most common. Wet trap values less than 75% on a sheetfed press are considered unacceptable. Although a high trap value is important, it is more important that the ink trap on production sheets match that of the OK sheet. Any change in ink trap causes changes in hue, saturation, and lightness of overprints. Such changes can be detected in the overprint color control bar when compared to those on the OK sheet. The following recommendations help to minimize trap problems:

- Use only inks that are balanced correctly for color strength. Trapping is improved if the ink film thickness increases slightly from one unit to the next. In order to increase ink film thicknesses in such a manner, the color strengths of the ink must be adjusted accordingly.

- Use tack-rated inks for wet-on-wet printing; that is, purchase a set of inks so that the highest tack-rated ink is printed on the first printing unit, the second highest tack-rated ink on the second unit, and so on. The difference in tack of consecutively printed inks should be only one or two tack units, as measured using an Inkometer.
- Make sure that the ink/water balance is correct and that the inking system is operating properly.

Hue error and grayness. Hue error is a term used to indicate the departure of a process ink from the ideal hue. To determine the hue error of an ink, density readings of the ink are taken through the red, green, and blue filters. The density reading are then used in the following formula to determine hue error:

$$\text{Hue error} = \frac{M - L}{H - L}$$

where M is the medium density reading, L is the lowest, and H is the highest.

Purity of a process color is judged by its freedom from gray. The following equation is used to calculate grayness:

$$\text{Grayness} = \frac{L}{H}$$

where L is the lowest density reading and H is the highest density reading. The lower the grayness of a process color, the higher its purity.

Print contrast ratio. Measurement of print contrast as a control parameter is increasing. High print contrast, an indication of good shadow contrast of a reproduction, yields better print quality. Printing conditions that cause print contrast to drop include excessive dot gain, low solid density, and fill-in due to insufficient water. Print contrast is calculated from a solid ink patch and a 75% tint patch, according to this formula:

$$\text{Print contrast} = \frac{D_S - D_{75}}{D_S} \times 100$$

where D_S is the density of a solid (including paper) and D_{75} is the density of a 75% tint (including paper).

Pressroom Lighting and Standard Viewing Conditions

Proper lighting is important in the pressroom. Light levels must be sufficiently high around the press to permit the press crew to install plates, blankets, and packing easily and to make the necessary press adjustments without eye strain. Having a light shining between each pair of press units is recommended. However, the lights should not be placed directly above the press, but off to one side. Aisles around the press should also be illuminated to make the printing plant safer.

In addition to lighting around the press, the tables or booths where press sheets are viewed must not only have sufficient lighting but must have lighting that conforms to recommended standard viewing conditions. To avoid misunderstandings, printer, supplier, and customer must agree on the illumination under which the print is to be viewed. Standard viewing conditions, consisting of standard lighting and surround conditions, are necessary to communicate the desired results and to ensure accuracy and consistency in color reproduction. In 1972, the accredited American National Standards Institute (ANSI), a committee of graphic arts and photographic industry representatives, issued specifications for standard conditions for evaluating the color quality of color originals, color proofs, and press sheets and for checking color uniformity between press sheets.

The standard viewing conditions are as follows:
- Color temperature of lighting—5,000 K (closely representing average white light)
- Color rendering index (how well a light source simulates daylight) of 90–100
- Level of print illumination—204.4 ± 43.6 footcandles
- Geometry of print illumination—angle that minimizes reflected glare
- Surround—matte, neutral gray (Munsell notation N8/)

Several companies manufacture viewing booths in which the lighting conforms to industry standards for illumination of the press sheet. For a detailed discussion of color viewing refer to GATF Technical Services Report 7223, *A Review of Color Viewing Conditions for the Graphic Arts.*

Electronics in the Pressroom

In recent years, electronic devices have been added to most modern presses to make operation easier and to improve print quality. Although the types of devices available vary from press manufacturer to manufacturer, the following

The Pressrun 295

The CCI computer console for a closed-loop inking system
Courtesy Graphic Systems Div., Rockwell International

CPC 2 quality control console
Courtesy Heidelberg Eastern, Inc.

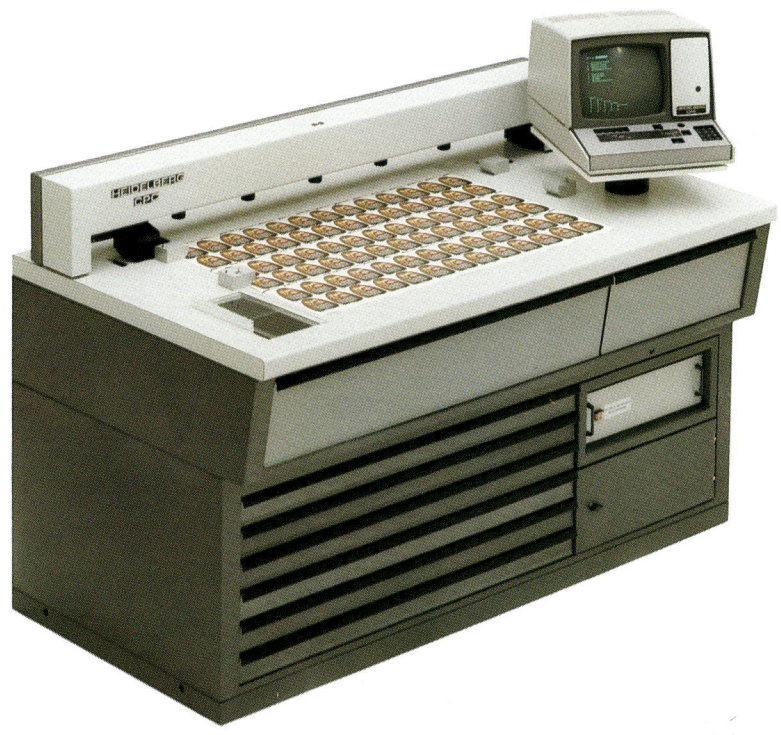

devices have become common in high-quality, high-productivity printing companies.

Remote Control Consoles

Most press manufacturers offer free-standing remote control consoles with their presses. A **remote control console** is a computerized device that enables the press operator to control a variety of press functions without leaving the inspection table. Among the functions controlled are inking, dampening, and image register.

The console usually includes a remote set of fountain keys, usually a tumble switch or push-button array numbered to press position. The press operator determines which fountain position is to be altered and depresses the appropriate button to decrease or increase ink feed. The drive system that adjusts fountain key position is either continuous or modulated. Usually, in case of electrical problems, the fountain keys on press can be manually adjusted. To take it a step further, some systems include an array of light-emitting diodes (LEDs) that shows the fountain blade profile. The details can be recorded on tape or punch card, allowing for automatic presetting of the fountain the next time the job is run.

Most remote control consoles allow the press operator to adjust the position of the plate cylinders.

Plate Scanner

Another auxiliary device is the plate scanner, which can be interfaced to an inking control console or record plate readings on tape or some other medium. A **plate scanner** is a device that measures the image area percentages at selected increments across the printing plate prior to mounting the plate on press. The information is recorded, often on a magnetic storage medium, so that it can be used to preset the ink fountain. Many plate scanners produce a printout that shows a graphic representation of the ink density of each individually controlled ink zone.

Scanning Densitometer

A **scanning densitometer** is a computerized quality control table that measures and analyzes press-sheet color bars using a densitometer. The results are compared with a prerecorded tolerance program, and a printout indicates the degree of variation. Ink fountain key adjustments and fountain roller adjustments can be made using the information provided by the scanning densitometer. The use of a hand-held densitometer to individually measure each patch of a color

The EPS plate scanner
Courtesy Graphic Systems Div., Rockwell International

The PSS plate scanner, which is an optional accessory to the Lithrone press line
Courtesy Komori America Corp.

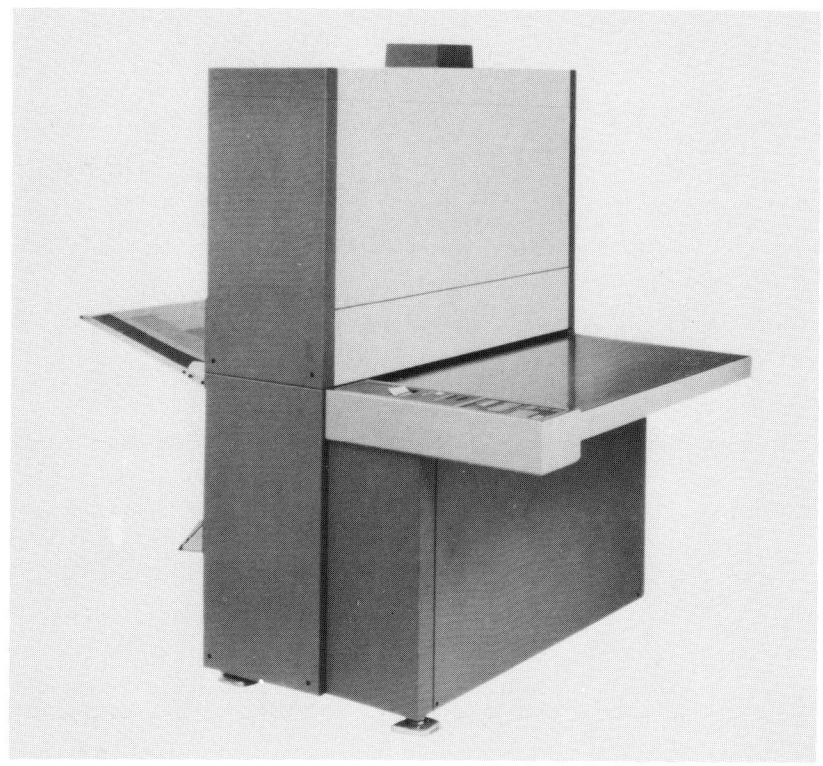

Solna plate scanner
Courtesy Solna, Incorporated

CCI automatic scanning densitometer
Courtesy Graphic Systems Div., Rockwell International

bar is eliminated, and it is no longer necessary to make pen-and-paper calculations because the computerized equipment does that. Some scanning densitometers also provide information on dot gain, contrast, slurring, and doubling. Most systems also provide a data printout.

SCR-41 scanning
densitometer
*Courtesy Tobias
Associates, Inc.*

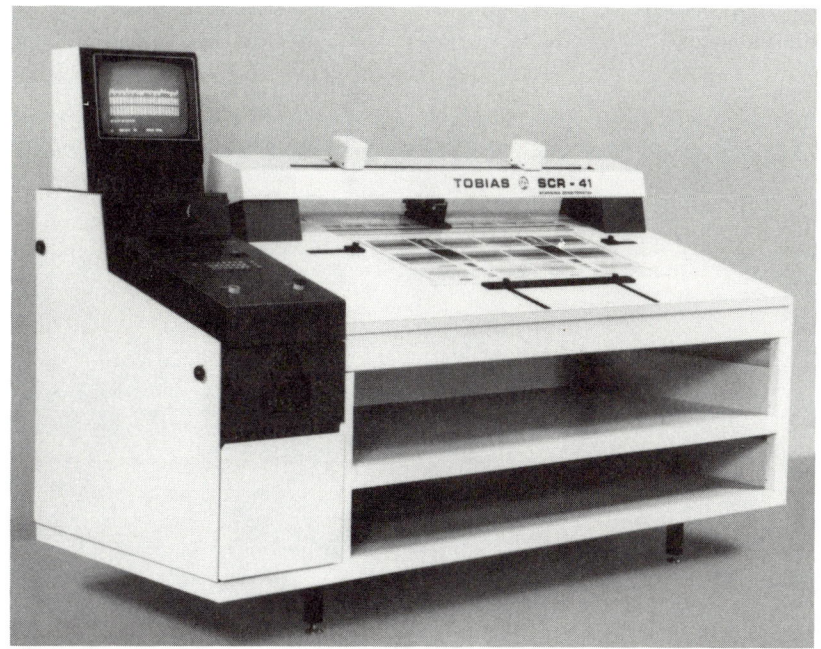

Microdot scanning
densitometer
*Courtesy Macbeth
Process Measurements*

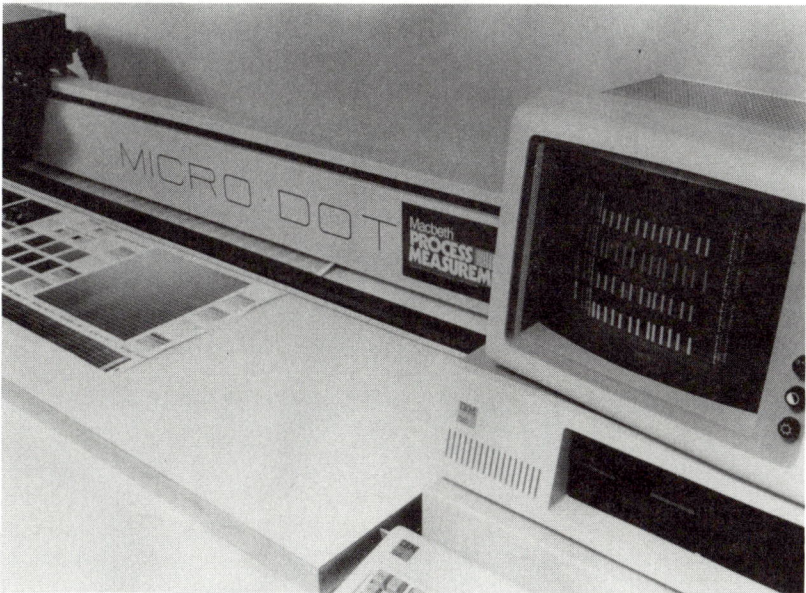

**Closed-Loop
Systems**

A closed-loop system combines a remote control inking console, scanning densitometer, and computer together to automatically control and adjust inking. In addition to inking, many of the systems can monitor solid and halftone density, dot gain, print contrast, and ink trapping. Unless the system has a press-mounted densitometer, the press operator still has to remove sheets from the press for measurement.

Cosar AutoSmart™ densitometer

Even with a closed-loop system, the ultimate control of the press remains with the press operator because a closed-loop system can not presently identify all process variables.

Unimatic C^4, a closed-loop inking system
Courtesy Miller Printing Equipment

PDC Printing Density Controller, which automatically monitors and adjusts inking
Courtesy Komori America Corp.

The control console for the PAC Print Aqua Control system, which monitors and controls the dampening supply
Courtesy Komori America Corp.

Glossary

air-blast nozzles Components of the sheet-separation unit that separate the top sheets of the pile.

air-cushion drum A device that supports the sheet on a cushion of air to lessen the chance that ink will smear on the press sheet. *Alternative term:* air-transport drum.

antifoaming agent A substance that prevents the buildup of foam in a dampening solution.

antisetoff compound An ink additive that prevents setoff either by protecting the ink surface or by shortening the ink (decreasing its gelling time).

antiskinning agent An antioxidant that counteracts the drying of sheetfed inks so that they do not skin in the can.

back-edge curl A curl in the paper that develops at the back edge.

backlash gear A thin second gear bolted to the spur gear to reduce play between gears.

bareback roller A form or ductor roller in a conventional dampening system that operates without cloth or paper covers.

basic size Sheet size in inches for a particular type of paper.

basis weight Weight, in pounds, of a ream of paper cut to its basic size, in inches.

bearer A hardened metal ring attached to the cylinder body or journal of the plate and blanket cylinders.

bearer-contact press A press that runs with the bearers of the plate and blanket cylinders in contact.

bimetal plate A negative-working multimetal printing plate that usually consists of copper electroplated on a base metal such as aluminum or stainless steel.

bladeless ink fountain A disposable sheet of polyester foil that is held in contact with the fountain roller by a series of small cylinders lying parallel to it.

blanket	See *offset blanket*.
blanket and packing height	The total thickness of the blanket and its packing.
blanket cylinder	The cylinder that carries the printing blanket and has two primary functions: (1) to carry the offset rubber blanket into contact with the inked image on the plate cylinder and (2) to transfer, or offset, the ink film image to the paper (or other substrate) carried by the impression cylinder.
blanket-to-blanket press	A perfecting press in which the blankets from two printing units are in contact, with the paper passing between the two blankets. Since each blanket acts as the impression cylinder for the other, no impression cylinder is needed.
blow-downs	A series of air holes, located near the top of the delivery, that assist in dropping the sheet onto the delivery table.
body	The relative term describing the consistency of an ink, referring mainly to the stiffness or softness of an ink, but implying other things including length and thixotropy.
bonding	The elimination of a difference in electrical potential between objects.
buffer	A substance capable of neutralizing acids and bases in solutions and thereby maintaining the acidity or alkalinity level of the solution.
catch-up	The problem that occurs when ink appears in the nonimage area due to insufficient dampening of the plate. *Alternative term:* dry-up.
chain transfer	A principal method of sheet transfer where sets of grippers riding on a chain transport the sheet from one impression cylinder to the next.
color strength	An ink's color power as determined by its pigment concentration.
compression set	The permanent reduction in thickness of a blanket or any of its component parts.

continuous-feed dampening system A ductorless dampening system in which there is a continuous flow of dampening solution from the fountain roller to the form roller.

continuous feeder A feeder that can be reloaded without stopping the press.

conventional dampening system A dampening system used for sheetfed offset lithography, consisting of a fountain, fountain pan roller, ductor roller, oscillator roller, and one or more covered or uncovered form rollers. The ductor roller intermittently contacts the fountain roller.

convertible perfector A perfecting press in which special transfer cylinders tumble the paper end for end between printing units so that the other side of the sheet is printed by the second unit. It has the capability, through transfer cylinder adjustment, to print either two colors on one side of the sheet or one color on each side in a single pass through the press.

corrosion inhibitors An additive to the dampening solution to prevent it from reacting with the plate.

crash bar A device that detects foreign objects on the feedboard and prevents their passage into the printing unit.

crystallization The drying of an ink to form a hard, impervious surface that interferes with dry trapping.

cylinder undercut The difference between cylinder body radius and bearer radius.

dampening solution A water-based solution that is applied to the printing plate before it is inked. *Alternative term:* fountain solution.

dampening system A series of rollers that dampen the printing plate with a water-based dampening solution that contains additives such as acid, gum arabic, and isopropyl alcohol or other wetting agents.

dead-weight micrometer A device that uses the dead weight of an anvil to obtain repeatable measurements on plate, blankets, and packing.

deep-etch plate — A seldom-used positive-working printing plate in which the image area is etched into the plate's surface. During exposure, the light-sensitive coating on the plate is hardened in image areas. The unhardened image-area coating is dissolved, and the unprotected image area is then etched with an acid solution.

delivery — The section of a printing press that receives, jogs, and stacks the printed sheet.

delivery cylinder — The cylinder after the last printing unit that powers the chain delivery and coordinates the transfer of the printed sheet from the last impression cylinder to the delivery gripper bars attached to the two delivery chains.

desensitization — In platemaking, the making of an nonimage area less receptive to ink by the application of a gum solution.

dimensional stability — Ability of a sheet to maintain its dimensions with changes in its moisture content or applied stressing.

direct infeed system — A type of infeed in which front guides stop the sheet and move out of the way at the proper time. No intermediate transfer device is used.

double-sheet detector — A device that can be set to stop the feeding action of the sheet-separation unit if more than one sheet of paper is being forwarded on a *single-sheet feeder*.

drier — An ink additive, such as a salt of cobalt or manganese, that acts as a catalyst to convert a wet ink film to a dry ink film.

dry trapping — The ability of a dry, printed ink film to accept a wet ink film over it. The wet ink dries by oxidation polymerization.

dry-up — The problem that occurs when ink appears in the nonimage area due to insufficient dampening of the plate. *Alternative term:* catch-up.

drying agent — An ink additive, such as a salt of cobalt or manganese, that acts as a catalyst to convert a wet ink film to a dry ink film.

drying section — Section of a papermaking machine where water is removed by passing the web over hot drying cylinders.

drying stimulator A substance—e.g., cobalt chloride—that complements the drier in the ink.

ductor or ductor roller A transfer roller that alternately contacts the ink or dampening fountain roller and the first roller of the ink train, often an oscillating drum.

ductor shock The vibration sent through the inking system when the ductor first contacts the oscillating roller.

duplicator Any press smaller than 11 × 17 in. (279 × 432 mm) without bearers (hardened metal disks attached to the ends of the cylinder or to the cylinder's journal).

durability The blanket's ability to withstand the pressure, tension, and physical abuse on the press.

durometer Instrument used in printing to measure the hardness of roller compounds.

dwell The length of time that the ductor roller contacts the fountain roller.

effective diameter The diameter of the bearer.

endplay Undesirable lateral movement due to poor fit between roller shaft and roller bracket.

extra-sheet detector A sheet detector on a *stream-fed press* that is set to trip if three or more overlapping sheets pass under it.

fan-out An expansion of the sheet near the tail edge.

feedboard A platform or ramp on which the sheet to be printed is transported to registering devices that properly position the sheet and time its entrance into the printing unit. *Alternative term:* feed table.

feeder The section of a sheetfed press where paper is lifted from the top of a pile table, forwarded on a feedboard to front stops, laterally positioned on the feedboard by a side guide, and fed into the first printing unit.

feeler gauge — A thin strip of steel ground to precise thickness and marked accordingly.

fingers — Devices that prevent the suckers in the sheet-separation unit from picking up more than one sheet at a time.

form roller — A device that transfers dampening solution or ink from an oscillator roller to the printing plate. Presses typically have one or two *dampening* form rollers and three to five *inking* form rollers.

forwarding roller — One of a series of rotating devices that transfer the sheet from the sheet-separation unit to the feedboard.

fountain — A reservoir for the dampening solution or ink that is fed to the plate.

fountain blade — A spring steel plate, steel segment, or plastic angled against the fountain roller.

fountain cheeks — Vertical metal pieces contacting the edges of the fountain roller and blade to form an ink-tight trough.

fountain height monitor — A sensing device, usually mechanical or ultrasonic, that checks the height of ink moving over the agitator.

fountain keys — A series of thumb screws or motor-driven screws or cams behind the blade that provide for variable inking across the fountain.

fountain roller — A metal roller that rotates intermittently or continuously in the ink or dampening fountain and carries the ink or dampening solution on its metal surface.

fountain solution — See *dampening solution*.

fountain splitter — A device that divides the ink fountain so that two or more inks can be used in the same ink fountain. Each ink will print a different section of the press sheet; e.g., red on the left side and blue on the right side.

front guide — One of a series of stops that halt the forward movement of the sheet on the feedboard. The front guides square the sheet in relation to the printing cylinders and determine the front margin.

fungicide — A substance that prevents the formation of mildew and the growth of fungus and bacteria in the dampening system.

furnish — Mixture of fibrous and nonfibrous materials created during stock preparation and used to make paper.

ghosting — The appearance of faint replicas of an image in undesirable places, caused by mechanical or chemical processes, other than setoff or show-through. *Mechanical ghosting* is caused by ink starvation or by a depressed area of the blanket. *Chemical ghosting* is the appearance of gloss or dull ghosts of images that are printed on the reverse side of the sheet and is caused by the chemical-activity influence that inks have on each other during their critical drying phases.

glaze — A combination of oxidized roller surface, embedded ink pigment, dried ink vehicle, and gum from fountain solution on an inking roller.

gloss — High reflectance of light from a smooth surface.

grain direction — In papermaking, the alignment of fibers in the direction of web travel. In printing, paper is *grain-long* if the grain direction parallels the long dimension of the paper and *grain-short* if it parallels the short dimension.

grammage — Weight in grams of a single sheet of paper having an area of 1 m^2.

gripper bite — A term that refers to the amount of sheet—margin—under the paper gripper of the impression cylinder.

gripper-bowing device — A device, usually part of an infeed drum, that compensates for the effects of fan-out by intentionally bowing the gripper bar as much as 0.008 in. (0.020 mm) at its center.

grounding — The elimination of a difference in electrical potential between an object and the ground.

groundwood — Mechanical pulp used in papermaking produced by forcing pulpwood against a revolving, abrasive grinding stone.

height above bearers	The height of the surface of the plate or blanket above the surface of the bearers with proper packing.
helical gear	A gear located on the blanket cylinder that has teeth cut at an angle.
hickey	An imperfection in printing due to a particle on the blanket or, sometimes, the plate. A *doughnut hickey* consists of a small, solid printed area surrounded by a white halo, or unprinted area. A *void hickey* is a white, unprinted spot surrounded by printing.
hold-down rods	Rods that are positioned so that they hold down the back corners of the sheet as it enters the feedboard.
hot-weather scumming	The tendency of ink to print in nonimage areas when the dampening feed rate is too low.
hydrophilic	Water-receptive, as in the nonimage areas of the printing plate.
hydrophobic	Water-repellent, as in the image areas of the printing plate.
image area	On a printing plate, the area that has been specially treated to receive ink.
impression cylinder	A cylinder that transports the press sheet and forces the paper or other substrate against the inked blanket.
infeed section	The section of a sheetfed press where the sheet is transferred from the registering devices of the feedboard to the first impression cylinder of the printing press.
ink absorbency	The extent that an ink penetrates the paper.
ink agitator	A revolving cone-shaped device that moves from one end of the fountain to the other keeping the ink soft and flowing.
ink drying	Process by which a sheetfed ink is transformed from an original semifluid or plastic state to a solid.
ink holdout	The extent to which paper resists or retards the penetration of the freshly printed ink film.

ink vehicle	A complex liquid mixture in which pigment particles are dispersed.
inker-feed dampening system	A continuous-feed dampening system that delivers dampening solution to an ink form roller.
inking control console	A computerized device that enables the press operator to control a variety of functions without leaving the inspection table.
inking system	A series of rollers that apply a metered film of ink to a printing plate.
intermediate rollers	Friction- or gravity-driven rollers between the ductor and form roller that transfer and condition the ink. They are called *distributors* if they contact two rollers and *riders* if they contact a single oscillating drum.
intermittent-flow dampening system	A descriptive term for the conventional, or ductor, dampening system used for sheetfed offset lithography.
knife rollers	Small-diameter hard rollers that help to keep the ink system clean by picking up ink skin particles, lint, etc.
lay	Position of the printed image on the sheet.
lift	A manageable amount of paper.
liquid drier	A drier in which metal salts are suspended in liquids such as a petroleum solvent.
makeready	All of the operations necessary to get the press ready to print the current job.
makeready book	A pile of press sheets consisting of both waste sheets (previously printed sheets) and clean, unprinted sheets.
masstone	The color of a thick film of ink. It is the color of light reflected by the pigment.
metering nip	The line of contact between the two rollers of an inker-feed dampening system.

misregister	Incorrectly positioned printed images, either in reference to each other or to the sheet's edges.
misregister, random	Misregister that varies from sheet to sheet.
mottle	Irregular and unwanted variation in color or gloss caused by uneven absorbency of the paper.
multicolor press	A press consisting of two or more printing units (each with its own inking and dampening system), a feeder, a sheet transfer system, and a delivery. Two or more colors can be printed on one side of a sheet during a single pass through the press.
multicolor printing	The printing of two or more colors, often one over another.
multiple-sheet proof	See *overlay proof*.
multiunit press	See *multicolor press*.
negative-working plate	A printing plate that is exposed through a film negative. Plate areas exposed to light become the image areas.
nip	The line of contact between cylinders.
non–bearer-contact press	A press in which the bearers of the plate and blanket cylinders do not run in contact; i.e., there is a slight gap—clearance—between the bearers.
nonimage area	On a printing plate, the portion that does not print.
off-press proofing	Proofing that is done photomechanically using light-sensitive papers (principally to proof single-color printing), colored films, or photopolymers.
offset blanket	A fabric coated with synthetic or natural rubber that transfers the image from the printing plate to the substrate.
offset lithographic press	A mechanical device that dampens and inks the printing plate and transfers the inked image to the blanket and then to the printing substrate.

offset lithographic press, web   A press that prints on a continuous web, or ribbon, of paper fed from a roll and threaded through the press.

offset lithography   A planographic printing process that requires an image carrier in the form of a plate on which photochemically produced image and nonimage areas are receptive to ink and water, respectively.

oleophilic   Oil-receptive, as in the image areas of the printing plate.

oleophobic   Oil-repellent, as in the dampened nonimage areas of the printing plate.

opacity   (1) The ability of a printed ink film to hide what is underneath. (2) The extent to which light transmission is obstructed.

oscillating form roller   A roller substituted for the first and, sometimes, fourth (last) form rollers of a press to reduce ghosting on a job.

oscillator   A driven inking or dampening roller that not only rotates but oscillates from side to side, distributing and smoothing out the ink film and erasing image patterns from the form roller. *Alternative terms:* oscillating drum or vibrator.

overfeed system   A type of infeed in which front guides stop the sheet and move away at the proper time. Feed rolls or vacuum belts drive the sheet against stops (front guides) on the impression cylinder.

overlay proof   A type of proof used in multicolor or process-color printing where pigmented or dyed sheets of plastic are registered to each other and taped or pin-registered to a base.

packing   (1) The procedure for setting the pressure between the plate and blanket cylinders. (2) The paper or other material that is placed between the plate or blanket and its cylinder to raise the surface to printing height or to adjust cylinder diameter to obtain color register in multicolor printing.

packing gauge   A device for measuring the height of the plate or blanket in relation to the cylinder bearers.

paste drier — A soluble drier that contains resins and plasticizers to achieve the desired body or viscosity.

perfecting — The printing of at least one color on both sides of a sheet in a single pass through a press.

perfector — A sheetfed press that can print at least one color on both sides of a sheet in a single pass. *Alternative term:* perfecting sheetfed press.

pH — A measure of a solution's acidity or alkalinity, specifically the negative logarithm of the concentration (in moles/liter) of the hydrogen ions in a solution.

picking — The delamination, splitting, or tearing of the paper surface due to an ink film's resistance to being split between blanket and paper.

pick resistance — Ability of a paper to resist a force applied perpendicularly to its surface before picking or rupturing occurs.

pickup suckers — Components of the sheet-separation unit that lift and forward the top sheet of the pile to forwarding rollers. The sheets are lifted by rear pickup suckers and are then transferred to the forwarding rollers by the forwarding pickup suckers.

pigment — Finely divided solid material that gives an ink color.

pile height — Maximum height of the paper pile in the feeder, usually 3/16 in. (5 mm) below the forwarding flaps at the front of the pile.

pile table — A raisable platform where the paper to be printed is loaded.

piling — Accumulation of material on the blanket or plate in such quantity that it interferes with print quality.

pipe rollers — Small-diameter hard rollers that help to keep the ink system clean by picking up ink skin particles, lint, etc.

pitch diameter — The working diameter of the gear attached to the cylinder journal.

plate and packing height   The total thickness of the plate and its packing.

plate blinding   The loss of ink receptivity in the image area due to an excessively acidic fountain solution.

plate clamp   A device that grips the edge of the plate and pulls it tight against the cylinder body.

plate cylinder   A cylinder that carries the printing plate. It has four primary functions: (1) to hold the lithographic printing plate tightly and in register, (2) to carry the plate into contact with the dampening rollers that wet the nonimage area, (3) to bring the plate into contact with the inking rollers that ink the image area, and (4) to transfer the inked image to the blanket carried by the blanket cylinder.

plate-feed dampening system   A continuous-feed dampening system that has separate dampening form rollers.

plate scanner   A device that measures the image area percentages at selected increments across the printing plate prior to mounting the plate on press, in order to preset the ink fountain keys.

plate scumming   The pickup of ink in nonimage areas of the plate.

play   Free or unimpeded movement.

positive-working plate   A printing plate that is exposed through a film positive. Plate areas exposed to light become the nonimage areas.

press section   Section of papermaking machine where water is removed from the web by pressing and suction.

printing plate   A flexible image carrier with ink-receptive image areas and, when moistened with a water-based solution, ink-repellent nonimage areas.

printing unit   The section of the offset lithographic press where the print is generated and applied to a substrate, usually paper.

proof	A trial print from a plate, film negative, or film positive to verify correctness and quality.
proof press	A printing machine used for making a proof.
pull	A group of inspection sheets removed from the delivery of the press.
ream	With a few exceptions, 500 sheets of paper.
reducer	An ink additive that softens the ink and reduces its tack.
refiner mechanical pulp (RMP)	Papermaking pulp produced by passing wood chips through a disk refiner instead of pressing the wood against an abrasive grinding stone.
refractive index	Measure of the ability of a pigment particle to bend or refract light rays.
register	The accurate positioning of images—either in relation to images on other press sheets or in relation to an image already printed on that press sheet.
register plate	A device that stops the lateral (sideways) movement of the sheet. *Alternative term:* register block.
release	The readiness of the blanket to give up the paper after it leaves the nip.
resilience	The ability of a blanket to regain its thickness after pressure on its surface has been removed.
reverse slip nip	The point of contact where two rollers are rotating in opposite directions in a dampening system.
roller cover	Absorbent cloth or paper that covers the rollers and helps to provide more continuous dampening by increasing the solution-carrying and solution-storing capacity of the rollers.
roller setting gauge	A device that shows the amount of pressure exerted by pulling the paper strip between the two rollers being set.
roller stripping	The failure of ink to adhere to the inking rollers.

roll sheeter	A device that cuts paper on a roll into sheets and sends them to the press feeder.
rotary drum	A type of infeed in which front guides stop the sheet and move out of the way at the proper time. Grippers on a rotating drum close on the sheet and transfer it to the impression-cylinder grippers.
safety bar	A device that detects foreign objects on the feedboard and prevents their passage into the printing unit.
scanning densitometer	A computerized quality control table that measures and analyzes press-sheet color bars using a densitometer.
scumming	The problem that occurs when a permanent ink image—usually dots—appears in the nonimage area.
sensitization	In platemaking, the making of an image area more ink-receptive.
separator brush	One of a series of brushes that prevent the suckers from picking up more than one sheet at a time.
sequestering agent	A substance that prevents the calcium and magnesium compounds in the dampening solution from precipitating.
sheet decurler	A device that is designed to take troublesome curl out of press sheets.
sheet detector, early and late	A device that detects the early or late arrival of a sheet at the front guides.
sheetfed offset lithographic press	A printing press that feeds and prints on individual sheets of paper (or other substrate) using the offset lithographic printing method.
sheet guide rods	Rods that are positioned so that they hold down the back corners of the sheet as it enters the feedboard.
sheet-separation unit	A device that uses both air and a vacuum to separate the top sheet from the feeder pile.
sheet steadiers	Weights positioned at the outside quarters of the feeder pile.

sheet transfer section — The section of the press that transports the press sheet between the impression cylinders on a multicolor sheetfed press.

shortening compound — An ink additive that reduces ink flying, or misting.

side guide — The third point of the three-point sheet-registering system (also including the front guides) on the feedboard, responsible for moving the sheet in the sideways direction to facilitate register.

single-color press — A press consisting of a single printing unit, with its integral inking and dampening systems, a feeder, a sheet transfer system, and a delivery. It can also be used for multicolor printing by changing the ink and plate and running the paper through the press again.

single-drum transfer — A principal method of sheet transfer where a set of grippers on a large-diameter transfer cylinder transport the sheet from one impression cylinder to the next.

single-sheet feeder — A feeder where only one sheet of paper (traveling at press speed) is on the feedboard at any instant.

single-sheet proof — A type of proof used for multicolor or process-color proofing where the printing colors are built up on a base through lamination and toning or other processing.

skeleton wheels — The series of movable disks that are mounted on a shaft of the delivery cylinder and positioned in nonprinting areas of the press sheet.

slip compound — An ink additive that improves scuff resistance of the printed ink film.

small offset press — Any press smaller than 11×17 in. (279×432 mm) without bearers (hardened metal disks attached to the ends of the cylinder or to the cylinder's journal).

smash — Undesirable localized compression of the blanket's surface.

smash-resistance — The ability of a blanket to recover from being momentarily subjected to excessively high pressure.

smoother	A device that helps to keep the sheet flat on the feedboard.
snowflaking	The tiny, white, unprinted specks that appear in type and solids.
specific gravity	Ratio of the weight of one material to the weight of an equal volume of water.
spur gear	A gear that has teeth cut straight across.
squeeze	Printing pressure between the plate and blanket cylinders. It is expressed as the combined height of the plate and blanket over their respective bearers on a *bearer-contact press* and as the combined height of the plate and blanket over their respective bearers minus the distance between the bearers on a *non–bearer-contact press*.
start-of-print line	A horizontal line that indicates the limit of the printing area. It is often engraved in the gutters about an inch behind the plate cylinder's leading edge.
stream feeder	A type of feeder section where a number of sheets of paper traveling slower than press speed overlap on the feedboard.
subtractive plate	A printing plate in which the light-sensitive coating also contains an image-reinforcing material.
successive-sheet feeder	A type of feeder section where only one sheet of paper (traveling at press speed) is on the feedboard at any instant.
suction plate	A device that holds the sheet by vacuum and then moves it against the register block.
suction rollers	Devices that slow down and steady the sheet as it enters the delivery.
supercalendering	Finishing operation in papermaking where the web of paper passes between a series of hard metal rollers and soft, resilient rollers that impart varying degrees of smoothness and gloss to the paper.
surface plate	A printing plate in which a light-sensitive coating applied to the plate surface is made ink-receptive in the image areas

during exposure and processing, while in the nonimage areas it is removed or converted to a water-receptive layer.

surface strength — Ability of a paper to resist a force applied perpendicularly to its surface before picking or rupturing occurs.

swing-arm infeed system — A type of infeed in which front guides stop the sheet and move away at the proper time. Grippers on a swing-arm mechanism close on the sheet and transfer it to the impression-cylinder grippers.

tack — Resistance of a liquid to splitting. It is measured by determining the force required to split an ink film between two surfaces.

tail-end hook — A curl in the paper that develops at the back edge.

temperature conditioning — Process of allowing paper to reach pressroom temperature before unwrapping the paper.

texture — In inkmaking, the hardness or softness of a pigment in its dry form.

thermo-mechanical pulp (TMP) — Papermaking pulp produced by preheating wood chips with steam prior to passing them through a disk refiner.

thixotropy — Characteristic of a material that causes it to change consistency on being worked.

three-drum transfer — A principal method of sheet transfer where three transfer cylinders are used to transport the sheet from one impression cylinder to the next.

through drier — A drier that dries the ink film throughout and does not form a hard surface.

tight-edged paper — A paper whose exposed edges have given up moisture to the atmosphere and shrunk.

tinting — The bleeding of ink pigment particles into the dampening solution. *Alternative term:* toning.

top drier — Drier that gives a very hard surface to the ink.

transfer cylinders	The paper-transport cylinders between printing units.
transfer devices	Any of several devices (often auxiliary cylinders with sheet grippers) that facilitate sheet transport through the press.
trimetal plate	A positive-working multimetal printing plate consisting of a top layer of chromium (the nonimage metal) and a bottom layer of copper (the image metal) electroplated to a base metal.
true rolling	A term often used to describe the condition when there is no slip in the printing nip.
two-sheet caliper	A device that can be set to stop the feeding action of the sheet-separation unit if more than one sheet of paper is being forwarded.
type-A durometer	Instrument used in printing to measure the hardness of roller compounds.
undercut	The difference between the radius of the cylinder body and the radius of the cylinder bearers.
undertone	The color of a thin film of ink. It is the color of light reflected by the paper and transmitted through the ink film.
unitack	A series of printing inks that have the same tack rating.
viscoelastic	A material, like an offset ink, that behaves as both a fluid and an elastic solid.
warp	The direction of maximum strength on a blanket.
water pan	A device that holds the dampening solution to be fed to the plate.
water stop	One of a series of devices that are set against the surface of the dampening fountain roller; commonly used to reduce the amount of solution reaching heavily inked areas of the printing plate.
wavy-edged paper	A paper whose exposed edges have absorbed moisture and become wavy.

wedges — Devices made out of wood or plastic that are used at startup to produce a neat pile in the feeder.

weft — The direction of minimum strength on a blanket.

wet ink film thickness gauge — A device that measures the thickness of the ink film on a roller.

wettability — The ease with which a pigment can be completely wet by the ink vehicle.

wetting agent — (1) In inkmaking, an additive that promotes the dispersion of pigments in the vehicle. (2) A substance, such as isopropanol or an alcohol substitute, found in a dampening solution, that decreases the surface tension of water and water-based solutions.

wet trapping — The ability of a wet, printed ink film to accept another wet ink film printed over it.

wire side — Side of the paper that is in contact with the paper machine's wire during papermaking.

Index

Absorbency, ink   207–208
Air bar   67
Air-blast nozzle   107, 112–113, 129
Air conditioning   211–212
Air-cushion drum   24, 139
Alcohol, isopropyl   70, 71–74, 95
Alcohol, safe handling of   73–74
Alcohol substitute   70, 74
Antifoaming agent   70
Antisetoff compound   223–224
Antisetoff spray powder   284–286
Antiskinning agent   224

Backlash gear   16
Bareback dampening roller   87–88
Basic size   204
Basis weight   204
Bearer   16
Bearer compression   147–148
Bench micrometer   150, 169
Blanket   161–181, 253–254
Blanket,
   compressible   164–167
   durability of   163–164
   effect of, on packing   146–147
   quick-release properties of   168
   resilience of   163–164
   sheet release by   163
   smash-resistance of   163–164
   solvent resistance of   164
   stretch and tensile strength of   164
   surface smoothness of   164
   use of slightly damaged   181
   warp and weft directions of   162
Blanket care   169–174
Blanket cylinder   2, 19–22
Blanket manufacture   161–163
Blanket mounting   176–180, 272
Blanket mounting bars   174–176
Blanket reel   20–21
Blanket selection   167–169
Blanket smash, recovery from   180–181
Blanket solvent   170–171
Blanket storage   169–170

Blanket thickness   149–150, 168–169
Blanket washing and reconditioning   171–173
Blinding, plate   75
Blow-down in delivery   140
Body   236
Bonding   73
Book, makeready   274
Brushes on feedboard   120
Buffer in dampening solution   69

Cady gauge   150, 169
Calender   202
Catchup   98, 243
Chain transfer   135
Clamp, plate   19
Closed-loop press control systems   299–300
Coating, paper   203
Coating, water-based   249
Color control bar   289–291
Color control during pressrun   291–293
Color matching   238–240
Color of print   275
Color strength   235
Compact Color Test Strip, GATF   289, 290
Compression set   167
Conductivity   77–79
Convertible perfector   10, 25
Corrosion inhibitor in dampening solution   69
Crash bar   123
Crystallization   246
Curl, back-edge   216–217
Cylinder,
   blanket   19–22
   delivery   28
   impression   22–23
   plate   16–19
   transfer   23–27
Cylinder low spot   39
Cylinder pressure   144–145
Cylinder setting   28–32
Cylinder undercut   188

Dampening   69–99
Dampening form roller   81, 82–85, 87–88, 253

Dampening fountain 80
Dampening metering on a conventional system 86–87
Dampening roller cover 82–85, 95–96
Dampening solution 69–79, 283–284
Dampening solution, refrigeration of 94–95
Dampening solution concentrate 70–71
Dampening solution conductivity 77–78
Dampening system,
  adjustments to conventional 85–87
  continuous-flow 88–94
  conventional 80–88
  maintenance of 95–97
  operating problems with 97–99
  preparing the 272
Dampening system washup 256, 267–268
Decurler, sheet 137
Delivery 1, 2, 101, 136–140
Delivery-assist device 139–140
Delivery cylinder 28
Delivery operation 284
Delivery pile, jogging the 138–139
Densitometer, reflection 286–289
Densitometer, scanning 296–298
Densitometry 286–289
Desensitization 69, 184
Diameter, effective 16
Diameter, pitch 16
Dimensional stability of paper 209
Distributor roller 43
Dot Gain and Slur Gauge, GATF 290–291
Dot Gain Scale-II© 289, 290
Double-sheet detector 114, 116–117, 129–130
Doubling 162
Drier, ink 224–225
Drum, oscillating *See* oscillator
Drying of an ink 225–231
Drying stimulator in dampening solution 70
Dry trapping 4, 244, 246
Dry-up 243, 280
Ductor dampening system *See* dampening system, conventional
Ductor roller 43, 44, 55
Ductor shock 47
Ductor timing 47

Duplicator 12
Durometer 63
Dwell 46, 87

Effective diameter 16
Electron-beam radiation 230–231
Electronic devices in the pressroom 294–301
Endplay 54–55
Environmental Protection Agency (EPA) 71
Extender 239

Fan-out 132–133
Feed tapes 118–119
Feedboard 103, 114–129
Feeder 1, 2, 101
Feeder,
  continuous 105
  single-sheet 101, 129–130
  stream 101–129
Feeder loading 104
Feeder operation 284
Feeler gauge 31
Fit 280
Floor layout 252
FOGRA PMS Print Control Strip 289, 290
Form roller,
  dampening 81, 82–85, 87–88
  ink 43, 47
  oscillating ink 48
  setting of, to oscillator 50–51
  setting of, to plate 52–55
Fountain blade, ink 44, 59
Fountain cheek 44
Fountain height monitor, ink 67
Fountain key 45
Fountain roller, ink 44, 45
Fountain solution *See* dampening solution
Fountain splitter, ink 65
Front guide 114, 117, 125–127
Fungicide 70

GATF Compact Color Test Strip 289, 290
GATF Dot Gain and Slur Gauge 290, 291
GATF Dot Gain Scale-II© 289, 290

GATF Quality Control Strip   290, 291
GATF Six-Color Control Bar   289–291
GATF Star Target   289–291
Gauge, packing   150–151
Gauge, roller-setting   51
Gauge, wet ink film thickness   48, 50
Gear, blanket cylinder   22
Gear, plate cylinder   16
Ghosting, gloss   246–247
Ghosting, mechanical   48, 49, 248
Glazed roller   57–59
Glazing   57–58
Gloss, ink   235
Gloss of paper   205–206
Grain direction   206–207
Grammage   204
Grayness   293
Gripper bite   126, 133, 135
Gripper bowing   132–133
Grounding   73
Groundwood   200
Gum arabic   69
Gum etch   96
Gumming   184

Halftone, plugging of   280
Hardness, roller   63
Hazard Materials Identification System (HMIS)   41, 73
Helical gear   16
Hickey   65, 216, 246
Hickey-picking roller   65–66
Hold-down device   118, 119–120
Hot-weather scumming   94
Hue error   293
Hydrophilic   183
Hydrophobic   183

Impression cylinder   2, 22–23
Impression-cylinder stop   132
Infeed   101, 130–135
Infeed gripper clearance   130, 131
Infrared radiation   231
Ink   219–251, 253

Ink,
   color strength of 235
   effect of, on packing 146
   opacity of 235
   optical properties of 231–235
   problems with 242–249
   quickset 231
   unitack 231
   working properties of 235–238
Ink absorbency 207–208
Ink additive 223
Ink agitator 65
Ink consumption counter 67
Ink cuff 61–62
Ink drier 224–225
Ink drying 225–231
Ink feed, adjustment of 45–47
Ink film thickness 48, 50
Ink fountain 43
Ink gloss 235
Ink handling on press 240–242
Ink holdout 207–208
Ink ingredients 221–225
Ink leveler 67
Ink setting 226–227
Ink vehicle 223
Ink viscosity 237
Inking control consoles 296
Inking system 2, 43–67, 272–273, 282–283
Inking system operation 55–56
Inking system problems 56–60
Inking system washup 256, 263, 266
Inkmaking 219–225
Integrated dampening system *See* dampening system, continuous-flow inker-feed
Intermittent-flow dampening system *See* dampening system, conventional
Isopropanol 70, 71–74, 95

Jogger 138–139

Kauri-butanol (KB) solvent 171
Kraft paper 142

Length, ink   236
Lift   104
Lighting, pressroom   294
Linting   244
Lithography, offset   1

Maintenance, inking system   60–65
Maintenance, press   32–38
Makeready   261–278
Makeready book   274
Marking   23–24, 28
Masstone   232
Material Safety Data Sheet (MSDS)   41, 73, 171, 263
Mechanical ghosting   248
Metamerism   240
Metering nip   89, 93
Milling   219–221
Misregister   125, 214–216
Molleton   *See* dampening roller cover
Mottle   248–249
Mylar   142

Nip   15
Nip, metering   89, 93
Nip, reverse slip   93–94

Occupational Safety and Health Administration (OSHA)   73
Off-press proofing   12
Offset lithography   1
OK sheet   263, 273–277, 281–282, 286
Oleophilic   183
Oleophobic   183
Opacity, ink   235
Opacity of paper   206
Oscillator   43, 44, 47, 50–51, 53–54, 55
Overprint varnish   249–250
Oxidative drying of an ink   227

Packing   18, 141–160, 188–189, 193–195, 254
Packing,
    arithmetic of   151–154
    determining proper amount of   145–148
    factors affecting   145–148
    problems due to improper   154–157

Packing gauge   150–151, 193–195
Packing material   142–144, 149–151
Paper   199–218
Paper,
   dimensional stability of   209
   effect of, on packing   146
   gloss of   205–206
   moisture content of   208–209
   opacity of   206
   temperature conditioning of   209–211
   tight-edged   210–211
   wavy-edged   210
Paper coating   203
Paper grain direction   206–207
Paper handling   209–213, 253
Paper problems   214–218
Paper properties   205
Paper requirements for sheetfed lithography   205
Paper storage   213
Paper surface strength   209
Paper weight   204
Papermaking   199–203
Perfector   10, 25
Perforating   181
pH, dampening solution   74–79
Picking   209
Pickup sucker, forwarding   107, 112
Pickup sucker, rear   107, 111–112, 113
Picture method of roller setting   52–53, 59
Pigment, ink   221–222
Pile   129
Pile height   107, 109, 129
Pile table   102, 103–105
Piling   216, 244, 245
Pitch diameter   16
Plant layout   251–252
Plate, printing   2, 183–197
Plate blinding   75
Plate clamp   19
Plate cocking   196
Plate cylinder   2, 16–19, 189–190
Plate dry-up   280
Plate finisher   196–197

Plate handling and inspecting   187–188
Plate height in relation to bearer   193–195
Plate mounting   190–193, 269–270
Plate mounting, preparation for   187–190
Plate preparation for storage   269
Plate runnability   196–197
Plate scanner   296
Plate scumming   75
Plate thickness, measurement of   149
Play   16
Polymerization in the drying of an ink   227
Premakeready   251–259
Press,
   bearer-contact   28–30, 153, 158
   blanket-to-blanket   10
   duplicator   12
   multicolor   5–10
   non–bearer-contact   31, 154, 158–159
   offset lithographic   1
   open-unit   3–4
   perfecting   10, 25
   printing unit of   15–41
   proof   12
   semiopen   5–10
   sheetfed   1
   single-color   3–4
   small offset   12
   web   1
Press configurations   3
Press functions, control of   282–286
Press maintenance   32–38
Press sheet inspection   279–282
Pressroom lighting   294
Pressrun   279–301
Print contrast ratio   293
Print Control Strip, FOGRA   289, 290
Print length adjustment   157–160
Print length gain   159–160
Printing pressure   144–145
Printing unit   15–41
Proof press   12
Proofing   12
Pulp   200–201

Quality control, material 255–256
Quality control devices available from GATF 289–291
Quality control during the pressrun 286–294
Quality Control Strip, GATF 290, 291
Quickset ink 231

Ream 204
Reducer 224
Refining 201–202
Refrigeration of dampening solution 94–95
Register 18, 125, 274–275, 280
Register block 114, 127, 128
Register problems 214–216
Relative humidity 208–209, 211–212
Remote control console 296
Reverse slip nip 93–94
Roll sheeter 105–106
Roller,
   bareback dampening 87–88
   ceramic-coated dampening 96–97
   dampening ductor 80
   dampening form 81, 82–85, 87–88
   dampening fountain pan 80
   dampening oscillator 81, 85
   forwarding 115
   glazed 57–59
   hickey-picking 65–66
   ink ductor 43, 44, 45
   ink form 43, 47
   knife 64
   pipe 64
Roller cover 82–85, 95–96
Roller hardness 63
Roller problem, ink 59–60
Roller removal and replacement 60–62
Roller setting, ink 50
Roller-setting gauge 51
Roller storage, ink 62–63
Roller streak 57
Roller stripe 52–54
Roller stripping 59–60, 75

Safety bar 123
Safety in the pressroom 39–41

Scanner, plate   296
Scanning densitometer   296–298
Scoring   181
Scumming   75, 94, 243
Separator brush and finger   111
Sequestering agent in alkaline dampening solution   75
Setoff   284–286
Sheet bridge   121
Sheet control   101–140
Sheet decurler   137
Sheet detector, early and late   123–125
Sheet guide rod   118
Sheet-handling mechanisms, setting of   270
Sheet-separation unit   102, 107–114, 129
Sheet steadier   110
Sheet transfer   101, 135–136
Sheeter, roll   105–106
Shortening compound   224
Side guide   114, 127–129
Side-guide marks   276–278, 280
Single-drum transfer   135
Six-Color Control Bar, GATF   289–291
Skeleton wheel   28, 139
Slip compound   223
Slow-down roller   139–140
Slurring   162
Smash   167
Smoother on feedboard   127, 128
Spray powder   284–286
Spur gear   16
Squeeze   144–145, 153–157
Standard viewing conditions   294
Star Target, GATF   289–291
Start-of-print line   19
Stiffening agent, ink   224
Stock control   253
Stripping, roller   59–60, 75
Supercalender   203
Surface rupture   217
Surface strength   209
Surface tension of water   71

Tack   237–238
Tail-end hook   140

Testing, material   254–256
Thixotropy   236
Three-drum transfer   135
Tinting   94, 243
Toning   243
Total copy center   14
Training, press crew   257–258
Transfer cylinder   5, 10, 23–27
Trapping   4, 5, 244–246, 292–293
Trial impression   273–276
Two-sheet caliper   *See* double-sheet detector

Ultraviolet radiation   229–230, 250
Undercut   18, 141
Undertone   232

Varnish, overprint   249–250
Vibrator   *See* oscillator
Viewing conditions, standard   294
Viscosity of an ink   237

Warp direction of blanket   162
Washup, dampening system   256, 267–268
Washup, inking system   256, 263, 266
Water pan   80
Water stop   87
Wedges in pile   140
Weft direction of blanket   162
Wet ink film thickness gauge   48, 50
Wet trapping   5, 244–246
Wettability of ink pigment   222
Wetting agent in an ink   223
Wetting agent in dampening solution   70, 75

About the Authors

Lloyd P. DeJidas, the GATF Production Department director and facility manager, supervises the mailing and in-plant printing operations at GATF, which includes the printing of textbooks, technical reports, and promotional materials originating at the Foundation. A contributor to numerous Foundation workshops, textbooks, and reports, Mr. DeJidas has worked at GATF since 1967. Starting as an apprentice and progressing through the ranks, he has held numerous press-related positions, including pressroom superintendent.

Thomas M. Destree is the editor of the Publications Division of the GATF Education Department. He supervises a staff of writer/editors in preparing material to be published in textbooks, reference books, audiovisuals, Learning Modules, technical and research reports, and promotional materials. A 1977 graduate of the University of Wisconsin—Stout, Mr. Destree contributed to several GATF textbooks, including the eighth edition of the *Lithographers Manual,* and Learning Modules.